Signifying God

Signifying God

SOCIAL RELATION AND SYMBOLIC ACT IN THE YORK CORPUS CHRISTI PLAYS

Sarah Beckwith

THE UNIVERSITY OF CHICAGO PRESS • CHICAGO AND LONDON

The University of Chicago Press, Chicago 60637
The University of Chicago Press, Ltd., London
© 2001 by The University of Chicago
All rights reserved. Published 2001
Paperback edition 2003
Printed in the United States of America
10 09 08 07 06 05 04 03   2 3 4 5

ISBN: 0-226-04134-4 (cloth)
ISBN: 0-226-04133-6 (paperback)

Library of Congress Cataloging-in-Publication Data

Beckwith, Sarah, 1959–
    Signifying God : social relation and symbolic act in the York Corpus Christi
plays / Sarah Beckwith.
        p.   cm.
    Includes bibliographical references (p.   ) and index.
    ISBN 0-226-04134-4 (cloth : alk. paper)
    1. York plays.   2. Mysteries and miracle plays, English—England—York—
History and criticism.   3. Christianity and literature—England—York—
History—To 1500.   4. Literature and society—England—York—History—
To 1500.   5. Christian drama, English (Middle)—History and criticism.
6. English drama—To 1500—History and criticism.   7. Bible plays, English—
History and criticism.   8. York (England)—Social conditions.   9. Social conflict
in literature.   10. Symbolism in literature.   11. God in literature.   I. Title.

PR644.Y6 B43 2001
822′.051609—dc21

                                                                                2001027513

For Sue
16 AUGUST 1942–22 APRIL 1998

For Christ plays in ten thousand places
Lovely in limbs and lovely in eyes not his
To the Father through the features of men's faces.
   Gerard Manley Hopkins

The crucified human body is our best picture of the
unacknowledged human soul.
   Stanley Cavell

It is impossible to have social relations
without symbolic acts.
   Mary Douglas

Contents

Acknowledgments

It is a pleasure indeed to come to the "last but not least" thing we write in books: our acknowledgments. It is not simply that now we can rest after long labors and put the book once again into the kind hands of others, but because now we can see how we have already done that time and time again, in conception, continuation, and completion.

Chapter 1 first appeared as "The Present of Past Things: The York Corpus Christi Cycle as a Contemporary Theatre of Memory," *Journal of Medieval and Early Modern Studies* 26, no. 2 (spring 1996), and is reprinted by permission of Duke University Press. Chapter 2 appeared in *Bodies and Disciplines: Intersections of Literature and History in Fifteenth-Century England,* edited by Barbara Hanawalt and David Wallace (Minneapolis: University of Minnesota Press, 1995), and is reprinted by permission of University of Minnesota Press. Chapter 3 appeared as "Making the World in York and the York Corpus Christi Cycle" in *Framing Medieval Bodies,* edited by Sarah Kay and Miri Rubin (Manchester: Manchester University Press, 1994), and is reprinted by permission of Manchester University Press. Chapter 5 appeared as "Absent Presences: Resurrection Theatre in York" in *Medieval Literature and Historical Inquiry: Essays in Honour of Derek Pearsall,* edited by David Aers (Cambridge: D. S. Brewer, 2000), and is reprinted by permission of Boydell and Brewer. The photographs of the stained-glass windows from All Saint's Pavement, York Cathedral, that open each part of the book were taken in June 1994 by John Twyning. They include the Ascension (p. iii), the Empty Tomb (pp. 1, 159), the Crucifixion (p. 21), the Resurrection (p. 57), and the Deposition (p. 119) and are reproduced with his kind permission.

I held the Delta Delta Delta fellowship at the National Humanities Center in 1994–95. To Kent Mullikin and his wonderful staff, as well as the Tri-Delt sorority, I have been looking forward to saying: Thank you, thank you, thank you. Jonathan (zoid) Freedman became a friend during that year, and his lively presence and supremely intelligent imagination have continued to be a source of delight. Thanks to the University of Pittsburgh for a summer grant enabling me to travel to York in 1994. I thank Philip Smith and Dave Bartholomae, Marianna Torgovnick, and Maureen Quilligan, my chairs respectively at Pittsburgh and at Duke, and Dean Bill Chafe, who allowed me to take the leaves necessary for the research and completion of this book and who granted me essential research funds.

Many people were kind enough to invite me to give lectures while I was conceiving this book. I received intellectual stimulus, immensely helpful comments, and the warmest hospitality from Tom Hahn, Derek Pearsall, Beth Robertson, David Nirenberg, Nicholas Watson, Tony Spearing, Clare Lees, Lynn Staley, Gail Gibson, Allen Frantzen, Karma Lochrie, Sepp Gumbrecht, Larry Scanlon, Susan Crane and Chris Chism, Ruth Evans, Patricia Badir and Mark Vessey, Eugene Vance and John Coldeway, Gillian Overing, David Wallace, Sybille Fischer, Miri Rubin, Julia Hell and George Steinmetz, and Mike Schoenfeldt. The conviviality and intellectual provocation of many of these occasions lingers in my memory.

Many of my colleagues in the English Department at Duke have been delightful, adventurous companions. They have made intellectual endeavor feel like an integrated activity in our lives together and with the students we teach. I thank Thomas Pfau, Michael Moses, Tom Ferraro, and Ian Baucom, who in their very different ways have been brothers in arms. They have also listened to, read, and commented on a considerable part of this book—and especially the chapters that now make up part 3. Leigh DeNeef has also been a trustworthy guide and a fount of wisdom from which I have frequently benefited.

How that old cliché "this book would not have been the same without" is animated by the presence of my friend and colleague David Aers. He has read and commented on all of this book with massive generosity and insight, with great sensitivity to what I wanted to say, and sometimes with an efficiency so awesome that it would be truly dreadful were he to expect *that* kind of reciprocity. A great deal of the book has been worked out whilst we have been teaching together and talking on topics of mutual fascination. Deeply suspicious of theater, but impelled by the demands of theology, he has always made me think about their difficult connections. Such as it is, it is a much better book for his constant stimulus and example.

I thank present and former graduate students at Duke, for the chance to teach them, be taught by them, and continue conversations as they publish their own inspiring work. Meghan Johnson and Joann Kleinneur were passionate and brilliant undergraduate students, the kind of students who make this vocation a joy as well as a discipline. It has been a pleasure to get to know Nancy Atkinson, who worked with me at Pittsburgh over the years. I thank Daphne Rosenblitt, too, for the intelligent creativity and skilled rigor of her patience from which I have learned more than I can say.

I am grateful for the superb readings I received from Andrew Cole and Chris Chism. Andrew commented on the manuscript with speed, attention to detail, and (as all his friends will attest) his own unforgettable way of putting things. He showed himself to be a wonderfully enthusiastic and generous scholar. Chris read the book with extraordinary insight and with the astonishing writerly eye that will show itself to such great effect in her own forthcoming book. Julie Paulson did the bibliography for the book, and I am immensely grateful for her work on it as well as her companionship on the trail of Wittgenstein, Cavell, and medieval drama.

I regret that I no longer live in close proximity to two friends who remain, despite geographical distance, vital interlocutors. Julia Hell has heard me talk about this book for years, and her support of it extended not simply to reading chapters and helping me see the gaps and flaws when I tried new arguments out on her, but also coming to see the Toronto version of the York plays in 1998. Her own work on memory in GDR and post-GDR literature has been something I have been both fascinated and educated by. Valerie Krips has also heard lots of versions of this work, and her own eloquence, massive warmth, and abiding interest in postwar English children's literature and psychoanalysis have been sustaining, and always fun and stimulating to boot.

Liz Clark, known for her legendary generosity, and Dale Martin were my boon companions and neighbors for a great part of the time of writing, and they helped to make the "Manchester Association" a real community.

Given his extraordinary and sensitive attention to acknowledgment, to its challenges, necessities, fears, and occlusions, it is only appropriate that I should thank one I do not know but must acknowledge: Stanley Cavell. Martin Stone and Toril Moi introduced me to Cavell's work, which I had first read with fascination and utter bewilderment as I came to this "new yet unapproachable America."

Martin Stone introduced me to Wittgenstein in two magnificent classes; and Toril and I have talked with each other and read together in ways I have found both stimulating and immensely insightful and useful. The writing of Fergus Kerr, Rowan Williams, and Denys Turner were also deeply illuminating for some of the perspectives I develop here. I feel gratitude to the great scholars of the York cycle, the living and the dead, for my work rests on so many of their indispensable labors. All York cycle scholars have especial reason to be grateful to Alexandra Johnston, Margaret Dorrell, and Richard Beadle, and now to the high-tech endeavors of Meg Twycross and Pamela King. I also thank the two anonymous readers who read the manuscript with great insight and generosity. I would also like to thank my meticulous, efficient, and wonderful editor, Randy Petilos, for his work and care, and Erin DeWitt for her excellent copyediting.

I am lucky to have two fine men for brothers and parents who have always thought that if things were worth doing, they were worth trying to do well. I thank them for having cared about my education from a young age.

Since 1996 Bart Ehrman, now my husband, has been my loved and loving companion. I am deeply grateful to him for reading numerous drafts of the chapters, and for his immensely shrewd comments about both the woods *and* the trees. I have appreciated his love of reason, intelligence, rigor, humor, and all-around sweetness in my life, which he has utterly transformed and enriched, as well as in my work.

Unfortunately, I can shift none of the ultimate responsibility for my words and mistakes on to any of the above helpmates. Such ineptitudes I acknowledge mine.

I dedicate this book to the memory of my beloved friend Sue Rankin, who died far, far too soon in April 1998. I wish very much that she could have felt the heft of this book in her hands and read these words, though they would not then need to have been written. I feel deeply grateful that I knew her, for the gift of her life and the gift, going on before, she made of her death.

Introduction

This is a book about the York Corpus Christi plays, the most lavish, long-lasting, and complex form of collective theatrical enterprise in English theater history.[1] In it I understand the plays as sacramental theater. How we present ourselves to each other (the classical domain of theater) and how we are present to each other (the domain of the sacrament) become, I argue, vital theological as well as theatrical resources in the York plays.[2] In them theater and sacrament become profound investigations of each other's opportunities and limits.

The York Corpus Christi Play is the only one of the four extant cycles that has indubitable links to the Feast of Corpus Christi. Even after the feast had been abolished in 1548, York's citizens frequently mounted performances on that day.

Produced possibly as early as 1376, when we have the first records of the "pageant-waggons" on which they played, the plays are "brought forth" by the trade guilds, written by anonymous clerics and regulated by the civic oligarchy, increasingly a mercantile group with interests as international middlemen and distributors. The only text we have from a performance history that lasted, off and on, until 1569, the date of the Northern Rebellion, is a civic document in which the original pageants, the "regnals," are entered as play text into a civic register in the last third of the fifteenth century.[3]

Although scholars have argued over quite how many of the pageants extant in the Register could possibly play on Corpus Christi Day, it is likely that many of them passed through between ten and sixteen stations appointed and approved by the city and played sequentially at each different station.[4] The claims over time and space are massive, in actual time and in represented time. From the entrance at Micklegate, past the Minster Gates, over some of the main trading districts in the Coney Street region, and at numerous other stations, until the last station at the Pavement, one of the main marketplaces of the city, the pageants process and play, transform and are themselves transformed by the places through which they pass. And they take most of a very, very long day. This temporal and spatial vastness are present in the story as well as the enactment, because the story performed moves from the beginning of time from God's creation of the world, through the birth, death, and resurrection of Christ through the harrowing of hell to the end of the world in future time. So although huge and cosmological, they also contain or rather double these other times and spaces with their own. We need to think, then, of an astonishingly polysemous theater with as much as a tenth of the city involved in the production—up to twenty Christs, twelve Maries, several different "Gods," and a few Satans wandering the city giving multiple performances at several sites. No physical markers separate a specific "theatrical" space from everyday life: there is no inherent, independent stage for acting.[5] Rather, the fictive localities of Calvary, Jerusalem, Herod's palace, Pilate's dais, and Lazarus's tomb are held in active tension with the public spaces of the city, and that tension is animated every time an actor assumes a role in the streets of York.

The task of understanding the York plays as sacramental theater is more difficult than it appears. In England, sacramental theater is now obsolete.[6] The forms of life that sustained it, as is clear even from my brief description above, no longer exist. The festive, occasional theater of Corpus Christi was intimately part of the social, cultural, economic, and political life of the medieval city, which are not separable from one another or from the meaning of Corpus Christi for the medieval people who celebrated it. Furthermore the Reformers' accusation that the medieval church was a theater constituted the most lethal, devastating, and successful way of undermining the plays' authority. In the process, the terms "sacrament" and "theater" became drastically revised, and that revision can only be understood in mutual relation.

Functionalist analyses of Corpus Christi ritual have made this hard to see because they imagine a perfect fit between social structure and expressive form, such that Corpus Christi festivity becomes the aesthetic mirror of medieval society and its ideal form. In part 2 (chapters 2 and 3), I analyze the interrelationship between social relation and symbolic act, showing how the organization of the Corpus Christi plays is one of the political mechanisms of labor regulation in the city.

Theater and church are deeply communal enterprises. Both give themselves over to the judgment of the community. Neither can be understood except as a performance of that community.[7] Each involves a sharing such that what they offer and how they are received are never separate from what they are. In the central section of this book, part 3 (chapters 4–6), I show how theater and sacrament work by means of each other to perform the body of Christ. Chapter 4 examines the complex interactions of theatrical signification through thinking about the actor's body as it plays Christ as sign and phenomenal body, and explores the theatrical resources of his "real presence." In the subsequent chapter, I look at the Resurrection sequences of the plays as a theological/theatrical exploration of eucharistic absence and presence. Chapter 6 shows the centrality of the sacrament of penance to this theater, and reads the trial and judgment plays as explorations of a penitential community.

It is one of the premises of part 3 that these plays do theological work. That theological work is not to be found as a set of contents, a doctrinal declaration. Indeed, part of the theological work the plays do is to render impossible the very notion of divine authority unrelated to a penitent community and the very notion of theological utterance unattached to the risks of conversation.[8] (There is no third-person utterance, no indirect speech in theater.) I hope to show that our received, deeply entrenched oppositions between church and theater, while fully comprehensible as the product of the particularities of English history, are themselves extraordinarily critically disabling. Unless we put sacrament and theater back into relation to one another, pre-Reformation theater is unacknowledgeable, missed in the very processes by which we think we know it.

In part 4 (chapter 7), I show in detail why the term "sacramental theater" is so oxymoronic in contemporary English culture. Reformers understood transubstantiation as a *pièce de théâtre*, and through such polemic, they understood theater itself as spectacle with the priest as its most consummate actor. The attack on the integrity of the sacramental system was devastating. Who would want to disclose herself in confession to one whose very being is dissimulation, who is concealed rather than revealed, for whom therefore the very possibility of a genuine response is foreclosed? Theater here is an accusation thrown at the Roman sacrament of the altar, made to expose the dissimulations that work to retain ecclesial power and not submit that power to judgment.

All theater is relentlessly and inevitably contemporary. Though it may conjure people who died long ago in a time and place dead to us, it does so only now and here, bringing the dead to life in the bodies of the living. The York Corpus Christi plays, as performance, have a contemporary life, and I have framed my book with first and last chapters that examine the forms this life takes. In 1951, after a gap of nearly four hundred years, the plays were revived in a still bomb-scarred city amidst the ruins of St. Mary's Abbey for the Festival of Britain. The setting of the ruins became a passionately defended locale for the regular subsequent performances of the York Festival, and in my first chapter I ask what versions of the past are required of them and what are the implications of this ruined history for contemporary medievalism.

In my final chapter 8, part 5, I return to the twentieth century. If reforming polemic saw the Catholic priest as the quintessential actor and if theater was, antitheatrically, the very medium of vituperation, then many modern encounters with these plays seem to have been interested in actors as priests whose self-giving alone will redeem the church and reform the very possibility of office. I explore the ramifications of this interesting reversal in an analysis of two explorations in the medium of film and fiction, *Jesus of Montreal* and Barry Unsworth's novel *Morality Play*, whose central metaphor for the life of Jesus and the office of priest is theater. In this chapter I also look at how two contemporary theater directors (Bill Bryden, Katie Mitchell) have striven to make Corpus Christi theater present to modern audiences in the setting of the professional, nationally subsidized theater.

The York Corpus Christi plays are sophisticated, textured, complex, and reflexive: these are not words conventionally used about this theater, and I have sought to show *how* those qualities are embodied in this theater rather than argue that they are, believing that such strategies of condescension merely reinforce their hold. If theater and sacrament teach us anything, it is surely that neither is an object to be known, but rather a process that demands our participation and our willingness to be known in the contingencies of our own biographies. "Nothing can be present to us to which we are not present."[9]

Part One

Ruins & Revival

1 The Present of Past Things

THE YORK CORPUS CHRISTI CYCLE AS A CONTEMPORARY THEATER OF MEMORY

Let us make noble use / Of this great ruin.
—John Webster, *Duchess of Malfi*, 5.5.110–11

The York Corpus Christi plays in their past and present productions have always argued over how and what to remember. Through the resources of theater, ritual, and liturgy, they narrate the Christian myth, and in this most fundamental of senses, they remember the life of Christ and the eucharistic imperative, the invitation celebrated in the Feast of Corpus Christi: "Do this in remembrance of me." But the very form of this remembering became profoundly alarming when it embarrassed and betrayed reformed understandings of representation: Corpus Christi theater became idolatrous when it was regarded as confining the limitless and potent God to the body of an actor, to his mortal gestures and banalizing mimicry, and when the actor's act was understood to be scandalously imitating rather than gestically signifying God. Religious theater, in a long struggle in which it was the vehicle as well as the object of argument, became profaning by definition, a betrayal and not a revelation of the mysteries of the faith, as those mysteries and that faith were themselves radically imagined anew. In a profound shift in the mnemonic landscape of the sacred, England's Blasphemy Laws rendered performance of religious materials both practically impossible and conceptually unthinkable.[1]

But the plays also remember and argue over memory, in the most tangible of ways, as they embody and transform the very shape of Corpus Christi in the plastic medium of the city of York. As the plays process through different stations, different places, different bodies, the shape and texture of Corpus Christi, the sacrament that is the church and all of Christian society, is twisted this way and that, transformed through its mediums of articulation. It is a ritual of remembrance orchestrated through a language of festivity that uses physical procession not just to display a social order but to fight over how it should be made up, how it wanted to be seen and hence remembered.

Technologies of remembrance are also part of the history of these dramas. Their confinement to a civic manuscript, made from copies of the "originals" owned by the trade guilds that produced and paid for the plays, is undoubtedly part of an attempt at control and censorship over extemporizing and unpredictable performances.[2] Once the manuscript was in existence—about a hundred years after these plays began to be performed—the performances were checked against the scripted version by a clerk, who recorded and monitored changes for the civic corporation that kept the document.[3] The memory of Corpus Christi, then, is argued over through the very forms and histories of its remembering.

Insofar as the York Corpus Christi plays are memorialized in English literary history, their northernness, their provinciality, their Catholicism, have often appeared to render them opaque, if not inexplicable to the literary histories that write the tradition of English literature in an Englishness that is unabashedly metropolitan, southern-dominated, and deeply Anglican. To walk around York as a southerner today is still to experience the sheer difference of a history written from rather than about the north of England.

It is precisely the ruptures, the profound discontinuities of the history of these plays, and the forms of cultural memory they inhabit that render them resonant for me as their historian. Their suppression, itself a massive attempt to reconstitute popular memory, is testimony to their spark and promise, and not just to their crudity and obsolescence, the danger of what and how they remembered. Their awkward, yet astonishingly successful resurrection after the Festival of Britain in 1951 indicates how densely and significantly they work in the very grains and arguments not just of English historiography, but of a necessarily expanded sense of the past as both fully contemporary and resolutely vernacular.

The York plays were performed off and on from 1376 to 1569.[4] After 1951 they were finally revived for the Festival of Britain and have been henceforth performed in York every three or four years.[5] They offer in their medieval enactment, Reformation suppression, and modern revival the most complex and various relations between the past and the present, the most nuanced and difficult versions of memory, that faculty of the soul Augustine called the present of past things.[6] This first chapter deals not with the story of their enactment or suppression (the subject of chapters 2 to 7), but with the revival of the plays in 1951 and with the contemporary past that the Festival of Britain inaugurates in the modern life of the cycle.[7] The strange story of the revival of these plays after an obliteration of nearly four hundred years will show the nature of our memorial and historical investment, as it also newly makes present that paradigmatically "past thing," the York Corpus Christi cycle. John Elliott in *Playing God*, which charts the modern stage life of the medieval "mysteries," prefaces his book with the following comment: "Ours is an age committed to the conservation of the past, yet few forms of art, dramatic or otherwise, have followed so tricky a path from oblivion to recognition as these fifteenth and sixteenth century biblical dramas."[8] As a rememoration, the contemporary Corpus Christi revivals in York offer us a way of looking at the framing of the medieval past in a contemporary city and at the specific past-present enactions at work there in the vaunted path from "oblivion" to "recognition." As such, it may also provide the means of exploring in a concrete setting the relation between historical loss and cultural reparation, which has recently been located as a vital psychic undergirding of medieval studies itself.[9]

THE FESTIVAL OF BRITAIN AND 1951

The *Official Handbook of the Festival of Britain* describes the sense of crisis and recuperation central to the conceptualization and mood of the festival: "Conceived among the untidied ruins of war and fashioned through days of harsh economy, this festival is a challenge to the sloughs of the present and a shaft of confidence cast forth against the future."[10] Held to commemorate the Great Exhibition of 1851, the Festival of Britain was principally located in four national centers—Glasgow, Belfast, Cardiff, and London—and twenty-two provincial centers.[11] Roy Strong describes the festival as a concerted attempt to construct a "new secular mythology" through which to constitute a future.[12] The very centerpiece of the festival was an ambitiously conceived exhibition on the South Bank that told a story about the continuity of Britishness, the unbreakable and profoundly informing link between Britain's landscape, arts, and people.[13] The British people were to be remade through the conjuration of a changeless and immemorial landscape, one that shaped them as indefatigably as they shaped it in an inescapable and fully mutual belonging. On the one hand, then, the British past was of comfortingly long duration, and this history was confirmed in and read through the indelible geography of its landscape. In this familiar but newly poignant relationship between landscape and time, between geography and history, the exhibition tells a story that is the stock in trade of romantic nationalism. Yet on the other hand, the festival staged the past as concertedly anachronistic. "The past was present only in the form of anachronism," remarks Raphael Samuel in his analysis of the festival as part of a contemporary archaeology of the past.[14] Willfully modern, relentlessly futuristic, the festival also sought to celebrate reconstruction. Adrian Forty declared it "a celebration of the achievements of the Labour Government," the architects of the postwar welfare state.[15] It was the Education Act (1944), the Town and Country Planning Act (1947), the National Insurance Act (1948) made manifest, beautiful, and material. The National Health Service was inaugurated on 5 July 1948, and it was the crowning glory of reconstruction, enacting a principle of welfare based not on the degradation of means-testing and selection but on the basis of universality—"flat-rate contributions and an equality of benefit for all as a bonding of a common citizenship."[16] The visionary legislation that inaugurated a historic change in the relation between state and people, and that was to sustain them from cradle to deathbed, has been rightly hailed as "the nearest Britain has ever come to institutionalizing altruism."[17] It was to be celebrated in the new-built environment, and the Festival of Britain, as well as celebrating a naturalized landscape, bodied forth the artificial triumphs of man-made reconstruction in concrete, brick, and glass. It was architecture, then, that was the predominant theme as well as the primary medium of the festival.[18]

The Festival of Britain took place between 3 May and 30 September 1951. In York the festival occupied the fortnight between 3 June and 17 June, and the relation between place and people was a vital understanding of the celebration. The archbishop of York, Dr. Cyril Garbett, opened the festival with a service at York Minster, and in his sermon he tried to thicken the time of the present through the reinvention of memory and the recovery of anticipation. Archbishop Garbett was not unequivocal about the modern, but hoped to celebrate the festival as the witnessing of the triumph of freedom over tyranny. He took as the text of his sermon the line from Psalm 16:6: "Yea, I have a goodly heritage," and located the goodliness of that heritage in York itself. The British love of freedom was ancient, he said. In the Middle Ages it was found in the trade councils and guilds, which protected the freedom and interests of their members. And in a continuation of this theme, as one newspaper reporter put it, "The whole city witnessed those characteristics of national life of which he had been speaking—freedom, authority and religion."[19] The festival strove to make material, to embody the hope of reconstruction, and the success of 1951 in York lay in the tight relationship between event and place that it created. By October of that year, a Conservative government had returned to power, and although this government maintained the consensus about the construction and maintenance of welfare,[20] it was nevertheless very soon possible retrospectively to see 1951 as a marker, an ending of Clement Attlee's Britain.[21]

The Festival of Britain in York was merely the beginning of an arts festival that has taken place subsequently every three years to this day, and the celebration of the very specificity of place was a central part of the desire to continue this newly invented tradition.[22] The "Report of the Board of the York Festival Society" ended with the following sentiment as they planned the events of 1954: "There will be nothing in this York Festival which does not have its proper place and justification. The buildings will not be adapted for the event, the event will adapt itself to buildings and grow in greater strength from that marriage of the site with the artistic creation."[23] That interrelationship between building and event, where the event marks the building but is constructed as simply molding itself to the preexisting exigencies of an already implacable site, becomes part of the essential mise-en-scène of the festival in York, but is particularly noticeable in the early years of revival. As the front page of the *Yorkshire Gazette* put it in June 1954, as the second festival opened, the plays "belong to York in a way that few other works of art belong to their places of origin."[24] The Corpus Christi plays were indispensable to the inextricable relation between place and event in many and various ways. For Archbishop Garbett, they were "like a silver thread" binding together the separate events making up the Festival of Britain.[25]

RESURRECTING THE CORPUS CHRISTI PLAYS IN YORK

Canon Purvis translated the plays from the manuscript, abbreviating them drastically so that they could be performed in three hours. They were staged every evening in the Museum Gardens between 3 June and 17 June 1951. Purvis's translation divided the cycle into two parts, massively cutting the Old Testament portions, which lasted a mere half hour. The first part took the narrative of the beginning of the world, to the nativity of Christ and up to the entry into Jerusalem; the second half could then be devoted to a narrative shaped around Judas's conspiracy, giving the greatest time and attention to the Passion, Resurrection, Ascension, and Last Judgement sequences.[26] The actors who played God and Christ were to be kept anonymous because Martin Browne, the director, felt that their personalities should not interfere with the object of their representation. But the actor playing Christ, Joseph O'Connor, was publicized because a local paper leaked his name. Browne used many amateur and local actors and kept the largest speaking parts for professionals. Keith Thomson, the director of the Board of Directors of the Festival, laid out some of the aesthetic and representational principles that governed the casting and production of the plays: "The first essential is that the actor should be a Christian. The man chosen must himself believe."[27] Thomson had been secretary of the Planning Committee of the Festival, and he was well connected: his grandfather had been archbishop of York. The then-archbishop of York, Cyril Garbett, had been less than enthusiastic about the production of the plays as religious drama.[28] Thomson arranged an informal meeting between the archbishop of Canterbury and the archbishop of York, and they agreed to the production of the drama on two grounds: first, that the plays be performed on sacred ground and as a religious rather than theatrical event, and, second, that Martin Browne should be the director of the plays. Martin Browne had been responsible for directing T. S. Eliot's religious theater and regarded religious theater as itself sacramental. As he said in a publication of 1936: "All religious drama . . . should strive to attain participation in a common experience vicariously suffered, whose perfect model is The Eucharist."[29] Browne was Director of Religious Drama for the Diocese of Chichester, an appointment that Bishop Bell had secured for him.[30] Browne, then, as Elliott remarks in *Playing God*, was "in the unique position as the professional director of an amateur theatre, responsible not to the authorities who had traditionally controlled drama in England but to an enlightened church leader."[31]

Browne used the ruins of St. Mary's Abbey as his stage. St. Mary's was the Benedictine abbey that lay on the northwest side of York just outside its city walls. This had originally been a five-apsed Norman church, rebuilt in the fourteenth century. A fragmentary nave still survives. Browne used the ruined north wall (about 150 feet long) as the backdrop to his production, deploying five of the eight available bays. The upper level of this wall was "heaven," and whenever God appeared, he was framed in the central arch. In the northwest corner, Browne raised a stage six feet above the floor with steps up to it; this corner stage also concealed a sepulcher. The lower floor was used for Pilate, the stable, and the priests; there was also a traditional hell's mouth to stage right. Eventually Browne used a multilevel open stage to facilitate movement, but he later remarks that "the mansions were better suited to the setting, which is powerfully dominated by the beauty of the ruined medieval architecture."[32] The medieval costumes were modeled on quattrocento paintings. Browne strove then for a pictorial effect; the actor playing Christ was praised in the reviews for "wisely relying on an evocative repose of face and figure."[33] The *Leeds Guardian* reported that the production had "the beauty of an old painting come to life."[34]

RUINED HISTORY

Browne was not unique in his attraction to sacred ruins as a setting for revivals of medieval religious theater. The Cornish plays, for example, were produced at Temple Church in Bristol, and Glastonbury was a site in 1970 for further sacred theater.[35] But the repeated choice of the ruins of St. Mary's Abbey for the production of the plays and the obsessive and absolute centrality that they assume in the history of these productions are indices of the function and texture of the past-present relations they enact. After the success of 1951, the plays were always, until 1992, produced in the ruins. When Tyrone Guthrie was asked to direct the plays, he refused to do the plays in the "petrified past of the ruins." He was forced to resign over the issue. For the Festival Committee, it was the abbey's ruins or nothing. In 1976 Joan Littlewood was asked if she would direct the plays. She agreed, on the condition that she could do them on wagons in the street and that they would be free.[36] However, the pageants were not done in the streets and that year the plays were not free. When in 1992 they were brought inside and put behind the proscenium arch in the Theatre Royal, the outrage was palpable. The *Yorkshire Evening Post* records letter after irate letter protesting the lack of tragedy, reverence, and power of the production, and many of the letters were exclusively concerned with the absence of the abbey ruins as set and backdrop.[37]

Why are the ruins particularly seen as the inevitable, fiercely defended natural locale for the plays? In her study of ruins in the poetic tradition, Anne Janovitz has noticed:

> The ruin provides an historical provenance for a conception of the British nation as immemoriably ancient, and through its naturalization subsumes cultural and class difference in to a conflated representation of Britain as nature's inevitable product. But at the same time ruin imagery cannot help asserting the visible evidence of historical and imperial impermanence, for the ruin has traditionally been associated with human and cultural transience.[38]

Ruins provide us with ancestors and not descendants.[39] It is when we are physically memorialized as ruined, cut off, decayed, and pilfered, that we appear to desire the medieval past that is also the contemporary past in York. The ruin offers itself as fetish to our nostalgia.[40] It is past persisting as residue, yet visibly in imminent danger, endlessly displayed and recovered because always about to be extinguished; shimmering with aura, utterly unique and tangible, yet always irreparably distant. The ruins are then a perfect physical emblem for our contemporary relation to the past. As the stubborn, repetitive, and ineluctably displayed site of this theater, they show our past in a "subtle play between its intractability and its disappearance."[41] They are, in fact, our form of modern memory, a besieged memory, a superb example of what Pierre Nora has called "*lieux de mémoire,*" places or sites of memory.[42] For Nora we build, commemorate, and obsess about places of memory because there are no longer real environments of memory: "The moment of lieux de mémoire occurs at the same time that an immense and intimate fund of memory disappears surviving as the reconstituted object beneath the gaze of critical history."[43] "Places of memory" stand then as besieged memory; they stand between and are produced by the opposition between memory and history, where memory is understood as that which is open to permanent revolution, a perpetually actual phenomenon tying us to an eternal present, and history is "the reconstruction, always problematic and incomplete, of what is no longer."[44] Nora builds on Maurice Halbwachs's crucial distinction between memory and history in his work on collective memory, wherein memory confirms the similarities between the past and the present, and history is the symptom of a deep fissure between present and past by which they become dense and opaque to each other.[45] Places of memory pay witness to a mnemonic crisis that has had us in its grip ever since the nineteenth century discovered a present "whose self-conception was defined by a disciplined obsession with the past."[46] In this understanding, history itself was predicated on its very opposition to, and systematic replacement of, memory. For history reveres and elucidates discontinuity, as memory renders the past continuous with and continuously and unnoticeably revised by and in the present. In history, recollection ceases to coincide with consciousness.[47] In this sense, Nora puts the extreme case that history is the delegitimation of the lived past: "history's goal and ambition is not to exalt but to annihilate what has in reality taken place."[48] History is parasitic on, as it seeks to revive the eroding traditions of, collective memory, the collective memory of the very groups that modernization fundamentally shatters and reorganizes. As traditional memory disappears, we fetishize its newly significant remains; we treasure the auratic value of this pitchfork, feel the texture of that decaying fabric, admire the functionless, splendid redundancy of this doorknob, the contingency and curve of that craftsmanlike shaping, wonder at the sheer endurance of this particular ruin, in which memory appears to be materialized. As Nora has said, we interiorize memory as an individual constraint because it is no longer a social practice: "Since the passage from memory to history has required every social group to redefine its identity through the revitalization of its own history, the task of remembering makes everyone his own historian."[49]

Lieux de mémoire are the most tangible sign of the split between memory and history, where the traces of a disappearing past are collected and made spectacular. Places of memory are "fundamentally remains, the ultimate embodiment of a memorial consciousness that has barely survived in a historical age that calls for memory because it has abandoned it."[50] They replace spontaneous memory because the sense of the past in this historical consciousness is that it is deeply endangered, about to disappear at any minute on a vanishing horizon. As Nora writes, "If history did not besiege memory, deforming and transforming it, penetrating and petrifying it, there would be no lieux de mémoire."[51] Like the ruins of the Corpus Christi revival, these *lieux de mémoire* are available in concrete experience, but also subject to the commodification of heritage regalia, the postcards, mementos, souvenirs, framing by "historical detail," the entire complex construction of a merely ostensible history, a sense of the past. They are *lieux* in three senses of the word—material, symbolic, and functional. These three aspects must always coexist; they must be concretely embodied, auratically symbolic, and functional in the sense that they do cultural work.[52] In them, finally, as Patrick Hutton remarks, history ceases to be a mnemonic reconstruction and becomes instead an archaeological deconstruction.[53]

Nora's analysis is an exquisitely seductive reading of the concrete forms taken by the renewed monumentalism of contemporary modes of rememoration. Not so much an end of history as an end of memory theory, Nora claims that places as memory can only be examined for the way they once did, but no longer do, refer to what he calls "true" memory. As such, his analysis has all the narcissistic pleasures of the nostalgia it so elegiacally invokes. In making such a decisive and absolute break between memory—homogenous, present-to-itself, continuous—and the destructive rampages of the malice of history, it enacts the break it merely seeks to analyze, and memory itself becomes the place at once of an absolute plenitude and of catastrophic loss. As such, it may be seen to exemplify rather than provide either an analysis or a history of modern memory. Or rather, like his exemplary forebear Ferdinand Tonnies, Nora has systematically transformed his account of traditional memory into a nostalgia for it.[54] But Nora's descriptions of "places of memory" resonate so well for York's reenactment of Corpus Christi—organic plenitude in petrified remains—because the ruins embody history as that simultaneous plenitude and catastrophe, so enacting our possession by the past and our dispossession of it, the place not so much of mnemonic reconstruction as of archaeological de(con)struction.

TOURIST NOSTALGIA IN YORK

The ruins, then, are not a momentary product of the Festival of Britain in 1951, but a constantly rehearsed aspect of the reenactment of the Corpus Christi plays in York.[55] The reenactment of these plays is effected against an intensified commodification of the past that develops and is also continuous with the ruined history enacted in 1951. These contexts are an inescapable part of the cultural history of the York Corpus Christi cycle. So when we go to see the revived York plays now, the revivals are an unavoidable part of a commodified heritage industry. If we go as professional medievalists to York, we arrive nevertheless as tourists. The Labour Group on the York City Council wanted to boycott the festival in 1980 because it wanted "entertainment for the masses," not a "jamboree for hoteliers and tourists."[56] But tourism is not so easily expunged from the commercial heart of the city.

As tourists, we are implicated in a paradox that is also played out in the concept and practice of "tradition." Structured by nostalgia, as Susan Stewart has said in her book *On Longing,* touristic nostalgia is a paralyzing structure of historical reflection, "a repetition that mourns the inauthenticity of all repetition."[57] It sets off a past characterized by its immediacy and presence. Constituting a "sadness without an object," it is

> always ideological—the past it seeks has never existed except as narrative, and hence, always absent, that past continually threatens to reproduce itself as a felt lack. Hostile to history and its invisible origins and yet longing for an impossibly pure context of lived experience at the place of origin, nostalgia wears a distinctly utopian face, a face that turns towards a future past, a past which has only ideological reality. This past of desire which the nostalgic seeks is in fact the absence that is the very generating mechanism of desire. . . . [N]ostalgia is the desire for desire.[58]

To visit contemporary York is to visit one of England's most beautiful cities, whose beauty is part of an intensive commodification and extension of the concept of heritage into more and more aspects of civic life. Indeed, York's museums may be understood to have pioneered approaches to the display and the commodification of the past. York's Castle Museum (1938) was the first of its kind, being one of the earliest museums to show dioramas of everyday life.[59] The Jorvik Viking Centre was a dramatic extension from the merely visual to an engagement of as many senses as possible in the search for the past's palpability. Visitors (as many as a hundred thousand a year) sit in moving trolleys, which take them through the reconstructed streets of Viking York through a regression sequence that transports people back thirty generations to the smells, sounds, and sights of a Viking settlement.[60] History is spectacle and tableau here; moreover the spectator is immobilized while whisked through the time-made-space of "the past" strapped into the moving trolleys. We move, and we move fast, but the past remains the same. Based on the excavations of the York Archeological Trust between 1976 and 1981, Jorvik purports to display what was uncovered in the waterlogged deposits of the Coppergate area, which made it seem possible to reconstitute, in archaeological terms, the entire material environment of Anglo-Scandinavian Coppergate.

One of York Archeological Trust's latest museums is Barley Hall, a reconstructed goldsmith's house. Historical records have provided it with a fifteenth-century tenant. Visitors can go through all the rooms and listen to conversations between the lady of the house (voice by Judi Dench) and her servant, overhear the craftsmen, and buy replicas of items that appear in a 1478 probate inventory. As Raphael Samuel remarks, the wall-hangings dyed in woad and madder would not look out of place in the haberdashery department of Liberty's or the Shaker Shop in Chelsea.[61]

These places are not merely museums in the sense of a particular building or institution, but are rather "potent social metaphors and the very means by which societies represent their relation to their own history."[62] York is itself now so museumized that very few of its features escape the construction of an imaginary and commodified past. The neo-Georgian public lavatories brought on the withering and curmudgeonly scorn of that indefatigable heritage-basher Neal Ascherson in *The Guardian* as he grumbled about the necessity of going to the bathroom, as it were, in heritage.

The past constructed by heritage is a past rendered alternative to, not continuous with, the present. The operations of heritage frame the past, bracket it off, put it in quotation marks, render it a homogenous site of leisure, literally, then, a past-time.

Interestingly enough, in this connection, the site of the production of the Corpus Christi plays after 1951, St. Mary's Abbey, was in the Middle Ages an archenemy of the civic authorities who controlled the production of the plays. Indeed, the abbey had its own competing procession to the civic dramas; territorial and juridical conflicts were endemic over the course of the medieval production of the plays. Furthermore, St. Mary's Abbey was commandeered as the headquarters of the Northern Council, which oversaw the demise of the very plays revived in the ruins of this former Benedictine abbey. "At the dissolution of the monasteries by Henry VIII," writes Francis Drake, in his topography of York written in 1736, "the site of this noble and rich abbey with all its revenues fell to the crown. And here it was that prince ordered a palace to be built, out of its ruins, which was to be the residence of the lords presidents of the North, for the time being, and called the King's Manor. That the very name and memory of the abbey might be lost for ever."[63] The sense of the historical located in the ruins then is gestural; they are there not to create a link with a verifiable past—the conventional sense, after all, of history—but rather to act as markers for an ineffable and constructed "past." As Peter Cramer has said of the effect of ruins:

> They encourage us to think two things at once. Abandoned and broken, they confirm our suspicion that the past is not recoverable, but equally, being still there, they have survived—they stimulate in us a reflection of this past which can only be done in the present. Together these two operations—one of losing, the other of re-possessing—give to time its familiar density; the knowledge that it consists neither in contingent events which peter out, nor in ideas living only in the mind, but in both.[64]

In this sense, ruins are ideal; they are a way of seeing and engage our feelings at the deepest affective level of where we see ourselves in history. They enact a sacramental version of the past that makes it continuous with and a part of the contemporary past of the heritage industry, inarticulable, vague, and mystical, encountered in the most exquisite and fleeting of experiences. Lying beyond words, they induce experiences that go without saying, for as the National Heritage Memorial Fund Annual Report of 1981 (HMSO, 1981) says, "We could no more define the new heritage than we could, say, define beauty or art."

Heritage has since the mid-1980s in Britain become part of a vital debate about the commodification of culture.[65] And it is a debate in which medievalists are intricately participant. For heritage, according to its critics, enacts the "glamour of backwardness,"[66] the love of and absolute inability to relinquish a feudal residue. Heritage in this reading is neo-feudal, and as such it is a symbol of "natural decadence, a malignant growth which testifies at once to the strength of the country's ancien régime and to the weakness of alternatives to it."[67] But for Samuel, heritage does not conform to this leftist demonology; it is, on the contrary, "one of the few areas of national life in which it is possible to invoke an idea of common good without provoking suspicions of party interest and it is also one of the few where notions of ancestry and

posterity can be invoked without bad faith."[68] Instead of class, it offers
place, Samuel suggests, rather as environmentalism offers the activist
and the reformist an alternative to the worn-out routines of party politics. But as Keith Thomas has pointed out in a recent review of
Samuel's book, Samuel perhaps overstates the utopian glories of heritage history.

Consider the following anecdote. When crusading fervor was
reaching its peak under King Henry II, many small Jewish communities in England came under pressure to "convert" to Christianity. Jews
were offered the choice of baptism or death. In 1190 the York Jews
rushed to Clifford's Tower, where, besieged by local people who were
incited by Robert Malebrisse, they committed mass suicide. The next
day besiegers gathered around the tower and persuaded those who had
survived to come out under a promise of clemency—if they converted.
It is thought that 150 were massacred on exit.[69]

Clifford's Tower is now owned by English Heritage, the English
quango started in 1983 under the second National Heritage Act, currently responsible for at least four hundred properties, which markets
their "unique selling propositions" aggressively. This is how English
Heritage notes the 1190 massacre on a plaque:

> In 1190 the wooden tower on the motte was burned down during anti-
> Jewish riots. It was replaced by another, also of timber which survived
> until 1228 when it was destroyed in a great storm.[70]

It is left to the Jewish community to place a single commemorative
plaque of their own at the base of the tower to honor and mourn the
murdered and anonymous Jews of 1190.

There is no room in the conception and practice of the "past" prof-
fered by heritage history to do more here than offer the massacre of the
Jews as anything other than a detail to explain, with a mindlessly casual
brutality, a particular aspect of the structure of the building, which
must be offered in an adiachronic and here amoral talismanic spectacle.[71]

COMMUNITAS

One of the conflicts acted out in the revival of the Corpus Christi plays
is between the plays as a theater local and participatory—in short, a
community theater staged by and for its participants—and the plays as

both an artistic spectacle and a tourist enticement.[72] In this sense, the plays are restaging a conflict that was always at the heart of their fascination and interest in the medieval period. But they also animate a conflict at the very heart of the transformation of memory performed from the 1950s in Britain to the '90s, the shared chronology of contemporary Corpus Christi performances in York. In the still bomb-scarred city of 1951, the production could evoke at once an old endangered nation, "where history is associated with tradition and belonging is based on cultural ideas of ancestral descent" with the modernizing society of postwar reform, "where history is associated with progress and state-led redevelopment, where belonging follows from citizenship and the political idea of consent."[73] The repetition enacted in the ruins at regular intervals is in some sense an attempt to establish, through repetition, a celebration of recurrence. This perhaps helps to explain the virtually inflexible attachment to the ruins despite the extraordinary variety of performances enacted against this setting. But such an attempted reenactment may also constitute both a refusal of capital's "ceaseless transformation of the innovative into the obsolescent" and an attempt to reritualize time and space in a "conscious recall of the prototypical."[74] The two images of hierarchy, tradition, and belonging, on the one hand, and of public egalitarianism and citizenship, on the other, have, as Patrick Wright notes, been defined "in polemical opposition since the war."[75] The restaging of the Corpus Christi plays in York is an attempt ideologically to supersede this opposition. *Communitas* is conjured, dreamed, sought for, embraced, every three years, and every three years once more stages the spectacle of itself: "The criticism has been laid against the York Festival that it offers little of interest to the ordinary people of the city, but wherever else this may be true, it cannot apply to the Mystery Plays."[76]

Throughout the history of the twentieth-century performances in York, there are debates about whether to employ professional actors, stars, outside directors, or local amateurs. For example, Edward Taylor, who directed the plays in 1969, used a local amateur cast.[77] The history of the productions displays the straddling of its historical situation. Desiring to embody community, the plays are only financially viable as part of an international arts festival scene. As such, they attract that exemplary postmodern type—the tourist—and enact the spectacle of community as his or her dream in a city where the past has now been rendered a homogenous and fully finished world that nevertheless exists adjacent to it.[78] The modern contradiction is expressed by Jude Kelly, the director of the 1988 festival: "Our aim was to create a popular programme of events which would encompass the national status of the Festival whilst broadening its appeal to the widest possible spectrum of York people."[79] In necessarily appealing to the tourist, the plays have to respond to the tourist's demands: "For tourists pay for their freedom—the right to disregard native concerns and feelings, the right to spin their own web of meanings, they obtain in a commercial transaction."[80] The production of the plays mime in exemplary form both the tourist's relation and practice of place, the dislocation of location, and the citizen's relation to it, which, in a familiar chiasmus, reverses that same relation to perform the location of and amidst dislocation. In enacting such contradictions, the plays give life to the desires and exclusions that also model the relation of medieval studies to "community."

MEMORY AS PLENITUDE OR CATASTROPHE: THE EXEMPLARY CASE OF MEDIEVAL STUDIES

We live, as Samuel has said, in an "expanding historical culture in which the work of inquiry and retrieval is being progressively extended into all kinds of spheres that would have been thought unworthy of notice in the past."[81] In this sense, as Samuel argues, history is precisely not the sole prerogative of the historian, but a social form of knowledge: "If this is true, the point of address in any discussion should not be the work of the individual scholar, nor yet the rival schools of interpretation, but rather the ensemble of activities and practices in which ideas of history are embedded or a dialectic of past-present relations is rehearsed."[82] The sense of the past at any given time is quite as much a matter of history as what happened in it, and if the argument of Samuel's book is correct, the two are indivisible.

The Corpus Christi productions enact the past as nostalgia, as utopia, as trauma,[83] as ruin. As such, they explore the repertoire of modern mnemonics and the varieties of relations of past to present that they inhabit. As nostalgia, they perform that "sadness without an object," bracketing off a past as a form of grief. As utopia, the very plenitude of the past will reproach our depleted presence from its fullness and animate, help to provoke the version of community it makes spectacular. As ruin, it is an august inheritance, brutally truncated. As

Richard Terdiman has said in his analysis of the modern memory crisis, these forms display memory as either too much or too little, as impoverished or exorbitant, excess or catastrophe: "Since the memory crisis of the nineteenth century cultural objects have carried the enigma of the past and its determinations as a particularly stressful and mystified content."[84]

But the very possibility of reparation for perceived loss is always an issue that is as aesthetic as it is social, for cultural reparation can only ever work its cure, remission, or homeopathy through symbolization. As Wendy Wheeler writes:

> What every successful manouever discovers . . . is that however historically contingent the re-invented self, there can be no contingency between the symbolic forms and the life that is lived. In other words, for successful mourning to take place, there must be ties which bind. Not only must there be the poetic coherence between the painfully altered "living" and the elegiacally transformed "dead" but there must also be a personal poetic; a coherence between what is thought and said on the one hand, and what is done on the other. This is not, and cannot be, an injunction to continue investments in something which can no longer be had. It is an injunction to find something good—and thus consoling—in the fact of shattering, loss and transformation itself. The "sign" which substitutes for the "thing" must, in other words, have sufficient integrity to bear the dead weight it carries.[85]

Whether the signs of Corpus Christi in contemporary York finally have that sufficient integrity, whether they are able to provide "mourning with solidarity,"[86] can be adjudicated only on much more concrete analyses of individual performances, their histories, and their receptions.

Part Two

Social Relation & Symbolic Act

2 Ritual, Theater, and Social Space in the York Corpus Christi Cycle

> God is only a figurative expression of the society.
> —Émile Durkheim

Christianity provides in the condensed symbolic economy of the passion an image of the body that converts the suffering of one individual into the redemption of the world.[1] In the Passion and Resurrection sequences of the York Corpus Christi cycle, that symbol which clerical culture had sought to establish as hegemonic (universal, yet exclusive to them through their rights of mediation and officiation)—Christ's body in the host—is subject to an inventive, brutal, and alarming series of reworkings.[2] The Passion sequence gradually comes to subsume the theatrical and ritual energies of the city of York, as over the course of its production, it comes to account for half of the cycle. It is the silent object of the competing juridical claims of the secular and ecclesiastical establishment, represented in the plays by Pilate, Herod, and Annas and Caiphas. The object of Judas's betrayal and subsequent remorse, Christ's body is ritually tortured in an agonizingly extended sequence culminating in the reconstruction on stage of the central icon of the culture—Christ on the cross, dramatically played as both reenactment of the crucifixion and a construction of its central representation. Mourned for longingly and with anguish and only eventually relinquished by his mother and Mary Magdalene, its absence in the tomb signifying its miraculous escape from confinement, the impossibility of its constraint, the wounded body reappears in the Resurrection sequences as the very proof of the sacramental system it underwrites, to become the vehicle of a drama of doubt, disbelief, and evidential testing. Groped by Thomas, whose fingering of Christ's hide[3] is extensively investigated, Christ comes back in his wounded shirt in the Last Judgement pageant, the final pageant, so that the Christian cosmology can complete the sequence it has followed in the

pageants, accounting for the very beginning of the world in its creation, as it looks forward and gives a rendition of its end. That symbol
of which every little piece was a *pars pro toto*, a synecdoche for the
whole, is subjected, then, both literally and symbolically, to extensive,
protracted, and vicious fracturing.

The York Corpus Christi pageants are an unprecedented encounter
with the central imaginary significations of late medieval culture.
Through their rearticulation of the body of Christ on the streets of
York, the representations that organize social existence in York are examined: "Who are we as a collectivity? [they ask.] What are we for one
another? Where and in what are we? What do we want; what do we
desire; what are we lacking?"[4] This chapter looks at some ways in
which the articulation of the body of Christ in the pageant plays of the
York Corpus Christi cycle points at and presses those questions, and at
some of the ways in which criticism has conventionally addressed and
thought about the ritualized social space of York itself. In looking at
the implications of such examinations, I want to show how and at what
cost certain understandings of ritual, in their analyses of these plays,
have severed culture from social and political relations, structure from
history, and ritual itself from theatrical practices. And I will argue that
the analysis of these pageants in terms of a theory of ritualization will
help us to see the way in which cultural reproduction is connected to
temporal change, spatial configuration, social relations, and political
form, both in the productions of York and in our critical reproductions
of this theater.

SOCIAL WHOLENESS, OR THE PART
FOR THE WHOLE

"Among all human communities," Aquinas following Aristotle reminds us, "the city is most perfect." And "because the things which
come into the use of humans are ordered to humans as to their end, it
is therefore necessary that the whole which constitutes the city is the
principle of all other wholes which can be known and constituted by
human reason."[5] The city is assured its composite status, its integrity
by that other "principle of all other wholes," Corpus Christi itself, according to the pioneering analyst of the celebrations of this theme in
late medieval English town life. In his article published in *Past and
Present* in 1983, Mervyn James writes:

The theme of Corpus Christi is society seen in terms of body. The concept of the body provided urban societies with a mythology and ritual in terms of which opposites of social wholeness and differentiation could be affirmed and brought into creative tension, one with the other. The final intention of the cult was, then, to express the social bond and to contribute to social integration.[6]

This approach is based on a particular interpretation of Durkheim by way of Mary Douglas; the body is the site for the close interrelation of symbolic classification, ritual process, and the formation of social solidarity.[7] This approach, brilliant and deservedly influential as was its elucidation in this particular article, has tended to reduplicate at the level of functionalist anthropology the very hegemony that the medieval theologies and politics of Corpus Christi sought to accomplish: social integration and unity in the name of a single administering body. Functionalist anthropology will thus reiterate the very clerical project it seeks to lay bare. In both cases, and they share a twin idealism, the hegemonic project that allows a part to speak for a whole will be rendered invisible, for that part will already have been mistaken for the whole. One can therefore hardly be used as an historical account of the other.[8]

James's appropriation of Durkheim has problems explaining and exploring the processes by which the town is reproduced as a whole. And his inability to do this is linked to the way in which his model of ritual derives from a holistic version of culture that cannot separate out or identify sociopolitical structures.[9] Neither is his model capable of engaging in any explicit way with the theatrical practices of the plays themselves.[10] This is perhaps not surprising, for the model of ritual wielded in these analyses is a better tool for examining and constructing a sense of overall structure than it is, say, at dealing with the manipulation of bodies in space in the individual pageants, or their sophisticated attention to the phenomenological dichotomy of the actor's body (simultaneously sign and signified).[11] And yet any understanding of the complex festivity of Corpus Christi should not avoid a more detailed confrontation with these pageants if it is to account for the ritual of Corpus Christi festivities and the manipulation of Christ's body at their center.[12]

In James's model, ritual is a discrete, identifiable object characterized in particular by its splitting of action from thought, and by the function of its action: the resolution of contradiction and the closure of social conflict.[13] The endemic fissures and tensions in late medieval urban life, between the mercantile oligarchy and an artisanate that it increasingly sought to delimit by repressive labor legislation, could all be assuaged by the sense of wholeness and participation both represented but more crucially generated by the composite, sacral, and unified body of Christ (see chapter 3). The body of Christ can unify in this view because it is itself invested with the intense levels of social interaction that surround it in the festivity, which is then invested in the object taken to represent collective ideals.[14]

The pageants that treat the ministry of Christ in the York cycle depict Christ's break with the Old Law via a demonstration of his superior scriptural knowledge (miraculously mediated) and his powers of salvific healing; and the drama is consistently self-conscious about its enactment and articulation of a prior text.[15] Thus Christ will tell Peter to fetch the ass on which he will ride into Jerusalem so that he can fulfill the prophecy, and yet this consciousness of scriptural precedent, particularly marked in the pageants most concerned with the move from the Old to New Testaments, disappears in the skinners' pageant of the Entry into Jerusalem. Here we are swept up in a process of ritual participation in which York becomes Jerusalem, and in which the lyrical and repetitive hailing of Christ as king is both a construction and recognition of him as such. Structures of belief, doctrinal considerations, are here utterly unimportant. The theatrical and ritual effect is one of being swept into an inevitable, visceral, and committed response to his passage. Exploiting the processional nature of the staging, the burghers in the play await the entrance of Christ; the blind man, the lame man, and Zacchaeus come out of the crowd to halt the procession, in such a way that Jerusalem and York are superimposed one on the other. Through the medium of Christ's passage, one has been converted into the other.[16] It is just such moments that James's model seems good at reading, but he is less successful at others. Indeed, we might say that his article examines the structural level of ritual organization in the abstract rather than the substance of the pageants in their performative practice. Part of the problem lies in the way he locates ritual as a discrete, autonomous object of study. For as Durkheim says in "Value Judgments and Judgments of Reality":

> Collective ideals can only be manifested and become aware of themselves by being concretely realized in material objects that can be seen

by all, understood by all, and represented to all minds. . . . All sorts of contingent circumstances determine the manner of its embodiment, and the object once chosen, however commonplace, becomes unique.[17]

But what precisely here is the object of representation? What, indeed, is the nominal object of festivity, of celebration? Who and what is Christ's body in the performance of the Corpus Christi pageants in York? At this point we will need to go beyond the notion of an integrated and wholesome body being traced onto the city as if it had no resisting shape, no already delineated contours, no marked and contested spaces to make a rougher surface, a more difficult screen on which to draw the shape and outline of Christ's body and the ideology that accompanies it.

SIGNIFYING GOD: SYMBOLIC PRACTICE

How is God signified? On the one hand, God as a supernatural concept underwrites the entire belief system and cosmology of late medieval culture. But on the other hand, it is the very impossibility of his representation that determines the way in which God as an imaginary signification might generate the creative mythologies through which that society looks at itself:

> Whatever points of support his representation may take in perceived reality, whatever his rational effectiveness may be as an organizing principle of the environing world for certain cultures, God is neither a signification of something real, nor a signification of something rational. . . . God is neither the name of God nor the images a people may give him, nor anything of the sort. Carried by, pointed at by all these symbols, he is, in every religion, that which makes these symbols religious symbols—a central *signification,* the organization of signifieds and signifiers into a system. . . . And this signification which is neither something perceived (real) nor something thought (rational) is an imaginary signification.[18]

God, or God as Christ, does not actually denote anything as such; but in the very vagueness and indeterminacy of that denotation, he may connote everything.[19] The symbol may be overdetermined through its very indetermination.[20] These hints from Castoriadis and Bourdieu may help us to extend the notion of ritual practice from Mervyn James to incorporate more precisely the ways in which cultural form is not so much imposed on the city of York but articulated by and through that city. In extending James's Durkheimian/Douglasian version of ritual into a reading of bodily practice, it will be possible also to overcome the dichotomy of ritual and theater that has bedeviled criticism of medieval Corpus Christi theater. For historians who have used the concept of ritual have by and large shied away from reading the pageants themselves; critics of the theater have been constrained by tenets of formalist literary criticism that are inadequate for performative readings. In the process we may be able to reconnect the political and aesthetic effects of the drama.

My argument is that ritual does not so much assert a set of monolithic beliefs as construct a series of tensions. As Catherine Bell has put it: "This orchestration is not a perfect and holistic order imposed on minds and bodies but a delicate and continual renegotiation of provisional distinctions and integrations so as to avoid encountering in practice the discrepancies and conflicts that would become so apparent if the whole were obvious."[21] This view further implies that ritual does not so much designate an object as a process of relation. As Bourdieu writes: "Ritual practice, which aims to facilitate passages and/or to authorize encounters between opposed orders, never defines beings or things otherwise than in and through the relationship it establishes practically between them, and makes the fullest possible use of the polysemy of the fundamental actions."[22] In such an understanding of ritual practice, no objective meanings can be assigned independently of material processes, and such meaning restores the practical moments of human agency that James's model of ritual has found hard to locate. Space, which is too simplistically conceived by Mervyn James as the tabula rasa of the procession, comes to have meaning through practice itself.[23]

INTEGRATION THROUGH DIVISION

The theoretical inflections of Catherine Bell and Pierre Bourdieu are not necessarily in complete opposition to the Durkheimian approach pioneered by Mervyn James. Durkheim, for example tends to use "sacred" as an adjective, not as a noun.[24] For him the sacred is arguably a situational rather than a substantive category: ". . . sacred and profane, are transitive categories; they serve as maps and labels, not substances; they are distinctions of office, indices of difference."[25] Such an understanding is not just one that is offered by contemporary theorists of ritual; it is also built into articulations of ritual practice in the late Middle Ages itself. Take, for example, an anonymous sermon on Corpus Christi that constructs itself quite conventionally around a scriptural text, gloss, and a series of exempla.[26] The text—"Whosoever eats my flesh and drinks my blood, will dwell in me and I in him. And therefore I will go to the place from which I came" (John 6:54)—is first translated from the Latin and then linked with the text from 1 Corinthians 11:29: "For he that eateth and drinketh unworthily, eateth and drinketh damnation to himself, not discerning the Lord's body." Then follow a series of exempla designed to make the point that the mass is not an empty rite, and the host not an object whose magic is preexistent. Its capacities for transformation depend upon the way it is approached; and such an approach requires preparation. One of the exempla concerns a woman who goes to mass out of charity in hatred of a poor neighbor. At the mass, her priest says he will withhold her "ryghtes" unless she forgives her neighbor and reconciles herself with her. She does this, but out of "shame of the world" rather than "awe of God." When after the service her hated neighbor comes to her house and she admits that she forgave only with her mouth and not with her heart, "the devil strangles her even there." The host will not magically resolve discord or disharmony. Its properties lie in the structures of relation that are established between the ritual participant and the ritual object. Though transformative powers might be ascribed to the host itself, they operate according to a mutual, and mutually structuring, relation.

It was such a relation that was subject, as here, to clerical definition and attempts at control. The ritual object is then not magically or ontologically efficacious. Catherine Bell, informed by both Bourdieu and Foucault, argues for a different understanding of ritual from Mervyn James, one which will see it as a practice whose self-differentiation is an intrinsic part of its efficacy. Ritualization will, according to her reading, involve the establishment of a privileged contrast, loosely homologized to suggest but never define solutions. In this way, sacred and profane (never in any case ontological referents for Durkheim) are produced through the very performance of their differentiation. So, in the York Corpus Christi plays, the body of Christ, the sacrament that is the ritual object par excellence, does not simply operate according to a static binary opposition: divinity versus humanity. Rather it catches in its network of association a range of oppositions that, because they are mutually constructed through the way the body of Christ conflates them, provide nuance, add to, and so defer any final signification. Christ's body alludes to numerous oppositions: inner and outer, transcendent and immanent, spirit and flesh, male and female, left and right, up and down, noisy and silent, just and unjust, passive and active, noumenal and phenomenal, public and private, hierarchical and collective, unified and multiplicitous, and so on.[27] Each set of terms invokes the others; they imply a loose coherence, but this is actually constituted by a "redundant, circular and rhetorical universe of values and terms whose significance keeps flowing into other values and terms."[28] Each set of categories transcodes and refers to the others, and meaning is constructed and deferred through those interrelationships. There is no definitive statement, then, nothing that may be subject to assent and denial. Integration is established paradoxically through division and ambiguity is essential to ritual's efficacy.

When the centurion comes rushing in to explain to his overlords the miracle of Longinus's regained sight in the butchers' Death of Christ pageant, for example, he declares that it is a "misty thyng to mene."[29] His words refer us back to that pageant where the unequivocal truths of the revelation of God in Christ have been asserted:

> O wondirfull werkar iwis,
> Þis weedir is waxen full wan
> Trewe token I trowe þat it is
> Þat mercy is mente unto man.[30]

And yet when we hear him again in the Resurrection pageant, the full complexity of the word "mene" becomes marked. For it carries the double significance of meaning, intention, and intermediary, and the very mistiness of the communication here is not an isolated incident in the Resurrection sequences but a central part of their ritual efficacy. It is as if the centurion's role is reflexively marked here to acknowledge, not merely that he is an intermediary, but that to mean something, to intend a meaning, is necessarily to have to go through the vagaries of representation, of mediation. What is meant needs to be meant by someone and understood by someone, and the complexities, difficulties, and frustrations of this "meaning" complicate greatly any simple act of witnessing that had seemed so simple in the "trew token of truth" asserted in the Death of Christ pageant. The other latent meaning of "mene" is doubt (surely contextually agitated here), and it is through the exploration of doubt and disbelief, of the difficulty of understanding, that a complex relation with the ritual object is established; and this, rather than the simple communication of the doctrine of the resurrection, is precisely the point of the extended sequence that contemplates the repetitive return of the wounded yet resurrected body.

We understand the body of Christ through the relation developed with it by Mary, Mary Magdalene, Thomas, the pilgrims at Emmaus, the other disciples. It is through this changed relation that new identities are formed. The continuous and agonizing return of Christ's bleeding body in these sequences, then, is not just the return of the incontrovertible proof[31] of the central doctrine that underscores the medieval sacramental system, but the insistence on its central cultural contradiction.[32] In the Death of Christ pageant, we are shown the central miracle that is the very axis of the play cycle: the regained sight that shows that we too can see that Christ is the sign of God. But it is neither the cognitive statement of belief that we are meant to understand by the time the play is over, or the mindlessly ritualized incantation,[33] which through its sheer repetition and formalization[33] will eventually manage to succeed in incorporating all in its ecstatic embrace. The plays as a whole consciously encode an argument about the relation of cognition to incorporation, and we need a model of ritual able to read the complexity of such interactions.[34]

CITY AS THEATER: ACTOR AND SPACE

In these sequences the body as the bearer of social and cultural meaning is absolutely central, not just because the pageants intimately concern a theology of incarnation and embodiment, but also because in theater it is the very body of the actor that becomes the chief vehicle of semiosis. If, as Robert Weimann has stated, "to explore [the] connections between the technical arrangements and the unformulated intellectual assumptions of the medieval theater is to find that there is no such thing as a unified or homogeneous concept of a stage,"[35] then that stage is articulated into being at the very moment when an actor assumed a role in the streets of York. Given that the acting area had no inherent symbolic significance, the "tension between fictive locality and public space"[36] is called into being through the body of the actor. Though the pageants are concerned with mapping the body in many and overdetermined ways, surprisingly there has been almost no attempt to develop a systematic understanding of the kinds of bodily inscription involved in the Corpus Christi pageants, nor the implications of such an account for an investigation of the interrelations of ideology, religion, and corporeal identity.[37] What is learned by the body is not (as Bourdieu has reminded us) what one has, but what one is.[38] Incorporating practices such as theater and ritual are powerful means of articulating the reproduction of the social order in habit-memory, in the innocent injunctions of the body's choreography. It is because the body somaticizes culture,[39] because the world is affectively as well as semantically structured[40] in powerful because mute ways, that "every group trusts to bodily automatisms the values and categories which they are most anxious to conserve."[41]

In addition, this is a processional theater whose very stage (or series of stages) is the city of York itself.[42] The topography of the city is spatially reorganized through the mutual restructuring of body and environment involved in this performative inscription. The route, for example—and so the shape of the city and the body that is mutually implicated—was subject to argument, and this had a direct bearing on who was able to control and profit from the ritual forum intended to encompass all its citizens. In 1399 the commons presented a petition to determine where the stations of performance were to be located. It requested that the stations be positioned at the doors of the important civic officials as well as at other more obviously public places.[43] In 1417 at a meeting described as the most representative meeting of the community that the *York Memorandum Book* has registered, the populace complained about the profit being made by those before whose houses the plays were performed:

> Since everyone bear his charge towards the upholding of this play according to his estate, it was therefore unanimously ordained that for the benefit of the commons the places for the performance of the aforesaid play would be changed unless those before whose places the play used to be performed have paid whatever was enjoined yearly to the commons for having this, his individual profit, thus. And it was ordained that in all the years following while this play is played, it must be played before the doors and holdings of those who have paid better and more generously to the Chamber and who have been willing to do more for the benefit of the whole commons for having this play there, not giving favour to anyone for his individual benefit, but rather that the public utility of the whole of the commons of York ought to be considered.[44]

The shape and timing and positioning of the performance of the Corpus Christi pageants, then, were subject to local bargaining in which the interests of private property and profit competed with the interests of "*tocius communitatis.*" The rhetorical conversion of individual profit to public-spirited generosity is a fascinating sleight of hand here and merits further consideration. For Charles Phythian-Adams, this is the demonstration of his dictum that "ceremony completed the transformation of wealth ownership into class standing for the upper levels of society."[45] But there may be more ramifications to such arguments than the principle of increasing ceremonial presence. The subtext of the 1417 meeting is the appropriation and definition of civic space as private property against a competing definition of common use. The scaffolds erected before the houses of the eminent in front of which some of the stations were to be located functioned virtually like private theaters in the public city space:

> Nevertheless, the mayor, the honourable men, and the whole said commons, by their unanimous consent and assent, order <that> all those who receive money for scaffolds which they may build in the foresaid places before their doors on public property at the aforesaid sites from those sitting on them shall pay the third penny of the money so received to the chamberlains of the city to be applied to the use of the same commons.[46]

The erected scaffolds rested, it was pointed out, on city property, and so the city should profit. It was a veiled protest against the conversion of communal drama into private entertainment and emblematic of wider contests in which the body of Christ was challenged to assume its universalizing, common, and generous invitation. In his analysis of the York Corpus Christi cycle as ritual, Richard Homan uses this incident as an indication of the "common interest prevailing over the interest of the few," a representation that ignores the rhetorical conversion of "individual advantage" into "public welfare," through the power of property and payment. For Homan, following James, this is an instance of "the Corpus Christi cycle's function as an arena in which actual conflicts could be ritually resolved."[47] Wealthy householders, through paying money to the city, could literally inscribe their own property into the route of the Corpus Christi pageants, because their houses were part of the processional staging of the cycle. The twenty-five surviving station lists between 1399 and 1569 indicate how this inscription was regularly invoked and exploited by incumbent mayors and the aldermanic elite of the city.[48]

Such arguments require a more supple and flexible conception of the ritual and theatrical carving up of space in York than is currently offered. They require of us the difficult task of thinking of the boundaries they delineate, in Georg Simmel's terms, as less a "spatial fact with sociological consequences" than a "sociological fact that is conceived spatially."[49]

The 1417 memorandum, for example, invokes the public utility of the whole commons, and yet by converting their wealth into their generosity, the rhetoric of the passage allows the maintenance of what are effectively private theaters within the public space of the city.[50] They function as private theaters in that the illustrious houses become the backdrop of the theater. These are the points that at least for the day define the shape of Corpus Christi, but because the space itself is rented out from the city council by private owners, who are making money by renting out seats on scaffolds erected on "community ground,"[51] it is riven with contradictory meanings. The space itself carries no essential meaning; it comes into being through the complex relation and actions of the ritual and theatrical practices through which it is enacted. The metaphor of the city as stage has been invoked before,[52] but we need to see in more concrete terms how the densely significant social space of the city and its topography can figure as part of the polysemousness of the theater.

By 1394 the route of the Corpus Christi plays seems already to have been established.[53] The contest over space and who was to control it can already perhaps be seen in the wording of that decree requesting that the pageants be played in their assigned stations and not at any others, and that there should be a fine if that decree was infringed.[54] Over the years the stations changed in number and position, and it would certainly be interesting to establish a more concrete sense of the meanings of those changes. Here I hope to establish how the city as stage might help us to conceptualize the kind of theater this is, how it might contribute to that sense of the sheer overdetermination that we have established as being central to the ideological mechanisms of this play's workings. Anna J. Mill and Meg Twycross have mapped out the location of the stations in some detail. From their work we can establish if we take, for example, some of the earliest records, those of 1398–99, as exemplary, that the Corpus Christi pageants first collected on

Toft Green outside of the city gates, and then passed through the following stations: Trinity Gates at Micklegate, the house of Robert Harpham, the house of John Gysburn, the end of Skeldergate and the end of Northstreet, the Castlegate end of Coney Street, the end of Jubbergate, the house of Henry Wyman on Coney Street, near the Common Hall at the end of Coney Street, the house of the late Adam del Brigg in Stonegate, the Minster Gates, the end of Girdlergate at Petergate, and, finally, the Pavement.[55] What is the (necessarily changing) significance of some of these sites? First of all we might say that the territory of the city itself (before any pageant, actor, or procession transforms it) was already hardly a single area of franchise. As E. Miller has said: "It was honeycombed with other franchises, some of them older than the liberty of the city."[56] One of the stations outside the Minster Gates represents the edges of one of these liberties, at which, for example the dean could hold a court for all transgressions "in the land of the court both within and without the city."[57] The Minster Gates then represent an area where the city's authority could not extend. The territorial marking of one of the stations at the gates of a minster that was itself not involved in the Corpus Christi procession[58] represented at once an enclosure of mayoral jurisdiction and a breach into the jurisdiction of the minster. It could thereby be a physical reminder that this interlacing of privilege and exemption—which, as Miller writes, "early manifested itself in disputes over the claim of the privileged churches that their property was exempt from the common burdens"[59]—was an irritant, sometimes erupting into a violent conflict.

Obviously there is some sense, then, in which the Corpus Christi pageants may be marking territory in the same way in which boundaries were "ridden." The ridings of the citizens and the mayor, for example, were requested by the citizens in 1465 "for that we may know our liberties and lose no part of our right that is due to the city."[60] These ridings did take place frequently (though not with annual regularity[61]) and were only stopped in 1830, because at this point, enclosure, outright extinction of common rights, as well as replacement by strays whose "boundaries were precisely known" and mapped, made the perambulations "unnecessary." The Corpus Christi procession and pageants may then mark space like the beating of the bounds ceremonies performed during Rogation Days, about three weeks before Corpus Christi in the liturgical calendar. The task of the Rogation

Days was to ratify boundaries, but they too display the ambivalence of festival in that they also offer the community license to transgress those boundaries.[62] The Rogation processions designate the common rights of the city; through priestly blessing they are sanctified; through the beating of the bounds they are inscribed in the physical memory of the processioners. E. P. Thompson describes a Rogation procession in which "small boys were sometimes ducked in the ditch or given a clout to imprint the spot upon their memories."[63] The Rogations designated the city as a political corporation with rights and responsibilities before the common law.[64] Thompson describes Rogation processions as examples of the contested nature of custom at the interface between law and agrarian practice. Custom, as Thompson in his pathbreaking examination shows, is at one extreme "sharply defined and enforceable at law, and (as at enclosure) . . . a property."[65] But it also depended on the "continual renewal of oral tradition, as in the regular perambulation of the bounds of the parish," and as such it passes into more blurred areas: "unwritten beliefs, sociological norms, and usages asserted in practice but never enrolled in any by-law."[66] Rogation ceremonies plotted out space, then, in such a way as to "imprint its topography on the popular memory."[67] They become indeed, historically, the very site of competing definitions of space as property as against use, away from a broadly feudal notion of custom as reciprocal obligation to a reification of usages into properties.[68] For "beating the bounds" conventionally signified at once a ritualization of space and a consecration of property.[69] When the 1547 royal injunctions curtailed many of the religious processions associated with "popery," the Rogation perambulation was retained. In 1559 Bishop Grindal refined the procession still further: it was to be carried out by the curate and "substantial men of the parish boundaries."[70] Grindal thus redefined the procession as a "perambulation" and restricted it to property holders.[71] In this reading, ceremony is not simply the confirmation or revelation of a preconceived holism, but rather a place of "unqualified class conflict."[72] In York the ceremonial ridings of the sheriffs are, after 1537, associated with the Corpus Christi productions.[73] Persistent attention is paid in the records of the city to the way disputes over the "commons" become an important theme of civic politics.[74] Miller documents the incidents of arguments between the citizens and Lord Lovell in 1479, between the citizens and St. Mary's Abbey in 1480, and those between

St. Nicholas Hospital and the commons in 1484, which erupted into riot in October of that year.[75] The city authorities tried to avoid disputes by seeking recognition of the citizens' common rights. Such "recognition" often took the form of an annual rent to substitute for the use of common rights, as for example when the vicars choral agreed to pay rent to the city to "extinguish the common rights" over commonage in the Vicars Lease.[76] The weavers rioted and took down the hedges surrounding the disputed land.[77]

The debate about the stations of the city may be seen as part of an endemic and long-standing argument over physical space, in which it was the literal ground of competing definitions, at once of possession and usage.[78] We need to develop a way of reading these plays and festivities, then, not as the reflection of a homogeneous collective understanding that will reveal the very principles of a social structure,[79] but in ways that make their spatial configurations, as they extend in time as well as space, a dynamic and component part of their articulation. If, as David Harvey says, space is a "source of social power,"[80] then its homogeneity can only be achieved through a total "pulverization and fragmentation into freely alienable parcels of private property, to be bought and traded at will on the market."[81] Festival, which insists on visibility, on publicity, makes claims on space in altogether different ways.[82]

The York Corpus Christi festivities reconfigure space, then; they argue over it in many ways. But we also need to be able to see how such reconfigurations will interact in a city that organizes its division of labor, its social polarities, in visible because spatial ways.

Generally speaking, we can talk about a concentration of the larger and bigger households with the greater retinues of servants in the central prosperous districts of York, while many poor suburban districts contained houses with only one person (frequently female).[83] In addition, as P. J. Goldberg points out, by about 1450–1500 the commercial sector, comprising the mercers and drapers who clustered in Fossgate and the parishes of St. Crux and All Saints, shrunk and appeared to become more closely defined.[84] This may well be a topographical enactment of an increasingly wide gap between the artisanate and the mercantile oligarchy, which it may have been part of the very purpose of the Corpus Christi celebrations to enact. As the commercial sector contracted the actual physical space it took up in the city, it extended its command over ceremonial space. Anna J. Mill's figures indicate that as the stations took in spectacularly less rent in the sixteenth century, there appeared to be more and more "freeplaces" commandeered for the use of officials and dignitaries.[85]

In addition, trades may well have been associated with certain specific sites that they filled with their wares, the physical tools of their trade, and the symbolic values that attached to them: the metal trades were to be found, for example, in Petergate and Coney Street, the drapers in Ousegate and Jubbergate, and the butchers were in the Shambles near the Pavement and had their own hall.[86]

But there were other ways in which the material space of York might have set up interesting interactions as the pageants rolled by the different temporary stages of their procession. As they passed the Castlegate end of Coney Street, they may have passed the prisons;[87] as they came onto the Pavement, that space would have signified the central marketplace of York, where not merely goods but people were traded, since servants had to collect here to sell themselves to new masters,[88] the place too where proclamations were made and punishments enacted. What significance would the Last Judgement have performed in such a place? Would it be different from the performance, say, of the Crucifixion or of the various jurisdictions that tried Christ in the plays? Would the differing versions of justice indict or underwrite (more likely both) the mayoral administration? And what if they were performed before the house of that mayor himself, John Gysburn? Gysburn was chased out of the city in 1381 by rioters who subsequently broke into the guildhall and swore in Simon Quixley as mayor.[89] Quixley and Gysburn were both rich merchants, but it seemed that Quixley had the support of the nonmercantile crafts.[90] The dispute was described as one between Gysburn and the "communitas."[91] If Gysburn had the pageants performing outside his door, he was claiming space in the city; although the way that space would be interpreted, as his house became part of the theater, would never be subject to his interpretive control.[92]

If we see and continue to devise ways of seeing the sheer ambiguous density of the interaction between city and theater as each transformed the other in the production of the York Corpus Christi cycle, then we will also see that the ritualization of the city is not about the imposition of a homogeneous kind of unity onto the city, but rather an implication of its webs of signification. The politics we need to talk about, then, will not be those of dominance and subversion or resistance and containment, but rather the politics of mobility and access.[93]

Far, then, from being the bounded, contained place that we have been used to thinking about, it would be hard to think of a theatrical space more polysemous then the stage provided by the city of York. But as I suggested earlier, it is not the essential meaning of the spaces themselves so much as the uses to which they are put, their construction through agency, that enhances our understanding of the multiple dimensions of meaning that they can inhabit. In the Corpus Christi pageants, overdetermination is the principle of the acting as well. There may be as many as thirty different actors playing, for example, Christ, as many as thirty playing Mary, and several different Gods. In each instance the identity of the performer, the actor, the persona, and the way it might be crafted in the individual pageant may all play against each other. And there is no determining the relation of the pageants to one another. It is hard to imagine that the processional order of the pageants would be the same order in which any spectator might want to observe them. The possibilities of perspective, of interrelationship, are at once bewildering and exhilarating.

One of the ways that the pageants work, then, is not so much through an assertion of doctrine or belief, but through the central manipulation of the symbol of Christ's body in ritualized performances. Such a structure helps to avoid those problematic areas that occur where awkwardnesses of doctrine are particularly foregrounded— such as the Purification pageant, where Mary, purest of the pure, untainted by the normal carnal sin attendant upon giving birth, must still be ritually purified, or the Baptism pageant, where Jesus (to the evident surprise of John the Baptist) must be baptized.[94] The paradox here is that the very foundation and legitimation of Christ's church on earth, Jesus himself, has to participate in the ritual structures that he supposedly actually instituted. The text registers this awkwardness, and it is not of course a problem that can be logically resolved at the level of belief, a problem that the cycle itself implicitly acknowledges in the Harrowing of Hell pageant. In response to Satan's subtle poking at the contradictions of the dispensation of mercy and the existence of hell, Christ responds quite unequivocally that it is not simply virtue, but allegiance and love, belief in his law, that are important to the attempt to stay out of hell: "Who will noght trowe, þei are noght trewe."[95] The plays themselves cannot altogether avoid the problem of belief, for they are, after all, partially concerned with commanding assent to those beliefs. However, theological readings of the plays that perceive them as sermons in drama can make no account of their symbolic working, for in such a view they merely encode simple messages whose "truths" will be passively absorbed by their audiences.[96]

One can, after all, only speak symbolically about Christ. If the symbolizing process involves a movement across a classificatory system, thus problematizing a region where language intersects with the world, a symbol may call both the describing language and the world into question. That is why the symbolic utterances that circulate around the symbol of Christ's body are the very densest sites of signification. It is because that symbol violates the classificatory lines of the system (and therefore the order upheld through those divisions and definitions) that contests for new configurations of meaning obsessively locate themselves here. But it is for this reason, too, that violent hierarchies may be reinscribed, as symbolic utterances paradoxically, through the very act of boundary crossing, reveal the lines of the system in the very act of rudely violating them.[97]

An interpretative practice, I have tried to suggest, based on a concept of ritualization rather than either ritual or doctrine and belief, might begin to understand and plumb the symbolic resources of the bodily symbol at the center of this drama and so help to articulate both its affective reach and its relation to structures of domination. (For the real power of a dominant model is "its ability to produce and reproduce itself, continually to impose the principals of the construction of reality."[98]) But it would not be sufficient to understand such a symbol through a set of cognitively understood binary oppositions; rather, these oppositions need to be seen as being articulated in and through the space that is actually only produced through social, that is, bodily, practice.[99] Such bodily practices are at once subject to diachrony and to intense theatricalization—to the simultaneity of production and communication rendered possible by performance.[100]

Such a reading might finally be able to begin to understand the defining religiosity of the Corpus Christi cycles. For we cannot, as in the discourse of rationalism, await some anticipation of an unambiguous set of symbols; rather, that ambiguity is central to the social mechanisms of Corpus Christi. And if, like Merleau-Ponty, we are able to see that "religion is not a veil for some other more true meaning which is hidden beneath it, even if it helps sustain a culture that is closed and narrow compared with a possible social existence,"[101] then we will see that religion is neither reducible to the orthodox doctrine "expressed" in these plays, nor is it simply false consciousness.[102] It does not finally constitute a doctrine to be transmitted, but a world of significance to be explored.

3 Work, Markets, Civic Structure

ORGANIZING THE YORK CORPUS CHRISTI PLAYS

Leaning back the spectator
Should see
How cunningly you prepare for him
Should see
The tin moon come swaying down
And the cottage roof brought in.
Do not disclose over much
Yet disclose something to him.
Friends
Let him discover
You are not conjuring
But working.
—Bertolt Brecht, "The Curtains"

In this chapter I argue that far from unifying the city of York, the Corpus Christi festivities are intimately bound up with a divisive political regulation of labor. York had a large percentage of its population involved in manufacturing[1] and the pageants seem curiously interested in the theme of labor. How is work understood, then, as York itself is remade on Corpus Christi Day? How does the political representation of the city connect with its cultural forms?[2]

In a Gary Larson cartoon, God is found with a large lump of plasticine on one side of him, surrounded on the other side by a series of plasticine snakes. He sits in the middle gleefully rolling out one of the more consequential of his creations. "Boy," he says, "these are a cinch."[3] Larson's visual humor works off an ancient theological axiom that insists there could be nothing approximating human effort, the labor of work, in the act of divine creation.

Standard commentaries on the creation of the world were in the habit of pointing out that God did not make the world like an artisan makes an object:

For the builder does not make the wood, but makes something from the wood, and so it is with all other craftsmen of this kind. But almighty God needed the help of nothing that he had not already made himself for carrying out his will. For if he was helped in making the things he willed to make by some other things that he had not made, he was not almighty; and to believe that is blasphemy.[4]

When God as "maker unmade," as alpha and omega, as the most primal of movers, creates the world in the York cycle, his act is to be understood as an act of creation, rather than a production of labor. And yet in the Fall of Angels pageant, God describes his own creation as "warke" with a repetitious insistence that can hardly be accidental:

> To all I sall wirke be ȝhe wysshyng.
> This day warke es done ilke a dele,
> And all þis warke lykes me ryght wele,
> And baynely I ȝyf it my blyssyng.[5]

This insistence on work is repeated with greater point and elaboration in the Building of the Ark pageant, where God does indeed become the master craftsman teaching the ignorant Noah the tricks of the trade of shipbuilding.[6] "Warke" that has itself up until this moment signified God's work of making the world, now comes to mean both the botched-up object of his work, the human, and simultaneously, the necessity to redo the work all over again: "Bot wirke þis werke I wille al newe."[7] The significance is worked alliteratively too in lines 35–36, where God says to Noah:

> I wyll þou wyrke withowten weyn
> A warke to saffe þiselfe wythall.

The notion of God's creation in the Augustinian and Anselmian sense is increasingly compromised by the analogy of God as master craftsman teaching Noah his trade. Noah knows nothing about "shippecraft," but God advises him in some detail (l. 66).[8] The work references continue insistently throughout lines 70, 87, 93, 95, 110, 115, 120, and with a newly charged meaning when it comes to mean the work of salvation in line 147. The reference to God as master craftsman is made quite explicit at the very end of the pageant:

> He þat to me þis Crafte has kende,
> He wysshe vs with his worthy wille.[9]

The meaning of the word for "work," then, is densely encoded to mean at once humanity as the object of God's work, the work of making humanity, the work of restoring it, and Noah's work of ark building and salvation. The hierarchies of creation insisted upon by Augustine and Anselm are here collapsed to foreground an activity seen in human and anthropomorphic terms.[10]

In the production of the Creation pageant staged by actors from the Department of Drama and Theatre Arts at the University of Birmingham in the Toronto York cycle production of 1998, Joel Kaplan's direction of the pageant brings out the twin meanings of mechanical labor through a theatrical theology of creation. This world is created "Noght by my strenkyth, but by my steuyn":[11] God's very words bring worlds into being, and as he speaks of the things he creates, they appear as beautiful artifacts ingeniously appearing from cantilevered foldouts emerging from every angle of the pageant wagon. As God speaks forth his creation, we the audience seem to see our old familiar world for the first time as it newly comes into being. The Birmingham staging movingly and brilliantly shows that God's creation can be our discovery, our recognition. And it does this using the theatrical coincidence that actors make worlds through voice, too. It is as if we see God saying, "Well, what a good idea, we'll have trees, and they can have branches and flowers," and it does indeed seem like a marvelous idea. This God is an actor with a mask on, a gorgeous gold mask with sunbeams radiating from its circumference. When he takes it off, as he was directed to do in the Birmingham play, we know that he is one of us, intimate with us, that his world is our world. The tensions between the beautiful artifice, the fabrication and mechanical movements of the pageant, and the creation of the world through the word, the voice, are in exquisite and moving tension. For God there is no tension between creation and labor. But new definitions of work come with our fall.

For the subsequent fall of his creation is the originary myth of the necessity of human labor, to be understood both as the pain of parturition and as the inauguration of a relentlessly finite existence: the rupture of culture from nature. Labor will be the end of a process in which reproduction—birth—will ineradicably be tied to death, and will serve as a reminder of the sundering of will and flesh. Furthermore, labor, in the sense of work, will be necessitated by the new relationship of humans and their environs. Nature is henceforth the medium that will have to be tended, worked, and cultivated for sustenance.

But it is not merely a regime of hard labor and sexual inequality that is inaugurated by the fall of God's creation, but a sacramental culture. For the architects of the sacramental system,

> the time of the institution of the sacraments is believed to have begun from the first moment when the first parent, on being expelled by merit of disobedience from the joys of paradise into the exile of this mortal life, is held with all posterity liable to the first corruption even to the end. For from the time when man, having fallen from the state of first incorruption, began to ail in body through mortality and in soul through iniquity, God at once prepared a remedy for restoring man.[12]

The sacramental system is part of the way in which fallen nature can be recuperated as redeemed culture. Sexual reproduction itself, for example, becomes part of that system through the sacraments of marriage, baptism, purification, and confession.

But if the York cycle is concerned with the moment of the fall as the inauguration of work, the subordination of woman to man through her sexual and maternal nature, and ecclesiastically sanctioned and administered sacramental culture, it is also concerned with the inauguration of shameful and acute self-consciousness. "Allas, what have I done, for shame! . . . Me shames with my lyghame," utters Adam after he has eaten the fruit in the Fall of Adam and Eve pageant.[13] The central moment of this pageant is not the transgression of eating the apple, that heinous and almost unthinkable act of disobedience, but an appalled understanding of self-consciousness as the facticity of the body itself. The staging makes this moment quite central. For we have seen Adam and Eve naked in the Garden of Eden throughout the pageant. All of a sudden we see them again, mediated by their own profound shame. Nakedness becomes before our very eyes the sign of sin and self-disgust. Though nothing has in fact changed in outward appearance, everything has changed in a new postlapsarian world, a world where costume and covering are an intrinsic part of human appearance.

In Hugh of Saint Victor's *Didascalicon*, Adam and Eve's shameful "aprons," sewn together from fig leaves, are the very first art objects.[14] It is not merely self-consciousness, work, sexual inequality, and sacramentality, then, that are the densely interwoven story of embodiedness as told in the Creation sequences of the York cycle, but the necessity of mediation and representation associated with covering, disguise, and pitiful lack. The careful attention of the York plays to the world of

making, and the world as made, is part and parcel of the cycle's elaboration of a politics of embodiment, its interest in the political regulation of the body, in a bodily epistemology, a theology of incarnation,
and a community created through praxis and self-representation, not
created ex nihilo. What is at stake in the attention given to the body
throughout this cycle? No longer the absolute and orthodox dividing
line separating God off from his creation, making, albeit necessitated
by the fall, is simply the term of reference in which the world can be
understood. Involved in this process, not only at the theological level
of the necessary reparation of incarnate humanity for sin, is the understanding of the body as the creative agency of knowing and doing. In
York this is no mere celebration of the physicality of humanity, but an
acute investigation of the kinds of identification enabled by Corpus
Christi, and of the kinds of political regulation necessitated by the
body as a central mechanism of imaginary social order.

The York plays' investigation of work that I have just briefly outlined may be usefully compared to the treatment that links the creation
story to Corpus Christi in the sermon that introduces the ordinances
to the York Corpus Christi guild.[15] This guild, founded in 1408, included august members such as the archbishop of York, the abbots of
St. Mary's in York, Richard, duke of Gloucester (later Richard III), as
well as nearly every citizen who could afford the two-penny annual
torch fee.[16] The sermon based on Matthew 26:26, "Hoc est enim corpus meum," conventionally read as the biblical inscription of the
sacrum convivium, the eucharistic feast, links the creation of the body
of Adam to the ideology of Corpus Christi as a sacramental unity:
"Likewise, having created, ruled, governed and endowed with a variety
of virtues that same first body, the Lord was able to fulfill the words
of this saying (that is, 'This is my body'), as a special presage of
unity."[17] Creation is linked here with order and with the formation of
humanity, not as an object of difference but as an extension of same-
ness, unity, and the immaculate reduplication of a perfectly conceived
social system. Where reproduction threatens or hints at the production
of difference, procreation before the fall ensures perfect and continuous integrity: "Thus, through the act of procreation, the harmoniously
formed body of every rational creature was to perpetuate in itself the
primal unity of creation, the concord of the state of innocence; all distinction or rebellion being dug out by the roots."[18]

Yet these glosses not only link the creation story with sacramentality in a very overt way, winding both meanings around the scriptural precedent for the institution of the *sacrum convivium,* but also betray a concern with preoccupations of cohesion and the specter of difference and distinction opened up by the formation of such a social body as the guild of Corpus Christi.[19] Central to the ideology of Corpus Christi as it is overtly articulated here is unity. All the metaphors that proliferate are about reproduction without difference.[20]

When Corpus Christi, the little host under clerical jurisdiction and subject to strict ritual control and construction, is extended into the drama of the town, it risks its own meanings, finding them difficult to guarantee. The parts that ideally come to make up the whole threaten to move in different directions. In extending "God's flesh" over and around and through the city of York, the hegemony of the host is as much threatened as confirmed. The ability of Christ's body to be a synecdoche for the composite society of York, for example, is questioned by the stresses on the borders and boundaries of that society. A bill presented to York council by a group of artisans excluded from the political governance of the life of their city reveals how thoroughly contested was the nominal community of council and commonality, but also how interrelated was the symbolic language of the body with arguments concerning the political structure of the polity:[21] "[F]or alsmuch as we ben all one bodye corporate, we thynke that we be all in-like prevaliged of the comonalte, which has borne none office in the city."[22]

Political power in the late medieval town, as Rosser and Holt have recently reminded us, was "largely an expression of economic influence."[23] The medieval urban economy was characterized by a complex and intricate division of labor in a small-scale economy. The power the merchant had over the craftsman was not the ownership of capital, but the control of a system of exchange.[24] As John Merrington has recently described it: "So long as the market depended on price disparities between separate spheres of production in which the producers were not separated from the means of production and subsistence, trade only existed in the interstices of the system, monopolising the supply of a limited range of goods, and was dependent on political indulgence."[25] The chief economic division in urban life was thus the one between the merchant and the manufacturing guilds. The division of labor imposed on the craft guilds was partly an expression of mercantile anxiety that feared "any situation in which a chain of operations, from the acquisition of the raw material to the marketing of the final product could be undertaken by the craftsmen themselves."[26] Tanners and butchers, for example, had easy access to raw materials, and they supplied other crafts with the raw material for their own production. It was therefore essential for maintaining commercial dominance to separate, for example, butchers, tanners, and cordwainers, just as it was important to separate millers and bakers, or for that matter, weavers, fullers, and dyers.[27] But because economic status alone (unlike the capitalist relations of production) could not sufficiently secure this mercantile power, the system of craft organizations developed to divide and control the nonmercantile body.

This view of the craft guilds is a very recent one among historians.[28] Although they were once viewed as a form of voluntary self-policing fraternal organization, recent research has indicated that they may rather be considered part and parcel of the repressive legislation of the late fourteenth century, a seigneurial reaction to the rising power and costs of labor.[29]

The economy was organized in terms of the household; it is partly the erasure of this fact in so many accounts of the socioeconomic life of late medieval towns that has tempted historians to see the mercantile-enforced fantasy of a division of labor as a late medieval reality.[30] The guild system underwent considerable expansion in the late fourteenth and early fifteenth centuries when the guilds became institutionalized as agents of the council. The labor statutes of 1363–64 introduced the principle of one person–one trade: "[A]rtificers handicraft people, hold them every one to one mystery, which he will chose betwixt this and the said feast of Candlemas; and two of every craft shall be chosen to survey, that none use other craft than the same which he hath chosen."[31] Swanson sees this 1363 statute as a composite part of the repressive labor legislation instituted in the 1351 Statute of Labourers and reenacted throughout the late fourteenth and fifteenth centuries.[32] The drive behind such legislation was simple: seigneurial reaction.[33] The legislation constituted an attempt to keep labor rates down to pre-plague levels, before labor scarcity had caused them to mount. By setting up a system whereby master craftsmen were in control of an artificially divided labor force, "the authorities effectively undermined the corporate identity which might develop amongst the artisans as a whole."[34] "It was not," according to Swanson, "a monopoly of manufacture that the council feared so much as a monopoly of distribution," because this was the very source of wealth creation in the towns.[35]

The select body of York consisted of the mayor and the council of twelve as well as a council of twenty-four. There was also a council of forty-eight, which was evidently rarely consulted. This was also known as the "commonalty." Where the identity of the "forty-eight" can be determined, it seems that they were representative of the crafts of the city, referred to in the *York Memorandum Book* as "les artificers."[36] As D. M. Palliser points out, during the fifteenth century this wider body came to consist of the searchers of the city's craft guilds.[37] Swanson points out that it is likely that as the searchers whose task was to supervise the products of the manufacturing guilds increased in authority as more powers were delegated to them by the council, "it must have seemed logical for them to take on a representative function."[38] The system of representation by guild hardly reflected the power of the guilds. It is rather an assessment of the authority of the council. Usually it is clear from the York records that the group of forty-eight was largely excluded from the political process. This political system was in constant turmoil virtually throughout the staging of the Corpus Christi cycles. In the revised constitution of 1517, a new common council was appointed whereby the role of the merchant body increased at the expense of the manufacturing guilds.[39]

Richard Homan has argued that there is one exception to this gradual and persistent process of exclusion. In the production of the Corpus Christi pageants, the group of forty-eight was regularly included in the decisions: Homan therefore reads this as an instance of a ritualized compensation for an actual political exclusion. The many instances of craft guilds protesting over their contribution to the production of the Corpus Christi pageants, he says, "can only be understood if the festival is looked at as a microcosm of the political and social structure of the town in which economic inequalities, unresolvable in fact, could be resolved, and most important, in which the central monopoly of the city government could be ritualistically put right."[40] But Maud Sellers does provide us with the crucial information, omitted by Homan, that the forty-eight were actually fined for their nonattendance at these meetings at which the organization of the Corpus Christi pageants was discussed. Their participation in the very meeting in which one ideal form of the body of Christ was going to be constituted was therefore financially and legally enforced.

The instances of quarrels over payment for the pageants are indeed emblematic of certain divisions between the trade guilds. Those divisions concern the dispute over the artificial division of labor through which their manufacturing activities were framed. So, for example, the sausagemakers protested that they would not put on their pageant because they could not afford the expense, unless they received help from those who made candles.[41] The mayor agreed that all those who made candles for retail should henceforth be compelled to contribute to the York Corpus Christi pageants. In this respect, the sausagemakers ensured that those who encroached upon one of their sidelines, the making of Paris candles from tallow, would be forced to pay for the pageant. Swanson even suggests that the guild of sausagemakers may have been created just so that they could bear the burden of a pageant.[42] If this is the case, then their protests expanded the numbers of those who would be responsible for payment by demanding that all members from other crafts who were not sausagemakers yet who sold sausages or their by-products, and all those butchers and butchers' wives who sold candles made of tallow, one of the main by-products of the butchers' trade, should be forced to contribute to the pageant.[43] On the one hand, this may be seen as a victory for the sausagemakers in revealing the artificiality (and injustice?) of the divisions imposed by the civic oligarchy. The production, they insisted, would be mounted by all who actually made and sold sausages. At the same time, it was, if not a recognition of the validity of the nonsensical category of sausagemakers, a necessary subjugation to the power of the definitions of the town government, and their ability to draw the lines delineating (constructing) the crafts.

The articificiality of the divisions of the civic body were thereby renegotiated, but only by acceding to a system of divide and rule whereby the artisanate were forced to compete with one another rather than perceive their structural common interests.

The craft system designed by the urban oligarchy was in this way a political machinery designed to prevent such a dangerous alternative body from forming.[44] The butcher's trade was in fact subject to the closest of regulations because butchers, as well as supplying the vital foodstuff to the city, were also in a position to supply and participate in many other trades (leatherwork, candle making, etc.), and so transgression of the boundaries established by the city seemed to be almost routine.[45] The particular ideological battle that the sausagemakers fought over their part in the pageant in 1417 was in fact lost, in that the pageant for which the sausagemakers had hitherto been responsible was amalgamated with several others in 1422.[46] Carrying the name of neither of the guilds nominally responsible for its payment and production, this pageant was to carry the arms of the city. Stevens reads this as a paradigm for the functioning of the cycle: individual sponsorship of the trade guilds could change, but the management of the city endured.[47] But it could also be seen as an ongoing strategic battle in which the guilds were constantly redefining the very nature of the parts they were to play, and for which they were to pay. It is indeed remarkable how much of the money financing the plays comes from infractions of the artificial division of labor set up by the mercantile oligarchy.[48] Regrators were fined and their fines went to the very craft guild they had undercut. Where craftsmen poached on the nominal craft of another, their fines went to support the injured guild's craft pageant.[49] These plays were in many ways financed by the persistent and systematic breaking of the lines of division established by the mercantile ruling body to separate one craft from another. If, as Swanson has written, "the burden of the pageants was instrumental in forcing a more rigid organization on the system of crafts guilds,"[50] one could also say, paradoxically, that the display of the wholesome and holistic corporate body of the town had been partly put together through the transgressive but systematic reordering of the mercantile drawing of, and fantasy about, this corporate body and its constituents.

If this logic is pursued, it then follows that it was in the interests of the town government to proliferate artificial divisions between the guilds: the more guilds, the more searchers, the more searchers, the more fines.[51] Fines went usually to the council and to the pageant,[52] and it was in this way that the production of the pageants was so intimately linked to the political regulation of work.[53] The craft system that emerges from Swanson's work suggests that although the records indicate a system in which a craft guild exists to transmit the skills of the trade in a master-apprentice structure, to maintain an actual distinction in function and control of craft and to perform/organize monopolies in manufacture, the craft system actually was revised by the mercantile body in the late fifteenth and early sixteenth centuries to protect the mercantile group whose own economic status was threatened.[54] The timing of the commitment of the "originals" (the play texts owned by the craft guilds) to the Register between 1463 and 1477 coincides with recession and with the decline in the York merchants' hold over overseas trade.[55]

Merchants lost their hold over the overseas markets, and diversifying away from wool they became much more invested in the market as regional distributors of manufactured goods.[56] This must have put them into a much more directly competitive position in relation to the craft guilds. The increased level of control over the production of the Corpus Christi pageants consequent on its transmission in the Register is in line with the intensified polarization in the relations of merchant and artisan in the recession of the post-1450s. Once again it was the organization of the pageants that operated as one of the vehicles of that polarization.[57]

This version of the interrelation of political and economic structure in the city of York should inform a different kind of cultural history of medieval theatrical production, as well, specifically, as a different account of the York plays themselves. For the conceptualization of late medieval towns as "non-feudal islands in a feudal sea,"[58] as defined by their putative exemption and immunity from feudal relations, has meant that the products of late medieval urban theater have been read as precursors of a Whig historiography, making of them a drama of bourgeois triumphalism. But as Rodney Hilton points out, the differing interpretations of the relation of urban life to feudalism derive from different conceptualizations of the nature of the structure of feudal social relations. If the determining features of feudalism are understood to be lord-vassal relations, characterized by private jurisdictions, then the town as an entity is consequently conceived as organized around the necessity to be free of seigneurial jurisdiction. But if, as for Hilton, feudalism is understood as a mode of production, the key relation is not within the governing class but between the landowning aristocracy, the expropriating class, and the peasantry who offer up surplus value in the form of rent, money, or labor. In this definition, as Merrington puts it, "urban 'capitalism' was both internal and external to the feudal mode—or more precisely, the latter was the *condition* for the former," since it was corporate urban autonomy that functioned like a "collective seigneur."[59]

The Marxist historiography of the feudal relations of medieval urban life informed by Swanson's detailed and precise articulation of mercantile-artisanal relations in York should render not only possible but imperative a reconsideration of the kind of culture ritually celebrated in the Corpus Christi plays.[60] In particular we need to develop a better way of thinking about the interrelation of the socioeconomic and the cultural. For our very conceptualization of culture is frequently "a-historical, non-processual and totalising."[61] Because it is so often understood as all-inclusive, culture has to be conceptualized as either autonomous or independent, or merely dependent, superstructural. But as Ellen Meiksins Wood has argued, in precapitalist societies "extra-economic powers, political authority, and juridical privilege had special importance because the economic power of appropriation was inseparable from them."[62] Cultural questions, then, are economic ones, and the distinction between base and superstructure that has been the source of such urgent debates, debates that intimately concern the relation of culture to the social, has to be reformulated.[63] Culture can no longer be the expression of a whole way of life, but must rather be conceived as the "very terrain of the political struggle over the reproduction or the transformation of the social relations of [pre]capitalism."[64] If, as I have argued here, the Corpus Christi pageants are themselves the very mechanism for the regulation of labor, trade, and manufacture in the city, then it is no longer possible to make the case that they are a cultural resolution of economic problems, at once the aesthetic mirror for York society and its ideal form. Neither are they an expression, a homology of the central mechanism of the "market" conceived in its quintessentially urban "function."[65] Rather, they are the cultural vehicles of sociopolitical life and the central means of their mutual articulation.[66]

How can this different understanding of the emphasis on work be reread in the plays themselves in the light of this account? My contention is that many of the pageants reveal and help to articulate an artisanal ideology that placed importance on manufacture, or on making, rather than on the control of exchange mechanisms, through the manipulation of networks of supply and distribution. The very public ceremonial designed to figure forth the body of the city as the wish fulfillment of its most illustrious members is therefore undercut by an emergent structure of feeling that will precisely emphasize manufacture as central.

It is the Crucifixion pageant that most articulates these themes of making, and of division and wholeness, in ways that have a very close bearing on the interaction between the city's political regulation and the sacramentalism that supposedly underwrote it. The Crucifixion pageant, mounted at the time of recording in the Register by the pinners, is famously a pageant about making: the making of the central

icon of late medieval Christianity, the body of Christ. If we take seriously Beadle and King's stage notes, it is possible to see the play first of
all working visually along a horizontal axis. As the pinners playing the
soldiers nail Christ to the cross, we cannot really see what they are doing. We know from their words that they are botching their job. They
make Christ fit the cross, rather than the other way around. The apoc-
ryphal story that the tree out of which the cross was made buckles and
moves in an effort to prevent the horrors of its destined usage is
brought into play here. Only when Christ is laboriously stuck in the
mortise, in the vertical axis, suddenly on display to the audience, can
we see the fruit of their labors. The twin axes of the play ask us first of
all to divorce means from ends, and then to see them brutally reunited.
The pageant constantly refers us to the crucifixion as work, and outra-
geously prolongs that work.[67] The soldiers understood to be acting under the aegis of an uncontestable authority[68] can conceive of their task
only in blind relation to this authority. They cannot see the whole
picture, and in not seeing it, they reenact the crucifixion itself as they
reproduce the very image of corporate holism signified by Christ's mu-
tilated body. The job of pinners is, of course, to make the joins, the piv-
otal points that both link and articulate the structure of the made
object. Their work is in fact to join things strongly and usefully together. When Christ in the second speech that cuts across the soldiers
to address the audience says: "What þei wirke wotte þai noght," the
costs of such a division are made to speak.[69]

The picture held up to York is the intimately familiar one that has
reproached the citizens from the walls of churches, from altarpieces
and retables, in flat and plastic form. Here it is seen again, but reconceived theatrically as the product of very human agency.[70] This is in
striking contrast to both the affective Christ of the devotional tradition and to the little wafer handled between priestly hands, synecdoche
for the whole of Christian society. Here the broken body of Christ is
understood in particular and intimate relations to the divisions enforced on the artisan body.

Rather than being the place in which the social and political polity
could reimagine itself, the body of Christ, ideally the universal church
and all of Christian society, was the ritual object, administered by a
closed caste that differentiated itself precisely by means of such administration. Some of the York Corpus Christi pageants nominally inscribe within themselves such an understanding of the sacrament. But

they fundamentally revise their understanding of sacramental culture: the sacrament is no longer the little wafer consumed by the celebrant. It is what the clergy represented it as being: the social world of York. But it is that world, not as an object, but as a process of relation. And in taking the sacrament at its word, some of these plays succeed in unlocking the emancipatory critique that is always the other side of its potent ideological force. Through the culture's central symbol of desire and suffering, the very limits of the satisfaction that the system of social labor provides are marked.[71]

For if it is the necessity of labor (rendered imperative by culture in the first place) that makes of humanity the creature who in transforming itself also transforms its environment, then it is this always excessive and non-self-identical creature who will permanently inhabit the gap between the actual and the possible. It is this gap between the actual and the possible that renders both inevitable and compelling the political struggle to "redeem what is possible from what is real, our reality being but the systematic obstruction of the possible."[72] That is also why we might celebrate the fig leaf, first art object, not so much as a deficiency, but as the very sign of human making.

Part Three

Sacramental Theater

4 Real Presences

THE YORK CRUCIFIXION AS SACRAMENTAL THEATER

My weight is my love.
—Augustine, *Confessions* 13.9.10

INTRODUCTION

Sacramental theater: the very term introduces itself as oxymoron. That the central sacrament, the body of Christ in the mass, *was* theater constituted the very bases of the searching and vituperative polemics of reform. Priests were actors conjuring in apish impostures God from a cake. The mass as theater was just so much hocus-pocus; the very term, nonsensical, rhyming, divorcing sound from sense, empties out the efficacy, the miraculous performative of "Hoc est enim corpus meum," the famous five words of consecration. And the fundamental indeterminacy of that little shifter "hoc" is seen either as the laughably reductive literalism, the merely stupid equation of a debased popular piety, or as an attack on the mendacious subtlety of scholasticism's exclusive, precise, fanatically, and fantastically defensive logic. The 1951 revival of the plays, which I explored in chapter 1, did not include the crucifixion.[1] The power and obscenity, the scandal of its enactment was still not yet to be countenanced. Yet the very force, the historical victory of this understanding of sacrament as theater has stood in the way of an analysis of theater itself as sacrament. The Corpus Christi plays of the late Middle Ages understand the sacramental relation between form and grace as *best* realized in theater. Theater is not so much inimical to the sacramental disclosure of God as the perfectly consonant form for the religion of incarnation. Precisely because sacraments are best understood as actions and not things, it is in the theater of dramatic action that they are best understood. In theater's phenomenality, in its central resource of the body of an actor, in the performance of sacrament as encounter and action, relation and *transitus* rather than object or thing, in its complex resemioticization of the sign, sacrament is no longer the little wafer held aloft between priestly hands but strives to fulfill and point toward the host's most ardent and outrageous claims—its most generously utopian aspirations to cause what it signifies, to perform a bond of love in the community of the faithful.

THE SACRAMENT OF CORPUS CHRISTI AS THEATER

Sacraments were conventionally described as signs of sacred things, the visible signs of an invisible grace. In the elaborated definition of Hugh of Saint Victor: "A sacrament is a corporeal or material element set before the senses without, representing by similitude and signifying by institution and containing by sanctification some invisible and spiritual grace."[2] In the eucharist that tension between the visible and the invisible, between palpable presence and ineffable mystery, is at its most difficult.[3] As Humbert of Romans put it in the thirteenth century: " . . . in all other sacraments Christ's power is spiritual, but in this one—Christ exists corporeally; and this is a greater thing."[4] This "greater thing" is the impossible constitutive claim and scandal of incarnation; the very form of the relation between visible sign and invisible grace was at the heart of polemical debates for centuries.[5] What does that neuter demonstrative pronoun point to? What is the "this"? Is it the bread that Christ breaks at the Last Supper? Is the pronoun referring back to its subject in Christ? Is it the event itself?[6] Berengar, who favored a spiritual understanding of the eucharist, was forced to make this recantation directed by Rome in 1059: "I believe that the bread and wine which are laid on the altar are after the consecration not only a sacrament but also the true body and blood of our Lord Jesus Christ, and they are physically taken up and broken in the hands of the priest and crushed by the teeth of the faithful, not only sacramentally, but in truth (non solum sacramento sed in veritate)."[7] The outlandish insistence not simply on figurative transformation but actual and corporeal transformation returned to both haunt and inspire the sacramental system that organized itself around this claim. In the later Middle Ages, questions were asked of patristic texts that they could not possibly answer. If the sign participated in the reality it represented and mediated participation in that reality, the distinction between a realist and a symbolist understanding of the eucharist is not operative. The idea that a sign could be a mere sign could arise only in a radically changed intellectual climate, a climate stressing causality rather than

participation. As William Crockatt puts it: "Once the notion of participation essential to an understanding of the relation between sign and
reality in the Platonic tradition has been lost, the language of figure,
sign and symbol appears to evacuate the sacraments of their reality."[8]
Aquinas then, according to Crockatt, was filling a theological vacuum
when he applied an Aristotlean principle of causality not in "order to
negate the symbolic character of the sacraments," but to make it clear
in the medieval context what was obvious in the patristic one, namely
that the sacraments as signs participate in the reality that they signify
and are not "mere signs."

Thus there might seem to be an almost irreducible tension between
visible and invisible in the sacrament of the eucharist when it is physical rather than metaphysical reality that is being considered. The doctrine of transubstantiation claims the greatest allegiance and the
maximum faith from participants in the mass precisely because of its
flagrant transgression of the evidence of the senses. The doctrine of
transubstantiation has it that the bread on the altar became the body of
Christ not simply figuratively but in reality; in the terms of medieval
Aristotleanism, the substance changed but the accidents remained.
And this was precisely the focus of controversy for scholasticism; for
many theologians that substance could change without accidents was
ridiculous. Even for those who understood that the impossibility
was precisely what made the substantial change a miraculous one, it
was still a miracle that was visible only to the eyes of faith. Aquinas, for
example, is very clear that "no bodily eye can see the body of Christ
contained in this sacrament."[9] The complexity of the existence of the
real presence under the appearances of bread does not translate all that
well into a pastoral program.

All historians of the mass stress the extent to which it became a
clerical celebration observed by onlookers, in which consecration, not
communion, was understood to be the most important moment.[10]
That visual theophany, that moment of turning, crucial yet not apparent, is more important than the communion of the faithful. The host
becomes an ocular communion as it is raised above the head after the
moment of consecration. Evidence of raising the host over the priest's
head is first apparent in Paris at the beginning of the thirteenth century. According to the constitution of Bishop Odo, priests should not
hold the host before their breast until they have said "this is my body"
and then elevate it so that it is possible to be seen by all. This practice

had as its primary motive the prevention of idolatry—for otherwise people would worship the host before it was the body of Christ.[11]

One might say that the mass was indeed theater, but as Anthony Kubiak has pointed out, though the mass is indeed grounded in theatrical ontology—for the "administration of the sacraments . . . represented the outward show of Christ's presence and power," yet "the problematic of appearances central to theatre" (that its illusion is embraced as truth) is inverted, for in the mass, "empirical reality is presented as an illusion that conceals truth (as, for example, when the actual presence of Christ is revealed *under the appearances* of bread and wine)."[12] For Kubiak, it was the "church's profound intuitive grasp of this oppositional identity between faith and illusion that forced it to repulse the drama."[13] To expose the mass as theater is to suggest then that the efficacy of its words are not operable, that they cannot cause what they signify for there can be no performatives in theater.[14] Discussions around the mass as theater then center around two related points: semiotically, under what conditions does a thing become a sign?[15] And phenomenologically, how does the appearance of things relate to their reality? To understand the sophistication of the metatheatrical exposition of Corpus Christi theater, to understand how consistently and reflexively it uses and puts pressure on signs as sacred things, on the relation between visible form and invisible grace, to understand not so much the sacrament as theater, but theater as sacrament, we will need to consider further how this theater engages and transforms these languages.

CORPUS CHRISTI THEATER AS SACRAMENT

It is a special property of theater that everything onstage is a sign.[16] When it enters illusory space and time, anything put onstage begins to signify, to point to, represent, become of or about something else. Consider, says Herbert Blau, an object in front of your eyes. "On stage it is no longer simple. A real chair used for a real chair in a 'realistic setting' remains, though a real chair, a sign for a chair. It is what it is not though it appears to be what it is."[17] And yet it is also the especial, unique property of theater that its signs are also in a very special way of the world. Theater, in other words, is peculiarly open to the world of objects;[18] its language consists to an unusual degree (and unlike fiction, painting, sculpture, film) "of things that are what they seem to be."[19]

The materiality of the signifier plays a constitutive role in theater for it relies very heavily on the iconic identity of its signs[20] in which there is similarity between the sign vehicle and the signified.[21] Moreover, theater relies on that most basic form of signification—ostension; to define an object, one simply picks up the object itself to show precisely what it is.[22]

Theater's polysemy, its complexity and power, resides in its consistent, reflexive, and systematic confusion of these two orders of representation, the illusional and the actual.[23] It is this confusion that Shakespeare's clown Launce comically enacts in *The Two Gentlemen of Verona* when he comes onstage with his dog Crab:

> Nay, I'll show you the manner of it. This shoe is my father. No, this left shoe is my father; no, no, this left shoe is my mother; nay, that cannot be so neither. Yes, it is so, it is so: it hath the worser sole. This shoe with the hole in it is my mother; and this my father. A vengeance on't, there 'tis. Now, sir, this staff is my sister; for, look you, she is as white as a lily, and as small as a wand. This hat is Nan, our maid. I am the dog. No, the dog is himself, and I am the dog. O! the dog is me, and I am myself. Ay, so, so.[24]

Keir Elam's comments on this passage analyze Launce's "metadramatic exposition" as a revelation not so much of the particular appropriateness of sign and sign vehicle (iconic identity), but the discovery that sign vehicles onstage are perfectly interchangeable.[25] Bert States's more nuanced exposition of this same passage calls attention to the comic resistance to semioticization of the real animal onstage: "The theater has, so to speak, met its match: the dog is blissfully above, or beneath, the business of playing, and we find ourselves cheering its performance precisely because it isn't one."[26]

During a conversation about medieval theater, a friend of mine told me another story about an animal that refused to play its part. He had seen a production of a Corpus Christi pageant, staging the journey to Bethlehem in which a real donkey had been used. Carrying the Virgin Mary, whose pure womb bears the very salvation of the world, the donkey strolls on with a massive erection.[27] States elegantly uses the dog, the real dog onstage, as I have more crudely used the donkey's triumphantly misplaced penis, as an emblem of "the cutting edge of theatre, the bite that it takes into actuality in order to sustain itself in the dynamic order of its ever-dying signs and images."[28] Its permanent spectacle is "the parade of objects and processes in transit from environment to imagery."[29] Theater, in short, is constantly caught at the boundary between its phenomenality and its terms of reference.[30]

And this includes its most complex and integral sign—the actor's body, there before us, as someone else for sure, but in the liveness of our co-presence. As I mentioned in chapter 3, in theater it is the very body of the actor that becomes the chief vehicle of semiosis, and his body also articulates the acting area itself in processional theater. The actor as dramatis persona is fictive, but the opportunity of theater is also its danger; the risk is that the actor really will trip up, forget her lines, come in on the wrong cue. "The stage actor performs in tension with the world of the audience, and each moment floats between victory and potential disaster."[31] Or as Blau puts it a little more melodramatically, taking up the actor's concept of corpsing. "He who is performing can die there in front of your eyes. . . . Of all the performing arts, theatre stinks most of mortality."[32] The performing body occupies, then, a paradoxical role as "both the activating agent of such dualities as presentation/representation, sign/referent, reality/illusion and that which most dramatically threatens to collapse them."[33] It is no wonder, then, that so many stories collect around this tension. In *The Theatre of God's Judgements,* for example, Thomas Beard tells the following anecdote: "In a certaine place there was acted a tragedie of the death and passion of Christ in show, but in deed of themselves: for he that played Christ's part, hanging upon the Crosse, was wounded to death by him that should have thrust his sword into a bladder full of bloud tyed to his side."[34] Beard turns this into his own allegorical morality play about the dangers imminent when Christ is played, for he reads the deaths occasioned by this playing as punishment for blasphemy.

This standing between facticity and semiosis of theatrical objects and bodies is the very mechanism of theater's capacity for transformation. The concretization of things and bodies onstage provides theater with its special power to show what it tells, and the simultaneity and coexistence of these modes will sometimes minimize, sometimes maximize the impact of those differences.[35] In the Wakefield Second Shepherd's pageant, for example, the delicate signification of the Christ child as the *agnus dei,* the paschal lamb at the center of the passing of Old to New Law, is compromised by his appearance as a bleating ram about to be devoured by the starving Mak and Gil in a parody of the eucharistic body. The attempt to pass off the lamb of God, tasty and eminently edible, as their newborn in a mock-nativity scene works characteristically in both directions. The concrete icon of the ram has overwhelmed its referent; this woolly, horned creature will simply not convince us that it is any newborn baby, let alone the Christ child, and it is not just Mak and Gil who are seen to be guilty of disguise.[36] It is above all the actor's body, simultaneously semiotic and phenomenal object, that in the York Crucifixion challenges the stability of representational levels of theater and exploits theater's capacity for disrupting the fixture between signs and their meanings.[37]

THE YORK CRUCIFIXION: THE BODY OF CHRIST AS SACRAMENTAL THEATER

There are twelve pageants in the York Corpus Christi cycle that concern the passion.[38] These scenes are boisterous and busy (to take up the infectiously alliterative language of the plays), composed of multiple levels and tensions, and scenically enormously complex. But their still center is the York Crucifixion, in which Christ's body is ritually tortured in an agonizingly extended sequence culminating in the reconstruction onstage of the central icon of the culture—Christ on the cross, dramatically played as both reenactment of the crucifixion and a construction of its central representation. Of all the composite cycle plays, only York has a crucifixion play that separates out the stretching and nailing of Christ on the cross from the other events at Calvary. In this pageant, four soldiers played by members of the guild of pinners crucify Christ. The pageant consists entirely of their actions and dialogue, which takes place on a plane of address oblivious to the surrounding crowd. Their dialogue, which orients itself entirely around the physical action of their job and its technical difficulties, its nature as a task, is broken across by two moments in which Christ speaks directly to the audience. Christ's first speech takes place as he willingly lays himself on the cross, and the action of the play takes place around his body on the horizontal plane of the pageant wagon so that it is invisible to view for most of the sequence. The second speech takes place as he has been erected to view. The action is belatedly separated from the perception of its effect, increasing the emphasis on what has been *done*. In a grotesque enactment and revision of the act of elevation, what the soldiers have been doing is now visible for all to see, and Christ utters the words of lamentation from the cross, echoing and making vernacular the liturgical "O vos omnes" from the responsorium for matins on Holy Saturday: "O vos omnes, qui transitus per viam, attendite, et videte / Si est dolor similis sicut dolor meus":

> Al men þat walkis by waye or strete
> Takes tente ȝe schalle no trauayle tyne
> Byholdes myn heede, myn handis, and myn feete,
> And fully feele now or ȝe fyne,
> Yf any mournyng may be meete
> Or myscheue mesured vnto myne.[39]

Here, Christ's body is the sign that looks back, the real presence that exceeds the parameters of representational space and confronts the audience's detachment with the familiar, deeply reproachful spectacle of a suffering caused by that very detachment.

The play is remarkable for its sheer theatrical economy; theater is purely and only the deed and its showing. The dialogue between the four soldiers is almost entirely functional, working to advance the task in hand, as in a spirit of cooperation they construct a perverted community of effort and action. The entire sequence famously dramatizes one central action, then—the laying on, the arduous stretching of Christ to the cross, and the brutal nailing of him on it. If, as we have seen, theater works through the very medium of the actor's body, and so has to process time at the speed of the actor's body,[40] there can be no more strenuous enactment of this principle in the history of the Western stage than this long, this excruciating, this almost endless interval of the time of crossing.

The main prop is the cross itself, which refuses the role designed for it—a reference to the legend in which the wood of the tree resists its use to crucify the son of God. In theater a prop is at once an object we look at and a tool put to use by performers; here the cross and Christ's body as an object of handling are the constant focus of attention, for the soldiers misplace the bores for the nails as the wood distends its shape, and they must wrench and pull Christ to fit the cross because the wood balks at its instrumentalization so emphatically.

The communication of the pain and difficulty of this crucifixion relies on the real physical risk of the actor, for the lugging up of a man onto a cross is a piece of theatrical virtuosity, as any actor who has played Christ will know. Will he fall? Is he safe? How does he stay up there? How painful is it? Does his body ache? This physical risk, the possibility of accident, of things not working, not going to script, of the physical world resisting our dearest designs upon it, is played out by the French Canadian film *Jesus of Montreal*, which I explore further in my final chapter. Daniel, the actor playing Christ, is on the cross and the ecclesiastical authorities (represented in the film by a priest who once played in Brecht's *Galileo* and who is also sleeping with the actress who plays Mary Magdalene) have sent in their police to halt the production. An enthusiastic and physically imposing member of the audience makes a running charge at one of the policemen to prevent him from stopping the show, and he crashes into the cross with Daniel on it. This inaugurates a "real passion" in the film. Daniel is pinned to the ground by the cross; he eventually dies and in a resurrection made possible by modern science, his body parts bring new life, new vision, new heart to those blinded in their failing eyes or dying of a weak heart. If theater existentially places the actor in a position of risk, of vulnerability because of its liveness and actuality, then at this moment of all moments that risk is fully palpable.

When I was back in England in the summer of 1997, I read a newspaper article with the title "Mystery of Actor's Final Fatal Role." A British actor who was playing Judas in a hotel production of *Jesus Christ Superstar* in northern Greece was hanged in front of six hundred holidaymakers. A stunt that he had performed several times before with a security belt did not operate as planned, and "the spectators looked on in horror as the spotlight picked out Mr Wheeler's limp body."[41] The corpsing that is a metaphor for the actor's bringing alive their characters has here taken on more sinister overtones as the actor falls prey to the very same fate as the character he depicts, by means of a fatal accident.[42]

V. A. Kolvé has talked about the ludic game of the "tortores" enacted in the ritualized dialogue.[43] The soldiers for nearly the entirety of performance talk their talk in strict order of rotation and in stanzaic form. The first break in the order of lines allotted to the soldiers (1, 2, 3, and 4) comes just after line 100, a break obscured in Lucy Toulmin Smith's edition, which ascribes the break to a scribal error and keeps to the ritualized order of the *ludus*.[44] Many commentators have pointed

out the intensely stylized nature of this scene, but Martin Bartlett, who
thinks like an actor about this pageant, points out that this break (the
only place where the end word breaks out of the rhyming scheme) occurs at the moment of maximum physical activity.[45] The first soldier
asks, "Sir, knyghtis, saie howe wirke we nowe?" and the ordered sequence breaks as the dialogue now moves across the soldiers more ran-
domly for two stanzas. This is the moment in the pageant in which the
soldiers are actually nailing Christ to the cross and then making him
fit, an action that involves carefully positioning themselves at all four
corners of the cross. It is a moment of intense physical activity. They
return to the rhyme scheme after the fourth soldier's pessimistic observation about the botched nature of their boring. Then begins the sequence in which they attach ropes to Christ's body to pull it onto the
shape of the cross and fix it to the nails that they have put in all the
wrong places.

The second moment in which the rhyme form breaks, as well as the
ritualized order of speakers, is when the soldiers are hauling the cross
up into its mortise at line 210:

III Miles: Owe, lifte!
I Miles: We, loo!
IV Miles: A litill more.
II Miles: Holde þanne!
I Miles: Howe nowe?
II Miles: Þe werste is paste.

Then back to the rhyming scheme. Bartlett's meticulously detailed argument implies that the disruption and resumption of the ordered sequence is structural to the scene itself.[46] The point is not that the scene
is either ludically stylized as Kolvé insists or innovative in its realism as
Clifford Davidson thinks, but rather a deliberate interplay between the
two. It is the pressure of performance that necessitates the break in
stylization. Because safely accomplishing the action of raising the cross
is crucial to the actor, Bartlett speculates that "the whole play might
have been written in strict order but the pressure of performing actions
that were potentially disastrous resulted in improvisation, which fed
back into text in the form of suitably 'realistic' dialogue."[47] I think
Bartlett's elucidation of these sequences is crucial in the light it sheds
on the tension and interplay between enactment and performance, and
between the man on the cross as both actor and Christ. His physical

risk is a component part of the play's design on our sensibilities. And this risk works off the constant, very tense interplay between what this scene shows and what it does, between what it connotes and what it denotes, between what it points to and what it actually is.

Even the play's most dense verbal puns enact themselves at the physical level. When Christ in his first speech from the cross talks about himself as being "pined," the pun works at the triple level. "Pinen" can mean to hurt, to suffer, and carries a penitential association. Souls are "pined" as in *The Pricke of Conscience* in which the "pyning" of the soul is understood to be a quickening of conscience. But it can also mean to strengthen, and this is another sense it has in the pinners' pageant. Pinners make pins that hold things together, strengthening them at the joints.[48]

What has been an act of the most malevolent destruction acting under the aegis of both the ecclesiastical and civic authorities, at their collusion and behest—the pinning of Christ—is at once his suffering, and through his suffering, an act of strengthening and joining. Their work—endlessly laborious, jobbing, divorcing the means of their act from the meaning of it, is turned to good use, and Christ himself is the tool, the instrument of salvation.[49]

The metaphor of Christ carrying the sins of the world is also given dramatic presence by the soldiers' heavy-duty grumbling about the weight of the cross. The cross indeed must be heavy, for Christ is burdened down by all the worldly sins for which he atones. The focus is on the suffering of the soldiers as much as on Christ then, as they bear the "wikkid wegt." This dramatic enactment makes material a glossing tradition, in which, for example, the writer of Hebrews puts Christ himself in the tradition of Aaron, at once high priest and sacrifice, "offered to bear the sins of many" (Hebrews 9:28), or Peter's first epistle, which glosses the atonement with an allusion to the text of Isaiah 24:20: "He himself carried up our sins in his body the tree" (I Peter 2:24).

As Paul Willis has pointed out, Christ himself cannot dramatize the burdens of sin, for he is necessarily a passive figure, affixed to the cross. But the soldiers can try to carry the cross, and in this invented action, they can show us the wicked weight of the sins of the world in the way that Christ cannot.[50]

Christ is now invisible; then visible. It is a miming of Elevatio. And in that raising, we are asked not to merge with Christ in the identificatory theater of passion, not to become him, or to enter or be at one with him, but to *bear a terrible witness* as we ourselves are addressed as participants at the scene of crucifixion.[51]

CONCLUSION

Someone stands in for someone else. Call it a structure of representation, a practice of substitution, a process of authorization or sacrifice— in all events the standing in is doubly descriptive. It describes at once the very economy of Christian redemption, that Christ is a body for us, that he stands in for both God and humanity—in God's place and on behalf of humanity, making possible the founding atonement. And it describes the seminal action of theater in which someone stands in for, represents someone else.

The York Crucifixion is paradigmatically theatrical: it reflects in its manifest content the structure of any theatrical event. That is, in it an actor stands in for a character who stands in for other characters.[52] Like Jerzy Grotowski's neo-Franciscan Poor Theatre and prefiguring it, one might say that it presents the audience in the person of an actor who stands "roughly in the relation of Christ to man in the Passion."[53] In this sacrificial closeness, the audience watches its delegate and its likeness, one who is there not just for the spectator but because of him.

Theater and Christian theology have a long history of antagonism, and the legacy of their abrasive relationship has shown itself in the bifurcated traditions that have developed in the criticism of Corpus Christi theater, in which practical aspects of dramaturgy have nearly always been isolated from questions of religious theodicy or devotion. But it is precisely in Corpus Christi theater that these two forms of standing in are seen in their most acute relation to each other.

The host, the little biscuit, is returned in this theater to a relation that is fully intersubjective, discovering Christ as the encounter between humanity and God. In doing so, this pageant almost uncannily predicts and performs some of the structures of relation currently being investigated by modern theologians of sacramentality. In his book *Christ: The Sacrament of the Encounter with God,* the Dominican theologian Edward Schillebeeckx discusses the way in which sacraments open up the possibility of falling in love with God.[54] Sacraments are symbols that cause through signifying, he says, echoing the Thomistic formulation (*significando causant*) and restoring its efficacy. They are like a kiss. For a kiss does not make love, but without it love cannot be made. Love is only ever both experienced and understood as such through such signs. They are necessary because the reality that they point toward is not knowable any other way. Christ, then, in this reading and in this playing is not simply a sign of love, but in the fundamentally donative nature of sacrament, makes it present and effects it. It is in the very signing that a sacrament causes, and it is in the causing that a sacrament signs.

The Corpus Christi pageants have found the means to explore the paradoxical and strenuous command to love through the semioticized, phenomenal body of Christ, and in doing so they have realized theater not as obstacle but as opportunity and resource. They have done this through the gap between visible and invisible that is at once welcome, incitement, invitation, and promise, but also exile, lamentation, and reproach, what we stretch across and what we fall between.

Medieval theologians, actors, and playwrights knew long before modern semioticians that all words for God must be used analogically. Since God cannot be understood propositionally, it is in the reach and resource of a symbolic language that he has to be not so much understood, as approached. The symbol of him, as I explored in chapter 3, is thereby overdetermined through its very indetermination.

"That is why," writes Thomas Aquinas, referring to the "hoc" of the mass's most significant words, "a pronoun is used," "thus signifying the substance in a vague way, without qualifying it, and leaving it without any determinate form."[55] It is this understanding that has been the very condition of possibility of the York Crucifixion and Corpus Christi as a theater of sacrament.

5 Presence after Presentness

THE THEATER OF RESURRECTION
IN YORK

Why do you look for the living among the dead?
—Luke 24:5

The dead come to life in the bodies of the living. It's a description of resurrection—and of theater.[1] Christ's presence after presentness, his risenness, the York Resurrection sequences teach us, is not *in* Christ, or in the reiterated belief of the first apostolic community; nor is it in the depiction of a preserved history, in a presumed reading of scripture, or in a propositional statement about the nature of God. It is a presencing of Christ in the community of the faithful. And since theater has no "transferable, autonomous existence" outside of the immediacy of performance, since the absolute contemporaneity of theater makes it an event that can occur only in the present, and since it is radically incomplete without its witnessing participants, the audience, York's Resurrection theater manifests the possibilities and resources of the insight that "nothing can be present to us to which we are not present."[2] The York pageants make both resurrection and community the inextricable and indispensable sources of eucharistic relation.

"Whom are you seeking?"—"Quem queritis?" This is how the angel addresses the three Maries who come in search of Christ's body after the crucifixion in the earliest form of medieval theater we know.[3] Who is Christ now and where is he? What is the nature of our quest? What does the object of our search tell us about ourselves as seekers? In the *quem queritis* trope, the resurrection is made manifest by an empty tomb, a plenitude and a promise by an absence, the glorious body by that container, the Easter Sepulchre with nothing in it. In the earliest phenomenology of theater, a presence is shown by means of an absence, a hole in nature.

Christ's presence in the eucharist is a form of presence in absence, as Paul Jones has recently recognized: "Without the reality of Christ's presence, redemption would be unavailable to the faith community.

Without the reality of Jesus' absence, the assertion of Christ's death, resurrection, ascension and *parousia* would be undermined. Both presence and absence are required simultaneously."[4] The late medieval dogmatic formulations about transubstantiation reduced the tension in the interplay between absence and presence. If Christ is really present in eucharistic consecration, the *parousia* is rendered superfluous and a substantial version of the eucharist replaces an ecclesial and communal one. In Jones's view, medieval eucharistic theology fails, as a consequence, to provide a theological justification for the absence of Christ. The elision of ecclesiological questions from this version of the eucharist has worked hand in hand in most criticism of Corpus Christi theater with an elision of an appreciation of the complexity of presence in that theater.[5] For it is in the drama of appearances and disappearances, exits and entrances, absences and presences, signification and reference in theatrical forms of life that the question central to sacramentality itself is asked: How do we encounter the glorified God who has withdrawn himself from our sight? The earliest Middle English forms of the word "theater" identify it as "a place for viewing, sight or view"; likewise, during the very period of the performance of the York cycle, the word for "vision" is going through crucial changes, from meaning the "action or fact of seeing or contemplating something *not* actually present to the eye, a mystical, supernatural insight" (my emphasis) to the "act of seeing with the bodily eye; the exercise of the ordering of the faculty of sight."[6] Though there is no theatrical theory as such in the late Middle Ages, for theater was not a separate "aesthetic" sphere of life but part of the material organization of public life, the plays themselves can be read as explorations of the relationship between the visible and the invisible central to sacramentality.

When contemporary Lollard sermons discussed the empty tomb sequences, they suggested that the question "Quem queritis?" should be asked of all Easter communicants and used to begin an extended meditation on the relation between the object sought and the seeker. The York Resurrection sequences, uniquely of all the extant Corpus Christi cycles, resituate the Easter tropes of *quem queritis* temporally and spatially between scenes of conspiratorial containment. The absence of the body of Christ becomes a commentary on prelatical authority because of Annas and Caiphas's attempt to contain the body of Christ in the tomb, to keep it mortified, not living.

The Resurrection sequences that mark the transition between

Christ as a living contemporary to a Christ who henceforth exists in memory—in the sacrament and in the church founded on and by those who witnessed his resurrection—use the resources of theater to explore the ecclesiological and theological implications of Christ's absence. In what follows, I explore the scriptural resources of the resurrection appearance stories, and their subsequent use both in the Easter liturgy and in Lollard treatments of these contexts, before indicating the pressures and opportunities of these contexts for York's theater of Resurrection.

SCRIPTURAL APPEARANCES

Moritur Christus ut fiat Ecclesia.

—Augustine

How and in what ways, and with what implications, can Christ be present after his death? The resurrection proclaims Christ's continuing presence in memory, in the church and in the sacrament, yet its implications trouble any facile continuity of the before and after. For insofar as the resurrection is about the possibility of restoration and redemption, the presence it offers must be connected with the losses of the past as they are owned by those who encounter it.[7] The resurrection is revealed to those who have also betrayed Christ, and their recognition of the continuity of Christ before and after Calvary is dependent upon the memory of their own infidelity.[8] If Christ's continuing presence is the guarantor of the church's identity, it cannot be as something to be administered as a quantified treasury of merit by them.[9]

Resurrection stories and ecclesiological implications have always had a peculiarly tight relationship, and hence resurrection beliefs raise questions about what the church is and in what it consists. In her work *The Gnostic Gospels*, Elaine Pagels declares that the New Testament accounts seem to support a range of opinions and asks why, therefore, did the second-century Christians embrace a literal view of resurrection. The advantage of a literal view of resurrection is that the witnesses could be restricted to a small band of persons whose "members stood in a position of incontestable authority."[10] Moreover, what they attested could not be verified. The controversy over resurrections, she claims, was "critical in shaping the Christian movement into an institutional religion."[11]

But if questions of ecclesiology and resurrection belief have been linked from the first, it is also clear that the resurrection stories themselves raise questions about testimony. Christ's risenness to the disciples, the stories continuously insist, is bound up at once with the possibilities of their own self-knowledge and with the possibilities of community. The very fact that, as Rowan Williams explains it, there is no "testimony outside of a group of believers" means that for him, "a resurrection appearance designed to prove the reality of Jesus' risenness, divorced from the establishment of the community's faith, can only be, at best, anomalous."[12]

The apparition stories of the New Testament offer a variety of perplexing and difficult encounters whose implications and possibilities are addressed in the York treatments. Mark has no apparition; his story ends abruptly in fear, unbelief, and rupture.[13] In Luke, Christ is the stranger met on the way to Emmaus, recognized only in breaking bread; in John, the gardener not initially recognized as "lord" by Mary Magdalene; and the stranger on the shore in Matthew.[14] He is a body that can both be touched (by Thomas), whose incredulous hands insist on groping Christ's side, and not touched (by Mary Magdalene) until he is ascended. The theme of otherness and unrecognizability seems to be one of the central features of the apparition stories.[15] Christ in one way or another seems constantly to be "not here." And it is for this reason perhaps that the empty tomb becomes such a powerful motif in the resurrection story. "The empty tomb belongs to nobody."[16]

Peter Carnley has spoken recently about how resurrection beliefs often concentrate on the cognitive element, making prayer and worship a "dutiful consequence rather than a response to his personal presence."[17] But it is impossible to speak of the resurrection in a dualist anthropology, just as it was impossible to tell by looking at Christ who he really was. The disciples could believe only when they acceded to, recognized in self-recognition, his demand. In this sense, faith is a virtue, a habit that must be endlessly practiced if it is to exist at all, and not simply a belief that witnesses have not deceived me.[18] Read in this way, the apparition stories of the New Testament offer a way of resisting at once, in Rowan Williams's words, "extremes of internalization (the resurrected body in the Eucharist as illustration of a doctrinal point) and depersonalization (the Eucharist as the confection of a life-giving substance)."[19]

HIDDEN AND REVEALED IN THE LITURGY

The origins and development of the *quem queritis* dialogue, so ostentatiously revisited in the York Resurrection play, are obscure and the evidence complex and contradictory.[20] The earliest extant texts of the holy rites of Easter week are preserved in the *Regularis Concordia* of Saint Ethelwold.[21] In that text written "ad fidem indocti vulgi ac neofitorum," the *quem queritis* dialogue is set within ceremonies in which the ritual objects of ecclesiastical worship, the host and the cross, are part of a reenactment of the events of passion week. Altar and sepulcher thus double as the place of the mass and the place of Christ's death. The cross is ritually buried as an antiphon describes the sealing of Christ's tomb. A vigil is held by two or three brothers. In the meantime, before matins, the sacristans take the cross and "put it in the appropriate place."[22] In the Visitatio ceremony described in the *Regularis*, one brother with an alb goes to the altar and sits there holding a palm in his hand. The other three brothers wearing copes and carrying thuribles "in imitation of those seeking for something" should go to the sepulcher. It is at this point that the dialogue takes place:

> Quem quaeritis (in sepulchro, o Christicolae?)
> Jhesum Nazarenum (crucifixum, o caelicola).
> Non est hic, surrexit sicut praedixerat; ite,
> nuntiate quia surrexit a mortuis.[23]

These rites thus frame the visit of the three Maries to the sepulcher in the midst of a reenactment of the burial (Depositio) and the reenactment of the resurrection (Elevatio).

In the Holy Week ceremonies as they are developed in the parish churches, a host as well as, or instead of, a cross is frequently reserved. On Maundy Thursday the priest consecrates three hosts because he cannot consecrate a host on Good Friday, Christ being then dead. Such features, along with the absence of the pax on Maundy Thursday (because Judas betrays Christ on that night with a kiss), weave the events of Calvary into a fully contemporary enactment. Indeed, Pamela Sheingorn has suggested that the Easter Sepulchre is "one prototype for the theatre's stage" and an "appropriate locus for the rebirth of Western drama."[24]

Every Easter week the resurrection of Christ is staged in a church that on Maundy Thursday was ritually stripped. Each of the altars is washed in water and wine and cleared of all its ornaments. Such stripping is allegorized as the stripping of Christ as for death, and by taking on some of his suffering ritually, the images and altarpieces themselves are anthropomorphized as the suffering God. After the Good Friday creeping to the cross, the priest takes off his mass vestments and brings the third host, which had been consecrated on Maundy Thursday in a pyx. The pyx and the cross had been kissed by people during the liturgy and were wrapped in a linen cloth and placed in the chancel. The sepulcher was covered in a cloth; it was censed and candles were burned before it and a watch placed around it with parishioners occasionally playing the soldiers minding the tomb.[25] On Easter morning the host is removed to its normal position in a hanging pyx above the altar and the cross is then placed on the altar at the north side of the church, after having been solemnly "elevated" from the sepulcher and processed around the church while the choir sings "Christus resurgens." Sheingorn notes that the Rites of Durham describe the cross from the Adoratio being joined by another "picture of our saviour Christ, in whose breast they did enclose with great reverence the most holy and blessed sacrament of the altar."[26] The kinds of images that seem to be associated with this practice indicate that the Elevatio had "become the public celebration of the Resurrection" and that the emphasis was very much on seeing the object raised from the Easter Sepulchre.[27] Texts such as the Rites of Durham and other evidence strongly suggest that there may have been specific images designed for this purpose. Sheingorn suggests that such images played no role in the Depositio but rather must have been "secretly inserted in to the Easter Sepulchre so as to be raised from it on Easter morning."[28] Later anti-Catholic sermons suggest even more elaborate images operating as puppets with vices in which Christ's legs spring out of the sepulcher as he gives a blessing with his hand.[29]

Eamon Duffy usefully points out that the "sepulchre was a part of the official liturgy of Holy Week designed to inculcate and give expression to orthodox teaching, not merely on the saving power of Christ's cross and passion but on the doctrine of the Eucharist."[30] The Easter Sepulchre and its ceremonies, he indicates, were the principle vehicle for the Easter proclamation of resurrection. Ronald Hutton agrees with Duffy on the centrality of the Easter Sepulchre in worship, telling us that "the Easter Sepulchre is mentioned in the majority of the parishes for which early Tudor accounts survive, and its popularity is demonstrated by the number of bequests made in support of it or its lights."[31]

The Easter rites of Holy Week, then, were themselves an astonishing play of presence and absence, exits and reappearances, affirmation and denial. The eucharistic body is a glorified body, and that complex eschatological temporality of a time past and a time yet to come are a component part of its absent presence and present absence. No wonder then that, according to John Mirk, "lewde men" were much more likely to ask questions about the services of Holy Church "of thys time" than at any other time.[32]

Having established that in late medieval liturgical rite the empty tomb is imaged as an Easter Sepulchre in which the cross and the host become objects of intense eucharistic worship, and in which the drama of appearance and disappearance is orchestrated in a set of visual metaphors that tie the reenactment of Christ's life to the rites and rhythms of ecclesiastical office around the time of resurrection, we might want to go on and ask two crucially related questions. First, why does the York playwright alone "adopt the method of the early Latin plays"[33] in resituating the Visitatio, and, second, why do Lollards return so persistently to that question about what is being sought at the empty tomb/Easter Sepulchre?

SURREXIT: NON EST HIC

It is in Wyclif's sermon on a verse from the last chapter of Mark that the most overt links are made between the empty tomb of the Markan tradition and the eucharistic rites of Holy Week. In a prolonged meditation, Wyclif points out that the angel's words to the Maries— "Quem queritis?"—are suited to Easter communicants: "Omnes enim qui ad ecclesiam hoc die venerint, ut sacientur ex isto viatico, Jesum querunt;"[34] He quotes 1 Corinthians 11:29 and suggests that the seeking and interrogation are indispensable at the Easter eucharist because the eucharist is approached for salvation and damnation according to the kind of charity in which it is held. But that charity does not inhere in the body as in an object. For he goes on to specify that Christ's body is hidden in the monument; the body, like Christ's body in the eucharist, is there sacramentally and cannot actually be seen. Hence the meaning of the words of the angel: "Surrexit; non est hic." Here Wyclif links the proclamation of resurrection that is used in the liturgical rites of Easter to proclaim the absence of a reified version of Christ's body:

Surrexit; non est hic. Necesse quidem est sic accipientibus eukaristiam quod in fide katholica instruantur et per consequens cognoscant quod Christus est sursum in patria quod secundum suam substanciam, et non est hic taliter sed sacramentaliter vel in signo. Sed quia fides per se est mortua, ideo necesse est quod spes et caritas comitentur.[35]

It is as if Wyclif here is highly aware of the simultaneous fact of Christ's body in the tomb as a dead body, and as an absent body; for both reasons he thinks that the question as to what is being sought by the Maries—who stand here for the faithful at Easter communion—is a vital one. For the dead body is Christ in his most fetishized form; and the absent body draws our attention to that part of the dialectic of sacramentality that much late medieval practice dismissed or had lost sight of. And so Wyclif uses the words of the angel to reflect back on the practices of the Easter rites, and in doing so he also reveals the extent to which the liturgical melding of tomb and sepulcher was a thoroughly worked and understood context for these passages.

In an English Wycliffite sermon on Easter Day that takes Matthew 27:1 as the central text, the author also makes the link between the Maries and Easter communicants:

And hit is seid comunly þat, as þese hooly wymmen hadden lefte þer formere synne, and take þeir fresch deuocion; so men schulden come to þe chirche to take þis hooly sacrament.[36]

Using Augustine's sermon "ad infantes" on the reception of the eucharist, he says:

And so hit is kyndely breed, as Powle seiþ, but hit is sacramentally verrey Godis bodi. And herfore seiþ Austyn þat þat þing is breed þat þine eyȝen tellon þe and þat þow seest wiþ hem. For it was not trowed byfore þe feend was loosid þat þis worþi sacrament was accident wiþoute suget. . . . But owre byleue is set upon þis poynt; what is þis sacrede host, and not what þing is þere.[37]

Here the author makes the visit to the sepulcher the occasion to allegorize the "stoone of unbileve" that stands in the way of those who would be witnesses to the resurrection and to the sacramental presence "in signo" of Christ's body and to castigate those who have perverted the old Augustinian understanding of eucharistic reception: "Crede et manducaste."

But perhaps the most obvious linkage of the tomb with the eucharistic connotations of the sepulcher in relation to anticlericalism is the reference in one of the Wycliffite sermons in which the guarding of Christ's body in the tomb is made analogous to the retention of Christ as word. For this sermon writer tells us that according to Matthew, Annas and Caiphas "dredded more þat þe name of Crist schulde growen among men."[38] So, this sermonizer tells us, after they have killed Christ, these men want to keep the truth of the Gospel and God's law from people, because it is by the light of those truths that they themselves will be exposed and revealed. In an idiom that puts them in the tradition of the best Lollard antifraternal satire, the writer says:

> And herfore þei seyn þat Godis lawe is false, but ȝif þei gloson hit after þat þei wolen; and þus þer gloos schulde be trowed as byleue of cristen men, but þe tixt of Godis lawe is perelous to trowe.[39]

The sermon continues to tell the story of the relations between Pilate and Annas and Caiphas in terms of a fairly careful linkage of the scriptural precedent to the relation between temporal and ecclesiastical authorities in the concealing of the word and the prosecution of heresy. Indeed, the writer makes an overt analogy between the high priests killing and then guarding Christ's body with the laws of the "newe religiows" who "make statutes stable as a stoon, and geton graunt of knytes to confermen hem."[40] The stone of the sepulcher is then the statutes that prevent unlicensed preaching, and the collusion of the secular arm is the specific target of attack. The statutes of stone, he says,

> þei marken wel wiþ witnesse of lordis, leste þat trewþe of Godis lawe hid in þe sepulchre berste owt to knowyng of comun puple. O Crist! þi lawe is hyd ȝeet; whanne wolt þow sende þin aungel to remeue þis stoon and schewe þi trewpe to þi folc?[41]

RESURRECTION THEATER IN YORK

The Empty Tomb Revisited

Both Meg Twycross and Rosemary Woolf have commented on the fact that the York Resurrection play is "an extended quem queritis."[42] The twin contexts sketched above—the liturgy's drama of presence and absence in the rites of Easter, and the Lollard interrogation about the nature of the object sought and the seekers—help us to understand why the York playwright chooses to resituate the *quem queritis* trope in this way. For in the York plays, the empty tomb scene is utterly redesigned from the earlier Latin drama by being resituated in the context of Pilate, Annas, and Caiphas's prelatical conspiracy, to guard and retain the body of Christ. Once the body has broken loose and the news of the resurrection has been uttered, they also conspire to keep all news of resurrection from reaching anyone's ears. Their act, then, is of a double retention—of the body and of news of its absence. It is clear from the Lollard sermons that these scenes are read as an indictment of the complex collusion of temporal and ecclesiastical authorities to prevent the dissemination of preaching of the vernacular word that had not been granted episcopal license. York asks this question as a pointed resituation of the body of Christ as a question of ecclesiology.

For the empty tomb that is visited by the three Maries is sandwiched temporally in the pageant between the two scenes going on in Pilate's hall, and spatially by its contiguity to the Visitatio scene. The pageant seems to run two parallel scenes with the soldiers as movers between the scenes; but unlike on the modern stage, these stations remain in close proximity throughout. In the staging of this pageant in the Toronto production, the action in Pilate's hall and the scene at the tomb were staged in the same place so that Pilate, for example, actually sat upon the very stage prop in which Christ later reveals himself to have been hidden. The effect of an actual physical containment is thus well suggested.[43] The tomb, then, is not a sacralized ecclesiastical space in which presence is wondrously manifest, but is rather framed by a conspiratorial act of containment and hiding. That hiding is a hiding at once of thing and word. The playwright's characterization renders Annas the high priest who constantly prefers that things not be talked about. Pilate, by contrast, is anxious to work out what has really gone on so as to be able to cover it up more effectively. As the pragmatist exponent of realpolitik in this scene, Pilate gets them to agree that they have all three killed Christ and done it legally. Caiphas agrees that they will "maintain" that "dede." "Maintenance" carries all the force here of its usage in the context of bastard feudalism. Maintaining the law is hardly a process of upholding it, but of bribery, corruption, collusion, and conspiracy. To Annas's statement that since the "pepull" also condemned Jesus to death "Nevyn it nomore," Pilate insists that it must be mentioned since nothing has been heard since his burial.[44] This is the ironical cue for the centurion, the first true witness of the crucifixion, who informs them that they have slain a righteous man. After the exit of the centurion, Caiphas reminds the others that Christ said that he would rise on the third day. They decide that they must guard the body:

> Wendis and kepis Jesu body
> With all youre myghte.[45]

In a roughly contemporary Resurrection play, the hiding of Christ's body under the direction of the bishops is stated by the expositor to signify the forcible maintenance of the Bible and Christ as word as a clerical preserve. Latter-day bishops are said to prevent "þe people, for reading of the Scripture, lest it make them Heretikes, unless they have a *Doctour*."[46] Whether this pageant is staged by locating the Visitatio sequence and the conspiracy in the same place, or in adjacent places, the effect is to make the empty tomb a place where the real followers of Christ are denied access to his body and where the dead body is a sign of ecclesial powers of containment. The Wycliffite texts previously cited make it clear that the guarding and the hiding of the corpse of Christ was understood in relation at once to the fetishization of the host and to the retention of the word in Latin—the prevention, then, of the dissemination of Christ. The ecclesiological implications are obvious. Retention and maintenance of the body is an indispensable part of their authority. Caiphas responds to the soldiers' news that Christ has escaped:

> Allas! þanne is oure lawes lorne
> For eueremare.[47]

The revelation that Christ is risen, far from confirming the truth of the church, is here the means of its exposure, which is why they must at all costs keep it hidden.

On the other side of the Visitatio, framed by Pilate's sleeping soldiers, is the even more ludicrous cover-up in which they all collude. Truth, Pilate concludes, must be bought and sold. The selling of truth was a vital part of contemporary ecclesiastical satire. And the playwright encodes this awareness rather explicitly as, for example, when Pilate calls Caiphas a "connyng clerke" and asks aid of precisely that cunning to help them cover up the absence of the body.[48] If the empty tomb points toward a plenitude located elsewhere, a risen Christ, then there are some searching explorations at work here about how that body is retained, confined, and hidden.

The centurion says at the beginning of the pageant:

> What may þes meruayles signifie
> Þat her was schewed so oppinly
> Vnto oure sight?[49]

The meaning may be unclear, but the sights have been "open" and available. Twycross points out that although the bishops and Pilate appear to be successful in sweeping the scandal under the carpet, the context of playing makes it clear that they have not succeeded because the audience has actually seen Christ escape from the tomb with their own eyes as the angels sing "Christus resurgens." "So Pilate and the Bishops are plotting to keep from them the truth of an event they have just witnessed with their own eyes."[50] The pageant has not simply "shown" us this, but through its modes of address, it has remade our relation to one another, because it has remade our relation to the body of Christ. It is not simply, then, that we have seen that Christ will not be contained, but that a new church that sidelines the episcopacy has occurred not so much before us, as between us. It is these structures of recognition that are also explored in the Mary Magdalene pageant.

Mary Magdalene

Perhaps it is also no accident that the York plays stage the first witnesses of the resurrection as outsiders to the community of the eleven apostles of Christ. Even here the message comes not as an extension of their community but from someone utterly marginal to it, a woman.[51] In the York Resurrection play, the playwright conflates the action of the Gospel accounts by sending off two of the Maries to spread the news of the resurrection while Mary Magdalene stays at the tomb because she cannot bear to leave the body behind, even though it is already absent.[52] *Quem queritis* is invoked again in moving and tender detail, now as an address not from the angels who guard the tomb, but from the resurrected Christ himself.

In the New Testament accounts of the appearance of Jesus to Mary Magdalene, we are dealing with a different kind of absent presence. Not a space in nature, but a person who is sentient and near; there, but not recognized as the very person sought. John's story can be read as a primal scene of recognition and self-recognition. In the pageant, this theme is explicated with yet greater force. For there Mary is, asking Christ the gardener who Christ is. Christ questions her as to what she would do with this dead body: "What wolde þou doo with þat body bare / Þat beried was with balefull chere?"[53] She would dry and anoint his body, she says, and the moment juxtaposes with tenderness and horror the uncanny presence (utterly particular, recognizable, embodied in *that* and only that shape and form) and absence (the corpse is not the body, it abandons and desolates us by the strangeness of its insentience). Here she is transfixed, caught at the bitterest reproach of absence to presence, for he *is* there, and yet is not there at all. At this point Christ calls her by name, and it is only in this hailing that she recognizes him.[54] It is as if by addressing her by name, by calling her, he brings her to a self-recognition simultaneously with the recognition of him. In a sense the appearance of Christ to her is a kind of a giving of herself to herself. Disclosure of God is also and crucially self-disclosure and is only effected in acknowledgment that is mutual, naked, and reciprocal. As in the Resurrection pageant, it is "sight" as insight, recognition that involves the direction of the will, the education of desire, the experience of knowing only as being known that must be communicated here for the play itself to live or die in the hearts and minds of its audience.

Augustine in his commentary on John unfolds some of the implications of the prior miscommunications and subsequent recognitions of this Gospel scene. Commenting on the exchange between Mary and the gardener, he says that Mary understands the question "why weepest thou?" as an injunction not to weep: "But she supposing [he] had put the question from ignorance, unfolded the cause of her tears. Because, she said, they have taken away my Lord, calling her Lord's inanimate body her Lord, meaning a part for the whole."[55] Mary has mistakenly localized the Lord in a dead body, an inanimate body, reading it synecdochally. The formulation of Augustine's analysis of misrecognition resonates eucharistically. She has called that dead body "her Lord" but calls him "Master": "When she then turned herself in body, she supposed Him to be what He was not, while now, when turned in heart, she recognized Him to be what He was."[56] The entire episode is used by Augustine to perform an object lesson in faith. Glossing Christ's "Touch me not, for I am not yet ascended to the Father," Augustine ponders why Christ was willing to be touched by the disciples before he ascended, but not in the case of this woman. He understands the words in the following way as an inward perception of the equality of Christ with the Father:

> But Mary might have still so believed as to account Him unequal with the Father and this certainty is forbidden her by the words, "Touch me not"; that is, Believe not thus according to thy present notions; let not your thoughts stretch outwards to what I have been made on thy behalf, without passing beyond to that whereby thou hast thyself been made. For how could it be otherwise than carnally that she still believed on Him whom she was weeping over as man?[57]

Augustine's reading here seems recognizable in another Wycliffite sermon, a sermon for Thursday of Easter Week on the text of John 20:11 (Maria stabat ad sepulcrum):

> Marie lovede here fleishli Crist; and he was not steyed in her herte as a bodi glorified, as he shal be after assencioun. And bifore þis ascensioun shal he not be fleishly tretid, for bi his ascensioun his body shal be goostly knowun, and not bi sich fleishly kissyng as Marie wolde have kissid Crist.[58]

Contrasting this passage with the Incredulity of Thomas episode, Augustine also contemplates the relation between belief and bodies, and the mislocation of faith as visible evidence, proof, or possession:

> He saw and touched the man, and acknowledged the God whom he neither saw nor touched. . . . "Jesus saith unto him Because thou hast seen me, thou hast believed." He saith not, "Thou hast touched me" but "Thou hast seen me," because sight is a general sense.

Augustine is keen to communicate the complexities of presence as a mutual event not reducible to physical proximity, or evidence divorced from all that it takes for acknowledgment. In the Mary Magdalene episode in particular, it is apparent that recognizing Christ comes from being recognized by him.[59]

The apparition stories and commentaries indicate the extent to which the question of the presence and absence of Christ is taken up as a question of sacramentality. But it is the actuality of encounter in theater that helps us to see and experience this drama as one of acknowledgment rather than knowledge. For what we have before our very eyes is all that has been missed. Like Mary, Christ is in front of us, but his presence is insignificant until woven into our memory. The continuity of Jesus with Christ will be part of a continuity of ourselves to ourselves; without that self-knowledge, belief in a risen Christ is a pointless and empty dogma, the visible witness of which is Mary Magdalene's love for a corpse.[60] Her recognition becomes to us, too, a communal achievement, one that has to be reexperienced, not merely repeated, for this version of presence to be real.

The Supper at Emmaus

Perhaps the most overtly eucharistic references in the Resurrection sequences of the York cycle emerge in the pageant that describes the episode of the travelers on the way to Emmaus. The travelers again describe to one another the narrative of Christ's crucifixion, a description that works simultaneously as a description of the pageant that we as audience have seen during the previous performance of the Crucifixion,[61] and their subsequent impatient and anxious awaiting. When a stranger enters their midst, they rehearse stories of crucifixion again, and their narrative returns almost inevitably to the empty tomb. They tell him that the women had reported that they had seen a light and a vision of angels. They said that "some of our folk" returned to the tomb to see it empty: "Þanne wiste þei þat wight was away."[62] At this point Christ approaches them, but it is not until he breaks bread with them and vanishes that they understand that this is he. Only the bread and his absence remain. It is as if, here, when they offer to share food with him, he shares himself with them. The bread is the token of this exchange and the precipitate of it. But what begins as a typical eucharistic scene—the breaking of bread that provokes acknowledgment—ends in the vanishing of the stranger, leaving the bread broken, the supper disrupted. What matters here is the act of recognition itself, and so it is as if the Emmaus encounter is staged as the very place where a fetishized host is figuratively exploded.[63]

The disturbing quality of these apparitions and their difficulty are stressed more emphatically in the York cycle than in any other. The risen Christ is not exalted or apotheosized but part of an encounter that is utterly bewildering because it is utterly ordinary. In some senses, then, it involves no extraordinary means at all of knowing and seeing.

RESURRECTION AND THEATER

O blessed body! Whither art thou flown?
No lodging for thee, but a cold hard stone?
So many hearts on earth and not one receive thee?
—Herbert, "The Sepulchre"

The occlusion of the resurrection from narratives and treatments of the humanity of Christ, the sundering of passion and resurrection, has recently been remarked upon by David Aers. He explores the implications of the centrality of resurrection to two of the most trenchant writers of the fourteenth century—Julian of Norwich and William Langland. The inextricability of passion and resurrection for these two writers, claims Aers, is a potent and intrinsically critical part of the way they revise the central narratives of their culture. As Aers explains it, in Langland's great poem *Piers Plowman,* the resurrection is encountered in the process of an interrupted Easter mass.[64] For Will, as for the figures in York, the glorified body is precisely not encountered as something that can be seen and contained, but is rather an encounter whose lineaments are difficult to discern. In the York Corpus Christi plays of Resurrection, these encounters are also strenuous and difficult to see; recognition (including self-recognition) is a component part of the Resurrection story.[65]

   In an article in which she discusses her experience of mounting a production of the Resurrection, Twycross discusses the particularities of audience response in this play. The audience, she points out, is "presented by an actual physical presence which had to be reckoned with": "The actors can solicit their attention, or they may pointedly ignore them, but they must acknowledge their presence."[66] The indispensability and palpability of the audience's presence are vital for understanding sacramental theater itself. Twycross states, "The playwright uses this physical closeness to extend, as it were, the terms of the contract between them. The characters (not merely the actors) are made to acknowledge the audience's presence."[67]

   I want to argue that this audience presence is an essential component of the defetishing of the host in Corpus Christi theater. The body of Christ is no longer that thing held between the priest's hands, the "object" of consecration, for the Resurrection theater that stages and presences that body has asked quite central questions about the relation between phenomenality and mystery, between seeing in terms of mere physical proximity and in terms of a necessary encounter that includes both knowing and being known. It has taken up the whole question of the emptiness of the tomb as a way of talking about sacramentality per se. God is neither dissolved into absence as nothingness, nor fetishized as a dead body contained and constrained to concealment and burial. He is rather endlessly disseminated in strenuous and difficult encounters where his strangeness forever reproaches our own constant temptations to idolatry.

The resources of the audience's presence are axiomatic to this performance of resurrection. For the resurrected Christ exists partly in a structure of relations, the communities of belief that are created by virtue of him. They can only take place, not as a fetishized memorial to an event that is already supposed to have happened, but by a perpetually relived and always present enactment.[68] But to be present, there must be continuity between the broken, failed community that has itself witnessed and participated in the betrayal of Christ and in the resurrected body. It is precisely in that painful remembering that the connection is established in a new community of virtue, one that will redeem the past by encompassing all its brokenness. To this extent, then, the eucharist must be a kind of absence in presence, a presence in absence, where absence is not simply something not there, nor something fully enclosed or contained in the objectual world, or in the concretion of a merely physical proximity.

Moreover, it is theater that is best suited to elucidate, portray, and embody the complexities of this relationship. In theater the "perseverance of memory must cross the threshold of performance."[69] Consequently there can be no tradition whose passing on can be guaranteed. It is theater's especial temporality to have no "transferable, autonomous existence" outside of the immediacy of performance; and medieval theater especially, as we have seen, makes us aware always of ourselves as audience, witness, spectator. The absolute contemporaneity of theater makes it an embodiment, a present event, which never simply refers to something happening elsewhere. As Erika Fischer-Lichte points out, this means that a theater performance that does not take place before an audience is not a theatre performance.[70] Audience is then a "constitutive part of theatre," and there, presence is real. We might say that nothing is seen in theater before we see it.[71] Herbert Blau suggests that as a result of this, "the drama is an extended meditation on the idea that whatever it is we're perceiving has already passed us by."[72] It is the "medium which keeps all significance continuously before our senses so that when it comes over us that we have missed it, this discovery will reveal our ignorance to have been willful, a refusal to see."[73] It is the very gap between the visible and the invisible in the sacrament (the visible sign of an invisible grace) that encourages us to think about the relation between intellectual, spiritual, and corporeal vision in a new way. In placing the body of Christ at once in the very body of an actor, and in the community of participation that was those who received, as well as that which was received, Resurrection theater embodies sacramentality through the resources of acknowledgment rather than knowledge, trust and imagination rather than doctrine.

The high priests have desired a dead Christ, and the doubling of tomb and sepulcher in the complex positioning of York's Resurrection plays indicates the extent to which that body is imaged as host, as the absent body of the empty tomb tradition, and as word. The great interest in the eucharistic body has led readers to underestimate the dialectic of absence and presence, whose theological implications animate vital meditations on the nature of the body of Christ as actualized in bonds of love, charity, and forgiveness. The resurrected Christ is a disseminated Christ, a gift who must be received to operate as such, a stranger who always judges the church who represents him, a Christ who travels. We might say that the resurrection in York's sacramental theater is not a factual hypothesis, but a truth function of the very difference it makes to the lives of those who maintain it.[74] The pageants are a criticism of the separation of passion from resurrection, of the obviation of penance as self-reflection and reparation, the obviation of the necessity that forgiveness be embodied in community, the obviation of the Christological and ecclesiological implications of eucharistic encounter. They are not, however, simply a meditation on eucharist as community, but an enactment of it. If theater, like resurrection, is the appearance of the dead in the bodies of the living, then its very liveness, our recovery from mortification, depends on the subtle linking of actor to actor, actor to audience, that sometimes happens in a theater whose only existence is the present. It is from this spectral yet palpable bond that our mutual recognition and self-recognition take on life and meaning together.

6 Penance, Presence, Punishment

We have lost and found the body of Christ in the complex space and time of York's Corpus Christi theater. We have seen the difference between a corpse and a body; we have understood Christ's presence to us in the evident bodies of actors, his absence in the eschatological temporality of the eucharist. But Corpus Christi theater (even though we have forgotten this) is a theater of the sacrament of penance as well as the sacrament of the eucharist.[1] I do not mean that this theater creates contrition in us (though it does if we are not heartless), nor that it merely refers us to an ecclesiastically derived definition of the sacrament by means of which we can be absolved (though it does this too). I mean that it reimagines the church as itself a performance of the life of Christ, in which he is rendered invisible or visible in communities of condemnation and persecution or love, forgiveness, and restoration. It is by examining the related intersubjective dimensions of penance and theater that we can further explore how the York Corpus Christi plays function as sacramental theater. Penance is not understood as secured through a treasury of merit founded on a distant past event and delivered through a monopoly of spectacular and quantified sacrifice; rather the story of the life of Christ and the community in whom and to whom it is reenacted are mutually constitutive.[2] If *penitentia* means both the sinners' contrition and the priest's absolution, it is also the most awkwardly but productively dialogic of the sacraments.

The severing of considerations of the sacrament of penance and the sacrament of the eucharist has pronounced implications for how we perceive the York plays as sacramental theater. The announcements of eucharistic unity in Durkheimian anthropology and in certain forms of theology are always fatally premature. In such accounts, atonement is either the achievement and function of ritual behavior or the doctrinal content of these plays. But to see how penance works as and in sacramental theater is to see again how theology and theater work through each other. In the York Corpus Christi plays, "the integrity of theological utterance does not lie in its correspondence to given structures of thought, its falling into line with authoritative communication, but in the reality of its rootedness, its belonging, in the new world constituted in the revelatory event or process."[3]

The obligation to receive the eucharist once a year was accompanied in the Fourth Lateran Council of 1215 by the obligation to be shriven for worthy reception of the host. The pastoral articulation of the practice of annual reception of the eucharist and penitential theology worked in conjunction. But if early penitential theology was markedly contritionist and remarkably focused on the relation between priest and penitent and the interior and voluntary movements of the will in the inviolable secrecy of confession, the liturgical and ritual aspects of Holy Week ceremony articulated absolution not so much as the sole prerogative of the priest, but as the reconciliation of the entire community that is the church. Penance was moreover not simply bound up with fundamental questions of ecclesiology, but also with vital disciplinary concerns in which the innermost movements of the will were put into play with a juridical apparatus that compelled exposure of that will within formulations of its choosing.[4]

If Lollards preferred to sever the link between the contrition of the penitent and the absolution of the priest, leaving absolution to God's omniscient and trustworthy discernment, late medieval penitential theology insisted on "confession of the mouth" to a priest as the central and saving link between contrition and forgiveness. Lollardy is an indispensable vector of my account of penance, not because I think that these are Lollard plays, but because it was in the combat against Lollard heresy that the penitential apparatus of the church was honed to become a punitive arm of the state. The York Corpus Christi plays perform the story of the man/God who turned his own punishment into penitence in the historical context of that story's tragic reversal, from penitence back to punishment. Through a scandalous and stunning exploration of a story at the mercy of its enactment,[5] Corpus Christi theater explores the two paramount arenas in which the late medieval penitential system most betrayed trust in its dispensation and authoritative claims: penance as a juridical apparatus and the substitution of the relation between priest and penitent for the embodiment of forgiveness in the bonds of community. In this theater, as for Wyclif, questions of ecclesiology are intrinsic to questions of sacrament, and

Corpus Christi's theater of penance is at the same time diagnosis, symptom, and attempted cure of the mutual failings of host and confession, of the infinitely costly reduction of the eucharist as Christ's gift in the church's possession of it.

KEEPING SECRETS, SHARING SHAME

After the Fourth Lateran Council of 1215, all Christians were enjoined on pain of excommunication to "faithfully confess all their sins at least once a year to their own priest and perform to the best of their ability the penance imposed."[6] These annual confessions were associated with Lent and were a preparation for the Easter eucharist, which was one of the very few occasions in which the eucharist was a communion and not a spectacle. The eucharist as the body of Christ is thus judge as well as redeemer. Preparation of the soul and reconciliation were central to worthy reception because receiving the eucharist meant enacting the body of Christ through living relations of love as known (and forgiven) creatures. This entailed not merely self-examination but actually restoring damaged bonds of love between people:

> For that we oweþ þat day to reseyue þe sacrament, ȝif that we be in discorde with any man, we moste firste be reconsilyd with hem, for ellis we take dome to us. . . .[7]

Penance is not merely then a psychologized form of forgiveness.[8] Penitential manuals understand sin as a breach at once of relations with God, neighbor, and church. The person out of charity needs to restore charity by coming either by himself or with his priest to the person he has harmed. Nor should the priest grant absolution if the person harmed refuses to forgive. The priest in fact should be concerned with truth and reconciliation, and one is seen as a component factor of the other:

> Synne is nogt foryeven un-to þat which was wrongfully with-holde and with-drawen be restorid ageyn, scilicet, ȝif he haue wherof and his power moue do it.[9]

In this sense, confession and penance are acts that concern the community as a whole.

Penitents were counseled to make their confession complete and entire, and to think about the nature of their sin, for penance was of no value without contrition and confession:

> of stede, of tyme, of perseveration, of dyversite and variacion, of person, þroug what manere temptacion, & of the grete execucion þat he haþ executyd with that vice.[10]

Such contrition is a reevaluation of one's past that does not divest oneself of it, an accounting for it by being accountable to it. But though it is an act that can only be willed and espoused individually, involving the self-searching that would recategorize one's own behavior in the vocabulary of "sin," penance and the eucharist were the only repeated sacraments, incorporated into the liturgical year.[11] Moreover, far from being isolated acts performed in the privacy of the confessional box, they were intimately part of a public, seasonal, annually repeated liturgical rhythm.

Both early medieval contritionist theology and modern critics have overestimated the purely psychological dimensions of the priest's interrogation of the sins of the penitent, at the expense of the communal and ritual contexts of annual confession. For even though confession was secret and private, it was done annually in the presence of the surrounding community as Easter communicants queued up to declare their sins, kneeling openly in church at the side of or in front of the priest.[12] The communal aspects of penance are further indicated by the fact that some of the penances enjoined were public, even if the confessions were not. Thomas of Chobham, for instance, distinguishes between private, public and solemn penance:

> Est preterea sciendum quod penitentia alia privata, alia publica, alla solemnis secundum quod dicitur penitentia "satisfactio," quia penitentia quae, est "confessio" privata debet esse nisi fuerit in iure extorta. Publica autem penitentia est que fit coram omnibus quia: qui publice peccat, publice peniteat.[13]

Some of the manuals that help instruct parish priests how to hear confession and enjoin penance describe complex balancing acts of adjudicating the boundaries between what should and should not be exposed. In some of the earlier penitential discussions, it was even a subject of contention whether secret penances for secret sins were sacramental.[14] For example, in *Speculum Sacerdotale* the priest is advised to deal tactfully with a woman who has committed adultery and does not dare fast in penance in case her husband becomes suspicious of her. The penance recommended in *Speculum Sacerdotale* enjoins common days of fasting only and so tactfully allows her to keep her secret and protects her from the prospect of her husband's rough justice.[15] This same text makes some rather remarkable concessions to killers whose crimes are not known:

> And ȝif eny man have done manslaughter the whiche is not openly knowe, then let hym do preuy penaunce and stonde nogt withoute the churche.[16]

A female suspected of smothering her own child is not protected in the same way: "let her stand without the church."[17] In such decisions the boundaries between private and public acts are being constantly adjudicated, indeed such adjudications would make no sense in today's post- and counter-Reformation contexts, where confession is not part of a public, liturgical, and judicial apparatus.

For confession was not simply a spiritual act but a juridical one, too. Any information given over to the priest during confession could land a parishioner in a court where only a bishop could grant absolution. Receiving the sacrament invited and sometimes incurred scrutiny and judgment; it might conceivably involve public penance and always carried that risk.[18]

Palm Sunday was the first day in which a penitent could receive Easter communion; it was also the day in which, in the liturgy of Palm Sunday, the prophets hail the sacrament as the risen Christ. And so penitential and eucharistic rites are tightly linked.[19] The most popular days for confession, though, appeared to be Maundy Thursday, Good Friday, and Resurrection Sunday; for despite exhortation, most parishioners appeared to have left as little a gap as possible for lapsing between shriving and reception of the eucharist. Those who were undergoing a public penance were excluded from the church on Ash Wednesday and accepted for reconciliation on Holy Thursday. Their discipline at the hands of the church consisted in lying prostrate at the foot of the cross and having their bare backs struck by the priest while he intoned the Miserere over them.[20]

Penance was conventionally understood in the tripartite form of "compunccion of the herte, confession of mouthe and satisfaccion of dede."[21] The voluntary subjection of the will and the earnest desire to renounce the sin were central to what it meant to acknowledge oneself as a sinful creature. But confession was also a legal obligation and sometimes the contritionist aspects that emphasized the movement of the heart fitted ill with the injunctions demanded by the church. Given the tragic risks of earthly forms of punishment and the notion that sin is itself a self-damaging act, a perfect penitential system would allow sin to constitute its own punishment.[22]

If medieval penitential theologians debated the distinction between penance and punishment where the relations of power are understood in different ways—sometimes sin is understood as a crime against a natural order, sometimes as an offense against authority—they also debated precisely where the sacramentality of penance actually lay. For some theologians, proper contrition would grant absolution; for others, the emphasis was all on the power of the words pronounced by the priest.[23] Each version of the sacrament moreover entailed a different ecclesiology and even a different theodicy. For if contrition alone, or confession to another, was sufficient for remission of temporal punishment, then the pastoral role of priest was being differently understood, as was the church in its relation to and dispensation of salvation. Was the office of priest more important than his virtue? Is it merely the sin of pride that stands in the way of confessing to a priest who appears more sinful than you are yourself? It is very easy to see why the sacrament of penance gave rise to acute anxiety at virtually every level: in it the most intense forms of self-encounter and self-knowing were articulated in the context of a hierarchy of authority and a communal belonging (on pain of excommunication, legally enjoined and judicially enforced) and where, therefore, the possibilities of being known or misrecognized carried with them enormous promise, massive hope (to be known *and* loved), and colossally fearful risk (to see penance work at the service not of truth but of power).[24] Penitential theology was "particularly susceptible to controversy"[25] because the three components of the sacrament—contrition, satisfaction, and absolution—make clear more than any other sacrament that sacramentality is a relation *between* laity and priest.

LEGISLATING SIN

It is Lollardy that once again helps to highlight many of the problems with late medieval penance, not only because in questioning orthodox views on penance, Lollards also challenged the very boundaries of the church in administering that sacrament, but also because in trying to isolate, identify, and eradicate Lollard heresy on the sacrament of penance as on other issues, the church chose to push its own penitential doctrines in distinctly punitive directions.[26] What was it that so troubled medieval Lollards about the sacrament of penance?

In the first instance, Lollards distrusted the sheer power conferred on priests, who were the beneficiary of so many of the secrets of others. Canon 21 of the Fourth Lateran Council had made strict injunctions about secrecy in confession. But as contemporary analyses of secrecy observe and as Lollards were well aware, it was the fact that the priest had the power to keep those secrets in the first place, rather than their content, that preserved his discretionary, quasi-magical power in relation to the secretive subjects.[27] Furthermore, the privacy of the priest (as well as the confessee) could also protect abuses of this jurisdiction. Lollards feared that this secrecy preserved priests from forms of public accountability:

> [M]en punyshen ofte en here in mennes courte full grevously for dedis þat men callen trespasses, & ȝit God is not wroþe with hem; but it may falle oft þat men erren & punyshen not þe trespasses of god, ne for þat it is don agens God, but for mennes wynnyng; or for þat it mise-likiþ them.[28]

This same tract also pointed out the contradictions between the voluntary nature of contrition, which alone can secure purity of the will, and its enforced nature, a contradiction greatly exacerbated if the priest is corrupt. For these reasons, some Wycliffite texts, referring nostalgically to a time when "men tolden *commynly* her synne,"[29] proposed that two priests should hear confession, thereby changing the nature of the relationship of priest and community. In this same tract the author glosses Psalm 22 ("þou god þat art my god, I shal synge to þe in an harpe") and moves the sacramentality of penance away both from the priest's "Ego te absolvo" and also away from the "covert operation" of either a purely individual contrition or a purely private confession. Sacraments, he says, are open and known. A merely private sorrow of the heart or this "privey rownyng late brought in" is not sacramental:

> [B]ut whanne a man wiþ contrite herte shriveþ him opynly to god or man, þenne his voice, þat is token of his holy sorowe of herte, may be called a sacrament, as men knowen þat discriven it.[30]

Here the voice of David, the confessee glossed in the Psalm, becomes the token of sacramentality, the visible sign of an invisible grace. In addition, says the author, any good deed that we do that springs from charity in a person's heart "may be callid a sacrament."[31] With one fell swoop, the complex system of tariffing, the trafficking in indulgences, the accounting of temporal punishment—central components of the penitential system—are disbanded, along with the apostolic authority for binding and loosing.

Such a Lollard redefinition of the sacrament was, naturally, widely construed as heretical. As the questions by which Lollardy was to be identified, codified, and captured were fine-tuned, it became a very mark of heretical resistance to ecclesiastical authority to believe "quod si fuerit debite contritus, omnis confessio exterior est sibi superflua vel inutilis."[32] Confession and penance became in this context the very tools of subjection and punishment (from the point of view of the Lollard offender). Consider, for example, the case of Gilbert Johnson, a parishioner in Coneygarth in York, who makes the following abjuration:

> I the said Gilbherte Johnson said and affirmed that I wold make my confession onlye to God omnipotente bot to no priest; also that nother Pope, Archbushope or ordinary haith auctorite to curse any man or woman.[33]

Johnson denies the authority of priests to hear confession and to excommunicate. This church, then, will not be defined and adjudicated by priests. A. G. Dickens, who records this case, gives a detailed description of Johnson's extraordinarily elaborate penances enjoined for the public statement of views:

> Johnson's penance was closely linked to the impending Rogation-week processions in the city of York. On the Monday of that week he had to precede the cross heading the procession from York Minster as far as St Mary's Abbey, and to carry a faggot on his left shoulder, a pair of beads in his right hand, having his feet and head bare and clad only in his shirt. At certain places on the route he must humbly undergo discipline at the hands of the Dean of the Christianity of York. On arriving at the high altar of St Mary's he had to say kneeling various prescribed prayers, and remain there until the end of high mass, then return with the procession to the Minster. On the Tuesday he must likewise go through the suburbs of York in front of the procession to the Friars

Preachers, and there hear the sermon before returning. On the Saturday after Ascension Day he was ordered to enter the market on the Pavement in York, similarly clad, and receive discipline from the same Dean at the four corners of the market-place—no doubt an even less attractive assignment. On the Sunday, Johnson must finally lead the procession, with the usual conspicuous accoutrements, around his own parish church of Holy Trinity in Coneygarth. And all this accomplished, he had finally to reappear before the vicar-general on the Friday before Whitsun and "submit himself to the will of the said vicar general": the probable point of this interview being to ensure the due completion of the orders.[34]

Several things are to be noted about these protracted and comprehensive penances. First, and most obviously, it is to the very authority of the priesthood he had denied that Gilbert Johnson must, most publicly, submit after his admission/confession. And his penitential punishment is spectacular, a veritable theater of penance. But this theatricalization is complexly woven into a pattern of liturgical show and institutional authority. He must process, both to be shown to and to be revealed as being a part of those very authorities he has denied, marking space with them. The penances indicate that he must do obeisance to all forms of ecclesiastical authority—the friar preachers, the Minster, the Abbey, and his local parish church. This authority must be visible within the public contexts of market as well as parish and is temporally as well as spatially protracted, from Rogation processions, which are conventionally associated with penance, to the Sunday after Ascension Day.

It is of course possible to resist the role scripted for the heretic in such punishments. In her book *London and the Reformation*, Susan Brigden tells of one Thomas Wiggins who receives his penance more in "scorn and derision" than in contrition; we might say that Wiggins is hereby theatricalizing his own penance.[35] In creating a gap between person and role, he can use his penance gestically to show forth the punitive authority of the church. If Thomas Wiggins is a Brechtian actor, Gilbert Johnson is meant to be a Foucauldian one; his own body is scripted as the medium of the inscription of ecclesiastical power. When two sheriff's sergeants drew blood in an altercation at the gates of the Minster, the chapter imposed a penance on them. But the city would not allow the men to perform the penance.[36] The fact that the city had no jurisdiction over certain areas of the city—for example, the Minster, St. Mary's Abbey, or St. Leonard's Hospital—was continuously irksome to the civic authorities, and in this instance they refused to allow the organs of civic authority to submit themselves to ecclesiastical authority.[37]

Gilbert Johnson's penance and the Lollard critique of the penitential system indicate many of the risks involved in the intertwining of penance and punishment in the late Middle Ages. When the Lollard William Thorpe writes about his questioning by Archbishop Arundel, where he is asked, among other things, on the sacrament of penance and the sacrament of the altar, the entire narrative of the trial is conducted to indicate the problems with confession when it is placed within the context of legal obligation (under canon law). The problem with penance was a problem with the church and involved ecclesiological questions. When asked to submit himself to the church, Thorpe ostentatiously submits himself "ful gladli to Crist þe head of holi chirche, and to þe lore and to þe heestis and to þe counseilis of every plesyng membre of him."[38] For him the church of the body of Christ is quite distinct from the archbishop's authority.[39] So when Malvern offers him the invitation,

> I undirtake if þu wolt take to þee a preest, and schryve þee clene, and
> · forsake alle siche opynyons, and take þi penaunce of my lord here for þe
> holding and techynge of hem, wiþinnne schort tye þou schalt be greetly
> comfortid in þis doynge[,][40]

it will involve submitting himself to an impossible authority, betraying his faith, his friends, his God, and himself. In writing a new form of confession, he seeks new forms of authorization, simultaneous with new forms of community—from the readers of a confession not told to Arundel, but narrated to that community.[41]

In Thorpe's narrative, Arundel appears to be cast as Caiphas, just as Gilbert Johnson explicitly casts priests in the role of Judas:

> Also I the said Gilberte did saye and affirme that preistes ar worse than
> Judas; whie, Judas sold Almyghtie God for xxxd, and prestes will sell
> God for half a penny.[42]

Both William Thorpe and Gilbert Johnson thus rewrite the roles of the clergy and give them new parts to play in an old story.[43] But if the question of penance was bound up with the question of the church, there are profound tensions within the Wycliffite ecclesiology.[44] Lollard critique had accurately diagnosed some of the problems in the late medieval penitential system, and it had seen those problems clearly in the abuse of power in the jurisdiction of penance and the subversion of community in the protected secrecy of confession. But in so ardently locating sins in the other, in its mesmerized contemplation of clerical abuse, it forgot the redress of community. And it overlooked the centrality of the reflexive and self-acknowledging practices of contrition at least in its own forms of worship.[45] As in the Wakefield Last Judgement play, hell is the world of the other. In the Wakefield play the wily devils, advocates in the grand assize who carry off the lawyers and doctors of the church, allow us to indulge the pleasures of exactly that which the sacramental system of penance had so carefully sought to avert: revenge and resentment as powerful ecclesiastical sinners finally get what they deserve, with us standing by on the side of God.[46] Moreover, the Lollard antipathy to performance disables any prescient or usefully diagnostic analysis of public games and sights. The only piece of Lollard theater criticism we have fundamentally misreads Corpus Christi theater as "reversing penance" and crucially underestimates its resources.[47]

But it is in fact to the Corpus Christi plays that we must look for an examination of the intertwining both of the juridical and the collective aspects of the sacrament of penance. The plays link juridical and communal questions precisely through a transformed understanding of the liturgy. Indeed the plays are best understood as a form of liturgy; they perform a story that "has no foundation other than the community that tells the story by which it is told."[48]

CHRIST COMES TO YORK: THE ENTRY INTO JERUSALEM

York's Corpus Christi theater calls upon its audience to recognize its collective character, as witnesses to and participants in the event of crucifixion, and examines the obstacles in the way of such an endeavor. In reenacting the life, death, and resurrection of Christ, it also examines our ineradicable implication in a community that is the very medium and product of our agreements and disagreements. We have already examined the complexity of the actor's body as a theatrical sign in the York Crucifixion to see how sacramental theater works in the register of the sign; we will now need to examine the Passion sequences as a whole, from Christ's Entry into Jerusalem to the Last Judgement, to see how the audience is the central theatrical object, to recognize how intersubjective dimensions of this theatrical working carry vital penitential dimensions.

Theologians have long recognized the centrality of narrative for Christianity. John Milbank, for example, comments that the story of the crucifixion is redemptive because it shows us the shape of sin as a refusal of pure love.[49] In his comments on the Fourth Gospel, Rowan Williams indicates that the account of the crucifixion expounds the judgment not by uttering words of condemnation but rather by a complex process of interaction. The words and work of Jesus inevitably come to involve a choice for or against him. In Williams's account, they force to light hidden directions and dispositions that would otherwise never come to view, and "thus make the conflicts and interests between people a public affair."[50] The Passion in York is an excruciatingly public affair as the audience does not so much watch as perform the crucifixion, that is to say crucify Christ all over again in their own time and in their own city. Corpus Christi theater in York animates the intersubjective dimensions of theater to show that the presence of Christ and his absence are utterly bound up with our presence to each other in bonds of charity. How then does York welcome Christ into its city on Corpus Christi Day, and how does such a welcoming, such a recognition, mutually constitute Christ and the penitential community as the body of Christ, the church?

In the Entry into Jerusalem pageant, which one critic has recently called the "conceptual centre of the cycle," the recognition of Christ as king is coincident upon the formation of a model community.[51] The Entry play enacts Christ's entrance into Jerusalem, marking the beginning of Holy Week and the entrance of Christians into the sacrifice of Christ. For in the liturgical cycle, Palm Sunday was the first day in which one could make confession to fulfill the annual obligation prescribed by the Fourth Lateran. In the Palm Sunday liturgy, the eucharist is borne by priests in procession, who are met by different parts of the congregation, representing the crowds who witness Christ's entrance into Jerusalem. In this liturgy, then, the eucharist is the Christ entering Jerusalem; in the York pageant's version of this play, the eucharist as it is recognized in liturgical ritual is represented in the body of an actor.

Nissé has recently given an illuminating reading of the play in which she sees it as part of the "afterlife of Lollardy," a concerted attempt to "stage an account of biblical narrative as a form of public political discourse."[52] As part of a heterodox project influenced by the vernacularizations of scripture, it outlines, she argues, an idealized account of principles of rule within the contexts of York civic society. She announces her investigation as a critical project that will be interested more in questions of governance than in devotional themes.[53] But the two are inseparable, as exegetical questions cannot be removed from liturgical ones. For the life of Christ is not a story to be explained in an extrinsicist manner but is an injunction and an invitation to be lived and performed. In this sense, understanding and transformation are coincident, at least a coincident sign of conversion. Nissé's account stresses the exegetical project of the plays: it is clear, for example, that the citizens must agree who Christ is before they welcome him into the city, and there is great stress in these parts of the play both on the clarity of the prophecy and on the very mechanisms of consensus. The nature and identity of Christ must be understood and mutually assented to, before Christ can enter Jerusalem/York. The triumphant "Hails" at the end of the Entry play are hails of welcome and of recognition. They succede Zacchaeus's confession and absolution before Christ ("Thy clere confessioun schall þe clense") and acknowledge this poor man as prophet, prince of peace, king, and "domysman dredful" summoning up his past and our future on a path that belongs both to him and to the audience at York.[54]

Christ's entry needs to be read in the context of the royal entries, which themselves borrowed from the liturgies both of Advent and of Palm Sunday.[55] The community constitutes itself as and around the body of Christ, as it will later become invisible as that body when it crucifies him. It is, of course, inescapably and actually the very same crowd that welcomes him that will also see him die. It is here, I think, that more than a set of principles of Lollard exegesis is being announced. For the church as the body of Christ is literally, visibly present when such an ideal community forms; but it dissolves or rather becomes invisible when it is hate rather than love that is being exemplified. Christ is enacted in the penitential community or destroyed within it; he is made not absent but invisible, by the depravity of the agencies that act in his name. What follows is a scandalous, devastating series of pageants in which the body of Christ is rendered utterly invisible insofar as it inheres in bonds of charity, even as it is most visible as a tortured body, the central icon of the church.[56] It is the juridical aspects of this relationship that are most profoundly put under scrutiny in the subsequent series of pageants.

COMING TO JUDGMENT: CHURCH, STATE, AND HERESY IN THE TRIAL PLAYS

The Christian narrative of the Gospels has always confronted its followers with the scandal that the "fulfiller of God's law had been condemned."[57] The York plays perform the passion with this appalling and salvific paradox in mind. The aldermen in the Entry play are eager for the new laws of Christ and the execution of Christ is understood as a defense of an "old law against a new."[58] The Passion sequence includes seventeen scenes of judgment between the Conspiracy (play 26) and the Second Trial before Pilate (play 33) (not including the Last Judgement).[59] The plays not only indicate a detailed, systematic knowledge of civil and canon law; they have an account of the law in which humanly administered law will itself be judged eschatologically in the light of Christ's Gospel and person. In the painfully extended sequence by which Christ is judged, he is put on trial four times—before Annas and Caiphas, before Herod, and twice before Pilate—before he is finally, inevitably, condemned to death.

In the plays, the jurisdictions of the courts are recognizable as the English criminal procedure "for charges of heresy brought by a cleric against a preacher (Christ) before a royal justice."[60] The charges leveled against Christ are ecclesiastical crimes: breaking the ecclesiastical laws, false preaching, apostasy, and so on. Excommunication was the usual penalty for persistence in these errors. In the plays, as Elza Tiner points out, Jesus is treated like an excommunicant who refuses to recant. What Tiner does not notice, however, is that contemporary Lollard doctrine pointed out unequivocally exactly what these plays enact: for they said that if Christ returned now, he would be excommunicated and tried as a heretic by a church that functions as anti-Christ. The plays seem fascinated by the complex legal process by which it becomes possible to execute this particular man. They have written a series of plays that read the passion story in terms of the contemporary processes by which the church and the state colluded to burn heretics to death.

The principle agents of so-called justice each talk about themselves in relation to the law. Thus when we first meet Pilate, he declares himself "granted" to "justifie and juge all þe Jewes."[61] Annas and Caiphas are depicted as detesting Christ because of the way in which he will confound their law ("Many lordis of oure landis might lede fro oure lawes") and are shown as frustrated by their awareness that it does not lie within their legal power to silence Christ.[62] As Annas explains to Pilate:

> O, sir Pilate, withouten any pere,
> Do way,
> 3e wate wele withouten any were
> Vs falles not, nor oure felowes in feere,
> To slo no man—yourself þe soth say.[63]

As bishops they can excommunicate ("curse" in Gilbert Johnson's words) Jesus and flog him, but they have no other recourse of punishment.

In the early fifteenth century, bishops were faced with the problem of how to punish heretics who had lapsed and who refused to recant again. The process by which Jesus is executed does not simply mark his relation to such a relapsed heretic—for this is how he is regarded by Annas and Caiphas—but indicates the canny strategies by which the church and the state appear inexorably to require the bodies of heretics.[64] And although Elza Tiner and Lynn Squires have pointed out the general similarities of heretic trials to the judgment of Christ in these plays, the specific parallels between the state-church machinations to burn the first heretics and the conspiratorial and collusive strategies by which Christ is bought to death in the Corpus Christi plays reveal not simply a sophisticated grasp of what jurisdictions do when they are under threat, but a profound sense that this is a sacramental perversion in which processes of reconciliation have turned into processes of persecution, prosecution, and execution. In this analysis they reveal the extent to which the eucharist is now defended by the church as a privileged jurisdiction; indeed in the York plays, the bishops are seen, like the archbishop of Canterbury at the turn of the fifteenth century, to be willing to use the death penalty to defend their version of the body of Christ. In York, one might say, the legal and dramatic imagination of the playwright has pitted one version of the body of Christ against another.

In the first decade of the fifteenth century, the church and the state unite to burn two heretics. The first, William Sawtre, is burned as a dry run, a test case—but illegally—just before De Heretico Comburendo is enacted in March 1401. The second is a layman, John Badby, in 1410, after Arundel's Constitutions had introduced comprehensive measures of censorship of vernacular devotional writing, lay literacy, and preaching, indeed spiritual curiosity per se. Tiner, in her examination of the legal procedure observed in these plays, has argued that the lesson they teach us is that "only by strict obedience to the law of the realm, i.e., both divine and secular law, is salvation possible."[65] But such a comment is blind to the complexity of the relation between divine and secular law, their depraved but entirely expedient imbrication. And it is only by understanding that specificity that the legal contexts of Christ's execution in York will be properly appreciated. In discussing some of the Lollard cases below, then, I do not intend to suggest that the York plays explicitly quote or mime these cases, nor that they explicitly make the analogy between Christ and a Lollard that is found in the Lollard tracts themselves. But I am suggesting that it is the context of the Lollard threat, which confronted the church with its own limits as a jurisdiction, that reveals how inexorably the penitential milieux of episcopal examination with its sanctions was converted into a "theater" of punishment, and, by means of the presentation of such men as William Sawtre and John Badby, to extend those limits.

The church had been seeking the help of the state against heretics since the 1380s.[66] In the 1380s they had succeeded in gaining "help" (the word by Caiphas to Pilate in Christ before Pilate 2: The Judgment) in the discovery of heretics, but they were still brought to justice in the ecclesiastical courts.[67] After the legislation of 1382, any bishop could commission sheriffs or other royal officers to imprison preachers summarily until they "will justify themselves according to reason and ecclesiastical law."[68] Although there was a right of appeal to the king's council, the church could take action on suspicion of unauthorized preaching, and in such actions it had the full support of the lay power. The York plays show the preliminary collusion of church and state in their difference from the Gospel accounts, in which Pilate is not present during the "conspiracy." On the other hand, Pilate's approval for the plans of Annas and Caiphas is, on the contrary, understood to be central to the treatment in the York plays.[69]

By the late 1390s, the church imagined that it had very little recourse against determined and lapsed heretics. It had been asking Parliament to "do what was necessary" to deal with the problem, but the death sentence pronounced on William Sawtre was by a specific royal edict, rather than parliamentary act. In examining the indecent haste with which Sawtre was sentenced to death, both McNiven and Strohm agree that Arundel and the king may have been after the bigger fish of the heretic-preacher John Purvey, who, in Strohm's words, "folded up like an accordion" after he was informed of the burning of William Sawtre.[70] McNiven comments on the dubious legality of the case:

> . . . in pre-empting the statute, the king and Arundel had to weigh certain delicate factors in the balance. They risked committing the crown to, and implicating the church in, a profound legal injustice. Could they justify having a man burnt to death for something which, whatever the wording of the warrant, was not yet a capital offence?[71]

In the complex collusion of archbishop and king in burning their first heretic, the law itself comes after the act of burning, because Arundel and the king want an example.[72] It is such concerted and conscious deployment of power in a legal fiction that casts aspersions on Tiner's hopeful statement that salvation is possible within the limits of the law.[73] Arundel appeared to want Sawtre dead, just as Annas and Caiphas want Christ dead, before, rather than as a result of, the trial.

It is Pilate's task to make this clear in the plays. When Pilate turns their desire for Christ's death back on them in the York plays, Annas and Caiphas note over and over again that their law does not permit them to kill Jesus. "Nay sir, þan blemysshe yee prelatis estate," Annas cautions Caiphas when his anger and his sadism threaten to become too overwhelming.[74] But Annas, also, directly asks Pilate, "domysman nere and nexte to þe king" to put him to death.[75] In the plays this is repeatedly seen as a question of jurisdiction, as Christ is passed from the ecclesiastical courts to the king's courts and then to the court of Herod. So, too, in the social setting of the plays, the bishops maintain a legal fiction whereby they do not actually execute the heretics.

It is just such a sanction that William Sawtre thought would protect him in his trial[76] and that Walter Brut appeals to in his letter of appeal to the king in 1391 after he is arrested by Bishop John Trefnant. "It is not lawful," he says, "for us to kill any man; as they said to Pilate when Christ should be deemed."[77] He goes on to make an elaborate comparison between Christ's law and the pope's law, demanding to be judged by the "truth of God's law," which he understands eschatologically. Thus the very context of the trials raises pointed questions of law and legality in relation to spiritual and temporal jurisdiction, questions about which those under trial show themselves to be acutely aware. There can be no simple appeal to the form of the law when that law itself is being carefully tailored precisely to secure the death of offenders. And it was jurisdiction that was at issue in the actual content of the heresy and in the ability of the church to defend itself against that overt attack on its jurisdiction. "How," asks William Swinderby in his appeal to the king's court over the bishop's court of Archbishop Trefnant, can the bishop of Rome in the jurisdiction of confession, let alone the heresy trial, "dareth to take upon him to be a judge before the day of judgement?"[78]

In the burning of John Badby, there is similar collusion between church and state. Prince Hal was present at Badby's burning. Indeed, at Badby's first cries of pain from the fiery barrel in which he was bound, the prince ordered a temporary arrest and offered Badby a little pension if he recanted. Badby refused to recant. The prince was there to show solidarity with an "affronted church."[79] With Badby, it appears, as a scapegoat, the counter in a long argument about the very nature of the church and a decisive and ironical answer to those Lollards who had sought lay intervention in the English church. It is in this "new horizon of judgement and punishment" that the specific treatment of the Trial of Christ plays needs to be seen.[80]

Over and over again as one reads these Lollard trials, it is the very definition of the body of Christ that is at issue. When priests judged confessions, Lollards maintained, they usurped God's jurisdiction. In *De Eucharistia,* Wyclif insists that the powers of jurisdiction claimed by priests created the virtual blasphemy of making God's clergy partners in bestowing forgiveness.[81] It is when confession becomes judgment that Walter Brut begins to see problems: "After this manner I esteem confession to priests very expedient and profitable to a sinner. But to confess sins unto the priest as unto a judge, and to receive of him corporal penance for a satisfaction unto God for his sins committed: I see not how this can be founded upon the truth of scripture."[82] So, too, for Brut, an antisacrificial understanding of the mass and criticism of ecclesiastical jurisdiction are united around an abuse of the body of

Christ in a penitential system: "[I]f Christ evermore sittith at the right hand of God, to make intercession for us, what need he to leave here any sacrifice for our sin by the priests to be daily offered?"[83]

In the plays the eucharist is not a place, a territory to be defended as a jurisdictional zone with exclusive rights and privileges, a spectacle with its own procedural protocols for defensive adjudication, but a doubled time and doubled space of failure as well as jubilation, of a hopeless past redeemed in a promising eschaton, not the object of justice and forgiveness but, through our own performance, its very medium.

If Christ is hailed as king in the Entry play, then these hails are grotesquely mocked and mimed in the series of Trial plays in which the body of Christ is broken as the community becomes unreconciled. The consecration of Christ as king in the Entry play is consciously undone in a ceremony of ritual torture, deconsecration, and degradation.[84]

> Hayle, comely kyng þat no kyngdom has kende.
> Hayll vndughty duke, þi dedis ere dom,
> Hayll, man vnmighty þi menge to mende.[85]

He is unmade as king and lord; it is vital that this naming and unnaming is a communal, authorized act, performed by the soldiers but for which they alone are not responsible. Such hails not only undo the recognition of Christ as king effected in the Entry play, but also consciously recall the way in which, only a few hundred lines previously, the same soldiers have hailed Pilate:

> Hayll louelyest lorde þat euere led ȝitt,
> Hayll semelyest vndre sylke on euere ilka syde,
> Hayll stateliest on stede in strenghe þat is sted ȝitt,
> Hayll liberall, hayll lusty to lordes allied.[86]

In the sequence of Trial plays, the law is examined as the very machinery of injustice, perverted by the protection of power, the display of wills that have entirely lost the good of intellect. Implicit in these dramas is the claim that any regime that administers law in this way and that converts truth to power will be a regime that crucifies Christ again. Through the figure of Pilate and the relationship of Pilate with Annas and Caiphas, the difference between sheer brutality and law, between authority and tyranny, is explored. Pilate in the Conspiracy and in the two plays of the Judgement before Pilate seems to be able to see quite clearly that Annas and Caiphas suffer from a rawness of emotion, an anger and a hatred that are not simply unseemly in the episcopacy but that are directly generated out of the perversion of their will rather than any relation to truth or justice. These bishops are "overcruell"; they even want to strike Jesus themselves rather than delegating the job. There is nothing legally admissible in the desire of Annas and Caiphas to crucify Jesus, Pilate keeps declaring, and hence it is the nasty specificity of that desire that is exposed. This is simply, he tells them, about "ȝoure maistrie."[87] But as soon as his own interests are closely touched, his own power addressed, and his own will interpellated, Pilate's high-minded defenses of the law evaporate rapidly. In the tilemakers' play, Annas and Caiphas persuade Pilate that Christ is usurping the kingly office and that they might therefore be dealing with a charge of treason. He immediately becomes appallingly and violently angry.[88] In the second trial, Pilate seems to have lost his legal inhibitions and is quick to command that Christ be scourged for a second time.

> Wrayste and wryng hym to, for wo to he be wepyng,
> And þan bryng hym before vs as he was beforne.[89]

There is no judgment available that has not been utterly corrupted by the protection of personal power and prestige, that is not vitiated by the wills of the judges. But in this world, the truth cannot be heard even when it is spoken, as Christ points out in the bowers' and fletchers' play: "Sir, if I saie þe sothe, þou schall not assente."[90] Christ, the word, is silenced, for truth is incapable of reception when its audience is so depraved. In the investigation of William Thorpe, speech is similarly rendered pointless:

> And þanne I was rebukid and scorned and manassid on ech side. And ȝit after þis dyverse persones crieden upon me to knele down to submytte me. But I stood stille and spak no wordis; and I stood and herde hem curse and manasse and scorne me, but I seide no þing.[91]

Thorpe's silence isolates the bullying of Arundel and his henchmen. Christ's silence, on which it is partly modeled, both encloses these powerful men in their own prison of words and reaches out to the present and witnessing audience so that it is not silence but communication. When Christ does speak, unbiblically, the words relate directly to what they, the words themselves, witness and effect:

> Every man has a mouthe þat made is on molde
> In wele and in woo to welde at his will,
> If he governe it gudly as God wolde,
> For his spirituale speche hym thar not to spill.
> And what gome so gouerne it ill,
> Full vnhendly and ill sall he happe;
> Of ilk tale þhou talkis us vntill,
> Þou accounte sall, þou can not escappe.[92]

Government and speech are brought together here as the vital medium of breaking and reconciliation. In these plays, words are converted to blows, to the breathless, rhythmical exhortations of measured, calculated, and ritual beating, to cruel imperatives that silence even prayer:

> II Miles: Swyng to this swyre to swiftely he swete.
> III Miles: Swete may þis swayne for sweght of our swappes.
> IV Miles: Russhe on this rebald and hym rathely rehete.
> I Miles: Rehete hym I rede you with rowtes and rappes.
> II Miles: For all oure noy þis nygard he nappes.
> III Miles: We sall wakken hym with wynde of oure whippes.
> IV Miles: Nowe flynge to þis flaterer with flappes.
> II Miles: I sall hertely hitte on his hippes
> And haunch.
> II Miles: Fra oure skelpes not scatheles he skyppes.
> III Miles: 3itt hym list not lyft vp his lippis
> And pray vs to have pety on his paunch.[93]

During these grueling sequences, Christ falls more and more silent and the body of Christ as the reconciled community becomes less and less visible as he is put to death in front of them. Ironically, that is to say, as his body becomes more and more visible as tortured and wrenched, so the body of Christ as the community of the faithful becomes more and more invisible. All torturers know how to unmake the bonds of human community. Here the soldiers, the bishops, and the king's justices try to make of the body of Christ a kind of countereucharist, dispersing not gathering, wrecking not making, isolating not uniting, in hatred not in charity. Torture, as William Cavanaugh has movingly elucidated, is the countereucharist par excellence. But in these plays as the body is unmade, so it is made again by the new community forming to sideline those who claim to speak in his name:

those who are viewing the very shape of sin—and its refusal and subsumption.

If these plays have systematically addressed the trial of Christ as the trial of a heretic, this is not because they make Wycliffite arguments. Indeed, the view of church-state relations as it is outlined in Wyclif's own writings renders priests "royal tenants" of the king. Wyclif's program of systematic disendowment offered no recourse outside of royal jurisdiction—even for the adjudication of sin and especially for the adjudication of heresy. As Aers has powerfully noted, what emerges in Wyclif's writings is a "fascinating convergence . . . between the Catholic Church in Lancastrian England and the heretical reformation programme of John Wyclif."[94] On the contrary, these plays have isolated and exposed just such a dangerous convergence in the sidelining of the collective, reconciliatory action of the body of Christ as a new community. For they seek no final redress (in scriptural fundamentalism, in the convenient location of newfound scapegoat anti-Christs, in a fetishism either of ecclesial power or royal jurisdiction) outside of the necessity of that body of Christ to be embodied, incorporated, in short, performed.

COMING TO JUDGMENT: THE ESCHATOLOGICAL ASSIZE

The only just judgment in the York plays is the great eschatological assize that takes place in future time. What is the play's strange temporality? Its tense seems to be the future anterior, and it is in this way that grace is never hypostatized. When the angel conjures the souls out of their graves, their goodness or badness cannot be discerned or secured on the basis purely of what they think they have done and of whether they consider their actions good or bad. Although strictly speaking this final judgment had already been made for each soul at the hour of death, this play, I believe, makes judgment as uncertain as possible so as to show it to be a genuinely divine mystery, which cannot be earned or presumed. For the good souls have certainly done bad things, as they are aware:

> Of oure ill dedis, lorde, þou not mene,
> That we haue wroght vppon sere wise,
> But graunte vs for thy grace bedene
> Þat we may wonne in paradise.[95]

But their goodness is rather defined by the direction of their wills, their awareness of the giftedness of God's creation, their sense of the availability of his mercy. Their sincerity comes not from a quantification of good deeds, but rather an awareness of their own sin and therefore of themselves as creatures in relation to God.[96] The bad souls are damned because they have so little sense of inhabiting God's creation that they look for ways not to know themselves, to hide from the imminent judgment; and since they have utterly lost the virtue of hope and the way it supports faith and love, they are filled with despair:

> What schall we wrecchis do for drede,
> Or whedir for ferdnes may we flee,
> When we may bringe forthe no goode dede
> Before hym þat oure juge schall be?
> To aske mercy vs is no nede,
> For wele I wotte dampned be we,
> Allas, þatt we swilke liffe schulde lede
> Þat dighte vs has þis destonye.[97]

Moreover this play deploys Matthew 25 to enhance the sense that unlike the rather minute tariff held on earth in penitential punishments, the good works that bring life are ones people have not even been aware of doing, for they have acted out of love and care for their fellow humans in the kindness of their humanity. When we *read* the plays, of course, we are given the dramatis personae, which tells us in advance of performance whether the souls are good and bad. But those who actually see the play (as opposed to reading it) have no way, outside of theatrical signification, to know whether the souls are destined for heaven or hell. The souls are onstage for several hundred more lines after their own speeches and before the angels part them into those destined for heaven and those destined for hell. It is thus costuming conventions, the evidence of the behavior of the actors, and the relation between word, deed, and sight that provide the dynamics of the play. And it is from their own words and more subtly their own attitudes toward themselves and God that they can be discerned as good or bad. Productions that emphasize this indeterminacy, then, are more in line with the spirit of the play. Comparison with the clear satirical identifications of the Wakefield Judgement, for example, indicates how austere and restrained is the York Judgement play.

This genuine indeterminacy is quite different, for example, from the judgment in the Towneley plays, where hell is constantly and instantly recognized as the place of *other* people.[98] The York play works in a much more concentrated way to bring into inexorable focus the possibilities of self-knowledge of the sinner and to ground his acts of charity in habitual forms of kindness to others. The judgment's temporality is at once in eschatological time (future anterior) and in the proleptic time of a past not fully acknowledged or caught up in the present.[99] And so judgment becomes "the object of fear as a future set in the past."[100] When they have given to the poor man, clothed the hungry, and provided water and shelter to the thirsty and homeless man, they were charitable and Christ was there among them. One is here reminded of the many Lollard critiques about the best image of Christ being the poor man.[101]

God himself sits down to the judgment as if to a final show, inviting "Mi postelis and my darlyngis dere" to "se þat sight."[102] All of a sudden in a shockingly metatheatrical moment, we as audience become part of the judgment; God and his apostles are sitting opposite us, overseeing all the souls at the eschaton, but it is us they face and view.[103] When Christ shows us his wounds again, it is to show that these are forms of judgment as well as mercy, for we have let this happen again in our city.

In the Last Judgement play, then, characteristically in York, the possibilities of scapegoating are ruled out about as scrupulously as they could be. The play remains eschatological even though it is being enacted in present time, and thus the city of God never becomes one that is transparently identified on earth as being the possession of any particular jurisdiction.

The eschaton is a crucial horizon in these plays, for it is in the eucharist that the church is "always called to become what it eschatologically is."[104] As an eschatological feast, the future breaks into the present in the eucharist; it has happened already and is yet to come.

THE CHURCH AS A DRAMATIC PERFORMANCE

The unmistakable kinship of the trial of Christ with the trials of contemporary heretics is a reminder of how close penance was to mere punishment when ecclesiastical authority was impugned. But the acute criticisms of these abuses in Lollard literature were not advanced in social and aesthetic forms that could address the communal and collective problems of reconciliation. Lollard texts indicate what can, in historical retrospect, seem a hopelessly naive faith in the powers of a lay ruler to reform the church. That that lay power ended up empowering the church to execute Lollards was merely one more brutal irony for this failed and "premature" reformation. And there were other massive naïvetés in the way in which their hermeneutic project founded and authorized itself. In the sequence from the Entry until the Last Judgement, the pageants in York try to address and redress the collective and the judicial aspects together. And in this sense the discussions that critics have had about the nature of the soteriology of the plays—what kind of satisfaction theory of atonement they imply—is moot. For such accounts, whether they are of the "devil's rights party" or the Anselmian satisfaction theory, entail universalistic and legalistic stories about salvation, which "make unnecessary the actual existence of a reconciled people."[105]

In his book on the interrelationship between church and state, Cavanaugh has talked about the body of Christ as something that is liturgically enacted, not institutionally guaranteed.[106] The blocks to seeing the church as itself a performance—as opposed to a program, a territory, a place—are deep. They include a dominantly dualist conceptualization of the church as a soul animating the body of the state, the cordoning off of the mystical from historical space and time, and the imagination of the soul as interior and only truly alive in the innermost recesses of human subjectivity. An entirely different ecclesiology, as well as an entirely different theater, is implied by a notion of the church as liturgical performance, one that holds the church up to the scrutiny and actuality of the present rather than guaranteeing its authority on the basis either of a past historical event or a text firmly relegated to the past. Cavanaugh gives us a definition that the Corpus Christi plays marvelously exemplify: "Because it is enacted liturgically, the church is a series of dramatic performances, and not a state of being. The church is not a constant presence, an identifiable site firmly bounded and policed by law."[107] The Corpus Christi pageants enact the church as a series of dramatic performances through which the visibility of the body of Christ is rendered in relation to the possibility of recovery of reception in liturgical action. For in these pageants, the life of the church is told with utter concreteness in relation to our response to and recognition of the passion and resurrection of Christ. As Milbank observes, the resurrection of Christ is about the foundation of a new community, and both these events are inseparably tied up with each other.[108] But if the eucharist needs a theater as much as a church to present itself, it is because that church has indeed come to be an "identifiable site firmly bounded and policed by law" and its liturgy is not so much performance of a new community as a defensive and thorough immersion in an old one that imagines Christ as its possession. Its liturgy has become bastardized.

Denys Turner has brilliantly illuminated the liturgical language of the eucharist by means of J. L. Austin's famous distinctions between illocutionary and perlocutionary acts of speech in performative language. Turner, working off Austin's distinction, is talking about the difference between "what your words effect in virtue of what they mean" and "what it is that your act of saying those words effects in virtue of being uttered."[109] We call performative contradictions those speech acts in which the two fall apart. The examples Turner gives are arguing at tedious length in favor of maximum participation in a seminar ("which the prolixity of your saying inhibits") and the British army officer whose actual words to an assembly of Welsh miners—"Behave in an orderly fashion or else"—provoked the very behavior it prohibits.[110] In each case the actual saying *does* the opposite of the meaning. Liturgies, Turner explains, are constituted by the interactions of performative utterances and uttering performances. He describes a preacher delivering an egalitarian sermon from an authoritarian pulpit in which "the total result is a social reality constructed upon the contradictoriness internal to the communicative act."[111] It is in the facts of this contradiction that worshiping members of this community are socialized. The ritual "effects a rupture between what the ritual signifies and what it effects," and in this sense may be understood to be functioning ideologically.

Turner is discussing here what signs can do under certain empirical conditions of their reception (which is a different question from that of the sacramental efficacy of the sign). In theatrical communication, a statement has the illusion of creating its own enunciative conditions; it is only the situation that permits the conditions of enunciation to be established that gives the utterance its meaning. This means that the theatricalization of liturgy, far from being an emptying out of liturgy's content, may be a way of examining the very conditions under which it can be efficacious. For in theater, all words are at the "mercy of their enactment," at the mercy of the contingency of their signifiers (which place, what time, which particular bodies of the actors, which unanticipated audience response, what weather). That is to say, the actual enactment and empirical conditions of reception are central in the theatrical act.[112] Rather than socializing us in a rupture between thing said and thing done, the very conditions of enactment and reception are seen to be a nonsuppressible component of the meaning.

Lollardy had tried to expose some of the performative contradictions of the act of confession and absolution (that it was supposed to be voluntary but framed by an injunction that made it essential on pain of excommunication, that its so-called voluntary speech act was thereby highly constrained by compulsion and therefore legitimate fear). In a different way, the York Corpus Christi plays radically conceive of the church as the body of Christ enacted among them, incomprehensible except as the very product and horizon of their agreements or disagreements. Where liturgy has become bastard liturgy, then, it is exposed as ideology.

But the Corpus Christi pageants are also an index of the extent to which, in Cavanaugh's words, "the visibility of the church in the communal performance of the sacrament had been replaced in the late medieval church by the visibility of the eucharistic object." Cavanaugh suggests that in the late medieval church, signifier and signified have exchanged places "such that the sacramental body is the visible signifier of the hidden signified, which is the social body of Christ."[113] By exposing these performative contradictions, this theater has reconsidered the relations between the juridical and the collective dimensions of the body of Christ. Far from celebrating sacrifice and punishment, in their utterly concrete refiguring of the foundation of a new community through the enactment of the death and resurrection of Christ, these plays actualize the body of Christ in its complex appearing and disappearing, absence and presence, past and future temporality. Far from conceiving of Christ's death as conferring benefit that is then administered by a priestly caste, punishment is revealed as a desperate, endlessly regrettable, chronically human failure, one that in these particular contexts is enacted in the service not of justice but of power.[114] Its failure ensures that Christ will be crucified again, and will continue to be as long as punishment is not converted to penitence, entailing an understanding of sin not as an offense against a power and a jurisdiction, but rather as that thing that damages human life as it alienates people from God and one another, in one and the same movement of alienation. The two cities of Jerusalem and York are not, then, separate times and spaces but are mapped onto each other. The dividing line between the two cities is actually invisible because it involves the capacity of each person to love what he loves.[115] The church is *not* identified as the city of God. Atonement to be such cannot be confined to a past time, a once-and-for-all. And neither can theater. But we are committed to this confinement if we regard either Christianity or theater as the imitation of a past or transcendent original.[116]

Milbank, in discussing the narrative forms of Christianity, has said that they are indispensable "not because they record and point us to a vision which is still available in its eternal presence, but because they enshrine and constitute the event of a transformation which is to be non-identically repeated and therefore still made to happen."[117] If the eucharist is not so much a thing, as a "performance which makes the body of Christ visible in the present,"[118] if it must therefore be intrinsically related to the sacrament of penance, then there could be no better description of Corpus Christi's relentless focus on the present community, its occlusions and possibilities as a body of Christ.

PART FOUR

Reform

7 Theaters of Signs and Disguises

THE REFORM OF THE YORK CORPUS CHRISTI PLAYS

... nothing can be present to us to which we are not present.
—Stanley Cavell, *Must We Mean What We Say?*

It greatlie offendeth, that some, when they do labour to show the use of the holie Sacramentes, assigne unto them no ende bot only to teach the mind by other senses, that which the worde doth teach by hearing.
—Richard Hooker, *Of the Laws of Ecclesiastical Polity*

We say "The expression in his voice was *genuine*." If it was spurious we think as it were of another one behind it.—*This* is the *face* he shews the world, inwardly he has another one.—But this does not mean that when his expression is *genuine* he has two the same.
—Ludwig Wittgenstein, *Philosophical Investigations*, no. 606

Corpus Christi theater has incarnated some of the central paradoxes of Christ's ministry on earth in a dramatic language from which the meanings of that ministry cannot be separated or extracted. Dragged through the streets that he blesses but in which he will be executed, Jesus, in the bodies of numerous actors, is put on the cross in Micklegate, and then again in Coney Street, and then again at the Minster Gates, and then again in the Pavement. He is horribly recognizable as an icon in the Crucifixion pageant, and then again barely recognized when he returns, a "presence after presentness"[1] in the resurrected body to the disciples, to Mary Magdalene, to Thomas, to the pilgrims at Emmaus, and above all to those souls who have never seen him at all in the bodies of the sick, the hungry, and the homeless. The eucharist, the word on the street,[2] has been performed not as a magic spectacle that confers merits through seeing, but as a drama of at-onement in which forgiveness has been embodied (or refused) but not bought or acquired. Those meanings lie *in* the enactment, not behind, beyond, or through it. That this should have been so hard to see among modern scholars is testimony to the fact that what accompanied the suppression of Corpus Christi theater was also the very means of its understanding.

If my argument is correct, or at least convincing, if it is retrospectively obvious, inevitable as soon as made, why has it been so hard to see? This chapter will deal with the question of the reform of the Corpus Christi cycles as the question of the extraordinary success of the legacy of reform in defining a way of seeing, and thus what it is possible to see in the picture that has held us captive.[3] To talk about the reform of the Corpus Christi cycle is to talk not simply about how and why the plays were no longer performed, but about the profound distrust of its means of representation, whose costs and consequences affect us most where we are most blind to them—in the inevitability of the assumption that religiosity (redefined as belief) can go on anywhere else but in the public and collective practices of a people. The inseparability of the twin reforms of church and theater lies precisely in the fact that far from being the mere side effect or object of the reform of the English church, theater was, in fact, one of the principle *mechanisms* of reform. But the force of this crucial interrelationship cannot be seen in isolation from changes in the ritual action of liturgy or from the vitally interanimating sign systems of ritual, theater, and liturgy as they parse the body of Christ.

Scholars have tended to read the chronically ambiguous phrase "This is my body" as if they knew what it meant outside of language games, as if, that is, the ritually enacted statement of the medieval mass meant the same as its theatrical predication in Corpus Christi festivity or the same as a dogmatically defended doctrine used to entrap heretics. The ritual and theatrical predications of this statement do not simply mean different things in the specific contexts of utterance or implication, but the ritual and theatrical forms are there to shape and determine the grammar of their form and meaning.[4] That is why questions of performance are at the very heart of questions of reform. The first section of this chapter will briefly recount the shape of suppression in York to see concretely how this theater ended and to give a schematic indication of some of the stories woven around this ending. The subsequent sections will attempt to unpick the grammar of eucharistic signification as it operates in performance (ritual, liturgical, theatrical) and show the costly implications of the replacement (as practice and hermeneutic) of a theater of signs by a theater of disguise.

My claim is that the separation of theology and theater, of religious and theatrical history, has been disastrous not simply for the mutual understanding of these disciplines but for their own internal self-understanding. Perhaps more modestly and pertinently, it has been detrimental for our ability to receive, re-create, and understand the most communal drama in our history. Indeed, in the currently dominant narrative of the transition from medieval to early modern theater that plays in Renaissance circles, there seems to be a double elision at work. The double elision is of any serious or sympathetic understanding of religion as anything other than a bald ruse of power; of theater itself as theatrical, as an embodied practice that is neither assimilable to text nor derivable from it. (It is the theatricality of theater, one might say, as well as the concrete, embarrassingly specifiable beliefs and practices of religion that new historicist conceptions of power have displaced and evaded.) That inextricably double elision, then, needs to be jointly addressed through studies of religion and theater—religion as theatrical, theater as religious—because they are integrally related.

Glynne Wickham announced several years ago that the reformation of the English church involved an automatic and inseparable reformation of the English stage.[5] We will never have a responsible history of the Reformation as a cultural revolution as long as we fail to understand both the transformations of these vital theatrical traditions and the centrality of the reformed project to their variations and concerns. Neither will we understand the grammar of medieval sacramental theater, whose mode of being was so transformed as to be rendered unplayable and virtually unreadable in the later idiom. But the difficulty in fact is not merely one of expertise and the bifurcations of specialisms. The difficulties of writing about the Reformation involve the massive lure and satisfaction of polemical writing and the strong (almost irresistible) temptation to take sides. For the sixteenth century is a century of intensely polemical alignment in which nevertheless it was utterly impossible to think of religion "as it is with us, a sectional and voluntary undertaking."[6] Hence, one side cannot leave the other side alone. Like a bad marital argument, one cannot simply relinquish one's partner to his own profoundly wrongheaded view, for the desire for union is too strong. The unity of religion, the definition of the church, the possibilities of salvation within that church—these stakes are too high to relinquish the argument. This is why Reformation history for so long followed ecclesiastical history in the mode of apologia and its generic counterpart, vendetta.[7] But taking sides when it comes to my particular question—why the Corpus Christi plays became unplayable and illegible—will mean condemning them to one of two forms of modern oblivion: nostalgia or obsolescence.

"THE LEARNED WILL MISLIKE IT"

First then, a bare chronology of suppression: in 1548, the year of the suppression of the Feast of Corpus Christi, the plays are moved to Whitsun.[8] In 1549 the pageants of the "Assumption, Coronation and Dying of Our Lady" are excised from the annual Corpus Christi performances.[9] An injunction of 1561 repeats the veto of the Virgin pageants.[10] In 1568 Matthew Hutton advises the mayor and aldermen after reading "the bokez" of the Creed play, formerly the play text of the now-defunct Corpus Christi guild, that the plays should no longer be played.[11] There are records of disagreement among the aldermen about whether to comply with his advice. In 1569, the year of the Northern Rebellion, the plays are performed for the last time, on Whitsun. In 1572 the archbishop of York, Grindal, requests to have a copy of the Paternoster playbooks that the council want to play.[12] The production takes place on the Thursday after Trinity Sunday, the Feast of Corpus Christi.[13] In 1575, there are records indicating that Grindal never returned the books to the aldermen.[14] The play scripts, which had been there to preserve a tradition of performance, became the instrument of their erasure.[15] The suppression of the plays is eventually effected then simply by impounding the texts of performance. As late as 1579, the council formulates requests to the dean and the archbishop for the production of the Corpus Christi plays.[16]

What does this bare chronology tell us? Twenty years after the first censorship of the play text, during the year of the Rebellion of the Catholic Earls, the council wished to see their plays staged on their proper day of celebration: on the feast day that had already been abolished.[17] Thirty years after the first censorship, some numbers of the council still want to stage a production of the Corpus Christi plays.

Two figures loom even in this stark chronology: Matthew Hutton, dean of York, and Archbishop Grindal.[18] And they are both testimony to the foreignness of reform to York, that it comes as extrinsic, an import of manners, ways of being from the outside. Dean Hutton's letter of 1568 is revelatory of the terms of that outsiderdom. With a remarkable mixture of disingenuity and condescension, he argues that it is simply not possible to reform the plays piecemeal:

> . . . as I finde manie thinges that I muche like because of thantiquitie, so see I manie thinges that I can not allowe, because they be Disagreinge from the senceritie of the gospell, the which thinges, yf they shuld either be altogether cancelled, or altered into other matter, the whole drift of the play shuld be altered, and therefore I dare not put my pen to it.[19]

Not daring to ruin the antique integrity of their drama that cannot simply be edited piecemeal, he prefers politely to suppress it altogether. Disavowing his own responsibility in actually executing state-driven preferences and policy, and perhaps knowing that fear works far better through suggestion since the imagination fills in the details and consequences of prohibition with alarming fecundity, he merely hints at "how the state will beare with it." The clarity of his alignment comes less from his overt statement that the learned will "mislike" a revived production than in the full-scale confidence with which he locates the ignorance of his simpleton addressees. Starting in an only superficially unctuous subjunctive mood, "yf I were worthy to geue your lordshipp and your right worhipfull brethren consell," his judgments are perfectly clear:

> suerlie my advise shuld be, that it shuld not be plaid. ffor thoghe it was plausible 40 yeares agoe, & wold now also of the ignorant sort be well liked: yet now in this happie time of the gospell, I knowe the learned will mislike it and how the state will beare with it I knowe not.[20]

The history of the plays is made antique in the very precision of Hutton's chronology of obsolescence: the decisively has-been of forty years.

Hutton's hint at "how the state will beare with it" was quite sufficient within the logic of the institutional underpinnings of reform. For after 1559 any attendance of mass where the body of Christ was made was deemed illegal—a denial of the Royal Supremacy. All subjects were enjoined to attend church services on Sundays and holy days on penalty of a fine of twelve pennies.[21] To enforce the Acts of Supremacy and Uniformity, the ecclesiastical commission in 1561–62 was asked to draw up a list of Catholics known to be opposed to the establishment.[22] The 1563 law had extended the scope of the earlier law to include not simply men of the cloth but all figures, such as schoolmasters, teachers, and persons engaged in the execution of the law. After 1574 aldermen were expected to take the Oath of Supremacy. In other words, recalcitrant officeholders were targeted for identification and dismissal if they were involved in the suspect practices of going to mass.[23] The Northern Rebellion and excommunication of Elizabeth by the pope, which thereby absolved the pope's Catholic subjects from allegiance to the queen, intensified the enforcement of uniformity. The appointment of Grindal as the archbishop of York in 1570 was part of that enforcement.[24] In 1570 the queen and president of the Council of the North and the archbishop can be found chastising the corporation for their reluctance to prosecute and stamp out religious offenses.[25] The repetition of various chastising letters complaining about the nonattendance at church of the corporation and the local gentry indicates the slowness of the corporation in responding to royal requests of this nature.[26]

There had been persistent attempts to reform the clergy and to persuade the corporation to act as agents in that reeducation. The bishop of Gloucester, John Hooper, was dismayed when he examined his clergy in 1551. Out of 311 clergy examined, a shocking 168 could not remember the Ten Commandments, and 34 could not say who was the author of the Lord's Prayer.[27] When Holgate was archbishop, he tried to rectify this situation; he ordered the vicars choral to learn Paul's Epistles (starting with Romans) by heart and saw that every one of them had a copy of the New Testament.[28] But as Claire Cross notes, the city fathers in the 1530s, '40s, and '50s in fact had very little contact with "university protestantism"; their contact was all with monks and priests, the bearers of the "old religion." It was really not until the 1590s that the aldermanic body could safely be said to be conformist, having been co-opted, silenced, crushed, or much more frequently, simply replaced. After 1578, when the state was having to deal not simply with "survivalism" but with mission Catholicism, the statutory fine for recusancy doubled to two shillings and recusants were forbidden to be inn holders.[29] The head searchers of each craft guild accompanied householders of their guilds to Minster sermons.[30] The onslaught on the practices of the "old religion" eventually succeeded.[31] Parochial clergy after 1578 were not henceforth charged with recusancy, and between 1577 and 1580 the aldermanic bench lost nearly all of its recusants.[32] Cripling, a bower who was mayor in 1580, tried to stage the Corpus Christi play in 1579, and was actually jailed by the Council of the North for recusancy.[33] He conformed but his wife and family remained recusant.[34] That left only William Allen, who by 1580 was bankrupt and no longer resident in York.[35] William Allen, elected mayor in 1572, had revived the Paternoster play and had placed the last performance at Harman, an alderman's door. Harbert and one Beckwith[36] were disenfranchised by the corporation for not participating in the performance.[37] The Housebook entries for 23 June 1572 detailing the business of an assembly at the Council Chamber make it clear that it was partly dealings that Harbert had had with the "foreyne Courte" of the Council of the North that was a major point of contention.[38] But after this civic defiance, Harbert himself succeeded Allen as mayor. The last traces of recusancy on the aldermanic bench seem to be the association that Henry May, mayor in 1586, had as stepfather to York's most famous recusant, Margaret Clitherow, herself pressed to death in 1586 for the treasonous charge of harboring a priest.[39]

SUPPRESSION / SURVIVAL?

It seems, then, that there is no direct and overt suppression of the Corpus Christi cycle in York.[40] Rather, religious uniformity is gradually attained by the slow replacement of people resistant to it, the steady, uneven, only retrospectively inevitable transformation (subject to changes of policy in the Henrician regime, intensified in Edward's, altogether reversed in Mary's, reversed again to something roughly like the status quo ante in the Elizabethan settlement); by a vitally changed relation between state, church, and locality; by the erosion of a culture of festivity that renders amateur and local performance meaningful to the audience who are also its players; by the extraordinary changes in the material fabric of the city and the changes in the very relations of space and time entailed by them.

Text

How does Hutton, the dean of York from 1567–89 and the archbishop of York in 1595, see these plays? In the first instance, it is important to notice the central role played by the text itself, which is now regarded as the sole arbiter of the play's content and suitability for performance. In perusing the text to establish the possibility of performance, Hutton might be seen to be acting as the city fathers had done for generations, as they checked the performances of the passing pageant wagons against the text registered in their civic register. But not quite; for Hutton seems to be looking for the doctrinal content of these plays, which I have been arguing is not derivable like a kernel from a shell. In so doing, he virtually ensures their obsolescence, for by examining the texts for doctrine, he indicates how little he understood the role of theater (its scope, its very nature) in the forms of communal life of the Middle Ages. Looking for indications of the "sincerity of the gospel," he sees the text as the guarantor of the doctrinal meaning of performance; the performance as and of eucharistic community is not an aspect he can see. No tinkering with such a text, no excision or editing will render it conformable enough. In any case, the Corpus Christi plays did not teach doctrine and scripture in any way Hutton would have recognized as instructional. Even the most exemplary heresy of Romanism— transubstantiation—was not a clearly identifiable, certainly not a characteristic feature of the York cycle.[41] If Hutton could not envisage a reform of the text to excise Roman doctrine and show forth a more evangelical understanding of the word, neither could he envisage a reform of the plays along the lines of liturgical reform. For Tudor liturgical reform is put into place precisely so that parishioners should share the same kind of worship with their English compatriots, not with the people of Yorkshire.[42] We have then with Hutton, not so much a deliberate policy of censorship of the range of civic drama in York as a conception of the spirit so profoundly at odds with the Corpus Christi celebrations in York that he cannot see them as religious, let alone admit them to the company of his own more godly spirit.[43] Hence the destruction of their *modus vivendi* for him is actually the unintended side effect rather than the principal object of reform. It is clear however that the "learned" who "will mislike" the plays are the vital new community of adjudication for the possibility of performance. As for Bucer in his *De Regno Christi,* so for Hutton it is "experts" alone who have the authority to decide on the suitability of performance:

> So that Christ's people, however may profit from religious comedies and tragedies, men will have to be appointed to the task of preventing the performance of any comedy or tragedy which they have not seen before hand and decided should be acted. They must be men both outstanding of their knowledge of this kind of literature and also of established and constant zeal for Christ's kingdom.[44]

The casual assumption that "knowledge" of "this kind of literature" is the exclusive domain of men of zeal and learning and that they can only correctly adjudicate such knowledge in circumstances utterly divorced from the communities that inhabit, claim, and judge themselves by means of the stories of performance—*this* barely noticeable yet devastatingly significant assumption of authority as the knowledge of experts will devastate, make invisible, the theater of Corpus Christi as a theater of acknowledgment, not knowledge.[45]

The legislation of performance shows that it was quite usual to regard a play as a public event rather than a text; hence threats to authority were regarded as proceeding from actors (*who* could assume roles) and places (*where* they could legitimately assume them) rather than texts.[46] Greg Walker comments on the formulations of the Tudor legislation against playing: "Whoever drafted the documents did not think of dramatic texts—unlike printed ballads, songs and rhymes—as sufficiently important to be specifically named among these other forms."[47] Playbooks were merely the means to check up on performances. And this is precisely what happened with the texts at York, which were the very means of suppression (by confiscation) rather than preservation.

We tend to think in exactly the opposite way about the authority of text and performance, understanding the authority of the performance to be authorized by the text. But it took a cultural revolution and much symbolic work for these changes to be effected.[48] Hutton, reading the playbooks of York's civic drama, may be understood then as performing his own historic role in such a cultural revolution, in advance of legislation that grants as it seeks to inhibit authority (hence necessitates censorship) to texts and their known authors. Quite unable, in his terms, to locate the authors, hence authority, of these texts, he simply retains the texts of performance.[49]

Occasion

When theater happens in no particular bounded-off place but in so many places in the city, then place has been overdetermined by time and occasion in potent and interesting ways. One of the ways in which place is transformed by time and by occasion is the patterning we call festivity.

Corpus Christi theater, until the Edwardian regime, had been related to the ecclesiastical calendar, and thereby indirectly regulated by the church. The abolition of the feast day of Corpus Christi in 1548 divorced the plays from the specific occasion of a holy day and from the repeated rhythms of the liturgical calendar.[50] And thus the roles of those who took their part in the story of the body of Christ no longer participated in the larger rhythm of a story not written by them or motivated solely through them, but to which and in which they wanted to find their relation. The connections made in this theater, then, between the church as an institution and the church of the body of Christ that extends beyond those jurisdictional and physical borders are lost, for there is no larger sanctioned relation to the transformation of space and time by the life, death, and resurrection of Christ.

In this sense, too, the "suppression of Corpus Christi theater" is a misnomer: Hutton could not suppress the theater because in some sense there was no "theater" to suppress. Corpus Christi theater in York, I have been arguing, is not a place but "a spatial story."[51] The double time of Corpus Christi as the city of God and the city of man, the complex presencing of the past, the way that the eucharist is taken out of a jurisdictional territory and disseminated in the community— all these are dimensions of eucharistic culture rather than the *ex opere operato* work of the sacrament of the altar. But the possibilities for their meaning are radically altered by the abolition of their feast day.[52]

Space/Place

The abolition of the feast day is part of a widespread change in the landscape of the sacred. The reorganization and suppression of the Corpus Christi pageants are part and parcel of a thoroughgoing reorganization of the spatial and public life of the city. Since theater uses the things of the world and since processional drama in particular has theatricalized civic space so completely and so richly, we will need to contemplate at once the total transformation of the material fabric of the city effected through reform in York. We will need also to think about how such drastic reorganizations change the very meaning of Corpus Christi not simply because its very raw material changes, but because the very meaning and organization of space changes, too.

Think first, then, about the church as ecclesiastical space and territory. Before the Reformation, York boasted the Minster, St. Mary's Abbey—one of the richest of the Benedictine abbeys in the north— forty parish churches, and as many as a hundred chantries, which bound the dead to the living and the living to the dead in songs of remembrance and hope.[53] In the years 1538–39, all the city's religious houses were abolished, expelling 61 monks, 61 friars, 12 brothers, and 4 sisters of St. Leonard's, as well as 4 canons and 9 nuns from St.

Clements. All the buildings were in the hands of citizens within a generation. In the reign of Edward VI, the chantries and guilds were abolished, a third of the city's parishes were amalgamated, and the internal fabric of the churches despoiled. In 1547 the corporation tried to see if it could exempt the Gild of St. Christopher and St. George from suppression, but this proved to be impossible. The corporation in addition tried to purchase en bloc the chantries but found it impossible to do so. The repositioning of the old relics and icons of the parish were at once acts of preservation and acts of desacralization. Parts of St. William at York, for example, were built into local houses.[54] Vestments were fashioned into bed hangings or clothes; service books into spice containers; Easter Sepulchres were converted into "a communion table at Castle Bytha, a bier for corpses at Stallingborough, a clothes press at Denton and even a chicken coop at Durrington."[55]

These changes are a decisive reorganization of the fabric of the city. How did these fundamental reorganizations of the space of the city affect the production of the theater? Corpus Christi plays and rituals are not the ritual expression of theological utterances;[56] they are the liturgical enactment of Corpus Christi. It is not simply then that iconoclasm destroyed the artifacts of this catholicity, but rather that if, as I have argued, the sacraments in the plays are precisely the performance of community, then the erosion of the collective spaces of the culture had a decisive effect on their playing. For this theater has worked by means of those collective spaces, articulating its meaning across them as it both deploys their immanent meanings and fluidly transforms them. Desire to stage the Corpus Christi plays is intimately connected to the issue of local self-governance and jurisdiction, and the very boundaries and bounds of that community. Patricia Badir has recently talked about the reorganization of the Corpus Christi pageants as part of a thoroughgoing project to redefine place as true space—abstract, conceptualized, and ready for state definition: "True space, as conceived by the state and church and as institutionalized across the North, would have been directly challenged by the symbolism of civic pageantry which converted the universality of Christian doctrine into symbolic capital localized upon the physical site and within administrative structures distinctive to the town."[57] For the space of an urban town, as she indicates, must be thought of as "more than a homogenous and static surface; it must be looked at as a space both strategically conceived and materially produced."[58] In this reading, theater and the acts and injunctions of the Reformed Crown competed in organizing the interrelations of buildings and people. Hence the vital importance of theater to the spatial reorganizations of civic life, for space is one of theater's primary modes. The theatrical event, Badir has usefully said, might be thought about as both "a representation of space and as producing representational space."[59]

I have already mentioned that the regulation of drama was originally in fact regulation of the space of operation (and not the text of performance), and the main concern appeared to be to restrict the place of playing. I think this is more than the simple worry about unruly behavior; it is an acute anxiety about the unpredictability of meanings when space is transformed through communal performance.[60] It is part, then, of a long-term experiment in separating space and theater so that not all space could be theatricalized.

Actors/Roles

Those who assumed roles in York on Corpus Christi Day did not make their living in this way; an amateur actor has a different relation to his role than a professional actor. As occasional, civic, and festive theater was gradually transformed, so acting as such increasingly became the professional prerogative of actors. After the Royal Proclamation of 1559, visiting players had to present their license to the mayor to perform, and if he granted them permission to proceed, they were invited to give their first performance, usually at his command and usually in the guildhall.[61] The late sixteenth century saw many prohibitions against acting, and although the licensing system was dropped, no commoner "could henceforth sponsor a troupe of players under warrant and the status of those players who did not enjoy the protection of a noble patron was finally compromised."[62] (The Whiggish myth of the triumph of Elizabethan theater misunderstands utterly the extent to which the localization and professionalization of theater under forms of profit, patronage, and privatization represent a drastic reduction of actors in sheer numerical terms and, more complexly, a drastic reduction in the dissemination of role-playing, festivity, and ceremony in the structures of everyday life.)[63] For far from being the proscribed vagabonds of the new statutes, allowable only by virtue of the patronage of great lords, in Corpus Christi theater, actors were men who participated in a story larger than themselves for a day and looked at their lives in relation to that story.

Not surprisingly, toward the end of the sixteenth century, playing tends to shift indoors rather than outdoors. Robert Tittler, for example, tells us that "by about the last third of the sixteenth century the most favoured site in the countryside [for theatre] became the banqueting hall of the aristocratic household; in the town, the inn and civic hall."[64] The entire relationship between actor and audience is changed in indoor theater; it gives actors at once more control over their actual playing space and a more standardized format of interaction with their audience. Indeed, if theater now takes place indoors and by actors whose specialized task it has become to act, then it is no longer a transformation of local people and places but something that will happen within defined spaces and roles. The constantly changing meanings enacted by the changing backdrop of the stational routes, for example, and the interweaving of one ceremonial form with another, for example, in the complexity of York's Entry into Jerusalem, is no longer available.[65]

But as well as being a reorganization of the fabric of the city, the acts regulating place and playing also are a symptom of changed relations between locality and center. The acts often cited as most central in "theater history"—"the renewal of the acts against retainers in 1572, the Act for the punishment of Vagabonds in the same year, the crown patent granted to Leicester's Men in 1574, the patent granted to the Master of the Revels in 1581, the forming of the Queen's Men in 1583, the Privy Council decree of 1598 establishing a new licensing commission for plays, and the Privy Council order for the destruction of all playhouses"—had the effect of making it difficult for companies to operate in the countryside unless they were protected by persons of rank.[66]

For the council in their tentative and deferential but hopeful approach to Hutton appeared to want something and to understand something altogether different from the same theatrical performance: a reaffirmation, perhaps, of who they were together. Part of the difficulty presented by those two thorns in the side of the council—Harbert and Beckwith—might, for example, be that they understood their allegiance as being to the competing jurisdiction of the Council of the North. I have pointed out the extent to which the Corpus Christi plays are themselves intimately and intricately about jurisdiction; they are critical of *all* forms of jurisdiction, but such criticism is not done within an evangelical and utopian program of reform, but rather a sense of a renewed polity through the dissemination of the body of Christ outside of any particular jurisdictions. It is the transformed places and spaces of the city, the fact that theater is not confined to any one place or space, that makes such dissemination so workable, so functional and regular a part of Corpus Christi festivity. But Hutton and Grindal represent figures whose allegiance is to the state and London and the university system, to an education understood as necessarily imported, and reform means to them an alignment of the culture of the locality with their own national one. To them the Corpus Christi cycles might simply have seemed arcane, certainly not capable of performing the body of Christ, which was to be done in a different memory of the life of Christ, in a liturgy, like the plays, performed in their own tongue, in a participation legally compelled.

By tracing out some of the changing and interconnected meanings of text, actor, and playing place, I hope to have shown how these categories stand in relation to one another in a rapidly shifting religious and theatrical landscape and some of the competing demands made of theater by its practitioners and prohibitors.

In our contemplation of Corpus Christi theater's ending, we have sometimes tended to ascribe our own version of theater to the Middle Ages. Then we have seen its disappearance as the result of hostility toward it. But the state did not know what theater in this sense was, so it could hardly suppress it. Furthermore, by postulating the eucharist as a communicable content, possession of the church rather than performance of it, we make it impossible to see the continuities between ritual and liturgy as well as between the Middle Ages and the Reformation. The combined effect of a back projection of the category of theater and of an understanding of the eucharist as a proposition located inside the plays as a doctrine means that reformers and critics alike have severed the very relations between ritual, liturgy, and theater without which these changes are themselves not understandable.

Michael O'Connell has recently made this illuminating comment: "That a popular and vernacular biblical drama should be assailed by the left wing of the English Reformation requires explanation."[67] I have tried to give some understanding of how such a vernacular drama was "assailed" in York, and I have imagined some of the conflicting conceptualizations of performance (and how they are organized around the categories of text, time and space, theater, and ritual) of the plays' defenders and detractors. I will now try to address O'Connell's question by further examining the changing interrelationships of theater and liturgy in sixteenth-century England.

For the thoroughgoing reorganization of the space and time of the fabric, the mode of organization, the regulation of time and space and festivity effects a radical transfer of authority away from a receiving community. In the sentimentalized forms of lament and retrieval we call nostalgia, such costs have yet to be fully reckoned.

THIS IS MY BODY: LITURGY, PERFORMANCE, AND THE BOUNDARIES OF THE CHURCH

In chapters 4, 5, and 6, I argued that Corpus Christi theater in York had as its primary premise that the "token of the body of Christ is not the thing tokened."[68] The pageants assume at once a noncoincidence of token and thing tokened and the radically ambiguating force of the demonstrative pronoun at the heart of the mass. That is the force at once of their symbolic energy and their liturgical power. As such, I have argued, they constitute a complex kind of para-liturgy; the very gap between an amateur (known) local actor and sacred role, and the juxtaposition of word and thing onstage help to make the Corpus Christi theater a commentary upon and an interaction with the liturgy of the mass and offices. In that they seek both to embody and to show the limits of the presence of Christ in the body of the faithful, they are also an emphatic extenuation as well as a diagnosis of the interrelationship between eucharist and ecclesiology. They are a complex metaphorical predication of the body of Christ, and as such are not reducible to orthodox doctrines that defend consecration and spectacle as the central moment and meaning of the mass as a priestly sacrifice.

It was the purpose of that revolution in ritual theory and practice that we call the Book of Common Prayer to attempt to disambiguate the horribly confused and scandalous references of this demonstrative pronoun, and thus to avoid the taint of a newly *Roman* Catholic doctrine and ceremony. Understanding some of the dimensions of this disambiguation are vital for our purposes not only because they radically affect our understanding of what "presence" is, but also because it is impossible to understand how the changes in the history of theater (as in the history of theology) can be conceived except by way of this central rite that was to be the authorized, state-mandated new performance of that body. In rendering unambiguous that "this," liturgical reformers undoubtedly succeeded in distancing the new communion from all traces of the doctrine of transubstantiation; but in so doing, they also perhaps succeeded in making it harder to see the conscious and concerted figuration of that "this" in the practices of Corpus Christi theater. The changed liturgy was an English liturgy inaugurating a changed relation to the mother tongue, a national liturgy inaugurating a changed relation to Rome, and a changed relation between eucharist and church.

The new liturgy was, as Judith Maltby has recently insisted, "work, intended not so much to be read in a passive sense, but to be used, performed, experienced."[69] Indeed the new prayer book throughout the second half of the sixteenth century and beyond produced endless disputes over the forms of continuity and discontinuity shared by the reformed church with the medieval church. Despite the attempt to locate areas of noncontention that would be *adiaphora*, things indifferent, it was precisely the ritual gestures, postures, costumes, and words of the formerly Latin mass and offices and their persistence in a common and enjoined liturgy that were at the center of all the major and most of the minor theological controversies of the sixteenth century. These revolutions in ritual theory and practice utterly changed the ritual landscape, the relation between sacred and secular, the orchestration of time and space in the older rituals, the landscape, that is, in which Corpus Christi plays were still performed and received until 1569.

The Book of Common Prayer of 1549 prescribed a service that was common to both priests and people in a common language. When laypeople followed mass books, they worked in parallel to the clerical liturgical action, coming together only at the moment of the elevation.[70] The priest's own books consisted in Breviary, Missal, Consuetudinary and Customary, Ordinal, Directory, Antiphonal, Gradual and Processional, which the BCP economically replaced.[71] It is common secondly because communion is in two kinds and shared by all, rather than solely by the celebrant as in the medieval mass. Although Thomas Cranmer had modeled the prayer book on the canon of the mass, there is no offering of the elements, but only the offering of thanksgiving to God and the sacrifice of self-offering.[72] The words of the canon are changed from this "oblation" to "these thy gifts and creatures," and the communion is commemorative only, a remembrance of a sacrifice, "full perfect and sufficient,"[73] that had happened long ago, and that is not renewed or repeated. Much emphasis was put on careful preparation for the sacrament. Reception of the sacrament, moreover, was only for the worthy. Cranmer keeps the phrase from the Sarum Rite "that they may be to us the body and blood of thy most dearly beloved son Jesus Christ" by interpreting the "to us" as those who "receive worthily."[74] There is no fraction and no elevation. Cranmer reforms the daily office into matins and evensong and distributes the scriptural readings so that they can be read continuously, the Psalms every month; the Gospel, Epistles, and Acts thrice a year; and the Old Testament annually. We, says Cranmer, "have mostly cut off Anthems, Responds, Invitatories, Chapters, and suchlike things as did brake the course of sacred reading, only retaining a few hymns which seemed to possess greater age and beauty than the rest."[75] In addition, he adds more vituperatively, "we have thus removed that re-cooked cabbage of the same sentences and chants repeated so often like a cuckoo, to the great convenience and relief of the readers."[76] Many of the phrases of great beauty Cranmer also kept and modified in his extraordinary collects (eighty-four in number) to the infinite enrichment of future generations.

Collinson has said that the BCP could itself be called "almost a piece of equivocation."[77] For although in many ways a full-scale attack on the notion of transubstantiation, the BCP still called the new service "Holy Communion commonly called the mass," and there were still crosses at all the words for bless and sanctify that were expunged utterly in the 1552 version. The BCP kept some of the saints' days of the preferred saints, but no intercessionary powers could henceforth be ascribed to them.[78] Many of the most mobile, dynamic, and moving of the ceremonies from the Sarum Rite had already been abolished. From 1546 there was no ringing of the bells on All Souls' Night, no veiling of the images during Lent, no creeping to the cross, no stripping of the images.[79]

The 1552 prayer book of Edward VI's reign, accompanied as it was by a wide-reaching and well-enforced campaign of iconoclasm and destruction, changed further the ritual experience of communion. Since 1547 inventories of parish property and furniture had been taken; Hutton's scrutiny of the church visitation records indicates the speed and ruthlessness with which the subsequent iconoclastic raids were carried out. In the 1552 prayer book, there was no possibility of reading in any version of transubstantiation—there was no "mass," no signs of the cross, no prayers for the dead, and no priestly vestments. The divorce of eucharistic fellowship from communion implicit in the doctrine of predestination was liturgically complete, the evangelism already present in the homilies utterly apparent: "What can be spoken more plainly, than to say, that freely, without works, by faith only, we obtain remission of our sins."[80]

Mary restored the Latin service, but it was in churches recently stripped and devoid of their ritual paraphernalia. The 1559 prayer book of the Elizabethan settlement restored vestments and placed back some of the ambiguity of the 1549 prayer book.

The early modern period, Edward Muir announces, is a most crucial period for ritual theory.[81] It was during the Reformation that a generalized concept of ritual emerges as a distinct activity. Ritual in this meaning is always of course someone else's.[82] Precisely because ritual forms present themselves as being invariant, any modification in them is perceived as a threat to their very existence and certainly undermines their ability to authorize. Indeed, rituals that are composed entirely of new elements are rarely attempted and nearly always fail. "A ritual which has never been performed before may seem to those present not so much a ritual as a charade," writes Roy Rappaport.[83] The Cornishmen who confront Cranmer in the prayer book uprising agree. Cranmer's new service is like a "Christmas game" to them.[84] When Cranmer hears that "we the cornishmen (whereof certain of us understand no English) utterly refuse this English," he is confronted by the fact that the language he had assumed to be "common" was in fact more alien, less familiar than the loved gestures and idioms of the Latin rite: "And standeth it to reason that the priest should speak for you, and in your name, and you answer him again in your own persons: and yet you understand never a word, neither what he saith, nor what you say yourselves?"[85] The heart, Cranmer thinks, "cannot be moved by words that be not understood," unless, that is, they are more like parrots than "true Christian men."[86]

The Book of Common Prayer was intended to be at once the index and instigator of conformity in the Elizabethan settlement. Elizabeth decided that church attendance, rather than reception of communion, was to be the deciding factor of conformity. It was not her desire or intention to "make windows into men's hearts and secret thoughts, except the abundance of them did overflow into overt and express acts and affirmations."[87] Rather every subject's public presence was the linchpin of the 1559 settlement.[88] For as J. L. Austin has brilliantly made clear, it is perfectly possible to accept publicly what one privately denies or despises, and such a denial will not vitiate the performance of a performative. The profound inextricability of our fundamental understandings of our relations to one another in trust and obligation, then, are bound up with liturgical acts and orders.

I have already mentioned that change in liturgy, because of its invariance and the role of that invariance in preserving that normative order, is so disturbing that the very efficacy of the ritual is in doubt. And so, too, is our very sense of who we think we are and how we grasp ourselves to be. It was no wonder that churchmen found it so hard to agree on *adiaphora,* for the very notion that how we comport ourselves—how we kneel, hold our hands and heads, coordinate our actions with one another, what we look like to one another—could be matters of mere indifference registers ignorance of how we love and live. Changes in ritual order, far from being superficial, are morally confusing and psychologically extraordinarily disturbing.

The commonality of the Book of Common Prayer was devised with the promise "to the intent . . . [that] your hearts and lips may go together in prayer."[89] "Of late," says Nicholas Ridley, "all men and women were taught, after Christ's doctrine, to pray in that tongue which they could understand, that they might pray with heart that which they should speak with their tongue."[90]

And yet to papists and puritans alike, the Book of Common Prayer might seem less a forum for commonality, certainly not the place where their lips and hearts came together, than the legally decreed and mandated forum that would deny them the public demonstration of their allegiances, loyalties, and loves. As Walsham has said: "In a period in which co-existence of differing versions Christianity was still philosophically inconceivable and the concept of toleration at least theoretically anathema, it is hardly astonishing that outward conformity should arouse such unease."[91] The compelled uniformity of religious worship in a newly national church creates a group of subjects overnight whose modes of being in relation to their maker and preferred patterns of worship render them treasonous subjects though nothing had changed in their own forms of life. And for those nonconformists whose religiosity was one of conversion, whose evangelical hearts would never find themselves, their godly ideals or the movements of the spirit in the merely outward forms of uniformly shared and uttered words, it was clear that the Elizabethan settlement would settle nothing at all.[92] Elizabeth's determination to be a Protestant queen and not the queen alone of the Protestants, in Lake's words, "opened up a gap between the inward and the outward, the real convictions of a person and his or her outward behaviour, a space, which it seemed to many contemporaries, could be exploited for all sorts of dissimulation and pretence by the faithless and the unscrupulous."[93] Both groups who felt that the liturgy created an impassable obstacle between their convictions and their public expression wanted that painful divorce lessened or obliterated.[94]

Arguments, then, about the forms of worship, the vestments of priests, the language of liturgy, the physical orchestration of space were about the ways in which liturgy authorized both the new form of church government and the national monarch of a church of England. Far from remaining indifferent to the painful gap between inner conviction and outward gesture, this gap helps create a chronic divorce between the heart and the lips. Such a gap produces distrust in the body, its actions, gestures, and behaviors as being the field of expression for the human soul.

ANTITHEATER'S AMPHITHEATER: BECON AND BALE'S ACTOR-PRIESTS

In ritual and in theater, actors enter into roles. In each aesthetic form, one sign stands for another. Ritual forms seek by various means—invariance, uniformity of practice—to use such standings-in as forms of authorization.[95] In them, identities are changed in ways that persist quite beyond the time of performance. Through the performative language regulated in ritual practice, men and women are married, men become tonsured priests, recreants become excommunicants, children enter and repentant sinners reenter the kingdom of Christ and the possibility of salvation. And such radically changed and charged identities are the point and purpose of the rituals. When a priest has been made a priest, he will not stop being one once the performance of his ordination or his own celebration of mass is over. The costume he wears will denote the totality of his role. In her injunctions issued before her first visitation in June 1559, Elizabeth, for example, requires that clergy wear full dress even when they appeared *extra sacra*, outside of their official capacity.[96] He is a priest (and better seen as such) even when he is not hearing confessions, saying the mass, or doing the pastoral work of his office. Or so we would prefer to think, which is why we do not like to think of him in the frockless state that would render him not merely naked but without solemn authority. But even though the social reach of rituals is indispensably pervasive, ambitious, and tenacious—precisely because ritual must be performed and because actors must be held up against roles that invariantly precede them and that are created through the performance—the reach may falter:

> Two years ago an old lady who was a neighbour of mine lay dying, and asked me to fetch the priest. He arrived but without being able to give communion, and, after administering the last rites, kissed her. If, in my last moments on earth, I ask for a priest, it isn't so that he can kiss me, but so that he can bring me what I need to make the journey to eternity. That kiss was an act of paternalism and not of the sacred ministry.[97]

The inability of this nouveau priest to perform the recognized and familiar death rites threatens his own imminent journey to eternity as it also renders him simply not believable, not recognizable as a priest (for *this* is what a priest does and he is not doing it).

Robert Fox, incumbent in the vicarage of St. Martin's in Marian York, liked a good drink or two. John Foxgale, the parish clerk, remembers and testifies that on Ascension Eve in 1554, Fox was so drunk that he could barely mumble the service. On 22 July 1555 he was so drunk he could not say evensong on Saint Mary Magdalene's Eve. Worse still, he could not administer the last rites to George Mason on Saint Stephen's Day after Christmas.[98] John Clerke, the scrivener and town clerk of York and principal scribe of the York plays in the Register, is one of those who testifies against Fox. His charges concern the detailed enunciation of Fox's drunken mauling of the Latin service.

> [He] hathe herde the said Sir Robert in redinge of his Servis pronounce and change Sentences in the same, as where he shoolde saye, "*per misericordiam dei in pace requiescant*" he sathe *per misericordiam in dei in pace requiescant* and in a nother sainge in the Evensonge where it is *sed volet (?) nimis etc* he called it *voluit nimis* and in many other places which he cannot now remember.[99]

It is important to note in this instance that it is not Fox's Latinity but his alcoholic stumblings that render the service both ridiculous and illegitimate, in Austin's terms, infelicitous. In what sense can he be understood to be performing his office? His inebriated slipups impugn his office and the church that speaks or misspeaks through his performance, and for his outraged parishioners, these careless mistakes put at risk their fearful path into the life beyond this one.

It is because of the terrible fragility of ritual authorization that the bond, the contract forged between actor and role in ritual, must not be glimpsed or reopened. In the tenth-century *Visitatio Sepulchri* in *Regularis Concordia* of Saint Ethelwold, the extra-liturgical ceremony for Benedictine use discussed in chapter 5, the instructions for service (stage directions) read that the monks who are in the "likeness of" the three Maries should be "vested in copes, bearing in their hands thuribles with incense."[100] Though they portray the three Maries who come in search of Christ's body, their vestments (costumes) indicate that they are not imitating the Maries or pretending to be them, for they never cease to carry the insignia of their office, never cease to be monks for the duration of the play/service. Both Innocent in the Decretals and Bishop Grosseteste in 1244 tried to place as absolute a wedge as they could between appropriate liturgical behavior and the *ludi théâtrale* that parodied them.[101]

The *Tretis of Miraclis Pleyinge* is concerned chiefly with clerical participation in interludes, and it understands such playing as threatening the very integrity of sacramental action. Since Sarah, daughter of Rachel, abstains from association with players, says the author, surely

> myche more a prist of the Newe Testment, that is passid the time of childehod and that not onely shulde kepe chastite but alle othere vertues, ne onely minstren the sacrament of matrimonye but alle othere sacraments and namely sithen him owith to ministre to alle the puple the precious body of Crist, awghte to abstene him fro al idil pleying bothe of miraclis and ellis.[102]

In the *Croxton Play of the Sacrament*, the very boundaries between liturgy and theater are fundamentally at issue. The unauthorized usurpers of liturgical action are stuck in the role of Jew, but the Jew is also a kind of defective actor fulfilling an unwitting role in the very script of a story (the crucifixion of Christ) he does not understand in his performance/parody of the liturgy. The figure of the Jew as actor allows for the liturgical action to be at once legitimate and illegitimate: having your eucharistic cake and eating it, too.[103] The play, it seems, must return us to the consecrated space of the church, as it forms into an episcopal procession, its Jews and merchants, and its actors converted and banished or transformed into the participants of ritual, its theatricality dispelled. The body of Christ is back in a mass, not in a play; the sacrament has become a real presence again. When you do have a bishop on stage, it is a good idea to get him back into the church and to banish the threat of theater's doubleness, its capacity to open up the gap between actor and role so tightly sealed in the performative actions and utterances of liturgical and ritual action.

No wonder, then, that the following prohibition accompanies the 1559 BCP as the legislators establish the legitimate performance of their newly national church and its authorized officers:

> And it is ordained and enacted by the authority abovesaid, that if any person or persons whatever after the feast of the Nativity of Saint John the Baptist next coming shall in any interludes, plays, songs, rhymes, or by other open words, declare or speak anything in the derogation, depraving or despising of the same book or of anything therein contained or any part thereof, or shall by the open fact or deed, or by open threatenings compel cause or otherwise procure or maintain any person, vicar or other minister in any cathedral or parish church or in chapel or in any other place to sing or say any common and open prayer or to minister any sacrament otherwise or in any other manner and from them is mentioned in the said book, or that by any of the said means shall unlawfully interrupt or let any person, vicar or other minister in any cathedral or parish church, chapel, or any other place to sing or say common and open prayer or to minister the sacraments or any of them in such manner and form as is mentioned in the said book, that then every such person being thereof lawfully convicted in form abovesaid shall forfeit to the queen our sovereign lady, her heirs and successors, for the first offense a hundred marks.[104]

This injunction is noteworthy for several reasons. First of all, there is an absolute separation between the approved liturgical form mandated by the Book of Common Prayer and any theatrical form. It is not that interludes as such are banned; merely that they must never quote or otherwise make reference to the Book of Common Prayer. Secondly, the authorized players for whom this form of worship is scripted, the celebrant priests at communion, must use only this form and no other in the church itself. The form of worship, thirdly, must not be interrupted. Fourthly, the authorized place of performance is legally determined. The strict regulations about performance should at once remind us of the continuity with the regulation of the medieval mass, a continuity necessitated by a quite similar relation between ritual uniformity and the authority of office, and they should remind us of the particular vulnerability of the authority of new rituals.

There are, of course, confidently contrary examples. Take, for example, this one of Thomas More's. "We say," he points out, "that the very body in forme of bread betokeneth and representeth unto us, the very self same body in his owne proper fourme hangynge upon the crosse." They, however, say that "nothing can be a figure or a token of itself." This, More thinks, is most peculiar:

> For if ther were but euen in a playe or an enterlude, the personages of .ij or .iij. knowen princes represented, if one of them now liked for his pleasure to playe his own part himselfe, dyd he not there his owne persone vnder the fourme of a player, represent his owne persone in fourme of his own estate.[105]

I talk of More's confidence here because I think it is clear that the analogy would never work if More felt that becoming momentarily a player would threaten the identity of the prince who plays himself, would reveal the identity of prince to be also one created as a sustained theatrical fiction. Rather, it is used as an example of the coincidence of the identity of the player with the one who is played. The interlude here is tellingly introduced to reinforce the prince's identity as the theatrical example subverts the gap opened up between the bread and the body of Christ in the mass.[106]

"Ritual and theatre," writes Michael Bristol, "have a long history of strained and sometimes openly hostile relations."

> This conflict between hieratic ceremonies and the meretricious performances of actors is however deeply equivocal. The manifest antagonism between the liturgical forms of religion and the dramatic spectacles of theatre are continually haunted by traces of a hidden complicity. The integrity of religious practice depends to a considerable extent, therefore, on the control of access to redemptive media.[107]

Such specific distinctions, antagonisms, and complicities are worth understanding, for they are profoundly and diagnostically revelatory of the tensions and transitions that these forms undergo in relation to one another. It is precisely because plays assume a gap between individual and role where ritual action formalizes roles, that one can be a standing threat to the other. When Falstaff interrupts the solemn coronation procession of his erstwhile companion, Prince Hal; when Lucio slanders the Duke at the public trial that ends *Measure for Measure;* when Claudio at the precise point of assent in the marriage service refuses to offer Hero his "I do," it is a fact that such grotesquely infelicitous interruptions would have rendered the rituals in which they are embedded inoperative as ritual (and that is precisely the force and point of ritual's ardent, emphatic conventionalism). And it is the simultaneous possibility of theatrical representation and the impossibility of ritual felicity that makes of them a complex investigation of the performative nature, say of kingship and of marriage for the participating and witnessing community: "Thus the doubleness which is only embryonic in ritual becomes the basis of theatre, where every coronation, marriage or trial is by definition, a mock-coronation, mock-marriage or mock-trial."[108] But it is precisely this endemic and embedded doubleness between actor and role that was made the subject of persistent and vitriolic criticism by the Reformers when they came to think about a medieval mass as the very ultimate measure and exemplum of theatricality. It becomes their aim to get their audience, the "massmongers," to see the mass through their eyes. They do this by systematically transforming ritual signification into disguise. If a painful gap between the inner movements of the spirit and the very possibility of their outward expression was opened up by that paradox, the converted liturgy, then such suspicion was a concerted and systematic part of an antitheatrical campaign that sought to render suspicious the entirety of Roman ceremony.

Thomas Becon was chaplain to that great architect of liturgical reform, Thomas Cranmer, archbishop of Canterbury. The purpose of his tract the "Displaying of the Popish Mass" was to compare the Lord's Supper with the Roman mass, and it is in this tract that we may begin to examine the function and purpose of the conversion of the priest into actor. The work is addressed to those who "have been so rooted from the beginning of your greasy priesthood in this wicked kind of massing."[109] Although Becon identifies several doctrinal points of difference between the reformed communion and the Roman mass, most notably the Catholic abomination of the mass as a sacrifice and the complete absence of preaching in the mass, his main task is utterly to delegitimate the ritual forms of Catholicism, to render ludicrous the solemn orchestration of its signs, costumes, and registers. His most concerted metaphor, then, is the priest as a player, and he encourages us to see the priest before he vests and after he unvests. What is this man except his costume? What is the mass without its trinkets and accoutrements, its smells, bells, and gorgeous gear?

> When Christ came to the table to minister the holy communion, he came in such comely apparel as he used daily to wear. But how come ye, in the name of God? that we may well see how well ye follow Christ in this behalf also. Ye come unto your altar as a game-player unto his stage. And as though your own apparel or else a fair white surplice, were not seemly enough for the due ministration of the sacrament, ye first put on upon your head an head-piece, called an amice, to keep your brains in temper, as I think. Then put ye on also a linen alb, instead of a smock, to declare how well ye love women, specially other men's wives; and that alb ye gird unto you for catching of a cold, though it be in the midst of summer. After this ye cast a stole around your neck, instead of a halter, which signifieth that ye will persecute and strangle with halter, or else burn with fire so many as speak against your abhominable apish mass. . . . Last of all come on your fool's coat, which is called a vestment, lacking nothing but a cock's comb. . . . This your fool's coat, gaily gauded, signifieth your pleasant fineness and womanly niceness, and your delectation in the verity or change of Venus's pastimes, because you will not be cumbered with one lawful wife. Thus as men well harnessed for an interlude, ye come forth to play hickscorner's part with your shameless, smooth, smirking faces, and with your lusty, broad shaven crowns, antichrist's brood of Rome. . . .[110]

Each garment is not only reconceived as a player's costume, so that the gap between the man and his assumed role is stressed, but it is also wrenched from its ritual context into the context of quite other significations. The smock with its ease of access and the vaunted celibacy of the priest (now understood as a refusal to be content with one wife alone!) are mere preparations for philandering: here is that figure of ecclesiastical satire with which we are familiar—the priest as lecher—but conjured economically through his costume. The stole that he dons to hear confessions is recast as a halter that he could traditionally escape through his neck verse, and it becomes the halter that he tightens around the necks of others once he has secured their guilt in confession. It is now the sign of his persecutory fantasies about and palpable hold over heretics. Becon depicts the priest's words as so many mumblings, breathings, blastings, and blowings, accompanied by kissings and genuflections, boppings up and kneelings down, and he divorces the actions from the word to render them spectacles without meaning.[111] The entire pamphlet works carefully through the order of mass familiar to us, say, from the Sarum or the York use; Becon wants us to see it differently. At the end of the mass, Becon shows us the priest greedily licking up all the droppings of the chalice; to Catholics this is, of course, a consequence of the doctrine of transubstantiation, but Becon renders it a sign of the priest's private gluttony: "When the boy or parish clerk cometh again with the *pax*, ye hold forth your chalice, like sir Ralph Rinsepitcher, for a little more drink. . . . After this ye return to the altar and take another lick or two of the droppings of the chalice, because ye would be loth to lose anything."[112] The end of the mass is the end of the play. Show over, costume off, the priest becomes the man he really is under the disguise of the vestments:

> After all these things ye truss up your trinkets, ye shut your book, ye fold up your corporass cloth, ye wind up your chalice, ye put off your fool's coat, your vestment, your stole, your fannel, your girdle, your alb and your amice; ye put out the candle, and solemnly making courtesy to your God that hangeth over the altar, ye trudge out of the church, either home, or else to the ale-house, being now at liberty all the whole day after to do what ye list with a safe conscience, to dice, to card, to hunt, to bowl, to bib, to make good cheer, to play revel-rout, to drink them all out, to set cock on the hoop, let the devil pay the maltman, to fish in Venus' pond, to sacrifice to Bacchus and what not.[113]

Becon wants us to see that the entirety of his office is in the playing. When it is all over, he can get down to the serious business of hawking and drinking.

The analogies of priest to player are a commonplace of reforming polemic. The aim of such analogies is to deauthorize the ritual performances of the mass as the centerpiece for ecclesiastical power. But insofar as the metaphor of theater is persistently elaborated, two features of theatricality alone are specified at the cost of others: disguise and spectacle. It is worth remarking here that this represents a significant attenuation of the mediums and mechanisms of theater, which has implications for the understanding and understandability of medieval sacramental theater. For Becon's privileging of disguise and spectacle as the two dominant aspects of theatricality significantly reduces the role of the audience's complicity in the very medium of theater, at least insofar as they can figure in anything other than the unattractive role of ignorant dupe. And it is precisely the actor-audience relation, the constitution of community through the obstacles and occlusions of charity as a eucharistic body, that has been the vital resource of theater to sacrament in the theater of Corpus Christi. Becon's analysis has implications that reach far beyond even his local and vitriolic delegitimation of the mass. Becon's savage satire of the Catholic mass certainly clears the way for a reformed liturgy, which, as we have seen, seeks to make the body of Christ truly common; his delegitimation of its predecessor helps to authorize ritual authority as the sole prerogative of the Church of England. But such strategies make it hard to see beyond disguise and spectacle as modes of playing, and thus made it harder to understand the constitutive links of a theater and a theology of the sacrament though a community of participation.

The principle at work in Becon's discursive attack on the mass is extended further into antitheater, in the conceptualization of ceremony as meretricious spectacle and concealment of the bilious ex-friar John Bale. Bale was highly likely to have been familiar with the idioms of Corpus Christi theater in its East Anglian and northern aspects. Trained as a Carmelite in Norwich, acquainted with heterodox groups at Cambridge University, he became a prior at Doncaster by 1530. By 1533 he had abandoned the religious life to become a secular priest and was rescued from his examination for heresy at the hands of Archbishop Lee of York by Thomas Cromwell, Henry VIII's principal secretary and an ardent Reformer.[114]

Written in 1538, *King John* is not only the first English history play; it is also the only extant play text of the Henrician reign for which a precise date of performance can be given.[115] Although not all of Bale's plays have survived, it is clear that much of his dramatic work is an attempt to replace and supersede the civic Corpus Christi dramas. Paul Whitfield White has argued at length for Bale's intimacy as actor, dramaturg, and playwright with the concerted dramatistic policy of iconoclasm inaugurated by Thomas Cromwell.[116] We know that *King John* was performed at Lambeth Palace for the archbishop of Canterbury, Thomas Cranmer, and Cromwell at Christmas 1538–39. It was also revised by Bale in the early years of Elizabeth's reign after his return from exile. The date of the play places it, then, after the Ten Articles of 1536, but also after the dissolution of the monasteries. Henry had embarked upon and also relatively quickly retreated from full-scale reform of the church, its sacraments, officers, and ceremonies. Auricular confession is still a sacrament; the doctrine of transubstantiation still holds; Henry still creeps to the cross; the mass is still Latinate.[117]

Bale's devastatingly iconoclastic play works its most inspired and brilliant agit-prop effects through a systematic figuration of ecclesiastical office as theater. And just like Becon, he intends our political education through the total way in which ritual forms are delegitimized theatrically. More insidiously because less obviously, theatrical signification is transformed and recoded before our eyes; once again its chronic side effect is the eradication of the community as the very address (audience and medium) of sacramental theater. If all Catholic clergy are only ever actors, the sole function of their theater, the only idiom of its possibility, is mimicry.

In Bale's theater, we see every ecclesiast in and out of his costume in the way we see actors in and out of their costume in metatheater such as *The Knight of the Burning Pestle*.[118] We see, then, *every* ecclesiastical costume as a disguise, not a ritually sanctified insignia of office that confirms the continuity of the sanctified role of the church's intermediary inside and outside the ceremony of performance. It is highly likely that *King John* was played with professional actors; it is also likely that some of the costumes used were the recently cast-off robes of the monastic houses.[119] When the play was performed again after the Elizabethan settlement, it was in the context of the Vestarian controversy in which Bishop Hooper had refused to be consecrated in a surplice and rochet as prescribed in the Book of Common Prayer. In 1559 vestments were restored, and by a 1560 order of bishops, a cope was to be worn in the celebration of holy communion.[120] Peter Stallybrass has recently pointed out the importance of the Vestarian controversy as a controversy over "what to wear."[121] In St. John's College in 1540–41, two green vestments, an old silk cope, and "half a decones cote" were turned into theatrical costumes.[122] Thus, Bale's theater may be seen as a piece of literal iconoclasm, in which formerly sanctified costumes and artifacts are emptied of sacred meaning, just like the conversion of service books into spice containers and the Easter Sepulchres into chicken coops I talked of earlier.[123]

Edwin Shepard Miller has made a detailed analysis of Bale's concerted parodies of Catholic liturgical ceremony.[124] In addition to par-

odies of Vespers, the liturgy, and the office of the dead, the most concerted and single-minded attack on Catholic ceremony targets the
penitential and disciplinary system. Every ceremony, but in particular
auricular confession, is used by ecclesiasts to suborn the state, the king,
and his subjects and to place them in the power of the church. I will
give two examples only from this all-pervasive parody. In the second
act of *King John,* Nobility asks Sedition to hear his confession, and after rehearsing the conventional forms of sinning such as breaking the
Ten Commandments and neglecting works of charity, and after being
catechized as to whether or not he is ignoring the new modes of religion, he is absolved—of "all obedience to the king." Absolution becomes an incitement to treason from which the church will relieve you
a priori, and it will be done in the name of the pope, not of God. Similarly, Sedition, who dwells in confession "undernethe bendicitee,"
pardons Clergye *a pena* and *a culpa,* from the guilt of the sin and from
the temporal punishment enjoined upon it.[125] When Usurped Power
confesses Dissimulation, the mode of catechizing functions as an investigation of whether Dissimulation has been guilty of preaching the
Gospel; if he did "thow shuldest haue no absoluccion."[126]

Every piece of ceremony is a parody of the liturgy. Liturgy itself has
its own built-in forms of parody such as boy bishops' processions, for
example, but here the reversals themselves are of the *positions* in the hierarchy. The boy playing the bishop sanctifies as it debunks the authority under which he rules; and the bishop himself is chastened by taking
the meanest part in the liturgical ceremony. The parody mocks preten-
sion but not authority for the role itself, which remains sanctioned,
cherished, and honorable. The role issues forth even more poignantly
and pointedly for being highlighted, as we see the boy in the seat of office. But when Usurped Power dresses as a Pope, Private Wealth for a
Cardinal, and Sedition for a monk, or when Dissimulation disguises
himself as a monk, we are led to believe that ecclesiastical robes are
only ever costumes.[127]

Disguise in plays is rare before the Tudor period.[128] Satan casts the
seven deadly sins as characters in the N-town play, but this is a verbal
not a performed allegory.[129] Lucifer appears as a gallant in *Wisdom
Who Is Christ,* the earliest play in the morality play genre to use disguise.[130] After Henry Medwall's brilliant play *Nature* in which Pride
dresses up as Worship, the disguise motif is an ubiquitous concern of
the Tudor interlude and the morality play.[131] These disguises are not
mere "devices" but a vital part of the plays' metatheatricality and wit.

For example, Aman can no longer be Vanity in the play *Godly Queene Hester* because one of the other characters has engrossed all the cloth, and so he is literally put out of a part.[132] In *Nature*, as John Alford has argued, Medwall's exploration of the ruse of disguise is a brilliant representation of our powers of rationalization, an exploration of the complex relation between our will and the world's possibilities in relation to our own dispositions.[133] Playwrights could not incorporate this literary device without its becoming, in its new context, a commentary on, an exemplification of, the essential dramatic art of impersonation.

Bale's costuming devices, his disguises differ from, say, the Marian play *Respublica*, in which there is a relation between oppression and reformation, between adulation, avarice, and policy and where the vice figures rename each other as they make their attack on the Republic.[134] When such costumes come off, the quality can be seen for what it is. In Bale's plays what is revealed is the absolute identity of ecclesiastical robe and disguise. Underneath their costumes will be power waiting to usurp, dissimulation that/who can only pretend, and sedition whose very nature is to suborn and whose essences can be concealed from us, but never transformed into anything else. The patterns of doubling and disguise are so tightly worked into the plays so as to make the theatrical logic and the theatrical economy, as Peter Womack has put it, speak the Reformation itself as the "victory of 3 actors over their bad other roles."[135] Hence Clergy doubles with Usurped Power and disguises himself as a pope; Nobility doubles with Private Wealth disguised as Pandulphus; Civil Order doubles with Dissimulation, who disguises himself as the historical personage Stephen Langton. Both the historical narrative and the forms of Catholic ceremony are themselves only disguises. Under the guidance of Imperial Majesty, Clergy promises to exile Usurped Power, Nobility undertakes to drive Private Wealth from the monasteries, and Civil Order will see to it that Dissimulation is hanged. One role destroys the other, so that Veritas will proclaim itself transparently. Theater itself is rewritten as antitheater: the exposure of the defrocked; the discovery of their true natures as deceivers.

The effect is an education in new forms of theatrical iconoclasm in which the role of community has been subtly but totally eradicated.[136] Commaltye indeed has only a tiny role in *King John*. The community exists only in its national dimensions as England the pathetic widow deserted by her husband and betrayed by her bishops to Rome, entering only at a moment of conflict, conceivable only for Bale as a bone in that conflict. Since there is no getting beneath the disguise of the Catholic ecclesiast in Bale's play, the bullying, relentlessly emphatic, but undeniable force of his theatrical logic is the obliteration of Catholic ritual and ceremony.

Both the lure of disguise in theater and the drive for it are epistemological: disguise poses identity as a conundrum. It says that there is a gap between what you see and what you can know; it unsettles and then satisfies our desires to close that gap by its logic of exposure. For most disguises, epistemological ambiguity disappears with their exposure. But in Bale's theater, the exposure is merely *to disguise as such;* disguise is what is uncovered. It is not that the actors are monks and ecclesiasts, but that the ecclesiasts are actors. Exposing them means uncovering—an actor. The epistemological lures and satisfactions of disguise in theater are provoked by monks as actors and exposed by actors as monks. The result is the perfect coincidence of theatricality with the ritual forms of the Catholic ceremonies and the ecclesiology that goes with it. A theater of epistemological doubt in a signifying language of appearance and reality replaces a theater of acknowledgment that uses the play of presence and absence as its signifying idiom, a presence and absence understood through and achieved by means of the community's availability to and presence to itself. Seeing theater as disguise, we banish its extraordinary resources as the very medium of disagreements and agreements that must be ours. Theater will no longer be a form in which we trust. The savagery of Bale's exposure is the savagery of a betrayed lover; it has all the intensities of rejection, all the affect of a felt betrayal of his past, where that "of" is understood as doubly genitive, moving two ways. The past we betray is the past we feel betrayed by. No wonder Bale produces a theater of such profound mistrust, such unstoppable suspicion, which, he can only pray, reform might end, for exposure certainly will not.

A Protestant Resurrection play provides my third and last example of the "amphitheater of antitheater" in which the implications of the transfer of authority out of the community of embodiment and into the scriptural story and its interpreter can be clearly seen. In an excellent account of this play, Nicholas Davis explains how the author's concern for the "literal" truth renders him anxious firstly about "the dramatist's obligation to localize events to which the Bible assigns no locale."[137] Secondly, since he has abandoned Christ's own address to the audience and the liturgical announcement of resurrection as extrascriptural, "he is compelled to express the significance as well as the fact of Resurrection." Thirdly, Davis points out, he charges the actual *moment* of resurrection with discursive significance (Davis's italics). This makes resurrection and theater a spectacle. And through this theatrical logic, it is also rendered theologically incoherent since the receiving community of recognition and misrecognition that I have examined as the central meaning of York's Resurrection theater can no longer find itself there. The Emmaus episode, whose eucharistic ironies were so central in the York Resurrection episodes, is replaced by the explanation of a character called Appendix, who now explains the episode as an assurance that Christ will find a way of speaking directly to the individual believer. Davis points out that it is crucially his commentary and not the action of the drama that sets up the analogy between resurrection and the free dissemination of the word. Because of his conceptualization of the relation between biblical text and performance, the playwright has had to make the action fit in with his understanding of biblical narrative as closely as possible, and hence any explanatory comment has had to be moved to the margins of the Appendix's words. This ancient story now is voiced through the textual apparatus of an "Appendix" and not the resources of wonder that I examined in chapter 5 and that T. G. Bishop has recently described as articulating not "the audience's ancient story, but the inner order to the story that shapes the audience's common present."[138] Davis observes that the author's attitude to the scriptures has the effect of isolating his commentator from the drama *and* rendering his presence necessary. Since the action of the play is precisely *not* transparent to the text of the Bible, Appendix's function "is partly to apologise for the very opportunities that the medium provides."[139] Yet the logic of his revisions is to produce a resurrection infinitely more spectacular than the complex immanences of Corpus Christi theater, a resurrection paradoxically shown to them but that is no longer available to them as a logic of their own immanent participation.

SIGNS AND DISGUISES

Think about the following conundrum:

> Question: What sign disappears as soon as it appears?
> Answer: The sign of disguise.[140]

The profound changes in ritual action in the manifold, sometimes self-canceling, but always far-reaching liturgical revolutions of the sixteenth century in England create a sense of a gap between inner conviction and outer conformity perhaps more effectively than the devastatingly iconoclastic theater of John Bale. These profound changes in the signifying systems of sixteenth-century religious culture have effects on the way in which a theater such as the vast ritual and cosmic drama of Corpus Christi can be understood, reenacted, and received. When we try to look behind and beyond what is in front of our very eyes, we will often miss precisely what is in front of them. The practices and habits of the substitution of a theater of disguises for a theater of the sign render the Corpus Christi theater hard to understand.

In his marvelous book on eucharistic practice, *In Breaking of Bread*, P. J. FitzPatrick writes about the difference between signs and disguises in relation to that amateur sleuth Sherlock Holmes. When Watson is utterly bemused that Holmes observes of a certain gentleman called Watson that he has been in Afghanistan, it becomes clear that there have been several legible signs (called clues when they appear in detective fiction) that have led to this observation: "He was a medical type with a military air (and hence an army doctor), had his face darkened by a sojourn in the tropics (the darkness was not natural, since his wrists were fair), and had been injured (an arm was stiff)."[141] The clues are signs that conceal nothing. But when we talk of disguise, "what needs to be seen is not the *significance* of what is there, but its *misleadingness*."[142] Thus when Holmes pretends to have a fever, he will not let Watson near him because he is disguised and fears exposure. In disguise what appears to be there and what is actually there "compete for assent," but this is not the case in Watson's appearance on his return from Afghanistan. Signs *can* be deceptive because a sign can signify more than one thing (and always does in theater), but there will not necessarily be competition between the sign and the significance we attach to it.[143]

In medieval Corpus Christi theater, for example, a mask is not a disguise but a sign. Whereas masks are used to conceal in Tudor morality plays and in court masques, in the cycle plays masks are specifically used with the supernatural characters for the purposes not of hiding, but of revelation. The mask enables the wearer to act on behalf of another for whom the mask is a sign. As Erika Fischer-Lichte writes: "Whereas the painted face is produced and interpreted as a sign of the unity of person and role, it is precisely the difference and distance between person and role which is constitutive of the meaning of the mask; for the mask is always indicative of two subjects, namely the one it signifies and the one it conceals."[144] In a masked performance the difference between the one wearing the mask and the one signified by the mask is neither eliminated nor ignored.[145] In other words, the mask is not a disguise; it is a theatrical sign par excellence, and it is used to denote the supernature of the characters so depicted. Jesus, for example, conventionally was fitted with a wig and a painted face, and God also appeared with a mask, as the Te Deum window in the York Minster seems to imply. Herod probably had a mask, and the devil's mask in the York Last Judgement play is given an elaborate description in the records.

But in the later sixteenth century, the significance of the mask as maintaining precisely the difference between the two subjects of actor and actant appears to be lost. Thus when the Diocesan Court of High Commission at York gives permission for the cycle at Wakefield to be performed if

> in the said playe no pageant be used or set furthe wherin the M(jest)ye of God the Father, God the Sonne, or God the Holie Ghoste or the administration of either sacraments of baptisms or of the Lordes Supper be counterfeyted or repreented[,][146]

"counterfeit" and "representation" seem to be used as synonyms rather than antonyms for each other, and idolatry and disguise are the specters raised by this theater. It seems at this stage that signs are being read as counterfeits or disguises. Similarly, in the Banns of the Chester play, we are told:

> sethence the face gilte doth disfigure the man yat deme
> A Clowdy coueringe of the man, a Voyce onlye to heare
> And not god in shape or person to appeare.[147]

"Disfigure" here carries the meaning of disguise, so it is as if the gilt covering is understood as a disguise of a God underneath which a man is concealed. Clearly, the masks in the cycle plays are not understood in this way. In the masked theater of Corpus Christi, the signifier and signified are physically differentiated by means of the mask, coexisting and not competing as signs. But the Wakefield and Chester examples imply that they come to be perceived as coverings and disguises in which the mask conceals or hides the actor who pretends to be the character he portrays. In these new conventions, the sign is something that we look past, behind, or through and not at.

In his study of the eucharist as ritual, FitzPatrick sees a confusion of signs with disguises in orthodox doctrines of transubstantiation as they were dogmatically defended in the Middle Ages as well as with the transignification theories of post-Vatican II sacramental theology. Their accounts, he argues at length, confuse signs with disguise, and the attraction of such schemas goes with "phenomenalism, that is, with a divorce between appearance and reality that is ultimately skeptical, a eucharistic presence that is insulated."[148] Even though the reforms I have been discussing are partly designed to attack precisely this version of what FitzPatrick calls the "Galileen Presence," their effect, I am arguing, is to widen both the perception and the actuality of the divorce between appearance and reality. The effect is at once a devastating erosion of trust in the shared, public nature of signs as the basis and product of our agreements and disagreements. As Kerr puts it, "The production of meaning retreats from the materiality of signs into the recesses of an invisible mind."[149] The mind retreats from the face as intrinsically expressive behavior is devalued, rather than understanding that "the body is the best picture of the human soul."[150]

The costs of this distrust, of this skeptical split between the outside and the inside, are enormous. Rituals themselves will now be read as externally coerced forms of hollow verbiage disconnected from our minds and hearts; or as the disguise of other ways of thinking, being, and doing. Trust in them is eroded and meaning is seen as always going on elsewhere. But as FitzPatrick has reminded us so powerfully, ritual action, including the ritual action of Corpus Christi theater that has become unreadable, is not reducible to a theory of knowledge or naming.[151] What becomes hard to understand, harder still to perform, is the redress of language in community as a consistent component of its sacramental concerns and their interweaving of our language and our lives together. For "we have no access to the divine, independently of our life and language," and "nothing else to turn to but the whole complex system of signs which is our human world."[152]

I have repeatedly argued that functionalism and dogmatism *find* community and publicness in Corpus Christi. But this, we might say, was not the achievement of the Corpus Christi cycles but their goal. And this might be like, as Stanley Cavell says, having sanity as one's goal.[153] To posit community as the achievement of Corpus Christi rather than its goal is paradoxically the ideal position for the skeptic to confirm his skepticism about this drama. For if community is already achieved, it will not be subject to my agreements or disagreements. I will not be in it. Either I will echo it as a pregiven script that is not mine, in which case my words will be hollow (I will be an actor), or I will imagine it as not being capable of expressing my own thought and imaginings, which I understand as too deep to be expressed and so understood (and so I will be mute). Both the fantasy of hollowness and of inexpressibility retreat from my stake in, my participation in, a community toward which I am accountable, and a community for which I share responsibility with others.[154] The difficulties we have, the condescensions we exhibit, toward the very form and shape of Corpus Christi are intimately tied up with such skeptical resistances, including our nostalgia for them, a subject to which I return in my final chapter.

PART FIVE

Revival

8 By The People For The People

THE GIFT OF GOD FOR THE PEOPLE OF GOD

> What then is it in the soul which causes it to take more pleasure in things which it loves when they are found and recovered than if it had always had them?
> —Augustine, *Confessions* 8.7

When John Doyle, director of the York Mystery Plays in 1996, announced that he had "seen his God," he meant Ruth Ford, the shopkeeper and amateur actress who was the first woman to take on the role of God in the York plays. The Venerable George Austin, archdeacon of York, was quotably outraged: the casting was "political correctness gone mad."[1] So, who, asks Charles Spencer in the *Daily Telegraph, could* or should play God? Jude Kelly thinks Prunella Scales would be a good contender, since she has such a good sense of humor. John Caird prefers Stephen Hawking, "all spirit and no matter, and very close to the stars."[2] The *Daily Telegraph* editorial of the same day in which Charles Spencer's copy appeared reassured: "The director, John Doyle, is not claiming that God is a woman; instead, he has cast a woman as God—a vital difference."

The difference, though vital, is one that provides far too thin a defense against theater's performative magic.[3] The working assumption of the first director of the York Mystery Plays, Martin Browne, as I said in chapter 1, was that the actor who played Christ must "look like" Christ.[4] The Blasphemy Laws made any representation of divinity or any discussion of theological issues onstage illegal: between 1569 and 1951, the York God is not played at all.[5] When he is, framed in the ruined arches of St. Mary's Abbey, the space of playing is considered to be as much part of the church as part of the theater; as I indicated in chapter 1, the insistence on the ruins as the backdrop for most of the plays' revival in the triannual arts festival productions is a longing for and an isolation from a past that is petrified in the ruins. The ruined, numinous space of production contains the scandal of enactment. Still, the relation between the actor and his role is dangerous: one must somehow "live up" to the part, and if something of the part will rub off on you the actor, perhaps something of you threatens to contaminate the being you are playing in the dangerous dual metamorphosis of acting.

Such suspicions attach to any playing of divinity, not merely playings of a medieval God. But for a long time in the twentieth century, it was precisely medieval Christs who were the only Christs allowed onstage. Until its repeal in the 1960s, the 1843 Theatre Regulation Act meant that all newly written plays had to be licensed by the lord chamberlain before they could be performed. This gave medieval plays the advantage of their antiquity, and in fact made them particularly ripe for revival since they could then be performed without the lord chamberlain's approval. Since it also meant that they were more likely to be performed in ecclesiastical rather than theatrical spaces, the relationship between the ecclesiastical and the theatrical seems particularly overdetermined in the case of medieval theater. For the very qualities (the fact, chiefly, that they were old and their authors unknown) that had rendered them obsolete appeared to make them suitable for resurrection in twentieth-century contexts. And since the Blasphemy Laws had prohibited the playing of God and the discussion of religious matters, virtually the only old plays that dealt with the life of Christ were medieval plays. It is for this reason that until 1966, the ban on the stage portrayal of Jesus had been lifted only for medieval Christs.[6] History in the shape of a past long over protects the stage Christ from the presentness of performance, for in post-Reformation England, a medieval Christ will signify a Christ separated off from the contemporary. It is precisely because the medieval stage Christ has been killed so completely that there is no danger of his coming to life.

In the later part of the twentieth century, it is at once versions of community and versions of heritage that compete to occupy the "medieval" space. By far the majority of contemporary productions of Corpus Christi plays are amateur; they are performed either as amateur parish acting or as conscious academic experimentation, and sometimes, as in the Toronto production of the York cycle in 1998, as both.[7] These productions, produced by academics, have also been extensively written about by them.[8] And so, in this chapter, I have chosen to concentrate on two major professional productions in which medieval community is a part of the contradictory articulation of the very con-

cepts of nation and people. I look at the two large-scale professional revivals of the Corpus Christi plays in the twentieth century in England:
Bill Bryden's workerist National Theatre production in the late 1970s
and '80s, revived "millennially" in 2000 at the Cottlesloe, and Katie
Mitchell's Royal Shakespeare Company production of 1996–97,
which, in opposition to Bryden's class-based populism, consciously explored Corpus Christi playing as a pre-Reformation *religious* heritage,
which iconoclasm had made inaccessible. But before I examine Bryden's and Mitchell's productions, I look at two fictional contempla-
tions—one a novel, Barry Unsworth's *Morality Play;*[9] the other a film,
Denys Arcand's *Jesus of Montreal,* in which priests and actors, church
and theater seem again peculiarly intertwined. Whereas the nationally
subsidized productions of Bryden and Mitchell have thought hard
about community, these two fictions focus particularly on the figure of
the actor-priest and seem to understand the actor himself as the only
possible location for authentic holiness. If John Bale and Thomas Becon had earlier evacuated the theater of community, they also used acting as the principle mechanism of a profound attack on Catholic
ceremony and the Catholic priesthood. What are the strange, changed
circumstances in which the theater can once again become "holy"?
From being the betrayer of Christ, how can the actor become (against
and above the church) the only authentic embodiment of him?

MORALITY PLAY: A PARABLE FOR THE THEATER

At the beginning of Barry Unsworth's novel *Morality Play,* set in
plague-ridden fourteenth-century England, a priest becomes an actor.
He does this initially because it is a disguise against discovery as a runaway priest, but by the end of his story, he has come to understand acting as, for him, a holier, less self-deceived existence. One spring
morning the priest, Nicholas Barber, a scribe who works for the bishop
of Lincoln's Cathedral in northern England, has left the cathedral
scriptorium on a whim. He begins to shed his first priestly costume almost immediately when he is discovered by the husband of a woman
with whom he is exchanging love for food. He meets a troupe of traveling players and, hiding to avoid discovery, watches Brendan, one of
the company, die without benefit of last rites even though he is the only
one present who can perform the office and shrive him in preparation

for death. Revealed by their dog, he is taken on as player to play Brendan's former role, the devil's fool, and so is "elected" to the company of
goliards (p. 12).

They travel to a nearby town, part of the fiefdom of Lord Richard
de Guise, hoping to raise enough money with their "Play of Adam" to
bury Brendan properly. Staying in an inn where one of the other guests
happens to be a King's Justice, they hear about the murder of the young
boy Thomas Wells, the latest in a whole series of murders of young
boys, and they hear that the suspect is a local heretic weaver's daughter.
Martin, the leader of the traveling troupe, decides that they will mount
a new play, not the "Play of Adam," but their own production of the
murder of Thomas Wells. It appears, partly through the course of their
own investigations, that the purse the weaver's daughter is accused of
having stolen from the boy (and that is supposed to supply both her
motive and the chief evidence against her) was actually planted in the
weaver's house by a monk, Simon Damien, who is Richard de Guise's
confessor, and that Damien is accessory to the murder of the boys he
procures for Richard de Guise's son, William. Damien's implication in
the murder is discovered accidentally, for Richard de Guise, hearing of
their show, demands a private performance in his Great Hall of the
"Play of Thomas Wells." Nicholas Barber, his identity now suspected,
is hauled out of this, their final show, where they are literally playing for
their lives, to give the last rites to a dying knight who was wounded in
a joust organized by de Guise. "Out of the playing-space now . . .
Nicholas Barber, a fugitive priest, sick with fear of death" (p. 163) gives
this dying knight holy oil and all the blessing he can, one mortal man
to another: "It was my own repentance I gave him, my own hope of
Heaven" (p. 165).

After these last rites, he escapes to find the Justice, assuming that
the Justice will "administer the King's Justice and set this foul wrong
right" (p. 173). But the Justice is not about to play the part Nicholas has
assigned him in his morality play, not there "for the sake of a dead serf
and a dumb goatgirl" (p. 173), but to limit the overweening power of
Richard de Guise, who has become rival to the monarch whom the
Justice serves. If he can find the son to be a rapist and a murderer, he
can defame de Guise and reduce his power. When Nicholas tells him
of the smell of plague the players had located in the house of de Guise,
it is for Nicholas a passing anecdotal detail to the real story he thinks
he is telling rather than a clue to the mystery. But by relating the smell

of disease in the house, he inadvertently gives the Justice the information he needs to implicate William de Guise and so to bring down his powerful father, for the Justice knows that Thomas Wells was already infected with the plague when raped by William. The book ends with the freeing of the falsely accused weaver's daughter, who escapes hanging by "merest chance, as an afterthought, a casual change of discourse in the play" (p. 187), and with the decision of Nicholas Barber not to return to the scriptorium, to the promising career offered to him by the Justice, but to "remain a player now" (p. 188).

The narrative of the book is made up of densely phenomenological descriptions of three separate productions of the new play written by Martin, whose interrupted and continually changing performances supply both the new clues that drive the plot as a murder mystery and provide an allegory at once of the birth of fiction and the "rise" of theater. The actors transform their script in each of the three performances. The boundaries between the fictional and the "real" shift minute by minute in the superb descriptions of the transformations and possessions of the actors, both their powers and vulnerabilities a product of the alchemical exchanges between actor and the highly interested parties of the audience. Martin predicts that his invention will be the future of drama: "It has been in my mind for years now that we can make plays from stories that happen in our lives. I believe this is the way that plays will be made in times to come" (p. 69). Their endeavor is a new kind of mystery play as much as a morality play, for as they try to make a play about a real thing, they find themselves encountering mystery rather than truth, and in doing a real thing, they make fiction. How can they play the life of a woman still living? "The woman who did it is still living, she is in the part herself, it is hers, no one else can have it" (p. 63). How can they play an unauthorized script, for "God has not given us this story to use, He has not revealed to us the meaning of it" (p. 64)?

In the subsequent performances of the "Play of Thomas Wells," the limits of play and world and of actor and audience become confused. Each interruption of the play enters its world, and the shape of both play and world change as a result. Each play leaves the actors more exposed to view, "closer to the people's lives" (p. 86), and so each time they perform, they create more space and structure between themselves and the audience—curtains, a tiring house in the middle of the stage.[10] The story has already been put together with the necessities of staging rather than truth in mind. Since they will have to double parts, Straw has to play the mother of the murdered boy unmasked and then double as the guilty woman in two masks—"an angel-mask for the deceiving of the boy, and a demon-mask for the killing" (p. 82). And since "we must make a scene of it" (p. 83), they decide to stage the murder (known to have happened) as an abduction of the boy by the woman to her house (for which there is no evidence at all). Thomas Wells's mother interrupts the first performance of the show, calling out, "It was not thus" (p. 93) as she sees Straw playing a lascivious temptress.

It is this interruption, and the utterly changed atmosphere it causes among the audience to whom Thomas Wells's mother has appealed, that changes the course of the play. For Martin interrogates the audience as to why Thomas Wells went with the woman, to "save" the play, to stop it from disintegrating completely in the light of the audience's interruptions. And the actors improvise a scene in which Springer as Thomas confesses that he was tempted by the woman. So here the play works like a blister around the wound to contain and protect the rupture in the play occasioned by its real-life interruption, and in preserving the fictional world of the play, new realities and meanings are busily forged and created. The "narrow avoiding of disaster" (p. 94) sets something free in the actors; "we were possessed" (p. 96). Stephen, the actor least likely to diverge from the scripted action, starts a manic improvisation in the middle of the performance and poses a riddle for the other actors and the audience: Why was the money not hidden after the murder? And the other actors again improvise answers; Springer, pulling off his mask, asks what brought the Monk to the place of discovery. This is left as a suggestive accusation at the newly devised ending to their play, an ending made all the more suggestive in that their prop for the Monk's purse supposedly "discovered" at the girl's house is now their collection purse in which they collect their copious earnings.[11]

It is in fact their own improvised reworkings of their planned play that lead them to the further mysteries of the murder of Thomas Wells. As if in the lightning, intensified energy of performance, they have found a problem to the Monk's story of discovery—how would he have "recognized" the woman as Margaret as he claims to have done, when it was cold and, as Nicholas said in the play, she would have been wearing a hood that would have made her unrecognizable? Before the second show then, they pursue further investigations so that they can perform the "*true* story of Thomas Wells" (p. 103; my italics).

Between the first and second performance, then, the actors turn investigators and discover three new things. Barber's visit to the girl's father, who has not yet appeared in the book, reveals that the Monk, Simon Damien, has himself planted the purse in the house of the girl's father, a heretic weaver, the better to silence his heretical views. Martin's visit to the girl in prison convinces him of her innocence (established in dumb show, for she is mute). Lastly, Margaret, Stephen's companion, who has now talked to the priest who buried Thomas, reveals that the boy had no sign of frost or freezing on him, which means that his body must have been discovered before the frost set in. In addition, Stephen has met the grave digger in the pub, who informs him that Thomas Wells is the fifth boy who has mysteriously been found dead or who has disappeared in the last year in the environs of the town.

When they next perform the "Play of Thomas Wells," it is with the purpose of implicating the Monk, Simon Damien, and restoring innocence to the falsely accused girl. The play has itself become the diviner and the medium of justice in their eyes. This time they determine that they will play the play as before until the moment when the woman, played by Straw, changes to her demon mask (p. 124). At this point Truth, played by Stephen, intervenes and questions the players, who will improvise answers to his questions, and they will perform the "true story" in mime.

Unfortunately, during this performance Stephen is too drunk to remember his lines and only hesitatingly begins his interrogations of the other characters. Another interruption comes from the audience as Jack Flint asks a member of the audience to confirm the truth of the statement made by Thomas Wells in the play that there is no hoar frost on him. As Truth begins to fumble his lines again, put off by the confusion caused by this real-life interruption, Martin takes off his mask, so "taking leave" of the character of Avaritia. As the interrogations and improvisations continue to implicate the Monk, another real-life entrance disrupts the show. The Monk himself, Simon Damien, is dragged into the yard. Not part of the action of the play and incapable of any other action, he lies dead over the back of a mule, his "costume" the white shift that penitents wear. Startled by the uncanny manifestation of the very man conjured in the portrayal, Barber tries to "save the play" again, this time by acting Good Counsel, who brings the tidings of death with a sermon on the theme of God's justice. Straw, as the woman, proclaims her innocence: "By hanging him they showed me innocent. Justice gives voice to the dumb" (p. 140). But yet again, an interruption has mistaken its own ending, the point at which it can close itself off from the world it depicts. Martin, still in the play, begins to speculate about who the murderer might now be after the death of Simon Damien. And he asks the audience who the Monk served, and the cast answers that he serves the Lord, Richard de Guise, as his confessor. It is at this point that the Lord's Steward enters the play arena to take the players off to perform their final show—at the house of Lord de Guise, whom they have just implicated in their play.

And so once again, the interruption is both produced by the play action and reveals its limits, what it does not know, as morality covers over mysteries it cannot anticipate or contain. The players decide to perform their play as simply as they can before the Lord. They will end with the Monk's death and will not inquire who killed the Monk. As the play unfolds, the terrifying audience of the Lord and his imposing, threatening reception alter the very meaning of Stephen's words as Truth, who "sets no store by gold or riches."[12] But Martin, "possessed" again, changes the ending. When Springer pronounces the last words, "Justice shows me innocent," Martin declares, "Pride makes an end, not Justice" (p. 159) and proceeds across the hall as Superbia: "Think you that Pride will suffer an end to be made without him, when he is the master-player of all?" (p. 160). As he advances on the Lord, Superbia begins to speak in the unmistakable metallic and deliberate voice of the Lord himself. Just as it seems certain that Martin will bring them all to perdition, another death interrupts the show and Nicholas, whom one of the women of the house thinks might be a priest, is called to give the last rites to the knight wounded in the jousting.

And so we leave the still unfinished final show, for so we think it is, about to bring doom to its makers, and escape with Nicholas, who finds his way back to the inn. Seeking out the Justice, he tries to bring another ending to the story, a just one. As we have seen, the ending we ourselves have been anticipating has been disrupted and then completed by this figure, the Justice, seemingly marginal to the workings of the play and of the novel, and now, it seems, involved in play makings of his own:

> You thought I was one of your company, one of the players, somewhat belated, come to put on the mask of Justitia in your True Play of Thomas Wells. There was the Monk and the Lord and the Weaver and the Knight. And now the Justice, who sets all things right in the end. But I am in a different play. . . . (p. 174)

As the priest-player explains to the Justice the process of discovery that lead the actors fumblingly, contingently, and yet inexorably to the scene of the crime, we see that truth has been revealed by the ungovernable processes of play, yet always outside of the anticipated script and action. As Nicholas explains it:

> We learned through the parts we were given. It is something not easy to explain. I am new to playing but it has seemed to me like dreaming. The player is himself and another. When he looks at the others in the play he knows he is part of their dreaming just as they are part of his. From this come thoughts and words that outside the play he would not readily admit to his mind. (p. 171)

Each attempt to end the plays has utterly misrecognized its own limits, just as we are led to misrecognize the characters who are in the play and those out of it in the novel's clever construction. In the penultimate chapter, Nicholas wonders "if there were not some larger play still, in which kings and emperors and popes, though thinking they are in the centre of the space, are really only in the margin" (p. 180).

The Justice believes that a priest who is a player is not such an unusual being. Martin himself has remarked earlier in the narrative that the church first makes God a player. The priests have in fact, as Martin points out, been implicated in theater from the beginning: "The priests played him before the altar, as they also play Christ and his Holy Mother and others, to help our understanding. As a player he can have his own voice, but he cannot take the voice of others" (p. 4).[13] Priests, as I explained in chapter 7, are forbidden playing in plays outside of the liturgy. Their identity as priests depends on this ban, as does the identity of liturgy itself as ritual, not theatrical action. The success of Reformation polemic, as I argued in chapter 7, was systematically to confuse the two, to make the one the vehicle of the other's permanent supercession. The Justice is fully aware of the claims behind the quite conventional association of priest with player and its critical force. But his claim in response to Nicholas is that though a "priest who is a player is not so infrequent," "a player who is also a priest . . . that is rarer" (p. 169). This is not merely a throwaway chiasmic witticism on the part of the Justice, but part of the novel's central and reorganizing claim for players and for priests. It is an argument at once for a new form of theater, a new form of priest, and a new form of confession called fiction.

For given the chance to return to Lincoln and to secure his former job in the cathedral scriptorium, Nicholas Barber asserts that he will not return "unless it was as a player":

> I knew little of the world, as the Justice had seen, but I knew that we can lose ourselves in the parts we play and if this continues too long we will not find our way back again. When I was a subdeacon transcribing Pilato's Homer for a noble patron, I had thought I was serving God but I was only acting at the direction of the Bishop who is the master-actor for all that company of the Cathedral. I was in the part of a hired scribe but I did not know this, I thought I was my true self. God is not served by self-deceiving. (p. 187)

He cannot return to a part he was unaware of even inhabiting, for to do so would now be a soul-destroying constriction. So he is not merely a priest who is really a player, a term usually ascribed to rather than espoused by its object.[14] He is a player who is also a priest, finally giving the last rites that he had earlier refrained from giving to Brendan out of fear of discovery as a runaway priest.[15] He has no such scruples when it comes to delivering the last rites at the castle, because he can now assume the authority of the player-priest since theater has been the vehicle of self-revelation, as of a justice adjudicated by the constant reengagements of play and world. We remember that at the beginning of the narrative, when he has been persuading the traveling troupe of the usefulness of his skills as a player, he informs them that he can hear confessions, expound the scriptures: "It is true I have no benefice and I am outside my diocese, *but I can still perform the office*"(p. 8; my italics). But the book has raised the question of what it might mean to perform the office, by which we might understand not merely the daily liturgical office of chanting and celebration, but the office of priest as curer of souls. What is "effective" or felicitous performance of this office, and what does it mean to perform it? By the end of the narrative, a play is interrupted and Nicholas is called as the only available priest to help a wounded man make the passage from life to death, and he finally espouses the life of a player-priest as the one authentic way of being a priest, a way of life that has eschewed both self-deception and the impossible deception of God, which is only another aspect of that self-deception. The book is in fact framed by the interrupted ritual of last rites, for though Barber cannot perform the last rites for Brendan, being much more concerned to remain concealed, undiscovered, he manages better when he is an actor rather than a priest. In the last performance the players give, Barber is called, literally, out of his role "onstage" to deliver the last rites to a dying knight. The book then is an investigation about how to perform the office, and so an investigation of the role of priesthood, taking the form at once of an interrupted ritual and a series of interrupted performances, where the boundaries between world and play are constantly called into question. In the transition from priest to actor, he becomes surrogate for the dead man, swapping clothes with him. The first and last role, then, in this morality play is Everyman, standing in for a role that precedes him, rehearsing for one that awaits him: the dead man. And it is his full assumption of his fear, his mortality, the role he can now acknowledge he shares with the dying man, that now authorizes and authenticates his office. Part of the point of the fictional novel *Morality Play* about the theatrical genre known as moralities, is that we are ignorant as to the limits of the roles that we play, for we do not know our own endings. The players made of their playing a diagnostic instrument of accusation and justice for the sins of others in their morality play. But in Unsworth's *Morality Play*, morality lies not in the accusation of others but in the full assumption of our own vulnerability as mortal.

If the book as a whole is a morality play, it wants us at once to understand morality as play, as discovered and understood in playing, and it wants us also to understand that pardon and revelation/self-revelation are truly intertwined, that the knowledge gained from playing is dependent on self-acknowledgment. For the book begins as a confession, whose openness and authenticity can alone guarantee absolution: "I will not hide my sins or what is the worth of absolution?" Any absolution granted through concealment of sin would itself be false currency. In a play of words, the heart of corruption in the medieval church, the systematic and legalized selling of indulgences—which obviated the cycle of penance and absolution by short-circuiting both contrition and satisfaction—transforms its meaning to indicate the reception and generosity of audience response: "It is the weakness of my case," Barber tells us at the beginning of the second chapter, "that I can seek pardon only by revealing the pass I had come to. But this in turn was the result of my own folly and sin. And so I seek indulgence for a fault by revealing faults anterior to it. And there are further faults anterior to those. *It is a series to which I see no end,* it goes back to the mother's womb" (p. 13; my italics).

Just as I have argued that York's play of Corpus Christi devises ways to perform the sacrament of penance at a collective level, to urge the contrition of penance and to condemn the falsification and scapegoating misdirection of its "satisfaction," so this narrative has seen that in the face of the complex perversion of the sacramental system, playing moralities to expose and probe the limits of role might be the only truly moral response.

The priest's habit has become "part of our common stock" (p. 30), not any longer solely worn or signifying the priest who dons it. The Monk who is supposed to hear the confessions of the Lord has acted as his bawd, procuring young boys whose lives are completely expendable.[16] As in Langland's poem, and as in the penitential delineations and concerns of the York Corpus Christi cycle, the abjuration of the role of honest confessor has effects on the integrity of the whole society.

Unsworth gives us a little parable for the theater within his parable for the theater. In the penultimate chapter, Margaret tells Nicholas Barber, our player-priest, about the story of the devil and the player:

> It took place before there were players, if we can imagine such a time. The Devil was casting about the world and he came upon a man of very virtuous life and sought to tempt him. He tried all manner of blandishment, the lusts of the flesh, the treasures of the world, fame and domination. All of these the man steadfastly rejected. The Devil was at his wit's end and could think of nothing more but to offer to make him a player. The man saw no harm in this and agreed and so he lost the bout and his soul was forfeit because a player borrows bits and pieces from the souls of others and in this pastime his own soul loosens and slips away from him and it is an easy matter for the Devil to scoop it up. And this has been the case for players ever since. (p. 179)

The book ends with Nicholas's decision to be a player-priest: "I would be a player-priest and I would try to guard my soul, unlike the player in the fable. And I would not again be trapped in a part" (pp. 187–88).

Nicholas has been trapped in his part in several senses in the book.

First as subdeacon, he has been trapped in a role. Later, too, as an actor, in a moment that in retrospective wrongly conceptualizes the player-priest, Nicholas contemplates the abjuration of the priest's habit (in that ancient pun) altogether, since the playing has emptied out the very meaning of the role for him at this instant:

> It entered my mind that I could get up, leave these scraps of travesty behind and walk away into the quietness of the morning in my proper dress of a priest, as I had been when I first came upon them. My condition was the same: I was cold and hungry and penniless now, as then. But I was confused between the playing of the thing and the living of it; it grieves me to say it but I am resolved to tell the truth, the habit of a priest seemed a travesty also, no less than the white robe that Stephen wore as God the Father or the false suit of Anti-Christ. (p. 86)

At this point he is an actor and not a priest, and the priest's robe has become a completely empty signifier, an actor's robe. But his desire to remain an actor—while also distinguishing himself from the actor in the fable who loses his soul to the devil—depends on his sense that acting can also be about the limits of role, rather than the subsumption of person within role.

The book is a fable of the origin of drama, as of fiction. Its originality lies in the way in which it has understood the interconnection of actor and priest, those ancient antitypes and alter egos, as a component part of the sacramental system of penance and its adjudication or travesty of justice. Revelation is essential to penitence, and in a world where the church cannot maintain its role as curer of souls, the relation between actor and audience, as established in new forms of participatory theater that weave the contemporary world into their renditions, will be vital. But revelation needs to include self-revelation and self-acknowledgment for morality not to be mere moralism. Both church and theater will be of the devil's party without such acknowledgment. The priest can only be a priest, then, on the basis of playing the morality play Everyman, there not to watch the death of another man, but ultimately to understand that his commonalty with that man lies in the only ending that he knows that they share.

Yet paradoxically, in allegorizing the origins of medieval theater, *Morality Play* is also inevitably a modern story about the actor and the actor's holiness. For its central insight—that the spiritual is best maintained, kept alive most honestly in the community of memory of the actor, not the priest—is also the central insight of a film made about a decade earlier than Unsworth's novel: *Jesus of Montreal.*

ANOTHER HOLY FOOL? THE ACTOR AS CHRIST IN THE COMMERCIAL AGE

In a brief introduction to the screenplay of *Jesus of Montreal,* a French-Canadian film made in 1989 in Québec, Denys Arcand talks about his encounter with a young actor in an audition. The actor apologized for the fact that he was bearded. "Je suis désolé, me dit-il, mais je suis maintenant Jésus."[17] Each evening this actor had been playing the stations of the cross up on the *montagne* of Montreal. How, ponders Arcand, can this actor at one moment be saying the lines "Celui qui gagnera sa vie la perdra," and the next day turn up for an audition for a beer commercial. In an interview Arcand discusses his film as a film about the "paradox of the actor": "He never knows where the role begins or where his personality ends."[18] As in the novel *Morality Play,* we have here a film fascinated by the interrelationship between church and theater, where one is a more authentic version of the other, where the boundaries between play and world are explored and collapsed through the central figuration of an actor who plays/is Jesus—of Montreal.

Daniel Coulombe is a thirty-year-old actor who is asked by Raymond Leclerc, the priest who is also the guardian of the Catholic shrine of the Communauté du Sanctuaire on the mountain at Montreal, to update a thirty-five-year-old passion play. Daniel agrees to undertake the task and collects a group of actors who are "resting" in various jobs. He first approaches Constance, an actress coincidentally having a surreptitious relationship with Leclerc, to help write and perform in the new passion play. He finds her at work in a soup kitchen. Typical of the film, the scene is replete with biblical references suggesting the discipleship of the apostles. Once he has persuaded Constance to be in the play, they go in concert to persuade Martin Durocher to participate. Durocher is dubbing a porn film, and here Arcand explores some intricate comic paradoxes. Since one of the other actors does not show up, Martin has to play the two men at once, and at the moment of maximal sexual excitement, muddles up the voices. Then comes René Sylvestre, recording the voice-over for a museum display about the origins of the world. Finally there is Mireille, recording a perfume commercial (the "unbearable lightness of being") shot by her ad man lover Jerzy.

The writing and staging of the play, then, is the new fellowship of Jesus; we see the actors outside as well as inside the play and are constantly, as in *Morality Play*, made to think about the transpositions and transformations made possible in that idiom. Each of the actors is already acting—one lying in the role of priest's lover, the others in the heritage, porn, or advertising industry. Nearly all of them are involved in the highly mediated world of film and modern technology. Daniel Coulombe is metaphorically the "real presence" in their midst, uncontaminated by their worlds, who catalyses them into forms of presence with one another in a eucharistic community. The film structures itself around three excerpts from the actual performance of the passion play. After the first performance, Daniel has accompanied Mireille to an audition for a beer commercial in which her ex-boyfriend and the audition team humiliate her; Daniel, in a reference to Jesus in the temple (the event that historically precipitates passion week), smashes in fury all the "sacred" camera equipment, the idols and emblems of their cult. In the second performance, Daniel is himself arrested from off the cross. He is charged, but, after having been examined by a psychiatrist who declares him more normal than the judge adjudicating the charge, released. In the third performance, the play and the story of the passion converge altogether. Raymond Leclerc, disgusted with the modernization he has requested because of its subversion of traditional church doctrines and anticlericalism, has been instructed to stop the performance, and the guards do so in the middle of the show. One furious spectator who wants to see the rest of the performance makes a running dive at one of the guards and in an unstoppable momentum crashes into the cross on which Daniel is fixed in the pose of crucifixion. Daniel is bound to the cross and cannot get off it in time. He is pinned to the ground, and so a "real crucifixion" is inaugurated. Daniel is rushed to first one hospital and then another. After a scene in the subway—the first time we see Daniel's identification with Christ as so total that we no longer know whether the words of Christ, prophet of the eschaton from Mark 13, are his or Christ's—he falls into a coma and dies. His body is then delivered over to a resurrection made possible by modern science. The Gospel scenes of restoring eyesight to the blind and restoring new life in the glorified body are actualized in the new eyes and new heart his body provides to a blind Italian woman and an Englishman.

The film itself has been shot so that during some of the performances, it is impossible to tell whether one is in the theater or in the cinema. This was a deliberate ambiguity that Arcand and the director of photography, Guy Dufaux, wished to exploit: "La caméra s'approche des personnages et les montres comme on ne peut pas les voir pendant une représentation théâtrale."[19]

In exploring its central metaphor of actor as Christ, church as theater, the film begins with a death that is not one. In a stark beginning—with no signs of staging—we hear Smerdiakov and Karamazov in a vehement argument: "Il faut détruire l'idée de Dieu dans l'esprit de l'homme," he announces, and we see Smerdiakov get up on a chair, put a noose around his neck, and kick the chair away. It is not until we hear a silence and then the loud applause and bravos of the audience that we are aware that this nihilistic despair ending in suicide is Dostoyevsky's *Brothers Karamazov* staged, and not an actual event. And Pascal Berger, the actor who plays Smerdiakov, in the film becomes parodically both "John the Baptist," whose "head" is wanted for a "L'Homme Sauvage" commercial by one of the film's advertising directors, and later the wild man of these ads displayed as the backdrop for Daniel's eschatological prophecies at the end of the film (and for the final strains of Pergolesi's *Stabat Mater* sung by the two women buskers). The film is framed by two deaths that are not deaths, and just as we have been made aware of the transposition of film to theater and then to film again, we are living very self-consciously in this film in highly mediated communities.[20] There is no way of avoiding this mediation, though Daniel's apostolic actors may attempt it through "alternative" theater.

Like *Morality Play*, the very nature of role and identity is probed in this film. The priest, Leclerc, declares himself to have been once "fou du théâtre." But he understands that as an escape from himself: "A l'époque, ça apparaissait comme une solution—une façon de s'en sortir." He once played in Brecht's *Galileo*, Brecht's depiction of the encounter of science with the church, but if he stood up to the church in the play, he is less successful in this later more actual ecclesial encounter with modernity. In showing the priest's concealment of his affair with Constance and the way he betrays the actors to the church authorities for fear of losing his very being—"a bad priest is still a priest"—we explore both the inauthenticity of his role as priest and his absolute subsumption of his identity to the role, precisely the problem of ecclesiastical office explored in *Morality Play*. Though he is a bad priest, he feels he would be nobody at all without that role; he is therefore overly identified with the role of priest. He is in bad faith. And in one idiom of this film's imagining, he is also, consequentially, imagined as a bad actor, too. For as Arcand has himself made plain in an interview during the early release of the film, Peter Brook and Grotowski were vital influences on the film's conceptualization of the actor. And in stage practice and performance theory, Brook and Grotowski were practitioners of poor or holy theater. In Grotoswki's handbook *Towards a Poor Theatre*, he thinks of the actor as embodying gift: "The actor makes a total gift of himself. This is a technique of the 'trance' and of the integration of all the actor's psychic and bodily powers which emerge from the most intimate layers of his being and his instinct, springing forth in a sort of transformation."[21] The actor's art is conceived as a gift, because he dedicates himself to stripping away the obstacles to communion, and such a training is a form of spiritual rebirth: "The actor is reborn—not only as actor but as a man—and with him, I am reborn. It is a clumsy way of expressing it, but what is achieved is a total acceptance of one human being by another."[22] Grotowski believes that theater is itself religious: "The theatre when it was still part of religion, was already religion. It liberated the spiritual energy of the congregation or tribe"[23]

If the priest is partly a bad priest, it is because he would be better off as a "holy actor" in poor theater. For the community achieved among the apostles of Daniel Coulombe is truly transformative. Mireille in particular is transformed from one who lives by the body, making money from her beauty in degrading ads, to a life of the spirit, transformed by love for Daniel and the new community into which she is welcomed. For her own beauty has been a mask and a disguise. Her initial awkwardness at being without her usual accoutrements and *maquillage* and her difficulties with the rigors and simplicities required in acting by Coulombe, are the prelude at once to better acting and to a new spiritual life. At their Last Supper, as they all share pizza on the mountain before the last show, she tearfully explains how utterly transforming her own partnership and collaboration in *Jesus of Montreal* has been. And at the end of the film when the aptly named Richard Cardinal, doubling as a Satan figure, shows them how they can start up a *compagnie théâtrale,* Mireille is the only actor who walks away from it, deciding not to participate.[24]

The film renders very complex its contemplation of the very nature of role-playing. On the one hand, when a Haitian woman interrupts the show during the raising of Lazarus ("Jésus, je suis à toi. Je t'appartiens. Pardonne-moi, Jésus"), she mistakes the actor for the role he is playing in a typical stage joke. Is she then supposed to be like the southern yokel in the story about *Othello* who tries to stop Othello from murdering Desdemona?[25] Or is this moment more like the extraordinary scene in the subway in which Daniel utters the prophetic words of Mark 13 when his identification with Christ is most complete? And yet at the same time, the moment of the proclaimed eschaton is also the moment where false prophets and anti-Christs *pretending* to be Christ people the world.

One might say that a great deal of Arcand's interest is bound up with the question of the performability of the passion and resurrection story in a double sense. To ask whether this story can be played in a way that makes sense is to ask whether it can make sense, whether it can be received, acknowledged as meaningful. And it is to take seriously the central point I have been trying to make in this book: that the passion story as theater necessitates a different understanding of what it means to live on.

The "resurrection" of the film is where the *"blague"* of the film works most seriously and profoundly. "Give us his body," says the doctor in the Jewish hospital (in English) to Mireille and Constance as they look upon him in a comatose and cruciform state. The reference is to the eucharistic, glorified body of the host, and to the "give us this day our daily bread" of the Lord's Prayer and, of course, to Christ in the tomb. The idioms of the resurrection as the supreme gift of God and the miracles of modern science converge in his words: "He's young, he's healthy, and he's got type 'O' blood. That's a god-send." In the film, Mr. Rigby wakes up with a healthy new heart and an Italian woman joyfully regains her sight; and we understand the gratitude with which such new heart, such new eyes are received. At once grotesquely literal, the film is also astonishingly moving at these moments as it combines resurrection and pentecost and the ministry of Christ all in one. The actor Daniel Coulombe has made a Grotowskian sacrifice for his art, and Christ's resurrection has taken on new life. These are medical prosthetics; but it is the donative nature of their giving that renders them miraculous. On the one hand, the possibilities of resurrection are predicated on the medical technology of organ transplant. The resurrected body is no longer the community of the faithful in the act of witnessing, but a restored prostheticized body. But the meaning and transformations of the film have been effected by moments that are to do with the "real presence" of actor to audience that, in the utterly mediated world of Montreal, exists as exiled and impossibly marginal to the secular world. Though Daniel's death has been accidental, such accidents are not incidental to the risks of live action. Such risks are part of the actor's self-giving, as I explored in chapter 4, and they are part of the thorough and total acceptance of the risk and vulnerability of God as human in Christ.

The film ends with an Easter moment of hope. Two buskers sing the glorious last words of the *Stabat Mater* in a setting by Pergolesi: "quando corpus morietur / fac ut animae donetur / Paradisi Gloria." (When [my] body is dead, grant that my soul be given the glory of paradise.) It is a beatific vision, longed and prayed for, from the dusty setting of the subway, with the "wild man," our travesty of harbinger, John the Baptist in the background. But as the camera moves away from the subway and the music sublimely continues, we move away from the analogical tomb of Christ (for the women, like the Maries at the tomb, sit where Daniel has "died"), and the camera moves from the earth through the skyline to the city, and finally rests on the empty cross on the mountaintop at dawn.[26]

The film works on the basis of the metaphor/actuality of the holy actor. And that is only operable because it articulates, in the complexities of a thoroughly mediated world, a new notion of "real presence" in the transformed group of actors who have made a new community among the corruptly idolatrous world of contemporary society. This time it is not so much that a priest has become an actor-priest as in *Morality Play*, but that the transformation effected by acting Jesus has inaugurated a new community of the faithful, a new church to renew an old corrupt church, ossified, static, blinded, and monumental like the statue around which Leclerc's old passion play is played.

We have been exploring the complexities of the metaphor actor/priest in two contemporary filmic and theatrical versions. It is definitely no accident that the most complete realization of the actor as holy fool, Daniel's total identification with Christ, is also effected in an idiom that insists most completely on the communicative network by which reality is made in the postmodern world—the medium of film, or more complexly, a film about a set of live performances where theatrical liveness is absolutely essential to their reception. Unlike the audience at Daniel's passion play, we as audience of the film are mechanically absent to his performances.[27] Theater performed in the age of film will often insist on the body of the performer, his display of muscular or nervous tension, as the very guarantor of authenticity: "Access to this risky reality is made possible by performance alone in a culture which transforms everything, including bodies, into commodity. Thus there's a pressure on the body to keep coming up with viable guarantees of the real."[28] This is part of theater's contemporary obsession with a "return" to ritual, and it is also where inevitably we rejoin a contemplation of specifically medieval revivals, to see what a modern theatrical medievalism might now look like. Let us turn from the novelistic and filmic representations of passion performance, then, to those of the professional National Theatre, to see how it thinks about the theatrical presence of the medieval Christ.

BILL BRYDEN'S THEATER FOR THE PEOPLE / BY THE PEOPLE

Bryden's production is the first, and Mitchell's (see below) the second, of the Corpus Christi plays to be set in the context of state-subsidized National Theatre. Transferred from its opening in Covent Garden to the Cottlesloe Theatre, the small theater in the round that is part of the massive National Theatre in the South Bank of London, Bryden's *Mysteries* become "the first commercially successful production of a medieval play outside a festival setting since William Poel and Ben Greet made a great profit from *Everyman* in the early years of this century."[29] The souvenir program to Bryden's production quotes an earlier critic of the drama: "Whatever may have been their original conception, they became in fact in the Middle Ages, of the people, by the people, for the people."[30]

It is not just within the context of 1951 and the arts festivals of the provincial north that the cycle plays provided the nation with the opportunity of revisiting its own ancientness in the context of a new understanding of the twin contexts of populism and nationalism and state subsidy in England after 1945. The populism ascribed to the plays that makes them so appealing and ripe for revival is forged through three ideological registers: people, nation, community.

The extraordinary success of the plays can be accounted for by the way in which the *Mysteries* accommodated what Womack has called the "frail consensual ideology of 'people's civilization'" which held together the competing models of state-subsidized theatre. The National Theatre, like the Royal Shakespeare Company, the Royal Opera House, and the English National Opera constructs its own public as a populist fiction designed for consumers who must imagine they are participants.[31] For here there are at least two competing versions of the people that both find themselves in the *Mysteries* of Bryden's production, one that locates itself in a national version of the people, and one that understands itself as a community rather than a nation. As Loren Kruger has noted, "the people" provide "no stable ground or ruling principle on which to erect a national theatre—but a battleground of intersecting fields on which the legitimacy of national popular representation is publicly contested."[32] For Kruger, a version of the people is essential to the very project of a national theater, and it is forged in the "contradiction between different class claims to transcend class." In the context of postwar Britain, it is also grounded in the construction of a fictional "public" for whom it caters. The famous publicity picture that opened the production puts the actors in workmanlike gear in front of the massive monumental architecture of the National Theatre South Bank complex and the vast space of St. Paul's: they are carrying a crucifix and it is Easter Sunday.[33] Contrasting sharply with the monumental facade of the institutional church is the "authentic spirituality now only able to be spoken as drama and play."[34] And since these monuments of national theater so blatantly do not appeal to the people, these theaters spawn their splits—the Other Place at Stratford, the Cottlesloe at the National, the Pit at the Barbican, their own rough theater, poor theater. The "Other Place," which is the name of the theater where *Mysteries* were produced in the Cottlesloe, is located, then, both "above and below the mainstream"—above because it is coterie art, below because it is a demotic challenge to elitism, a claim on behalf of the "people" against the prior appropriation of that term for monumental nationalism.[35] The *Mysteries* are esoteric enough to be coterie, a distinctly minority taste; but they are also distinctly noncanonical.

Owned by no known author, they appear rather to belong to a place and a people understood as a prenational locality, in short, a community.

Community is thus a second version of populism profoundly animated in and by Bryden's production. As part of postwar British nostalgia, community finds itself as a presence that is not one, "a self-apprehension of lost-ness."[36] Community theater becomes highly active during this period, and this version of community—amateur theater, theater in education, taking theater to the streets and to the people—is set against the fictional public theater subsidized by the state. Because medieval theater has historically been so tied to occasion and festivity, it appears to provide the ideal locus for these kinds of fantasies about the relation of place to community. And, indeed, insofar as the "medieval" becomes a force in drama of this kind of period, it appears in these guises.[37]

Bryden's *Mysteries* are based on a text prepared by the Yorkshire poet Tony Harrison, which consists of an amalgam of the York and Wakefield texts, with York predominating.[38] That the plays were highly invested in a demotic idiom is witnessed by the "folk" elements embedded within the old texts—folk dances such as the polka and maypole dances, Bob Dylan songs played on a guitar, as well as songs taking the form of ballads and refrains. But it is not simply a folk idiom. Bryden's theater is a concertedly workerist theater. God famously appears in a forklift truck; Cain and Abel are butchers; and all are dressed in laborers' gear of one kind or another. The *Mysteries* were produced during the time of the miners' strike in which Thatcher sought to break the back of England's most powerful union. This battle was in the very heartlands of South Yorkshire, where policeman on "overtime" rates of pay were sent up in droves to ensure that blacklegers could safely replace the striking miners to keep the mines running. In London there were supporters for the strikers asking people to "dig deeper" in their pockets to support the striking miners as their allotted strike funds ran out and as they and their families experienced great hardship. "Dig deep for the miners" expressed at once the dignity and hardship of a form of manual labor that always had a very special place in British industrial relations and trade union history.

In his play, Bryden made the miner's light the central prop of his passion play. Harrison altered the script of the York plays to cut from Christ's second lamentation on the cross in the Crucifixion pageant to the centurion's speech in the Resurrection pageant, which in the York plays is spoken to the conspirators, Caiphas, Annas, and Pilate. In Bryden and Harrison's version, Christ is hoisted high on the cross, where he has been pulled up by the soldiers (their version of the elevation). The centurion's words are spoken by a miner, and the light coming from his yellow miner's helmet catches the face of Christ in his beam. He asks, "What may these marvels signify / That here was showed so openly / Unto our sight?" and our sight is illumined by his probing spotlight as Christ is held in its beam. This motif of darkness and light is also used in the Harrowing of Hell sequence in the Doomsday play, where the opening stage directions give us a stage in total darkness; then we see God's miner's lamp illumining the head of Jesus, followed by the "lights from various miners' lamps [that] rake the darkness of limbo."[39] The light from the miner's lamp that had illumined Christ on the cross "rakes the gloom seeking for a way in" and the "light falls on the face of Adam."[40] The light continues to circulate and plucks out the relevant characters as they speak one by one. A song sings of the light that divides the darkness. It is first sung individually from different points in the room and then by all the inhabitants of hell in unison. But the voices come from all around us, not from one place. So Bryden has found an amazingly economic way of choreographing both sound and light to bring in an image that refers back to the crucifixion, but also to the creation itself, where God divided light from darkness.

In this drama, the mobility of the medieval performances is communicated by making the audience process: they are manipulated by the actors throughout the show. The performances in fact are even more intimately processional than the medieval processional performances in York. For both actors and audience are moved around each other in a larger space that offers them considerable freedom of movement while nevertheless containing and framing them all.

Bryden's *Mysteries* were initially given ecstatic reviews.[41] Bernard Levin talks about the effect of the sheer mobility of space as well as the astonishing mixture of the demotic and the cosmic that the plays achieved: "It is this wielding of actor, audience, play and story into one whole that gives the performance its unique quality—and I wish there were another word for performance, for it diminishes the thing that has been created as a place which we visit to see a play, and of a play as that which we visit a theatre to see."[42]

They were usually less popular with academics, who tended to prefer their own more "authentic" versions. Recently, too, it has become fashionable to attack Bryden's historic revival of the *Mysteries*.[43] Critics attack, in particular, his lack of a sense of a "religious feeling" and the substitution of a romantic conception of a worker's community. Meg Twycross has recently proclaimed:

> . . . the National Theatre's *Mysteries*, which have arguably done more than any other production, the York Mystery Plays included, to popularize mystery plays in Britain, tried to draw on a spurious sense of community created by appeals to a romantic nineteenth-century trade unionism that never was, as a substitute for the religious fervour and knowledge that the director probably rightly felt had gone for ever.[44]

But what if Bryden had been aiming not so much at imitating the guilds that put on the production, but at the very principle of anachronism at the heart of the medieval plays. He would then have rescued a vital part of their legacy, which I talked about at length in my third chapter: the imbrication of these pageants in the world of making. Such creation, invention, fabrication, and production—what we inherit and what we can make—are all examined as part of the world of human responsibility and labor. Such considerations, of course, do not exclude the "religious," which is always, in these modern criticisms, understood as a numinous, unembodiable force—a supervague form of awe.

Katie Mitchell, however, explicitly attempted to restore the religious heritage of these plays.

KATIE MITCHELL'S *MYSTERIES*

For Katie Mitchell, medieval theater elicits not simply fantasies of the interrelationship between place and community, but also a relationship to a lost Englishness and a specifically pre-Reformation culture. When Mitchell became director at the Other Place, Stratford's theater in the round, she inaugurated an entire medieval season entitled "Moral Mysteries." It consisted of a new production of *The Mysteries* (the first professional production of the Corpus Christi plays since Bryden's version), which Mitchell herself directed in collaboration with the dramaturg Edward Kemp. Also produced at the Other Place that season was *Everyman*, a production directed by Théâtre de Complicité's Kathryn Hunter and Marcello Magni.

What are some of the assumptions, rationales, and effects of the Mitchell/Kemp production? What fantasies does it enact or perform in relation to medieval theater?

Mitchell had spent some time working with Gardzienice theater in Poland and had been impressed not only by living in a Catholic culture where the plastic and material traces of a pre-Reformation religious culture had not been so completely obliterated, but also by some of the techniques of the theater group. In an interview reproduced in a booklet put out by the RSC to coincide with the "Moral Mysteries" season, Kemp and Mitchell each give complementary reasons for being attracted in particular to medieval theater. Mitchell described her own long-standing fascination with pre-Reformation theater: "My preoccupation was with pre-Reformation culture, and with the social and political impact of the Reformation. I was wondering what cultural memory might be; trying to see, by looking backwards, how we might move forwards culturally."[45] In her production of *III Henry VI* and Heywood's *Woman Killed with Kindness*, reviewers had noted how her strong sense of the culture's religiosity animated both productions. Kemp himself looked to medieval plays to expand a sense of a cultural inheritance and in particular of "Englishness" before empire and before industrial revolution and, indeed, before Shakespeare.[46] Mitchell similarly records in this interview an appreciation of the cultural ramifications of iconoclasm: because of the Reformation 96 percent of art was destroyed.[47]

Nonetheless, the production they ended up producing was extremely Protestant. It is worth considering why. Why is it that after starting with these desires and assumptions, they inexorably moved away from any specifically medieval understanding of community, theater, or culture?

The Mitchell-Kemp *Mysteries* is loosely based on the N-town cycle, but as they worked on the script, they became more and more uncomfortable with the medieval versions of the life of Christ that they saw in these cycles. They decided they were not going to work at the medievalism by means of the conceptualization of the actor, either as amateur, as in some of the York festival productions, or as Bryden had done by making his actors workers. And as Mitchell said, "Once we had removed the medieval context, we came face to face with the content—proselytizing Catholicism—which is certainly something I have great difficulty subscribing to."[48]

In an interview conducted with Katie Normington, Katie Mitchell explains their more and more distant relation to the medieval past: "We thought that we were going to do medieval mystery cycles, then we realized we couldn't do medieval mystery plays because we couldn't subscribe to the ideology at any level, particularly when we went back to the source material."[49] Mitchell and Kemp, in other words, were deeply embarrassed by what they imagined of the play's medieval context. Furthermore, they wanted to avoid the taint of heritage versions of medievalism at all costs:

> It seemed that we were in danger of building some quaint medieval time-capsule at the end of the millenium inevitably compromised by lack of knowledge, coloured by twentieth century prejudice. A piece of heritage theatre, perhaps entertaining in the shallowest sense, but devoid of any attempt to fully engage either with material or with our audience, both abandoned behind an opaque barrier of medievalism.[50]

Bryden's version of the *Mysteries* had been produced at the very beginning of the massive realignment of the past we call "heritage," which I explored in chapter 1. It was unlikely to have been a pressure on his own conceptualization of the medieval communities of performance. Mitchell and Kemp, on the other hand, were working in a culture (the culture I explored in my first chapter) where the past was highly mediated, presenced, and packaged in the eternal homogenous present of heritage that has always found medieval Britain richly auratic. To avoid the embarrassment of the belief systems that they perceived to be operating in the plays, they "started to reconstruct the project from the bottom up."[51] Hence they went back to a study of the Gospels and the Old Testament and denied their characters any knowledge that they, the actual historical figures, would not have had in the context of their historical origin. Unlike medieval actors who operated in permanently double time, the time both of the represented and representing figures, they sought to make their characters biblical, thus sealing off the present of the audience in its bond with the actors' present. The entire cosmological superstructure is thereby removed; in Kemp and Mitchell's *Mysteries*, there is no Fall of Angels and no Satan. Neither is there a Resurrection or a Last Judgement. In this way the theology of the plays—including the indispensable connections between reconciliation and punishment (chapters 5 and 6) available in the York plays as a story of witnessing—is obliterated. Jesus is constructed like a

"Stanislavskian character."[52] And having stripped away the medieval context, the dramaturge and his co-conspirators are forced to reconstruct the life of Christ from the principles of the scriptural text in true fundamentalist fashion with none of the mediating structures of the authorizing community.[53]

Scripture, mediated through the rubrics of nineteenth- and twentieth-century scholarship, replaces community as the authorizing agent of the plays. In such an understanding, it is no longer possible to see the plays as a counterliturgy (see chapter 6), in which performers and participants explore their own community as the body of Christ (see chapters 4 and 5). Ironically, then, all the talk about actors' community, the co-created work that has gone into the making of this play, is rendered empty: community has been edited out from the beginning in a reconstruction of theater as the search for origin. The play ends with Jesus kissing each one of his disciples and requesting them to follow him; they then all walk off in different directions at once. Kemp himself states the banal point: "The thrust of our story was one of human responsibility, for ourselves, each other and the rest of creation. . . ."[54] Yet precisely this kind of highly individualistic conception of personhood means that they cannot see how the medieval plays work with notions of corporate responsibility in the body of Christ. Thus when Kemp blithely declares that the historical "Jesus'" mission was a failure, that "he died and the kingdom of God was not seen on earth," he has utterly failed to appreciate the nature of eschatological temporality in the eucharist, that the complexities of the recrucifixion of Christ in theatrical time in York (not Calvary) is a component and constitutive part of the very meaning of these plays.[55]

In a sense, Kemp and Mitchell have unwittingly subscribed to every liberal Christian unexamined prejudice, which makes it so hard to see the interconnections between this theater and a theology of incarnation. Medieval Corpus Christi theater never authorized itself from the historically derived text, or indeed the play text of performance, but as I have been arguing, understood scripture as intrinsically intertwined with the communities who performed it. In Kemp and Mitchell's reading, the Gospels are "fraught with ideologically unsavoury baggage,"[56] and the play they have ended up producing is the kind of play produced at the extreme end of secularism where not even theater (as in *Jesus of Montreal*) can perform a community of the faithful.[57]

This contrasts with the efforts of Hunter and Magni in their production, which succeeded in making a medieval play live where Kemp and Mitchell did not. Their production rendered the play at once more medieval and more contemporary. Of all the medieval plays they could choose from, they chose the austere Dutch morality *ars moriendi* play *Everyman* and out of it created an extraordinarily moving meditation on our confrontation with death. The performance I saw enlivened versions of penitential theology that were not even remotely abstract. Instead of receiving the abstract names of the dramatis personae— Good Deeds, Strength, Goods, and so on, and representing them in characters that derived the meaning from the names, Hunter and Magni used the characters and their relationships to discover the virtues and vices as ways of knowing ourselves morally, socially, and spiritually. In their production, the moral, the social, and the spiritual were of a piece. Mitchell and Kemp stripped away to the origin so that the source and meaning was in some other and founding historical context (which, in fact, is created by the liberal academy) and in some original source of the scriptural text completely bare of the accretions and ranges of meanings through which these stories were lived out and lived by in concrete historical settings; Hunter and Magni imagined the names abstractly written on the dramatis personae sheet as a set of utterly embodied relations between people.[58] No wonder, then, that they succeeded in making their characters present to us in the way that Kemp and Mitchell failed. In this way, we understand what the very nature of Good Deeds is through discovering it, rather than from reading it off a page. And we see, too, the main theological point that Good Deeds are ineffective without an act of the will. Thus Good Deeds only comes alive when Everyman has experienced contrition. The theology and the theater work absolutely hand in hand and through each other. Kemp and Mitchell, on the other hand, distrusted and were threatened by medieval theologies of the passion: "Christ conquers death, either literally or metaphorically, by teaching people how to make a better use of life. I think part of the problem people have with Christianity is that it seems to be very death-driven and obsessed with what will happen to you after you die."[59] Kathryn Hunter's interview on the other hand makes it clear that she has no crippling version of medievalism, or indeed of Christianity, to stand in the way of the play's direct and moving address to us.[60]

Hunter describes how austere the play originally felt, "but as soon as we said 'these are people with specific relationships,' then it became released." Feeling that actors go dead if asked to play concepts, they "treated every scene in terms of relationship, and invented a community so that there is always a relationship to play."[61]

The utterly contemporary feel of the play and yet its felt sympathy, say, with medieval penitential theology derive from these fundamental theatrical instincts and traditions. Hunter is not embarrassed by medieval understandings of penance.[62] The abstract name of a virtue or vice becomes a pattern of recognition that is biographical and existential. Hunter essentially trusted to the simplicity of the play and understood profoundly that here theology and theater are not enemies, but only understandable through each other.

But Kemp and Mitchell never seemed fully to understand the complex kinds of agencies that had produced the Corpus Christi plays in the first place. They conceived them as an exercise of an outmoded and now outflanked ecclesiastical conspiracy. So what was "medieval" about their production? It is a question that they asked themselves as they readied their production for performance. The only answer Kemp gives at the end is that they retained the Middle English language. All the new parts that Kemp has put together from Jack Miles's "biography" of God, from the Nag Hammadi Library (the recently discovered collection of Gnostic writings), from liberation theology—all the books that they took down after they had put away Augustine and Aquinas—are assimilated to a sort of pseudo–Middle English style. Thus Kemp queries: "The question could well be asked, in what sense does the place at which we have now arrived have any connection to the medieval mystery cycles which were our starting point?"[63] His answer seems to be the language. But it is here that we see medievalism functioning most securely as heritage because Kemp understands "medieval" not at all in terms of the concrete, utterly specific meanings available in Middle English, but as a vague, deracinated sense of what Middle English sounds like—well, sort of medieval.[64]

Except that it is performed in "Middle English," this is no longer a medieval passion play; it is produced in a language that has no concrete specifiability, but that is vaguely archaic, a little like the homogeneity of the heritage time they were so anxious to avoid. Kemp and Mitchell have ducked and evaded all the hard issues by which old words and dead people can be brought alive through the bodies of the living. No wonder their "medieval" is a version of heritage created not in spite of their very best and most earnest intentions, but perhaps even because of them.

And so, in a way, this final example of a failed production is a poignant mark of the challenges and difficulties of revival. It is no small wonder that the "religious" dimensions of Corpus Christi theater are so difficult to revive comprehensibly. That is not to say that *we* don't believe in the things that *they* believed in, but rather that our forms of life cannot sustain the forms of presentness and the profound obstacles to presentness that are explored by the mutuality of community and eucharist in the medieval plays. For that reason, they are hard to make present to us and hard for us to acknowledge. They appear to us in a time to which they do not belong, perpetually estranged, chronically anachronistic, ghosts threatening to make play actors of us all. And because our recovery of these plays will always transform what we find, each finding will be a refounding.[65] Perhaps it is in this way that we might love these plays and learn from them, and take pleasure from such loving and learning, more than if we had always had them.

Notes

INTRODUCTION

1. Given that I am making an argument about sacrament and theater, the question might be asked why I chose to mount it around the York cycle, rather than any or all of the other three extant cycles, Chester, N-town, and Towneley. The kind of story I want to tell here—the interrelationship between a text and a place *over time*—is hard to tell with any of the other cycle plays. And though I certainly would not like to pronounce in advance on the ingenuity of future scholars to devise ways of telling such a story, I considered the following facts: N-town did not necessarily have anything to do with Corpus Christi festivities and, like the Towneley cycle, cannot securely be located. The Chester cycle, once understood as the most antique, is in fact the youngest; none of the manuscripts of the entire cycle predate 1575. In addition, there seemed to me to be no need to go over the ground so very well trodden in other comparativist projects such as Martin Stevens's in his *Four Middle English Mystery Cycles: Textual, Contextual and Critical Interpretations,* and Kathleen Ashley's in her eagerly awaited work. Whereas I have concentrated, for reasons that I hope will become obvious, on penance and eucharist, I hope that other scholars might feel interested in taking up explorations of the other five sacraments in relation to the cycle plays and to medieval drama generally and over the period of the Reformation's reduction of the sacraments from seven to the scripturally derived two, baptism and eucharist.

2. I will occasionally use formulations like "we" and "our" in this book. These are *not* to be read as unconsciously insular or arrogantly and unwittingly exclusivist. They are rather invitations to imagine us, that is, you and me, in relationship; they are not attempts to speak for you. For admirable clarification on this matter, see Toril Moi, "I Am a Woman," in *What Is a Woman? And Other Essays,* p. 231. Moi is working with the profound insights of Stanley Cavell, who argues that the procedures of ordinary language philosophy, which involve asking "what we say when," do not presume agreement among native speakers, but rather provide the means for exploration of the extent of that agreement. See Stanley Cavell, *Must We Mean What We Say?,* pp. 14, 68. Stephen Mulhall comments on Cavell's arguments in the following way: "The first-person plural form of claims about what is ordinarily said when makes manifest the fact that sharing a language, being able to speak to one another, is in part a matter of being able to speak for one another; communication hangs

together with community" (Stephen Mulhall, *Philosophy's Recounting of the Ordinary*, p. 11).

3. The plays produced in York are usually known in the records as "ludus Corporis Christi." The modern editors (L. Toulmin Smith and Richard Beadle) call them "the York Plays," and I alternate between the singular and plural usage.

4. The *Ordo Paginarum* of 1415, compiled by Roger Burton, from the *A/Y Memorandum Book* (a record of the administrative decisions of the city's governing body) lists fifty-two pageants; see *Records of Early English Drama: York* [hereafter *REED: York*], edited by Alexandra F. Johnston and Margaret Rogerson, 2 vols. (Toronto: University of Toronto Press, 1979), vol. 1, pp. 16 ff. A later second list gives fifty-six, see *The York Plays*, edited by Richard Beadle (London: Edward Arnold, 1982), p. 25. For the early history of the cycle, see Peter Meredith, "The York Cycle and the Beginning of Vernacular Religious Drama in England," in *Le Laudi Drammatiche umbre delle Origini*.

5. I am quite aware that there is no such thing as "theater" in the Middle Ages. The term "drama" was not really used until early in the sixteenth century, and "theatrum" was reserved for the theater of classical times. I have found it not only convenient but heuristically useful to take temporary advantage of this particular anachronism, for cultures do not always have words adequate to what they indicate, innovate, and invent. In those instances, the watch-cry of anachronism becomes a critical blindfold. See the introduction to Joan Copjec's *Read My Desire: Lacan Against the Historicists*. And for a recent discussion, see William W. West, "The Idea of a Theater: Humanist Ideology and the Imaginary Stage in Early Modern Europe," in *The Space of the Stage*, edited by Jeffrey Masten and Wendy Wall.

6. As, of course, it is decidedly not in many Catholic cultures. A comparative analysis that understands the spatial as well as temporal coordinates of historical narrative would be a fascinating project.

7. "This book," says Julian of Norwich, "is begunne be Gods gift and His grace, but it is not yet performed (*The Shewings of Julian of Norwich*, edited by Georgia Ronan Crampton [Kalamazoo, Mich.: Medieval Institute Publications, 1993], p. 154).

8. Rowan Williams writes, "Theology . . . is perennially liable to be seduced by the prospect of by-passing the question of how it learns its own language" (*On Christian Theology*, p. 132).

9. Stanley Cavell, "The Avoidance of Love: A Reading of King Lear," in *Must We Mean What We Say?*, p. 346.

CHAPTER ONE

1. The Blasphemy Laws of 1606 attempted to prevent the "abuse of the Holy Name of God in Stage-plays" (*Statutes of the Realm*, 9 vols. [London, 1810–28], vol. 4, part 2, p. 1097). For further comments, see chapters 7 and 8.

2. In 1476 more experienced actors were appointed to audition the actors

and plays, and in the 1460s–70s each trade guild responsible for the production of a pageant was required to deliver the play script to be recorded in the Register in which is contained the only extant version of the cycle as a whole; see *REED: York*, vol. 1, p. 109; and *The York Play: A Facsimile of British Library MS Additional 35290, Together with a Facsimile of the "Ordo Paginarum" of the A/Y Memorandum Book, and a Note on the Music by Richard Rastall*, edited by Richard Beadle and Peter Meredith (Leeds: University of Leeds, 1983). See David Mills, "Chester's Mystery Cycle and the 'Mystery' of the Past," *Transactions of the Lancashire and Cheshire Historical Society* 137 (1988): p. 13, for some comments on the unsuccessful nature of these attempts, and for a strong reading of the transformation understood by the technology of the scribe, see p. 4: "the creation of a play-book may well signal the end of a cycle as a living art-form."

3. This can be documented from 1501 at the latest, when we know that the common clerk checked the performances against his script in the Register as they passed through Holy Trinity Priory Gate (*REED: York* [1501], vol. 1, p. 187, and [1538], vol. 1, p. 263). For further details on John Clerke, an important secretary of the Register, see Peter Meredith, "John Clerke's Hand in the York Register," pp. 245–71.

4. This date, 1569, is also significantly the date of the Northern Rebellion. The play that year was performed on Whit Tuesday rather than Corpus Christi Day, which was no longer celebrated; see Eileen White, *The York Mystery Play*, p. 26. For details about the "end" of the Corpus Christi plays, see Harold C. Gardiner, *Mysteries' End: An Investigation of the Last Days of the Medieval Religious Stage*, and below, chapter 7. There were several attempts on behalf of the citizens of York to revive the plays in 1579 and 1580, but 1569 remains the last recorded year for a production of the cycle; see Gardiner, *Mysteries' End*, p. 75.

5. The York Festival's productions of the plays have taken place in 1951, 1954, 1957, 1960, 1963, 1966, 1969, 1973, 1976, 1980, 1984, 1988, 1992, 1996, and 2000, when Greg Doran directed a millennial production in the Minster in July.

6. Augustine, *Confessions*, translated by Henry Chadwick (Oxford: Oxford University Press, 1991), 11.20, p. 232–33. Augustine famously suggests that neither the future nor the past can safely be said to exist. They both inhabit the present, which is then divided into "a present of past things, a present of present things, and a present of future things."

7. I do not deal here, then, with questions of medieval memory as they are explored and utilized in these plays, but rather with the issues raised by the uses of Corpus Christi in and for the contemporary past after 1951. The question of medieval memorialization has recently been explored by Mary Carruthers in *The Book of Memory: A Study of Memory in Medieval Culture*.

8. John Elliott, *Playing God: Medieval Mysteries on the Modern Stage*, p. vii.

9. I am referring to Louise Fradenburg's essay "Voice Memorial: Loss and Reparation in Chaucer's Poetry," pp. 169–202, which uses the psychoanalytic

literature of mourning to explore our psychic investments in medieval pasts and the versions of history those investments sometimes realize.

10. *Official Handbook of the Festival of Britain*, p. 3.

11. Roy Strong suggests that another major precedent for the 1951 Festival of Britain was the British Empire Exhibition held at Wembley in 1924, a few years after another cataclysmic and worldwide war. Roy Strong, *A Tonic to the Nation: The Festival of Britain 1951*, p. 6. The festival, however, was willfully insular, turning away from empire (as empires turned themselves into self-determining nation-states) as it also turned from the entire context of Europe.

12. Strong, *A Tonic to the Nation*, p. 6.

13. The guidebook to the exhibition eulogized in the following way: "The land, endowed with scenery, climate and resources more various than any other country of comparable size, has nurtured and challenged and stimulated the people. The people, endowed with not one single characteristic that is peculiar to themselves, nevertheless, when taken together could not be mistaken for any other nation in the world" (quoted in Strong, *A Tonic to the Nation*, p. 35). Despite the strange mixture of bashfulness and arrogance in this statement, the celebration of insularity was consistent—the cafeteria served no foreign foods, for example.

14. Raphael Samuel, *Theatres of Memory*, p. 55.

15. Quoted in Strong, *A Tonic to the Nation*, p. 8.

16. Peter Hennessy, *Never Again: Britain 1945–51*, p. 128.

17. Hennessy, *Never Again*, p. 132. Hennessy, making the important point that the service was organized around an ethical imperative and so moved beyond the notion of a progressive administration or socialist planning, cites Aneurin Bevan: "Society becomes more wholesome, more serene, and spiritually healthier, if it knows that its citizens have at the back of their consciousness the knowledge that not only themselves, but all their fellows, have access, when ill, to the best that medical skill can provide" (p. 132; from Michael Foot, *Aneurin Bevan: Volume Two 1945–60*, p. 105).

18. Hugh Casson makes this point in Strong, *A Tonic to the Nation*, p. 81: "Architecture in its fullest sense, i.e., places not buildings, so long the Cinderella of the arts, became the true princess of the Festival." Brian Aldiss reinforces Casson's perception with his own recollections (Strong, *A Tonic to the Nation*, pp. 183–84), as does Rayner Banham: "If one tries to recall the experience of the South Bank as an inhabited environment, if one looks at the backgrounds to the family snaps and the surviving footages of film, the landscaping is omnipresent in a way that it was not at any other great expo—you saw it (often obstructing the view), smelt it, walked on it and with varying degrees of legality sat on it" (quoted in Strong, *A Tonic to the Nation*, p. 189).

19. *Yorkshire Evening Post*, 1 June 1951. And I think there should be no condescension to such sentiments and no obliteration of the savage contingencies in which they were voiced; after such barbarism, the desire for such civilization

is not merely understandable, but imperative if that civilization seeks to grace itself by that name.

20. It is indeed hard to remember how little the word "welfare" was then contaminated by the associations it now has of dependency, passivity, and scrounging, the success of an onslaught on its most fundamental principles of universality of care and access as the bond of common citizenship. For an excellent analysis of the loss entailed by our prospective abandonment of one of "our great achievements of the twentieth century," see Will Hutton, "Stopping the Rot in a State of Decay," *Guardian Weekly*, 1 October 1995, p. 11.

21. See, for example, Michael Frayn's famous description of the festival reprinted in Michael Sissons and Phillip French, eds. *The Age of Austerity: 1945–51*, p. 331.

22. The concept of the "invented tradition" is developed by Eric Hobsbawm and Terence Ranger, eds., *The Invention of Tradition*, p. 1: "'Invented tradition' is taken to mean a set of practices, normally governed by overtly or tacitly accepted rules and of a ritual or symbolic nature, which seek to inculcate certain values and norms of behaviour by repetition, which automatically implies continuity with the past." See below for further reflections on the theme of the specific role of the medieval in the dialectic between tradition and modernity.

23. "Report of the Board of the York Festival Society," 14 October 1952, *York Festival Collection*, York City Library.

24. *Yorkshire Gazette*, 11 June 1954.

25. *Yorkshire Evening Post*, 1 June 1951.

26. Martin Browne usefully describes the production in his article "Producing the Mystery Plays for Modern Audiences," p. 12. Although this modern division truncates the role of the Old Testament sequence, it appears to share the interest that the cycle has in the Passion and Resurrection sequences, which take up the lion's share of the manuscript as it appears in the Register.

27. *Northern Echo*, 17 October 1950. Thomson went on to add that the actor who played Christ needed considerable histrionic ability and some stamina, and that the actor should "conform to the common idea of what Christ looked like." Thomson received an MBE in the New Year's Honours List in 1952.

28. Elliott, *Playing God*, p. 75.

29. Elliott, *Playing God*, p. 60.

30. Elliott, *Playing God*, p. 58.

31. Elliott, *Playing God*, p. 59.

32. Browne, "Producing the Mystery Plays," p. 11.

33. Herbert Read in *New Statesman and Nation*, 9 June 1951; cited in Elliott, *Playing God*, pp. 78–79.

34. *Leeds Guardian*, 15 June 1951; cited in Elliott, *Playing God*, p. 80. The *Yorkshire Evening Post*, 4 June 1951, mentions that after the performance, "people didn't know whether or not to clap" and records that the plays largely met a

"silent reception." The ecclesiastical setting clearly inhibited the sense of entertainment and enhanced a sense that these plays were a form of religious worship.

35. Paula Neuss, "God and Embarrassment," in *Themes in Drama*, vol. 5, *Drama and Religion*, edited by James Redmond, p. 250. See also Martin Browne's comments on his production of a shortened version of *Ludus Coventriae* in the ruins of the bombed medieval cathedral in Coventry in "Producing the Mystery Plays," p. 14. The occasion was the consecration of the flamboyantly modernist new Coventry Cathedral (described by Bevis Hillier as the apotheosis of festival style, in Strong, *A Tonic to the Nation*, p. 10), which opened out from the ruins of the old cathedral.

36. *Yorkshire Evening Post*, 27 July 1976.

37. See the leader in the *Yorkshire Evening Post*, 1 July 1992, and the letters pages for the entire month. Ian Forrest directed the 1992 production in a revised script using the writer Liz Lochhead, who emphasized both the humor and the alliterative force of the original. The production was designed to ask the key question: How would Christ fare were he to land in contemporary Britain? (see *Yorkshire Evening Post*, 15 June 1992).

38. Anne Janovitz, *England's Ruins: Poetic Purpose and the National Landscape*, p. 4.

39. See Robert Harbison, *The Built, the Unbuilt and the Unbuildable: In Pursuit of Architectural Meaning*, p. 99: "The ruin mentality appears frivolous, fixated on surface, not substance. It is in fact deeply pessimistic, counting more ancestors than descendants, sure without thinking that it inhabits a decadent phase."

40. For the metonymic logic of the ruin as fetish in postwar British melancholy writing, see Ian Baucom, *Out of Place: Englishness, Empire and the Locations of Identity*, especially chapter 5, "Among the Ruins." To be English in the postwar period, remarks Baucom, "is often to be a member of the cult of the dead . . . or a member of a cult of ruin" (p. 175).

41. Pierre Nora, "Between Memory and History: Les Lieux de Mémoire," translated by Marc Roudebush, p. 17. This is a translation of the introduction to the project that Nora directed, working with forty-five historians in a massive and compendious attempt to chart a history of the collective memory of France through its representations, published in France as *Les lieux de mémoire*, 7 vols., now available in English as *Realms of Memory*, translated by Arthur Goldhammer, 3 vols.

42. Nora takes his term from Frances Yates, *The Art of Memory*. See the note in "Between Memory and History," p. 25. Yates explores the *loci memoriae* by which classical rhetors remembered their speeches in the tradition of Cicero and Quintilian.

43. Nora, "Between Memory and History," p. 12.

44. Nora, "Between Memory and History," p. 8.

45. Maurice Halbwachs, *On Collective Memory*, translated by Francis J.

Ditter and Vida Yazdi Ditter, p. 78: "General history starts only when tradition ends and the social memory is fading or breaking up." Memory for Halbwachs concerns the continuities between past and present; history establishes differences.

46. Richard Terdiman, "Deconstructing Memory: On Representing the Past and Theorizing Culture in France Since the Revolution," p. 15.

47. Richard Terdiman, "Deconstructing Memory," p. 14.

48. Nora, "Between Memory and History," p. 9.

49. Nora, "Between Memory and History," p. 15.

50. Nora, "Between Memory and History," p. 12.

51. Nora, "Between Memory and History," p. 12.

52. Nora, "Between Memory and History," p. 14.

53. Patrick Hutton, *History as an Art of Memory*, p. 149.

54. This assessment of Ferdinand Tönnies's massively influential book *Community and Society*, translated by Charles P. Loomis, is Terdiman's, in a particularly rich chapter of his book *Present Past*, p. 44. For a medieval historian's view of Nora's nostalgia, see Patrick Geary, *Phantoms of Remembrance: Memory and Oblivion at the End of the First Millennium*, p. 11.

55. The sacralizing effect of the ruins is sometimes echoed in a story that I have seen repeated several times as I read through accounts of the festival productions in the local newspapers. Here is the most elaborated example of a trope of reporting the productions that becomes extremely familiar, in the York City Library Scrapbook of the Festival, Box Y394: "As he shouldered the cross the contralto fluting of a blackbird broke on the air, perfectly timed, every strain so clearly defined that it might have been providing a solo to the soft music coming from the back of one of the stands. But when the music stopped the blackbird went on, and as the cross was being erected a songthrush joined it, and a blackcap joined an aria, almost like a nightingale. It was strange and awesome. When Christ was taken from the cross another strange thing happened. Blackbird, thrush and blackcap ceased, and the screeching of an owl wrung the darkness of the night. Nature had fitted itself to the Christian story."

56. *Yorkshire Evening Post*, 6 December 1980. The attempted boycott took the form of refusing to nominate members to serve on the Festival Board, which was supposed to be made up of twenty-one members, thirteen council members, and eight "experts," who were to report to the committee.

57. Susan Stewart, *On Longing: Narratives of the Miniature, the Gigantic, the Souvenir, the Collection*, p. 23.

58. Stewart, *On Longing*, p. 23. In this respect, the psychic structure of nostalgia is deeply melancholic in the sense in which Freud understands melancholia in "Mourning and Melancholia," in vol. 14, *The Standard Edition of the Complete Psychological Works of Freud*, edited by James Strachey. Melancholy responses to grief occur when the object loved (the person, past, thing) was not conceived as separate from oneself, but rather was understood as mirroring,

narcissistically, the self's sense of itself. Loss is then accompanied by the shock of separateness, by the acknowledgment that that past, person, thing was actually other, for otherness itself is suppressed in narcissistic loving. This form of grief, because it concerns the very boundaries of the self, is usually understood to be much more primitive than mourning. "What melancholy must work through is not so much the loss of a particular object that one loved and cared for—an object that had appealed to one's pleasure principle—but rather the loss of a fantasy of omnipotence" (Eric Santner, *Stranded Objects: Mourning, Memory and Film in Postwar Germany,* p. 3). Nostalgia thus displays its melancholy in a mode of grieving that takes the form it does because the past it laments was only ever, is only ever, a narcissistic mirroring—but a mirroring whose loss painfully affects a sense of power and being in the world. Nostalgia, in short, defends itself against impotence through melancholic disavowal. In lamenting a past it never had—for us, as for Proust, all paradises are forever lost—it can continue to maintain a fictitious mirror of potency. "Through the past we venerated above all ourselves" (Nora, "Between Memory and History," p. 16). On the suppression of alterity in versions of the past in medieval studies, see Fradenburg, "Voice Memorial."

59. Samuel, *Theatres of Memory,* p. 182.

60. For details on Jorvik, see Jeremy Silver, "Astonished and Somewhat Terrified: The Preservation and Development of Aural Culture," in *The Museum Time-Machine,* edited by Robert Lumley, pp. 170–95.

61. Samuel, *Theatres of Memory,* p. 195.

62. Robert Lumley, introduction to *The Museum Time-Machine,* p. 2.

63. Francis Drake, *Eboracum: or, The History and Antiquities of the City of York, From its Original to the Present Times* (London, 1736), book II, chap. 4, p. 574. Drake, like the spectators of the York plays, is moved by the ruins: "The present condition of this once magnificent pile of Gothick architecture is very deplorable; there being now only so much left of the cloisters . . . but we say with the poet that it looks great in ruin, noble in decay" (p. 577).

64. Peter Cramer, *Baptism and Change in the Early Middle Ages c. 200–c. 1150,* p. 247.

65. One early influential analysis of heritage was that of Philippe Hoyau, translated as "Heritage and the Consumer Society: The French Case," in *The Museum Time-Machine,* edited by Lumley, pp. 27–35, in which he argues that an imaginary model, the past, takes shape around three major models—the family, conviviality (community life, festivals, etc.), and the spirit of place (patois, architecture, cultural ecology, etc.). Patrick Wright has usefully and resonantly extended Hoyau's analyses within the specifically English context in his *On Living in an Old Country: The National Past in Contemporary Britain,* and in his earlier essay, cowritten with Michael Bommas, "Charms of Residence: the Public and the Past," in *Making Histories: Studies in History, Writing and Politics,* edited by Richard Johnson et al., pp. 253–301.

66. See the extended polemic of Tom Nairn, *The Enchanted Glass: Britain*

and Its Monarchy. And see Neal Ascherson's analogy: "One of the marks of the feudal *ancien régime* was that the dead governed the living. A mark of a decrepit political system must surely be that a fictitious past of theme parks and costume dramas governs the present" (Ascherson, "Why Heritage Is Right-Wing," *Observer,* 8 November 1987; cited by Samuel, *Theatres of Memory,* p. 265).

67. Samuel, *Theatres of Memory,* p. 261.

68. Samuel, *Theatres of Memory,* p. 246.

69. R. B. Dobson writes about the massacre in *The Jews of Medieval York and the Massacre of March 1190.* The York massacre is, as Dobson says, "virtually the only episode in the history of the medieval English Jewry to have been recorded in some detail by contemporary or near-contemporary Hebrew sources" (p. 21).

70. David Uzzell, "The Hot Interpretation of War and Conflict," in *Heritage Interpretation,* edited by Uzzell, 2 vols., vol. 1, p. 43.

71. In March 1995, 2 million daffodils were planted around Clifford's Tower in memory of the York massacre of 1190. In 1988 a conference held at York called "The Splitting of the Ways" also reexamined Christian-Jewish relations in the local context of York.

72. Sometimes the plays in the festival productions are amateur, for example, in John Doyle's 1996 production. Sometimes, too, a "star" is brought in to attract the crowds, for example, Ian McShane played the devil in the 1963 production, though this is probably before he became famous to English audiences as the laddish but delightful antique dealer Lovejoy; Victor Banerjee (Aziz in *A Passage to India*) played Jesus in 1986; in 1980, in a gesture that blatantly combined local interest with "star" attraction, Christopher Timothy—the actor from the immensely popular series set in the Yorkshire Dales and adapted from James Heriot's *All Creatures Great and Small*—played Christ. For some further reflections on casting the supernatural characters, see chapter 8.

73. Patrick Wright, "Heritage and Danger: The English Past in the Era of the Welfare State," in *Memory: History, Culture and the Mind,* edited by Thomas Butler, p. 174.

74. Paul Connerton, *How Societies Remember,* p. 64.

75. Wright, "Heritage and Danger," p. 174.

76. *Yorkshire Evening Post,* 11 June 1966.

77. Program for the 1969 Corpus Christi Productions, *York Festival Collection,* York City Library. The director's program notes state: "For the first time in four hundred years, the plays will be acted throughout by amateur players drawn from York and Yorkshire. . . . The stories will once again be told by the people of York for the people of York."

78. It should be added here that many directors of the plays have attempted to utilize some of the critical energy of the strategic anachronisms of the medieval enactments. Stephen Pimlott, who directed the plays in 1988, said in the program notes: "Perhaps I should have asked the Archbishop of York to

play Caiphas, the Judiciary to take on Christ's Trial, the Territorial Army and the Police to supervise Christ's arrest and the control of the crowd." Ian Forrest, who directed the plays in the Theatre Royal in 1992, said he wanted to brush the biblical and the medieval past up against the contemporary by asking: "How would Christ fare if he landed up in contemporary society?" (*Yorkshire Evening Post*, 15 June 1992). In posing that question, he was addressing an issue both directly posed by English Lollardy and enacted in a long tradition of medieval performance in York.

79. Festival Program of 1988, *York Festival Collection*, York City Library. That year Jude Kelly took the performers of the plays into schools and community centers.

80. Zygmunt Bauman, *Postmodern Ethics*, p. 241.

81. Samuel, *Theatres of Memory*, p. 8. Fradenburg has recently provided us with an analysis, based on the psychoanalysis of mourning, of the losses that structure our forms of desire for the Middle Ages. The textual object of medieval studies, she claims, "has acquired its value insofar as it is, in some profound way, lost to us by its very pastness; critical and scholarly acts accordingly gain their legitimacy by means of reparation, by making up for that loss, by recovering an impossible relation to the alterity of the West's own past" (Fradenburg, "Voice Memorial, p. 173). However, such a sense of loss is not merely a nasty habit of a few medieval scholars, though medievalists may enact it out with exemplary force. Indeed, the reasons that might distinguish the loss of a past identified as "medieval" from the historical identification of other pasts remain to be specified and explored. The "sense of loss" identified by Fradenburg is in fact part of a much wider debate on contemporary structures of temporality, as Samuel's own work so richly suggests.

82. Samuel, *Theatres of Memory*, p. 8.

83. For trauma as a symptom of historiography, see Cathy Carruth, ed., *Trauma: Explorations in Memory*, p. 5. For Carruth, it is the simultaneous and total literality of the flashback in trauma and the necessary delay in knowing that constitute trauma as a pathology of history itself: "The traumatized, we might say, carry an impossible history within them, or they become themselves the symptom of a history they cannot entirely possess" (p. 5).

84. Terdiman, "Deconstructing Memory," p. 35.

85. Wendy Wheeler, "After Grief? What Kinds of Inhuman Selves?" p. 90.

86. Adapted from Eric Santner's aphorism: "Mourning without solidarity is the beginning of madness" (Santner, *Stranded Objects*, p. 26). For further reflections on the necessity to make distinctions that enable qualitative judgments about both past cultures and our own relation to their pastness, see my brief comments on psychoanalysis and medieval studies in an earlier version of this chapter in *Journal of Medieval and Early Modern Studies* 26, no. 2 (spring 1996), p. 371. Here I argue, following Terdiman, that psychoanalysis must itself be understood as part of a "memory crisis," which complicates "the apartheid of fact and interpretation that some forms of contemporary analysis gesture

toward in their facile reduction of all historicisms, with consequent scorn for the empirical, to positivism. Not all historicisms are positivisms: not all forms of reparation are forms of disavowal."

CHAPTER TWO

1. Dorinda Outram, *The Body and the French Revolution*, p. 1.

2. Alexandra Johnston reminds us that we need to think in terms of discrete Passion and Resurrection sequences rather than the full cycle, for the records indicate that this was in fact the most common mode of production in England as a whole ("The Continental Connection: A Reconsideration," paper presented at "The Stage as Mirror: Civic Theatre in Late Medieval Europe" [Penn State, March 1993]. Reprinted in Alan E. Knight, ed., *The Stage as Mirror: Civic Theatre in Late Medieval Europe*).

3. *York Plays*, p. 371.

4. These questions are the ones used by Cornelius Castoriadis to describe the necessary "social imaginary" through which any society is instituted. See his *The Imaginary Institution of Society*, translated by Kathleen Blamey, pp. 146-47, and below.

5. Aquinas, *Commentary on Aristotle's Politics*, translated by Susan Ziller, Cary Nederman, and Kate Langdon Forhan, in *Medieval Political Theory—A Reader: The Quest for the Body Politic 1100-1400*, edited by Cary Nederman and Kate Langdon Forhan (London: Routledge, 1993), p. 137.

6. Mervyn James, "Ritual, Drama and Social Body in the Late Medieval English Town," p. 4.

7. James specifically cites Mary Douglas, *Natural Symbols: Explorations in Cosmology*, on p. 6 of "Ritual, Drama and Social Body."

8. Sometimes it must be said that the subtle and dynamic complexity of James's article is reduced in its reproduction. See, for example, Eamon Duffy's recent invocation of James to underwrite his location of "traditional religion" in the late Middle Ages: "Mervyn James has written eloquently of the way in which the Corpus Christi procession in late medieval communities 'became the point of reference to which the structure of precedence and authority in the town is made visually present.' This was the 'social miracle', the sacramental embodiment of social reality" (Eamon Duffy, *The Stripping of the Altars: Traditional Religion in England c. 1400-c. 1580*, p. 11). It is possible to see in this sentence the swift move from "late medieval communities" to, in James's words, "the structure of precedence and authority in the town" to Duffy's "social reality" itself. In the process there is an erasure of an understanding of the mechanisms of representation by which the part has come to stand for the whole.

9. See also Charles Phythian-Adams's pioneering discussion of ceremony in the "life-cycle" of the Coventry citizen in "Ceremony and the Citizen: The Communal Year at Coventry, 1450-1550," in *Crisis and Order in English Towns, 1500-1700*, edited by Peter Clark and Paul Slack, p. 106, where the "fit" that functionalism describes between social structure and expressive form is eluci-

dated: "This exploratory analysis will seek first to demonstrate some simple congruities between Coventry's late medieval social structure (that relatively enduring but adaptable framework of institutionalized positions and connective relationships) and its ceremonial or ritualized expression in action, in time—with respect to the local calendar—and on the ground." In the process Phythian-Adams explains that in his examination of the "perennial" customs of Coventry 1450–1550, "known structural modifications . . . have to be sacrificed at the altar of brevity" (p. 106). But given Phythian-Adams's dense and pioneering analysis and the development in book-length form of the role of ceremony in Coventry, it is, I would say, the altar of synchrony, rather than brevity, that underlies the principle of omission. Phythian-Adams has recently reconceptualized some of the problems of the very versions of community and locality of which he was such an eloquent exponent in his *Rethinking English Local History*. See especially p. 25, where he discusses the difficulty of the relation between function and structure in the local historian's designation of his or her object of study: "Having defined a territory and then having discovered a community within it, the danger is that he will relate the community once again to the territory."

10. For a recent wide-ranging and interesting discussion of one possible way of conceiving the interrelation between ritual and theater, see Anthony Gash, "Carnival and the Poetics of Reversal," in *New Directions in Theatre,* edited by Julian Hilton, p. 93, which I also explore in chapter 7. Gash criticizes both Barber's understanding of "festive comedy" and Donaldson's understanding of "the world upside down" and more recent new historicist understandings of "staging carnival" for an insufficient observation of the distinctions between ritual and theater. Gash develops a poetics of reversal from a nuanced reading of Bakhtin, Empson, and Rossiter.

11. The reference to the "phenomenological dichotomy" of the actor's body is from John Harrop, *Acting,* p. 80.

12. Mervyn James does not look at the possibilities of staging, or at the version of the pageants that we have in the Register. This is a constitutive, structural omission, rather than an accident or oversight. His model of ritual cannot read theatrical practices, because those practices complicate functionalism's understanding of social orders as social systems. For Mervyn James, "this structure projected the nature of the society whose world view it expressed" (James, "Ritual, Drama and Social Body," p. 16). Where James talks about the play cycle, he uses it to distinguish that part of the festivity from the more rigid and hierarchical principles at work in the procession. The argument is that the "temporal mutation" within the urban body could work itself out through the more fluid medium of the play cycle as a "necessary complement to the Corpus Christi procession, which defined the static order prevailing in the urban world" (p. 18). James is quite clear, then, that the play cycle as the means of registering change "provided a mechanism by means of which status, and the honour which went with status, could be distributed and redistributed with a

minimum of conflict resulting" (p. 18). The play cycle is the vehicle of diachrony precisely so that the procession itself can reveal "the static order prevailing in the urban world" (p. 18). But it is only by conceptually separating the synchronic from the diachronic, that such an "order" can be analytically understood. It is temporal change itself that is the price James's model pays for its location of order.

13. See Catherine Bell, "Discourse on Dichotomies: The Structure of Ritual Theory," pp. 97–98. For the famous and founding Durkheimian distinction between belief and rite, see Emile Durkheim, *The Elementary Forms of the Religious Life*, translated by Joseph Ward Swain, p. 51.

14. See Lynn Hunt, "The Sacred and the French Revolution," in *Durkheimian Sociology: Cultural Studies*, edited by Jeffrey C. Alexander, p. 27. Mary Douglas's brilliant conceptualization of the interactions between body and society are usefully discussed by Jean Comaroff and John Comaroff, "Bodily Reform as Historical Practice," in *Ethnography and the Historical Imagination*, p. 79. For an inspired reexamination of Douglas's central paradigm, see Peter Stallybrass and Allon White, *The Politics and Poetics of Transgression*.

15. It is possible that there is some degree of self-consciousness here about the pursuit of a preordained script. Such self-consciousness may be particularly acute at those moments of transition from "old" to "new"; see especially The Annunciation and the Visitation, *York Plays*, pp. 110–17; The Purification, pp. 149–60; and Christ and the Doctors, pp. 174–81. The commitment of the play texts to the Register and the "keeping" of the Register are very much in the interests of oligarchic control against *ex tempore* performance and traditions of improvisation.

16. See Alexandra Johnston, "The York Corpus Christi Play: A Dramatic Structure Based on Performance Practice," in *The Theatre in the Middle Ages*, edited by Herman Braet, Johan Nové, and Gilbert Tournoy, p. 372, where she describes the way the Entry into Jerusalem pageant is modeled along the lines of a royal entry, and for further discussions on the Entry, see chapter 6.

17. Durkheim, *Elementary Forms*, p. 94.

18. Castoriadis, *The Imaginary Institution of Society*, p. 140. For Castoriadis's refutation of the adequacy of functionalism, see pp. 119, 124, 130, 136. See especially p. 122: "A functionalist may consider it self-evident that, when a society provides itself with an institution, it gives itself at the same time, as something it can grasp, all the symbolical and rational relations that this institution carries or produces—or at any rate, that there can be no contradiction, no incoherence between the functional 'ends' of the institution and the effects of its actual functioning, that whenever a rule is set down, the coherence of each of its innumerable consequences with the set of all the other previously existing rules and with the ends that are consciously or 'objectively' sought is guaranteed." Castoriadis's words above may be read as an extended gloss on Durkheim's statement "God is only a figurative expression of the society" (Durkheim, *Elementary Forms of Religious Life*, p. 226, taking that statement in

an uncharacteristically [for the Durkheiminan tradition] nonfunctionalist direction).

19. Castoriadis, *The Imaginary Institution of Society*, p. 138. And see Kenneth Burke, *The Rhetoric of Religion*, p. 15, for the necessary link between indeterminacy, polysemousness, and the simultaneous foundation and antifoundation established through "God" in the symbolic system: "Since 'God' by definition transcends all symbol systems, we must begin, like theology, by noting that language is intrinsically unfitted to discuss the 'supernatural' literally. For language is empirically confined to terms referring to physical nature, terms referring to socio-political relationships and terms describing language itself. Hence all words for 'God' must be used analogically—as were we to speak of God's 'powerful arm' (a physical analogy), or of God as 'lord.'"

20. Pierre Bourdieu, *Outline of a Theory of Practice*, translated by Richard Nice, p. 110.

21. Catherine Bell, *Ritual Theory, Ritual Practice*, p. 125. The influence of this work on the formulations I am making here is pervasive.

22. Bourdieu, *Outline of a Theory of Practice*, p. 120.

23. See Henrietta Moore's use of Bourdieu in *Space, Text and Gender: An Anthropological Study of the Marakwet of Kenya*, p. 77.

24. See William Paden, "Before the 'Sacred' Became Theological: Rereading the Durkheimian Legacy," pp. 11, 14, 17. See also Durkheim's analysis of the "churinga," in *Elementary Forms*, p. 141; and Jonathan Z. Smith's comments on these passages in *To Take Place: Toward Theory in Ritual*, pp. 106–7.

25. Smith, *To Take Place*, p. 105.

26. The sermon is from MS Royal 18 B. xxiii and is reprinted in *Middle English Sermons*, edited by Woodburn O. Ross. Early English Text Society, o.s., 209 (London: Humphrey Milford, 1940), pp. 61–69.

27. These binary oppositions are not cognitively understood schemata but learned through the bodily practice through which that space comes to have meaning in the first place.

28. Bell, *Ritual Theory*. See also Bourdieu, *Outline of a Theory of Practice*, p. 120.

29. *York Plays*, p. 345.

30. *York Plays*, p. 330. The rest of the passage is worth quoting in full: "Full clerly consayue þus I can / No cause in þis corse couthe þei knowe, / Ʒitt doulfull þei demyd hym þan / To lose þus his liffe be þer lawe, / No riȝte. / Trewly I saie / Goddis sone verraye / Was he þis daye, / Þat doulfully to dede þus is diȝt."

31. What possible kind of proof does this constitute in theater's simulation of miracle in any case?

32. See Burke, *The Rhetoric of Religion*, p. 2: "For regardless of whether the entity named 'God' exists outside his nature sheerly as a key term in a system of terms, words 'about him' must reveal their nature as words."

33. By far the most sophisticated, imaginative, and compelling version of

ritual as formalized repetition is articulated in Maurice Bloch, *Ritual, History and Power: Selected Papers in Anthropology*. His version of ritual restricts its usage as a "special strategy" of "traditional authority" (p. 45). The literature on ritual is now vast. For a preliminary survey that usefully reviews "the turn to history" and the questions it has raised for anthropology, see John Kelly and Martha Kaplan, "History, Structure, and Ritual," pp. 119-50.

34. One would have to think at length about the significance of the commitment of the "originals" to text in the Register and of the tensions around *ex tempore* performance frequently expressed in the records of performances to explore this more fully. I wish to stress here, though, that the Durkheimian model of ritual as expounded in James has not much room for such examinations.

35. Robert Weimann, *Shakespeare and the Popular Tradition in the Theatre*, p. 77.

36. Weimann, *Shakespeare and the Popular Tradition*, p. 80.

37. But see Peter Travis, "The Social Body of the Dramatic Christ in Medieval England," and Clare Sponsler's recent book, *Drama and Resistance: Bodies, Goods, and Theatricality in Late Medieval England*.

38. Bourdieu, *Outline of a Theory of Practice*, p. 73.

39. Peter McLaren, "On Ideology and Education: Critical Pedagogy and the Politics of Empowerment," pp. 175 ff.

40. Lawrence Grossberg, "Teaching the Popular," in *Theory of the Classroom*, cited in McLaren, "On Ideology and Education," p. 175.

41. Connerton, *How Societies Remember*, p. 102. He goes on to say: "They will know how well the past can be kept in mind by habitual memory sedimented in the body."

42. The most concerted and developed attempt to work through an analysis of the city as stage to date is the chapter on the York cycle in Stevens's *Four Middle English Mystery Cycles*, pp. 17-87.

43. *REED: York*, vol. 1, pp. 11-12, and translation, vol. 2, pp. 697-98. For a detailed examination of the stations of the York Corpus Christi play over the course of its performance, see Anna J. Mill, "The Stations of the York Corpus Christi Play," pp. 492-502; Meg Twycross, " 'Places to Hear the Play': Pageant Stations at York, 1398-1572," pp. 10-33; Eileen White, "Places for Hearing the Corpus Christi Play in York," pp. 23-63; and White's unpublished doctoral dissertation, "People and Places: The Social and Topographical Context of Drama in York 1554-1609" (University of Leeds, 1984). See also David Crouch's essay, "Paying to See the Play: The Stationholders on the Route of the York Corpus Christi Play in the Fifteenth Century," pp. 64-111, read after this chapter was completed.

44. *REED: York*, vol. 2, p. 714; *York Memorandum Book: 1376-1419* (hereafter *YMB*), edited by Maud Sellers (Durham, Eng.: Surtees Society, 1914), vol. 125, p. xlv, and Latin, p. 64: "cum unus quisque juxta statum suum onus sum portet pro ipso ludo sustinendo, unanimiter, igitur, ordinaverunt pro utilitate

communitatis quod loca ad ludendum ludum predictum mutentur, nisi ipsi, ante quorum loca antea ludebatur, aliquod certum quid solverint communitati pro ipso comodo suo singulari sic annuatim habendo, et quod in omnibus annis sequentibus, dum ludus ille ludi contingerit, ludatur ante ostia et tenementa illorum, qui uberius et melius camere solvere et plus pro commodo tocius communitatis facere voluerint pro ludo ipso ibidem habendo, non impendendo favorem alicui persone pro aliquo commodo singulari, sed tantum quod consideretur utilitas publica tocius communitatis Ebor."

45. Phythian-Adams, "Ceremony and the Citizen," p. 63.

46. *REED: York*, vol. 2, pp. 713–14. *YMB*, vol. 125, p. 63: "nichilominus maior, probi homines et tota communitas predicta eorum unanimi consensu et assensu ordinarunt quod omnes illi qui pro skafaldis, quas ante eorum ostia super solum communitatis edificant in locis predictis, de supersedentibus monetam recipiunt, solvant tercium denarium monete sic recepte camerariis civitas, ad usum communitatis ejusdem applicandum. . . ."

47. Richard Homan, "Ritual Aspects of the York Cycle," pp. 313. And see his adjacent comments, where he states that the festival of Corpus Christi must be looked at "as a microcosm of the political and economic structure of the town in which economic inequalities, unresolvable in fact, could be resolved, and most importantly, in which the central anomaly of the city government could be ritualistically put right" (p. 313). Homan's formulation here is surely a very precise instance of the way in which functionalist ritual theory conceives of cultural facts as working in support of a structure that preexists their articulation. As Robert Ulin puts it: "The intersubjective constitution of meaning of cultural facts is reified as logically reconstructed rules for the technical maintenance of a total social system" (*Understanding Cultures: Perspectives in Anthropology and Social Theory*, p. 19). The effect of such constitution is to render totality "coincident with nature" (p. 20).

48. Most of the station lists are derived from entries in the Chamberlains' Books, which give the amounts paid by householders for having the play performed before their house; see White, "Places for Hearing," p. 48.

49. Cited in David Frisby, *Simmel and Since: Essays on Georg Simmel's Social Theory*, p. 105, from "The Sociology of Space," originally published as "Soziologie des Raumes," *Jahrbuch für Gesetzgebung, Verwaltung und Volkswirtschaft* 27 (1903): 27–71.

50. Thus it accentuates the already contradictory space of the street. For an analysis of the street facade's function, see James Holston, *The Modernist City: An Anthropological Critique of Brasilia*, p. 118: "It defines by containment and separation interior and exterior, private and public, house and street (and all that is associated with these contrasting domains of social life) and yet provides for numerous kinds of passages between them. As a selectively porous divider, therefore, the street facade constitutes a liminal zone of exchange between the domains it holds apart."

51. See Mill, "Stations," p. 493. Also see White, "Places for Hearing";

Twycross, "'Places to Hear the Play'"; and Crouch, "Paying to See the Play." The uniformity and stasis of the stations from year to year has been exaggerated.

52. Most extensively by Martin Stevens.

53. Mill, "Stations," p. 492.

54. *YMB*, vol. 120, p. 47. The pageants should be played "in locis antiquitus assignatis et non alibi sed ut sicut premunientur per maiorem ballivos et ministros suos."

55. See Mill, "Stations"; Twycross, "'Places to Hear the Play"; and White, "Places for Hearing."

56. E. Miller, "Medieval York," in *Victoria History of the Counties of England: A History of Yorkshire, the City of York*, edited by R. B. Pugh, p. 38.

57. Miller, "Medieval York," p. 38. In addition, Miller tells us that in 1250 the king's justices were forbidden to try pleas concerning the minster or its tenants anywhere but at the minster door.

58. See Douglas Cowling, "The Liturgical Celebration of Corpus Christi in Medieval York," pp. 5–9, for details of the competing Corpus Christi processions in York. As well as the procession regulated by the corporation of the city, there were two other processions, one associated with the Minster and one associated with St. Mary's Abbey (pp. 6–7).

59. Miller, "Medieval York," p. 38.

60. Miller, "Medieval York," p. 315.

61. Miller, "Medieval York," p. 315. They had to be requested again in 1485.

62. See François Laroque, *Shakespeare's Festive World: Elizabethan Seasonal Entertainment and the Professional Stage*, translated by Janet Lloyd, p. 14.

63. E. P. Thompson, *Customs in Common: Studies in Traditional Popular Culture*, p. 98.

64. For a fascinating analysis of the relation between Corpus Christi and Rogation processions, see Steven Justice, *Writing and Rebellion: England in 1381*.

65. Thompson, *Customs in Common*, p. 98.

66. Thompson, *Customs in Common*, p. 100.

67. Laroque, *Shakespeare's Festive World*, p. 13. The literal imprinting on physical memory is often effected by means of beating—especially children, who will carry the limits, the bounds, into the future and so ensure their contours, or by tripping them up by the heels, hence "beating the bounds" (p. 13).

68. Thompson, *Customs in Common*, pp. 127, 135. Enclosure is thus, as Thompson classically describes it, the "climax" of this reification of usages as properties (p. 136). Roger Manning reminds us that there is no "clear and unqualified" definition of property in any legal dictionary or works of any legal writer before the eighteenth century (*Village Revolts: Social Protest and Popular Disturbances in England 1509–1640*, p. 5).

69. Laroque, *Shakespeare's Festive World*, p. 13.

70. Keith Thomas, *Religion and the Decline of Magic*, p. 72.

71. David Underdown, *Revel, Riot and Rebellion: Popular Politics and Culture in England 1603–1660*, p. 47.

72. Thompson, *Customs in Common*, p. 175. At least, Thompson so defines it "at the point when commons were enclosed."

73. *REED: York*, vol. 1, p. xvi; and p. 263: "Item it is agreyd that Master Shyrryffes of this Citie shall Ryde uppon Corpuscristy day with men in hernesse accordyng to the ancyent Custome of this said Citie."

74. See Miller, "Medieval York," pp. 82–84.

75. Miller, "Medieval York," p. 83. It was Richard III who seemed to spark off the incident of 1484 when he asked the council to give up common rights in a close belonging to St. Nicholas Hospital. The council agreed with the provision "if the commons will agree to the same." The commons disagreement took the unequivocal form of a riot. See *York Civic Records*, edited by Angelo Raine, 8 vols. (Wakefield: York Archeological Society Record Series, 1938–52), vol. 1, pp. 89, 102–5.

76. Miller, "Medieval York," p. 83.

77. Miller, "Medieval York," p. 83, *York Civic Records*, vol. 1, pp. 107–23. The leading rioters were imprisoned by the mayor, and under pressure from the king, who threatened to replace the civic authorities unless they could keep the peace, the council and the commonalty relinquished their common rights in Vicars Lease.

78. The classic account of the redefinition of property in the seventeenth century is C. B. Macpherson, *The Political Theory of Possessive Individualism: Hobbes to Locke*. See also his "Capitalism and the Changing Concept of Property," in *Feudalism, Capitalism and Beyond*, edited by Eugene Kamenka and R. S. Neale, p. 105, where the conceptualization of property under precapitalist conditions is discussed: "a) Whereas in pre-capitalist society property was understood to comprise common as well as private property, with the rise of capitalism the idea of common property drops virtually out of sight and property is equated with private property—the right of a natural or artificial person to exclude others from some use or benefit of something. b) Whereas in pre-capitalist society a man's property had generally been seen as a right to a revenue, with capitalism property comes to be seen as a right in or to material things, or even as the things themselves. c) There is a change in the rationale or justification of private property; before capitalism, various ethical and theological grounds had been offered; with the rise of capitalism, the rationale came to be that property was a necessary incentive to the labour required by the society."

79. See Don Handelman, *Models and Mirrors: Towards an Anthropology of Public Events*, pp. 9, 12.

80. David Harvey, *The Condition of Postmodernity*, p. 239. Harvey develops four dimensions of spatial practice: accessibility and distantiation, appropriation of space, domination of space, and production of space (see p. 222).

81. Harvey, *Condition of Postmodernity*, p. 385. The classic text here is Henri Lefebvre, *The Production of Space*, translated by Donald Nicholson-Smith.

82. The literature on festivity is increasing at a rapid pace. Here I confine myself to mentioning three recent works that examine the interrelationship between ritual and space in densely socially located ways. Roberto DaMatta effects a comparative analysis of carnival in Rio and New Orleans in his *Carnivals, Rogues and Heroes: An Interpretation of the Brazilian Dilemma*, translated by John Drury. Mono Ozouf provides a nuanced Durkheimian reading of the reconfiguration of festivity in the French Revolution in the brilliant *Festivals and the French Revolution*, translated by Alan Sheridan. Finally Don Handelman examines the Palio of Siena in his *Mirrors and Models*, pp. 116–35, as part of the development of an anthropology of public events. The power of these analyses is that though they are interested in examining the material relations of power in festive space, they refuse to do so in terms of blanket or ahistorical descriptions of the essential activity of festival. To me, they are therefore exemplary models for the possibilities of reimagining the York Corpus Christi festivities.

83. See P. J. Goldberg, "Urban Identity and the Poll Taxes of 1377, 1379 and 1381," p. 197.

84. P. J. Goldberg, *Women, Work and Life-Cycle in a Medieval Economy: Women in York and Yorkshire, 1300–1520*, pp. 64 ff.

85. Mill, "Stations," p. 499. By 1486, she points out, it seems to be established that the Pavement, the last station, will be rent free. The station at the common hall, she says, is by the early years of the sixteenth century reserved for the mayor and aldermen. This of course precisely ties in with the decisive reorganization of the systems of representation in 1517 whereby a new common council was appointed in which the role of the merchant body increased at the expense of the manufacturing guilds. See Heather Swanson, *Medieval Artisans: An Urban Class in Late Medieval England*, p. 123; and Jennifer Kermode, "Merchants, Overseas Trade and Urban Decline: York, Beverley and Hull c. 1380–1500," pp. 51–73.

86. Goldberg, *Women, Work and Life-Cycle*, pp. 69 ff.

87. The Ousegate "kidcotes," the set of cells that are recorded at least in 1435 as standing beside the doorway of a chapel (Miller, "Medieval York," p. 92).

88. Goldberg, *Women, Work and Life-Cycle*, pp. 176–77. Also see Jean-Christophe Agnew's illuminating comments on the situatedness of markets in his *Worlds Apart: The Market and the Theater in Anglo-American Thought, 1550–1750*, p. 18: "These markets were, in every possible sense of the term, *situated* phenomena; that is to say, they were assigned to precise sites—in space and time—in societies where the particularities of place and season were intricately linked to the dominant patterns of meaning and feeling, and where the configuration of the landscape was itself used as a mnemonic repository of collective myth, memory, and practical wisdom."

89. Miller, "Medieval York," p. 81.

90. Miller, "Medieval York," p. 81.

91. Miller, "Medieval York," p. 81.

92. The point about performances outside Gysburn's door is inevitably speculative. The first records of performance are from 1376; the identification of Gysburn's house as a station is from a list of stations dating 1398–99 (see above). By then, Gysburn is of course long dead; see Miller, "Medieval York," p. 98, where he is cited as leaving money for the repair of bridges in 1385. We cannot know, then, if Gysburn's house was used as a station during his life and hence before the time it appears in the records. It remains a possibility that Gysburn's house served as a station in the 1380s. I am indebted to an anonymous reader for this point.

93. Doreen Massey, "A Global Sense of Place," in *Studying Culture: An Introductory Reader*, edited by Ann Gray and Jim McGuigan, p. 235. Place, as she puts it, will not then be "bounded, homogenized . . . having a special history based on a long internalized history but constructed out of a particular contestation of social relations." She articulates the critical consequences: "If places can be conceptualized in terms of the social interactions which they tie together, then it is also the case that these actions are not motionless things, frozen in time. They are processes" (p. 239). It is less likely, in this way of thinking, that place will be misidentified as community.

94. In the Purification pageant, the needlessness of the ritual for the purposes of purification is pointed out by Joseph, *York Plays*, p. 154. Mary insists on participating in the ritual to fulfill the law and as a "sample of mekenesse." In the Baptism pageant when John points out that Christ is clean and does not need to be baptized, Christ says that "Mankynde may noȝt unbaptymde go / Te endles blys." And since he is an example to mankind, he has to be baptized too (pp. 183–84). See also the Harrowing of Hell pageant, pp. 341–42.

95. *York Plays*, p. 341.

96. In chapters 4–6, I attempt a theological reading that is also sensitive to social and dramatic form.

97. I am borrowing lines here from the conclusion to my book *Christ's Body: Identity, Culture and Society in Late Medieval Writings*.

98. Moore, *Space, Text and Gender*, p. 170.

99. For Bourdieu's decisive rejection of the location of incorporation at the level of representations such as body image, see his *The Logic of Practice*, translated by Richard Nice, pp. 72–73.

100. Tadeusz Kowzan defines the art of performance in ways that resonate with this discussion of ritualization: "This is what the circumscribed definition of performance implies: a work of art which must, by necessity, be communicated in time and space" *Littérature et Spectacle*, p. 24).

101. Maurice Merleau-Ponty, *The Visible and the Invisible*, edited by Claude Lefort (Evanston, Ill.: Northwestern University Press, 1968), p. 48.

102. See DaMatta, *Carnivals, Rogues and Heroes*, p. 62, for a discussion of ritual in relation to Marx's *camera obscura* image of ideology in *The German Ideology*: "In all ideology men and their relations appear upside down as in a *cam-*

era obscura" (*The German Ideology*, in *Collected Works*, vol. 5, p. 36). See also Tony Gash's discussion of this same image in relation to the characteristic role of reversal as it is ascribed to ritual, in "Carnival and the Poetics of Reversal," p. 94. Stuart Hall discusses ritual as a "metaphor of transformation" in his memorial essay for Allon White in *Carnival, Hysteria and Writing: Collected Essays and Autobiography*, pp. 1–25, in relation to the theme of "the festival of revolution," especially pp. 1–2.

CHAPTER THREE

1. For the comparative figures, see Nigel Goose, "English Pre-Industrial Urban Economies," pp. 24–25; Charles Phythian-Adams, *The Fabric of the Traditional Community*, fig. 5, p. 16. Goldberg estimates that roughly one-fifth of the "economically active population" was employed in the manufacture and sale of food and drink, and more than half in occupations associated with leather or metal crafts, textiles, clothing, or mercantile trades collectively (Goldberg, "Urban Identity," p. 213, and table 8, p. 211). See also D. M. Palliser, "The Trades Guilds of Tudor York," in *Crisis and Order in English Towns 1500–1700*, edited by Peter Clark and Paul Slack. It is, of course, not, strictly speaking, possible to treat manufacture as a specialism separate from trade in the urban market of the late Middle Ages, but it is in the interests of the merchant class to separate them as much as possible, since mercantile dominance establishes itself on the basis of establishing a position as both suppliers of raw materials and distributors of products. The handicraftsmen and retailers did not necessarily concede the point of view of mercantile wholesalers. David Harris Sacks describes the viewpoint of Bristol's craftsmen who "rather than seeing the conduct of trade as a separate craft, . . . saw it as an aspect of every craft" (Sacks, "The Corporate Town and the English State: Bristol's 'Little Businesses' 1625–1641," p. 92). For them, the freedom of the city precisely meant the freedom to trade, and they regarded mercantile monopolizing as a usurpation of their ancient rights of citizenship. Although there is no purely economic separation, then, between trade and manufacture, the increasingly wide gap yawning between mercantile and trade guilds in York is central to articulating the class relations of the precapitalist economy of the city and to the role of the Corpus Christi productions in that articulation.

2. Peter Travis has written about the interconnection of the social, political, and economic through the figure of the body of Christ in "The Social Body of the Dramatic Christ in Medieval England," pp. 17–36. On the interrelation between the cultural form of the Corpus Christi cycles and their socioeconomic status, see also John Coldeway, "Some Economic Aspects of the Late Medieval Drama," in *Contexts for Early English Drama*, edited by Marianne G. Briscoe and John Coldeway, pp. 77–101; and Lawrence Clopper, "Lay and Clerical Impact on Civic Religious Drama and Ceremony," in *Contexts for Early English Drama*, edited by Briscoe and Coldeway, pp. 102–36.

3. Gary Larson, *The Far Side Gallery*.

4. Augustine, *City of God* 12.26; quoted in Christopher Kirwan, *Augustine.* Augustine is partly responding to Plato's statement in the *Timaeus* that "every cause that is an agent must be a craftsman." In the *City of God*, the problem of creation brings in train the difficult problem, origins—why did God decide to create the world when he did, for example; to phrase the question in the magnificent formulation of the *Confessions:* "What was God doing before he made heaven and earth?" (*Confessions*, Book II.10, p. 228). The problem of origin here inevitably entails the question of finitude, for to posit a beginning is to posit a point where God is not. See also Anselm's denial that God could be a craftsman in the *Monologium*, translated by Sidney Norton Deane (La Salle, Ill.: Open Court, 1951), p. 58; and Michael Camille, *The Gothic Idol: Ideology and Image-Making in Medieval Art*, pp. 27 ff.; and for a treatment that deals specifically with the issue of mimesis and fabrication in the mystery cycles as inaugurated in the Fall of Angels pageants, see Robert Hanning, "'You Have Begun a Parlous Play': The Nature and Limits of Dramatic Mimesis as a Theme in Four Middle English 'Fall of Lucifer' Cycle Plays," pp. 22–50. It is also worth remarking at this stage the way in which the Gospel of John echoes the opening lines of Genesis: "In the beginning was the Word, and the Word was with God, and the Word was God. The same was in the beginning with God. All things were made by him; and without him was not anything made that was made" (John 1:1–3). John is here suggesting that Christ also had no beginning, being coextensive with God. See David Lawton's comments in his *Faith, Text and History: The Bible in English*, p. 9.

5. *York Plays*, p. 53, ll. 158–59. Other references to "warke" occur in the same pageant at ll. 15–17. In the Creation pageant, the word occurs in one variation or another at ll. 49, 53, 94, 124, and 125.

6. See the comments made by Richard Beadle and Pamela King remarking on the puns on "mark(s)" (ll. 64, 68) and "craft" (l. 150) in *York Mystery Plays: A Selection in Modern Spelling* (Oxford: Clarendon Press, 1984), p. 15. My own sense of the linguistic slippage at work here is that it works to blur rather than to preserve the distinction between divine artificer and medieval craftsman.

7. *York Plays*, p. 79, l. 24.

8. See also here Richard Beadle, "The Shipwright's Craft," in *Aspects of Early English Drama*, edited by Paula Neuss, pp. 50–61. And for a recent contemplation of the role of work in the York cycle, see Kathleen Ashley, "Sponsorship, Reflexivity and Resistance: Cultural Readings of the York Cycle Plays," in *The Performance of Middle English Culture: Essays on Chaucer and the Drama in Honor of Martin Stevens*, edited by James J. Paxson, Lawrence M. Clopper, and Sylvia Tomasch, pp. 9–24.

9. *York Plays*, p. 82, ll. 150–51.

10. See the reference to Hugh of Saint Victor's hierarchy of creation/creativity that was to become standard in Camille, *The Gothic Idol*, p. 35.

11. *York Plays*, p. 54.

12. Hugh of Saint Victor, *On the Sacraments of the Christian Faith*, trans-

lated by Roy J. Deferrari (Cambridge, Mass.: Medieval Academy of America, 1951), p. 150.

13. *York Plays,* p. 67, l. 110.

14. Hugh of Saint Victor, *Didascalicon* I, translated by J. Taylor (New York: Columbia University Press, 1961), chap. 9, p. 55; cited in Camille, *The Gothic Idol,* p. 40. Camille's discussion is extremely pertinent to the issues discussed here (see pp. 27–73).

15. This guild had nothing to do with the official Corpus Christi pageants, but they did put on their own "pater noster" plays and so on. See Alexandra F. Johnston, "The Guild of Corpus Christi and the Procession of Corpus Christi in York," pp. 372–84.

16. Johnston, "The Guild," pp. 372–73.

17. "quapropter creatione. possessione et gubernatione de ipso primo corpore humano virtutum varietate sic dotato poterit dominus thematis verba verificare velut singulare unitatis presagium videlicet. *hoc est corpus meum*" (Paula Lozar, ed. and trans., "The 'Prologue' to the Ordinances of the York Corpus Christi Guild," pp. 100, 101).

18. "cuiuslibet creature rationalis per propagacionem genite primordiale principium omnimodam unitatem et concordiam creatam pro statu innocencie in se gerendo omnen discreciam seu rebellionem radicitus extirpando" (Lozar, "The 'Prologue,'" pp. 100, 101).

19. See Theresa Coletti, "Reading REED: History and Records of Early English Drama," in *Literary Practice and Social Change in Britain: 1380–1530,* edited by Lee Patterson, p. 275, for an examination of the interrelations between the guild and city in relation to shared access to a Corpus Christi shrine whose keys were held by the guild.

20. My reading here differs from Coletti, who sees such metaphors as expressing the "paradoxical relation of wholeness and differentiation . . . central to the civic mythology of Corpus Christi" (Coletti, "Reading REED," p. 276).

21. For the terminology of the frequent term "*communitas*" in the civic documentation, see Maud Seller's comment in *York Memorandum Book: Vol. 1 (1376–1419),* p. iv. Susan Reynolds has criticized the way in which "communitas" is readily translated into the term "corporation" by constitutional historians and sees this as a function of nineteenth-century struggles for municipal reform and popular government (Reynolds, "Medieval Urban History and the History of Political Thought," pp. 14, 17). However, at stake for Reynolds is perhaps an even more deep-rooted organicist notion of medievalism, for, as she writes, "unlike people in the middle ages (so far as I understand the middle ages) we live in an age of ideological conflict about political principles" (p. 20). For two recent cogent critiques of the conceptions of community, medieval and modern, see R. M. Smith, "'Modernization' and the Corporate Village Community in England: Some Skeptical Reflections," in *Explorations in Historical Geography,* edited by A. R. H. Baker and D. Gregory, pp. 140–79, 234–45; and Miri Rubin, "Small Groups: Identity and Solidarity in the Late Middle

Ages," in *Enterprise and Individuals in Fifteenth-Century England,* edited by Jennifer Kermode, pp. 132–50. And finally for a recent examination of the organic analogy as it develops around the concept of *communitas,* see Anthony Black, *Political Thought in Europe: 1250–1450,* pp. 14–24.

22. Cited in Swanson, *Medieval Artisans,* p. 123. See also R. B. Dobson, "The Risings in York, Beverley and Scarborough, 1380–1," in *The English Rising of 1381,* edited by R. H. Hilton and T. H. Aston, p. 130, where he mentions the representatives of nearly all the craft guilds uniting in 1381 in opposition to the *probi homines* to create a formidable if temporary coalition of "all craftsmen, sellers of victuals and workmen (omnes artifices, victualium venditores et operarii) in the town." In fairness to Dobson, it should be noted that he is at pains to point out that such a coalition is unusual. Nevertheless I think that 1381 could only have been a ghastly specter of the kinds of corporate bodies that could form around political alliances utterly at odds with the fantasies of the ruling oligarchic body.

23. Richard Holt and Gervase Rosser, introduction to *The English Medieval Town: A Reader in English Urban History 1200–1530.* See John Merrington, "Town and Country in the Transition to Capitalism," in *The Transition from Feudalism to Capitalism,* introduction by Rodney Hilton, p. 178, who characterizes such "co-incidence of political and economic relations of subordination" as being grounded on and limited by "the overall parcellisation of sovereignty . . . which defined the feudal mode." On the relationship of the political and the economic generally within precapitalist societies, see Ellen Meiksins Wood, "Capitalism and Human Emancipation," pp. 3–20, and below.

24. So Marx in *Capital,* III, ch. 48, writes: "Capital is not a thing, but rather a definite social production relation, belonging to a definite historical formation of society, which is manifested in a thing and lends this thing a specific social character. . . . It is the means of production monopolised by a certain section of society, confronting living labour power as products and working conditions rendered independent of this very labour power, which are personified through this antithesis in capital. . . ." "Merchant capital," however, according to Marx, "cannot determine the basic nature of society, but rather superimposes itself upon societies whose essential character is determined independently of it. Merchant capitalism is not a definitive social and economic system, but rather a mechanism of control over the exchange of products for money" (p. 333). These distinctions are crucial in the Marxist historiography of the "transition from feudalism to capitalism." See Maurice Dobb, *Studies in the Development of Capitalism; The Transition,* Introduction by Hilton; and Robert Brenner's important articles with the ensuing arguments reprinted in *The Brenner Debates: Agrarian Class Structure and Economic Development in Pre-Industrial Europe,* edited by T. H. Aston and C. H. E. Philpin.

25. Merrington, "Town and Country," p. 181.

26. Rodney Hilton, *English and French Towns in Feudal Society: A Comparative Study*, p. 101.

27. Hilton, *English and French Towns in Feudal Society*, p. 101.

28. Swanson puts the case most forcefully, and with the most detailed attention to York, but the view is also articulated in Hilton, *English and French Towns in Feudal Society*, pp. 72, 101. R. B. Dobson, in a paper that I heard while drafting this chapter, is in substantial agreement with Swanson but believes that craft organizations could retain some residual political influence in the city (" 'Artificeres Belonging to Corpus Christi Plaie': The Social Context of the York Mystery Plays," delivered at "The Stage as Mirror" conference [Penn State, March 1993], and now published as "Craft Guilds and City: The Historical Origins of the York Mystery Plays Reassessed," in *The Stage as Mirror: Civic Theatre in Late Medieval Europe*, edited by Alan E. Knight, pp. 91–106). The literature on guilds is complex and conflicted, not least because of the difficulty in semantics — "guild" was not a self-ascribed term for the craft guilds. The conventional criticism defines three types of guild: mercantile guilds controlled trade, craft guilds oversaw industry, and religious guilds spiritually sustained their members. For these distinctions, see Benjamin McRee, "Religious Guilds and Civic Order: The Case of Norwich in the Late Middle Ages," p. 70 n. 2. The standard earlier works of reference are J. Toulmin Smith, *English Gilds*, Early English Text Society, o.s., no. 40 (London: Humphrey Milford, 1870); Charles Gross, *The Gild Merchant: A Contribution to British Municipal History*, 2 vols. (Oxford: Clarendon Press, 1890); Stella Kramer, *The English Craft Gilds: Studies in Their Progress and Decline* (New York: Columbia University Press, 1927). See also, Anthony Black, *Guilds and Civil Society in European Political Thought from the Twelfth Century to the Present*. I am grateful to Virginia Bainbridge for allowing me to read the opening chapter of her dissertation, before it was published as *Gilds in the Medieval Countryside: Social and Religious Change in Cambridgeshire c.1350–1558*, in which guild historiography is discussed. For a recent demurral to Swanson's thesis, see the two articles by P. J. Goldberg, "Craft Guilds, the Corpus Christi Play and Civic Government," in *The Government of Medieval York: Essays in Commemoration of the 1396 Royal Charter*, edited by Sarah Rees Jones, pp. 141–63, and "Performing the Word of God: Corpus Christi Drama in the Northern Province," in *Life and Thought in the Northern Church c. 1100–1700*, edited by Diana Wood, pp. 145–70.

29. Swanson, *Medieval Artisans*, p. 114. Swanson's book, a dense and detailed account of artisanal activities and relations in York, provides rich new material for any future readers of the York cycle. The argument is also made in succinct and abbreviated form in her article "The Illusion of Economic Structure: Craft Guilds in Late Medieval English Towns," pp. 29–48. Swanson establishes a prehistory for her argument in the work of Dobb, *Studies in the Development of Capitalism*, p. 97, and Mrs. J. R. Green [Alice Stopford], *Town*

Life in the Fifteenth Century, 2 vols. (London: Macmillan, 1894), vol. 2, pp. 145–57 (Swanson, "The Illusion," p. 30).

30. It is, as Swanson emphasizes, the erasure of the "vital role of women in the domestic production unit" that has been historically invisible and that partially accounts for the willingness to read the official civic version as economic reality (Swanson, *Medieval Artisans,* p. 6). Swanson stresses that the division of labor imposed by the merchant elite was everywhere transgressed: "Artisans worked in the service industries, kept livestock, ventured into the victualling trades, in short took every opportunity they could to make a little extra money. The diversity of their work disappears in official records, perhaps intentionally, for the civic authorities fully recognized that it was by trade and not by manufacture that even a modest fortune was to be made" (p. 6). See Martha Howell, *Women, Production and Patriarchy in Late Medieval Cities,* for the positioning of women in the economies of late medieval urban life.

31. *Statutes of the Realm,* vol. 1, p. 379; Swanson, *Medieval Artisans,* p. 112. In his paper "Craft Guilds and City," Dobson suggests that the York mayor and aldermen were coming under increasing governmental pressure to rationalize craft guilds, partly as a response to the engrossing activities of the London grocers, who were developing a monopoly over foodstuffs.

32. Swanson, *Medieval Artisans,* p. 114. See also the excerpts from Knighton's Chronicle in *The Peasant's Revolt of 1381,* edited by R. B. Dobson (London: Macmillan, 1970), pp. 59 ff. N.B. Goldberg, *Women, Work and Life-Cycle,* p. 336, comments that women were specifically exempted from the statute of 1363.

33. The terminology here should make it plain that such a view works against the understanding of medieval towns as "non-feudal islands in a feudal sea" (M. M. Postan, *The Medieval Economy and Society,* p. 239), a view that, as Merrington says, reads "the progressive role of the urban bourgeoisie backwards into history" and poses the market as "the *only* dynamic force, the principle behind all movement, all change" (Merrington, "Town and Country," p. 173).

34. Swanson, *Medieval Artisans,* p. 113; and see her further comments on pp. 3 and 172: "Ultimately artisans have to be seen in terms of their relations with the merchants who formed the ruling elite; by organizing artisans into formal guilds, by excluding them from political power, the merchants gave definition to the artisan class." As Dobson points out, from the 1370s and 1380s onward, the governing body begins systematically to call in the ordinances of as many crafts as possible (Dobson, "Craft Guilds and City," p. 102). Examples of such ordinances registered in the *YMB* by the civic clerk are printed in *YMB,* vols. I and II. See also Swanson, *Medieval Artisans,* p. 112.

35. Swanson, "The Illusion," p. 43.

36. *YMB,* vol. 1, pp. 35–36, 39, ix; Swanson, *Medieval Artisans,* p. 121; *REED: York,* vol. 1, pp. x–xiii.

37. D. M. Palliser, *Tudor York,* p. 68. See also the introduction to *REED: York,* vol. 1.

38. Swanson, *Medieval Artisans*, p. 121. See also the comments of Champion in "The Gilds of Medieval Beverley," in *The Medieval Town in Britain*, edited by P. Riden, vol. 1, pp. 58–59, for further comments on the roles of the searchers in articulating the guilds as agents of town government.

39. Swanson, *Medieval Artisans*, p. 123. See also Jennifer Kermode, "Urban Decline? The Flight from Office in Late Medieval York," who discovers that the putative "flight from office" is less a symptom of "urban decline" than an example of a council "keeping the lower orders out of high civic office and making a profit at the same time" (p. 195).

40. Homan, "Ritual Aspects of the York Cycle," p. 121. It is quite unclear how the unresolvable "in fact" could be resolved in ritual. For a recent critique of such an account of ritual consensus, see Claire Sponsler, "The Culture of the Spectator: Conformity and Resistance to Medieval Performances," pp. 15–29; see also Kathleen Ashley's recent investigations of ritual theory in her introduction to a special issue of the *Journal of Ritual Studies* and the essay by Ashley and Pamela Sheingorn in that collection, "An Unsentimental View of Ritual in the Middle Ages or, Sainte Foy Was no Snow White," *Journal of Ritual Studies* 6, no. 1 (winter 1992): 63–85; see also Rubin's comments on James in her "Small Groups," p. 145, and my chapter 2.

41. There is no extant version of the sausagemakers' pageant, but there is an entry for 1432 in the *YMB* that mentions their pageant, The Hanging of Judas: "in qua representatur quod Judas Scarioth se suspendit et crepuit medius" (*YMB*, vol. 1, p. 155). It appears that the sausagemakers may have gone in for a bit of facetious and grotesque advertising for their trade by representing Judas's intestines as a string of sausages. For further details of such "advertising," see Alan Justice, "Trade Symbolism in the York Cycle," pp. 47–58.

42. Swanson, "The Illusion," p. 44; and see *YMB*, vol. 1, pp. 155–56.

43. *REED: York*, vol. 2, pp. 715–16. As Goldberg points out, the manufacture of tallow candles appears to be a "feminised craft," citing evidence from Coventry that wives manufacturing and selling candles in Coventry were also requested to make a contribution toward the smiths' pageant (Goldberg, *Women, Work and Life-Cycle*, p. 133).

44. See Swanson, *Medieval Artisans*, p. 173; and Dobson, "Craft Guilds and City."

45. For the fluctuating fortunes of the victualing industry in relation to the mercantile elite, see Swanson, *Medieval Artisans*, pp. 24–25. By the late fifteenth century, it was in fact impossible to keep the butchers out of office altogether.

46. *YMB*, vol. 2, p. xlvii.

47. Stevens, *Four Middle English Mystery Cycles*, p. 23. This episode becomes for Stevens emblematic of the "self-perpetuating civic institution generated by the Corpus Christi pageants" (p. 24).

48. Beadle describes the sources of funding: "yearly contributions from non-members of gilds who gained income from practising the skills of the

play-owning craft; special payments made on becoming a master in a play-owning craft, or on becoming a member of a gild: a percentage of fines levied for infringement of gild ordinances; and contributions from crafts which did not have plays in the cycle" (*York Plays*, p. 31); and see M. Rogerson, "The York Corpus Christi Play: Some Practical Details," pp. 97–101.

49. See, for example, *YMB*, vol. 1, pp. 66, 155–56, 185–86; vol. 2, pp. 102–4, 123–24, 167, 179, 297. *York Civic Records*, vol. 3, pp. 14, 47, 61, 65–66. See also Swanson, *Medieval Artisans*, p. 120.

50. Swanson, *Medieval Artisans*, p. 120.

51. Swanson points out, for example, that the bow stringers in York seem to have existed as a craft simply to make provision for the searchers (Swanson, "The Illusion," p. 43).

52. Swanson, "The Illusion," p. 44; and *YMB*, vol. 2, p. 104.

53. Dobson cites the example of Durham, where the town craftsmen were not formally organized at all before the middle of the fifteenth century. It was the organization of the Corpus Christi pageant that was the mechanism by which they were regulated and formalized (Dobson, "Craft Guilds and City," p. 100). He notes the similarity to the York case and suggests that between 1370 and 1470 the gradual internal consolidation of the structure of guilds is coincident with the development of the Corpus Christi plays.

54. See Swanson, "The Illusion," p. 47. The common council was henceforth to be constituted by major and minor crafts, the major crafts having two representatives and the minor crafts, one. Swanson points out that "major" and "minor" are in this instance "social and not economic distinctions," that is, political manipulations disguised as social categories to ensure economic dominance (p. 47). Such arguments indicate that we need to think through the relations between the categories of the "political" and the "economic," whose separation might itself be seen as a product of a capitalist social formation (see below).

55. For details about the Register, see *York Plays*, introduction. Kermode describes the transitions in import-export patterns of the merchant oligarchy in "Merchants, Overseas Trade, and Urban Decline," pp. 51–73.

56. Kermode, "Merchants, Overseas Trade, and Urban Decline," p. 58.

57. Beadle points out that we are aware of the activity of the common clerk in "keeping" the Register from between 1527 and 1554, and his presence at the first station of Corpus Christi from as early as 1501 (Beadle, "The York Cycle: Texts, Performances, and the Bases for Critical Enquiry," in *Medieval Literature: Texts and Interpretation*, edited by Tim William Machan, p. 107). His role was to check the plays he actually saw against the now authoritative Register, so it may be surmised that the commitment of the play texts to the Register is very much in the interests of oligarchic control, and of written texts over the habits of *ex tempore* performance and traditions of improvisation.

58. See above, n. 41.

59. Merrington, "Town and Country," p. 178.

60. Lee Patterson has been one of the few literary scholars who has incorporated the Marxist historiography of feudal relations into his map of late medieval literature; see "The *Miller's Tale* and the Politics of Laughter," in *Chaucer and the Subject of History*, pp. 247–54.

61. See Gerald Sider, *Culture and Class in Anthropology and History: A Newfoundland Illustration*, pp. 4–8, for an examination of the anthropological concept of culture; also cited in Beckwith, *Christ's Body*, Introduction, n. 11, from which I extrapolate the comments here; and see my article "Ritual, Church and Theatre: Medieval Dramas of the Sacramental Body," in *Culture and History: Essays on English Communities, Identities and Writing*, edited by David Aers, pp. 65–90, for an attempt at an account of *The Croxton Play of the Sacrament* in sociocultural terms and for a critique of the nostalgic sacramentalist holism that so often comes into play when the concepts Corpus Christi, culture, ritual, and "medieval" are put together.

62. Wood, "Capitalism and Human Emancipation," p. 12. Wood's most dense, brilliant, and careful arguing of these points takes place in an earlier article, "The Separation of the Economic and the Political in Capitalism," pp. 65–95. The "rigid conceptual separation of the 'economic' and the 'political,'" she writes, has "served *bourgeois* ideology so well ever since the classical economists discovered the 'economy' in the abstract and began emptying capitalism of its social and political content" (p. 66). Her reconsideration of the relation between base and superstructure is avowedly indebted to the "political" Marxism elucidated by Robert Brenner, whose articulation of "the origins of capitalism" emerges out of his consideration of "the unintended consequences of relations between non-capitalist classes, the outcome of which was the subjection of direct producers to the *imperatives* of competition, as they were *obliged* to enter the market for access to their means of subsistence and reproduction" (Ellen Meiksins Wood, *The Pristine Culture of Capitalism: A Historical Essay on Old Regimes and Modern States*, p. 10). For a further consideration of the relation between base and superstructure in relation, specifically to the questions of class raised by E. P. Thompson, see Ellen Meiksins Wood, "Falling through the Cracks: E. P. Thompson and the Debate on Base and Superstructure," in *E. P. Thompson: Critical Perspectives*, edited by Harvey Kaye and Keith McClelland, pp. 125–52.

63. See Stephen Rigby's discussion of the "fundamentalist" and "dialectical" version of "base and superstructure" and his comments at the end of his book *Marxism and History*, pp. 182–86, 301: ". . . whilst much of the most interesting Marxist historical work is concerned with pre-industrial society, it is precisely in this area of historiography that Marxism, with its emphasis on the social constraints on politics and ideology, has had least impact." Raymond Williams, in his seminal essay "Base and Superstructure in Marxist Cultural Theory," has put the matter best when he writes: "One of the unexpected con-

sequences of the base/superstructure model has been the too easy acceptance of models which appear less crude—models of totality or of the complex whole—but which exclude the facts of social intention, the class character of a particular society and so on" (Williams, *Problems in Materialism and Culture: Selected Essays*, p. 36).

64. John Brenkman's formulation in "Theses on Cultural Marxism," p. 25. See also the debate on economism, "cultural marxism," and socialist humanism, inaugurated by Richard Johnson's essay "Thompson, Genovese and Socialist-Humanist History," pp. 79–110; and the ensuing debates, especially Simon Clarke, "Socialist Humanism and the Critique of Economism," pp. 137–56. See also Harvey Kaye's account of this argument and its implications in *The British Marxist Historians: An Introductory Analysis*, pp. 18–22, and his chapters on Maurice Dobb and Rodney Hilton, pp. 23–69, 70–98, where both are read in terms of their contribution not only to historical studies, but also to a tradition of theoretical work. Kaye refutes Johnson's analysis of the break between economistic and cultural Marxism, and Dobb is a key figure in that refutation.

65. Miri Rubin has examined the historiography of medieval urbanity, questioning both the understanding of towns as "natural ceremonial spaces" and our conceptual reduction of them to a function and nature conceived either along the lines of "mentality" or market (Rubin, "Religious Culture in Town and Country: Reflections on a Great Divide," in *Church and City 1000–1500: Essays in Honour of Christopher Brooke*, edited by D. Abulafia, M. Franklin, and Miri Rubin, pp. 10, 20, 21).

66. For a discussion of the conceptualization of the interrelations of class, gender, and the concept of culture in British historical work, see Stuart Hall, "Marxism and Culture," pp. 5–14. In surveying the work of *History Workshop* as well as the contribution of the Centre for Contemporary Cultural Studies, he reminds us that "one of the most serious theoretical and intellectual problems confronting the new concern with culture is how to conceptualize the areas of ideology, culture and consciousness without giving way, slipping back, to idealism" (p. 8).

67. *York Plays*, ll. 25, 26, 47, 66, 127, 143, 153, 181, 240, 250, 261, and "trauayle," l. 300.

68. *York Plays*, p. 315, Pageant XXXV, l. 5.

69. *York Plays*, p. 322, l. 261. See chapter 4.

70. It is striking how in the world of devotional prose there are only two actors, Christ and the human worshiper of Christ. Though we are asked to identify with the suffering of Christ, we are never asked to look at the social agents of brutality as we are here in the York pageant of the Crucifixion (see chapter 4).

71. Brenkman, "Theses on Cultural Marxism," p. 30.

72. The formulation is again Brenkman's, "Theses on Cultural Marxism," p. 27.

CHAPTER FOUR

1. Sister Bernarda Jacques, "Ancient Magic Distilled: The Twentieth Century Productions of the York Mystery Plays," p. 348. For Browne's 1951 production, see also Elliott, *Playing God,* pp. 71–82, and my chapter 1.

2. Hugh of Saint Victor, *On the Sacraments of the Christian Faith,* p. 155.

3. This gap is theologically and ecclesiologically essential: to close it is always idolatrous and so utterly compromises the nature of the sacrament. In an Augustinian ecclesiology of the body of Christ, the church is a prefiguration of the *civitas dei* and will only be revealed eschatologically. Outward membership of the church is no guarantee of salvation; those who are not members of the visible church may in fact be among its members. I elaborate these points in chapters 5 and 6.

4. Humbert of Romans, *Sermones,* fol. 59rb; cited by Miri Rubin, *Corpus Christi: The Eucharist in Medieval Culture,* p. 36.

5. See Rubin, *Corpus Christi;* Beckwith, *Christ's Body;* and Gary Macy, "The Dogma of Transubstantiation in the Middle Ages," pp. 11–41.

6. See Thomas Aquinas, *Summa Theologiae* 3a.75.3, 3a.78.2–5, on the grammar of the words of consecration. All citations from the *Summa* are from the Blackfriars bilingual edition (London: Eyre and Spottiswoode, 1964–80). For recent meditations on the indeterminacy of *"hoc,"* see Robert Sokolowski, *Eucharistic Presence: A Study in the Theology of Disclosure,* p. 82; and Catharine Pickstock, *After Writing: On the Liturgical Consummation of Philosophy,* p. 261.

7. *Reg Gregory VII Das Register Gregors VII,* 2 vols., edited by E. Casper (Berlin: MGH Epistolae selectae II fasc. 1–2, 1920–23), VII, VI, 17a, II, pp. 426–77; cited in Rubin, *Corpus Christi,* p. 20. This famous document that becomes known as *Ego Berengarius* is quoted by Lanfranc, "Liber de corpore et sanguine domini, vol. 150, *Patrologiae cursus completus: series latina,* edited by J.-P. Migne (Paris, 1841–64), cols. 410D, 411A.

8. William Crockatt, *Eucharist: Symbol of Transformation,* pp. 116–17.

9. "Now faith has to do with unseen realities, and just as he offers his divinity to our acceptance as something that we do not see, so in this sacrament he offers his very flesh to us in like manner." In the Latin: "Et quia fides est invisibilium, sicut divinitatem suam nobis exhibet Christus invisibiliter, ita et in hoc sacramento carnem suam nobis exhibet invisibili modo" (Aquinas, *Summa Theologiae* 3a.75.1).

10. But for some recent demurrals, see Virginia Reinburg, "Liturgy and the Laity in Late Medieval and Reformation France," pp. 526–48; and Eamon Duffy, "Lay Appropriation of the Sacrament in the Later Middle Ages," pp. 53–68.

11. Camille, *The Gothic Idol,* p. 217; and see D. S. Devlin, "Corpus Christi: A Study in Medieval Eucharistic Theory, Development, and Practice," pp. 183–86; and V. L. Kennedy, "The Moment of Consecration and the Eleva-

tion of the Host," pp. 121–50; Edouard Dumoutet, *Le désir de voir l'hoste et les origines de la dévotion au saint-sacrement*, pp. 37–38, cites Odo's constitution: "Praecipitur presbyteris, ne cum in canone inceperint qui pridie tenentes hostiam nimis alte ita quod possit videri a populo sed quasi ante pectus detineant donec dixerint: 'Hoc est corpus' et tunc elevent eam ita quod possit ab omnibus videri."

12. Anthony Kubiak, *Stages of Terror: Ideology and Coercion as Theatre History*, p. 50.

13. Kubiak, *Stages of Terror*, p. 49. Kubiak sees theatricality as entirely bound up with the dialectic of appearance/reality rather than absence/presence. I hope to make this complex interrelationship pertinent to the histories of church, sacrament, and theater in more detail in the subsequent chapters.

14. J. L. Austin, *How to Do Things with Words.* "A peformative utterance will for example be in a peculiar way hollow or void if said by an actor on the stage." I will refrain from commenting on (and will take up in my next book) Jacques Derrida's words on this passage, which are by now one of the main conduits through which J. L. Austin passes into literary studies (Derrida, *Limited Inc.*, p. 16).

15. Discussed by Stephen Greenblatt in "Remnants of the Sacred in Early Modern England," in *Subject and Object in Renaissance Culture*, edited by Margreta de Grazia, Maureen Quilligan, and Peter Stallybrass, p. 341. When Aquinas analyzes sacraments, he *first* discusses them as signs: "Signs are given to men. Now it is characteristic of men that they achieve awareness of things they do not know through things which they do know. Hence the term 'sacrament' is properly applied to that which is a sign of some sacred reality pertaining to men; or—to define the special sense in which the term 'sacrament' is being used in our present discussion of the sacraments—it is applied to that which is a sign of a sacred reality inasmuch as it has the property of sanctifying men" (*Summa Theologiae* 3a.60.2).

16. "All that is on stage is a sign" (Jiri Veltrusky, "Man and Object in the Theater," in *A Prague School Reader on Esthetics, Literary Structure, and Style*, edited by Paul Garvin, p. 84; cited in Bert States, *Great Reckonings in Little Rooms: On the Phenomenology of Theater*, p. 19). See also Fernando de Toro, *Theatre Semiotics: Text and Staging in Modern Theatre*, translated by John Lewis, p. 70; Erika Fischer-Lichte, *The Semiotics of Theater*. For some elegant elaborations, see Umberto Eco's examination of the stage drunk's weaving between an icon, index, and symbol ("Semiotics of Theatrical Performance," pp. 107–17).

17. Herbert Blau, *Take Up the Bodies*, p. 249.

18. States, *Great Reckonings*, p. 34.

19. States, *Great Reckonings*, p. 20.

20. Keir Elam, *The Semiotics of Theatre and Drama*, pp. 21 ff.

21. Elam draws on the work of Charles Pierce, *Collected Papers*.

22. Elam, *The Semiotics of Theatre*, p. 29. More interestingly, States quotes

Peter Handke, saying, "In the theater light is brightness pretending to be other brightness, a chair pretending to be a chair and so on" (States, *Great Reckonings*, p. 20; from Peter Handke, *Kaspar and Other Plays*, translated by Michael Roloff, p. 10). And see also the powerful opening pages of Bruce Wilshire in his study of phenomenology and theater, *Role Playing and Identity: The Limits of Theatre as Metaphor*, pp. ix–xv. On the role of spatial and temporal deixis in theater, see Toro, *Theatre Semiotics*, pp. 13–14. Thanks to Jody Enders for recommending Bruce Wilshire's book to me.

23. See Jean Alter on the permanent co-presence of the performative and the referential, "experienced in the form of an inherent duality of theatrical activity; on the one hand, its reference to a story that takes place in a mental space outside the stage; on the other, its display of real performances on stage" (*A Sociosemiotic Theory of Theatre*, p. 31).

24. William Shakespeare, *The Two Gentlemen of Verona*, edited by Clifford Leech (London: Methuen, 1969) (Reprint, London: Thomas Nelson and Sons, 1997), 2.3.15 ff.

25. Elam, *The Semiotics of Theatre*, p. 14.

26. States, *Great Reckonings*, p. 34. For further comments on this *locus classicus* of theatrical theory, see Meredith Anne Skura, *Shakespeare the Actor and the Purposes of Playing*, pp. 160 ff.

27. Thanks to Phil Smith for recounting this tale to me. There are no doubt many other such stories that such an anecdote spawns. I welcome anecdotal evidence from my readers of other stage "accidents."

28. States, *Great Reckonings*, p. 36.

29. States, *Great Reckonings*, p. 40.

30. See Stanton Garner, *The Absent Voice: Narrative Comprehension in the Theater*, pp. 27–28.

31. Bert States, *The Pleasure of the Play*, p. 30.

32. Blau, *Take Up the Bodies*, p. 83. "Corpsing" is the word actors use to describe what happens when one actor makes another lose control, turning him, as Skura writes, "into a mere body no longer able to perform wonders" (*Shakespeare the Actor*, p. 27).

33. Stanton Garner, *Bodied Spaces: Phenomenology and Performance in Contemporary Drama*, p. 44.

34. Thomas Beard, *The Theatre of God's Judgements* (London, 1631); quoted in Anne Righter, *Shakespeare and the Idea of the Play*, p. 17. Righter comments that this "show" occasions three violent deaths and represents for Beard the vengeance of God, "who can endure nothing less than such prophane and ridiculous handling of so serious and heavenly matters." For a series of fascinating and unexplored references to the penitential ramifications of "playing" Christ in a "somer game," see Siegfried Wenzel, "Somer Game and Sermon References to a Corpus Christi Play," pp. 274–83.

35. Alter, *Sociosemiotic Theory*, p. 27.

36. See *Second Shepherd's Play,* Play 13 of *The Towneley Plays,* 2 vols., edited by Martin Stevens and A. C. Cawley, vol. 1, Early English Text Society, s.s., 13 (Oxford: Oxford University Press, 1994), pp. 126-57.

37. Weimann, *Shakespeare and the Popular Tradition,* p. 413.

38. Wakefield has six; Chester, four.

39. *York Plays,* p. 321.

40. States, *The Pleasures of the Play,* p. 76: "Everything that passes in theatre must be actable, as opposed to merely speakable."

41. *The Guardian,* 20 August 1997, p. 9.

42. This article did not rule out either murder or suicide. Jody Enders has recently explored the boundaries of violence in medieval theater in her book *The Medieval Theater of Cruelty: Rhetoric, Memory and Violence,* and in particular her article "Medieval Snuff Drama," where she discusses an incident in Tournai in which an actor playing Judith allegedly actually beheaded a convicted murderer who played Holofernes. Chapter 6 should make it clear that I do not think the York plays operate like the theaters of punishment Enders describes.

43. V. A. Kolvé, *The Play Called Corpus Christi.*

44. Smith's note reads, "Here the rubricator put twice 'ii Miles.'" As the previous order of the soldiers in speaking has been 1, 2, 3, 4, I have altered these two so as to continue that order, making what was I Miles at [1.105] to accord with it" (*York Plays,* edited by L. Toulmin Smith [Oxford: Clarendon Press, 1885], p. 352).

45. Martin Bartlett, "The York 'Crucifixio Cristi,'" p. 10. I am indebted to Bartlett's illuminating and precise exploration of this pageant for this point (*York Plays,* p. 317, ll. 97 ff).

46. Bartlett, "The York 'Crucifixio Cristi,'" p. 27.

47. Bartlett, "The York 'Crucifixio Cristi,'" p. 23.

48. The following are selections from the *Middle English Dictionary's* (*MED*) listings for the word "pinnen": "1. to fasten or affix with a pin, peg or nail, affix in a prominent position. 2. to pen, or impound, imprison, confine, and used figuratively of God, to restrain (his retribution). 3. to establish something firmly in position, wedge, fill in the joints of masonry with stone or mortar"; and for the verb "pinen": "1. to torment, to torture to death, to crucify, to torture someone so as to extract a confession. 2. to torment one's body as in penance, inflict penance on oneself, endure penance. 3. to cause pain, to hurt, to endure pain. 4. to cause somebody grief" (Sherman M. Kuhn, ed., *Middle English Dictionary, O–P,* p. 948). A "pinere" is a torturer; a "pinner," a maker of pins (pp. 950, 953). "Pining" is "inflicting torment, the suffering or torturing of Christ, and penitential suffering and penance."

49. Perhaps there is a notion latent here like the one developed by Aquinas out of John Damascene: that of the human life and nature of Christ as instrument of the divine person who has taken on that nature, Christ's humanity as God's perfect tool.

50. Paul Willis, "The Weight of Sin in the York Crucifixio," p. 114.

51. See René Girard, *Things Hidden Since the Foundation of the World*, p. 223: "The surest way to miss the link between the cure (the crucifixion and its aftereffects) and the disease (the structures of scapegoating violence upon which all human social arrangements have depended) is to read the passion story with an eye to locating and denouncing those most responsible for it. If the responsibility belongs only to some of us, we are back in the world of religious categories and scapegoats." See also Pamela King, "Spatial Semantics and the Medieval Theatre," in *The Theatrical Space*, vol. 9, *Themes in Drama*, edited by James Redmond, pp. 45-58.

52. For the concept of "standing in," see Wilshire, *Role Playing and Identity*, p. 23.

53. States, *Great Reckonings*, p. 110. And see Jerzy Grotowski, *Towards a Poor Theatre*.

54. Edward Schillebeeckx, *Christ: The Sacrament of the Encounter with God*.

55. See *Summa Theologiae* 3a.78.6 for the full sentence: "Et ideo signanter non dicit Dominus, 'Hic panis est corpus meum,' quod esset secundum intellectum secundae opinionis; neque, 'Hoc corpus meum est corpus meum,' quod esset secundum intellectum tertiae; sed in generali, 'Hoc est corpus meum,' nullo nomine apposito ex parte subjecti, sed solo pronomine, quod significat substantiam in communi sine qualitate, id est forma determinata."

CHAPTER FIVE

1. See Joseph Roach's resonant preface to his book *Cities of the Dead: Circum-Atlantic Performance*, p. xiii: "In the name of memory, I hope that I may be forgiven this nostalgia for presence on the plea that, as a practical matter, the voices of the dead may speak freely now only through the bodies of the living."

2. Fischer-Lichte, *The Semiotics of Theater*, p. 6; Stanley Cavell, *Disowning Knowledge in Six Plays of Shakespeare*, p. 116. This last quotation is taken from Cavell's astonishing essay "The Avoidance of Love," a meditation on Shakespearean tragedy as registering the philosophical and affective dimensions of skepticism. These views are developed in *The Claim of Reason: Wittgenstein, Skepticism, Morality and Tragedy*, esp. p. 428. For a consideration of the constitutive incompletion of theater discourse, see Anne Ubersfeld, *L'école du spectateur*, p. 11.

3. "Quem queritis" is a responsary sung during Easter mass reenacting the visit of the three Maries to the tomb of Christ after the crucifixion. It is often understood as constituting the "rebirth" of "Western drama." For comments on the *quem queritis* trope in this respect, see Kubiak, *Stages of Terror*, p. 48: "In the history of theatre's disappearance, in theatre's history *as* disappearance, the medieval theatrical silence suggests a particularly intriguing historical moment during which a body is seemingly positioned at theatre's focal/vanishing point. Indeed, the disappearance of theatre in the early middle ages and its reappearance within the medieval church—first in the ritualized drama of the

Mass, and later as the theatricalised trope known as the Quem Queritis—were realised through the performative magic of the absent/present body." For the difficulties of liturgical scholarship around the *quem queritis* trope, see Andrew Hughes, "Liturgical Drama: Falling between the Disciplines," in *The Theatre of Medieval Europe,* edited by Eckehard Simon, pp. 42-62. And for a recent discussion that came out too late for me properly to consider its findings in this study, see Michal Kobialka, *This Is My Body: Representational Practices in the Early Middle Ages.*

4. Paul Jones, *Christ's Eucharistic Presence: A History of the Doctrine,* p. 9. See also pp. 105, 111. The absent-presence/present-absence relation has recently been brilliantly revisited by Denys Turner in his essay "The Darkness of God and the Light of Christ: Negative Theology and Eucharistic Presence," in *Catholicism and Catholicity: Eucharistic Communities in Historical and Contemporary Perspectives,* edited by Sarah Beckwith. For Turner the eschatological temporality of eucharist as the glorified body is central to its absent-presence: ". . . Jesus has been raised and we have not. If, therefore, Jesus will always be with us, present, it can only be as he who is raised can be present to those who have not been raised—and being raised and not being raised are conditions of embodiment." See also Pickstock's comments in her *After Writing* on the eucharist as the undoing of the metaphysical dichotomy of absence and presence: "This genuine outwitting of metaphysical dichotomies is possible because, according to a reading of the Eucharist as an essential *action,* and not as an isolated presence or merely illustrative symbol, the (mystical) unknown is not reductively confined to a negative nothing—which amounts to the known—but is traversed as a genuinely open mystery which, by being partially imparted through the sign, and therefore recognizable *as* mystery, has a positive—but not fetishizable—content" (p. 253).

5. See my previous chapter and also Anthony B. Dawson, "Performance and Participation: Desdemona, Foucault and the Actor's Body," in *Shakespeare, Theory and Performance,* edited by James Bulman, pp. 29-45.

6. *OED.*

7. Rowan Williams, *Resurrection.* This is a central formulation of Williams's profound book; see especially his chapter "Memory and Hope: Easter in Galilee." Williams's thoughts have everywhere helped to shape my thinking on the Resurrection theater of Corpus Christi.

8. Williams, *Resurrection,* p. 41: "The resurrection of Jesus, then, is not simply the raising and restoration to the world of his past identity. . . . Equally importantly, it is the 'raising' of the past identity of those who have been with him. The risen truth shows us the self-deceptions which have drawn us into the vortex of destructiveness."

9. See, for example, the utterances about the benefit conferred by seeing the host in John Mirk, *Mirk's Festial: A Collection of Homilies by Johannes Mirkus,* edited by Theodor Erbe, Early English Text Society, e.s., 96 (London: Kegan Paul, Trench, Trübner, 1905), pp. 169-70; and David Aers and Lynn

Staley, *The Powers of the Holy: Religion, Politics, and Gender in Late Medieval English Culture,* pp. 26 ff.

10. Elaine Pagels, *The Gnostic Gospels,* p. 12; citing K. Holl, *Der Kirchen begriff des Paulus in seinem Verhaltnis zu dem der Urgemeinde,* in *Gesammelte Aufsätze zur Kirchengeschichte* (Tübingen: J. C. B. Mohr, 1921), vol. 2, pp. 50–51. See also Pagels, *Gnostic Gospels,* p. 12: "What the apostles experienced and attested their successors cannot verify for themselves; instead, they must only believe, protect, and hand down to future generations the apostles' testimony." For a further elucidation, see Elaine Pagels, "Visions, Appearances, and Apostolic Authority: Gnostic and Orthodox Traditions," in *Gnosis: Festschrift für Hans Jonas,* edited by B. Aland, pp. 415–30. Here Pagels specifies two traditions of interpretation of resurrection apparitions; an orthodox tradition expounded by Ignatius, Irenaeus, and Tertullian that attests the reality of resurrection and a gnostic, heretical tradition that uses the elements of New Testament tradition that lend themselves to interpretation as visions (p. 415).

11. Pagels, *Gnostic Gospels,* p. 30.

12. Thomas's failure is in demanding a special, individual assurance of resurrection, a proof other than the testimony of a group of believers (Williams, *Resurrection,* pp. 102–3). See centrally his argument that if the apparitions were "fundamentally experiences of restoring grace, they take their places in a concrete, shared human history of hope, betrayal, violence and guilt, and are 'evidenced' *not* by individual report but by the continuing existence of the community in which this history is caught up and redeemed" (p. 118). And for the crucial link between eucharist and resurrection, see pp. 118, 121. For some further reflections on the interrelationship between eucharist, forgiveness, community, and redemption, see Juan Segundo, *The Community Called Church,* pp. 15, 19, 25 ff., 45.

13. This is of course on the assumption that this gospel ends at 16:8. A longer ending was added some time in the second century C.E.

14. Luke 24:13–35; John 20:11–18; Matthew 27:28. In Luke, he also shows up behind locked doors, no longer in disguise. For further discussion of the apparitions in the New Testament, see Raymond Brown, *The Death of the Messiah: From Gethsemane to the Grave,* 2 vols.

15. Williams, *Resurrection,* p. 83. See also Aers and Staley, *Powers of the Holy,* pp. 46, 72, for important perceptions on the unrecognizability of the risen Christ in Wycliffite writing and in *Piers Plowman.*

16. Nicholas Lash, *Easter in Ordinary: Reflections on Human Experience and the Knowledge of God,* p. 211.

17. Peter Carnley, *The Structure of Resurrection Belief,* p. 27. See also his comments: "The failure of the historical model, in other words, has an important positive impact upon our understanding of the structure of resurrection belief: it saves us from a purely past-centred approach to Easter faith which would allow us to conceive of it merely as a propositional attitude, relating us only to a set of statements asserting 'what happened' in the past" (p. 365).

18. For a recent contemplation of understandings of faith in late medieval English writing and in critical reflections on that writing, see David Aers, "Faith, Ethics and Community: Reflections on Reading Late Medieval English Writing," pp. 341–70, now reprinted in his *Faith, Ethics and Church in English Writing 1360–1410.*

19. Williams, *Resurrection*, p. 58.

20. Pamela Sheingorn, *The Easter Sepulchre in England*, p. 14. Pamela King explores some of the vital interconnections between Corpus Christi theater and liturgy in her article "Calendar and Text: Christ's Ministry in the York Plays and the Liturgy," pp. 30–59.

21. The text is easily accessible in *Medieval Drama*, edited by David Bevington (Boston: Houghton Mifflin, 1975), pp. 27 ff. This late-tenth-century manuscript designed at Winchester for Benedictine use is also edited by Karl Young, *Drama of the Medieval Church*, vol. 1, pp. 259 ff.; and translated by Thomas Symons, *Regularis Concordia* (London: Nelson, 1953). Walther Lipphardt publishes all known versions of the Visitatio in *Lateinische Osterfeiern und Osterspiele*, 7 vols.

22. The location of the *quem queritis* trope as part of the Easter mass or the Vigil mass is debated by scholars. See O. B. Hardison, *Christian Rite and Christian Drama in the Middle Ages: Essays in the Origin and Early History of Modern Drama*, esp. Essays V and VI; and Clifford Flanigan, "The Liturgical Drama and Its Tradition: A Review of Scholarship 1965–1975." The Visitatio is not in the Sarum Missal, and it is the Elevatio ceremonies that seemed to really influence the subject of the Easter Sepulchre. Indeed the Visitatio is not in the York rites either, and apart from its earliest appearance in the *Regularis Concordia*, it recurs in England only in the Barking Ordinal of the fourteenth century.

23. *Medieval Drama*, edited by Bevington, p. 27.

24. Sheingorn, *Easter Sepulchre*, p. 3.

25. The rites are so described by Eamon Duffy, *The Stripping of the Altars*, pp. 29 ff.

26. Sheingorn, *Easter Sepulchre*, p. 57.

27. Sheingorn, *Easter Sepulchre*, p. 58.

28. Sheingorn, *Easter Sepulchre*, p. 58.

29. Sheingorn, *Easter Sepulchre*, p. 59. She notes the representation of a resurrected Christ carved in an Easter Sepulchre at Patrington in Yorkshire that has a strong resemblance to a puppetlike figure, "both lively and stiff—i.e., ungainly as if a jointed puppet." Barnabe Googe, translating Thomas Kirchmeyer's *Regnum Papisticum* (1553), gives us a savagely pilloried Protestant account of some of these images in *The Popish Kingdom, or reigne of Antichrist written in Latine verse by Thomas Naogeorgus, and englyshed by Barnabe Googe* (1570): "An other Image doe they get, like one but newly dede, / With legges stretcht out at length and handes, upon his body spreade: / And him with pompe and sacred song, they beare unto his graue, / His bodie all being wrapt

in lawne, and silkes and sarcenet braue, / The boyes before with clappers go, and filthie noyses make. / The Sexten beres the light, the people hereof knowledge take: / And downe they kneele, or kisse the grounde, their handes held up abrod / And knocking on their breastes they make, this woodden blocke a God. / And least in graue he should remaine, without some companie. / The singing bread is layde with him, for more idolatrie" (fol. 51V; reprinted in Young, *Drama of the Medieval Church*, vol. 2, pp. 525–37).

30. Duffy, *Stripping of the Altars*, p. 31. He points out that it represented the most solemn worship of the host, "in many communities far more elaborate even than the Corpus Christi procession."

31. Ronald Hutton, *The Rise and Fall of Merry England: The Ritual Year 1400–1700*, p. 22.

32. Mirk, *Mirk's Festial;* cited by Duffy, *Stripping of the Altars*, p. 28.

33. Rosemary Woolf, *The English Mystery Plays*, p. 275.

34. John Wyclif, *Sermones*, edited by Johann Loserth, 4 vols. (London: Wyclif Society, 1887–90), vol. 1, Sermo XXIV, p. 164.

35. Wyclif, *Sermones*, p. 164.

36. *English Wycliffite Sermons*, edited by Anne Hudson and Pamela Gradon, 5 vols. (Oxford: Clarendon Press, 1988–90), vol. 1, Sermon 46, p. 431.

37. *English Wycliffite Sermons*, vol. 1, Sermon 46, p. 431. The author of the sermon is using Augustine's sermon "ad infantes," Sermon 272: "Ista, fratres, ideo dicuntur sacramenta, quia in eis aliud videtur, aliud intelligitur. Quod videtur, speciem habet corporalem; quod intelligitur, fructum habet spiritalem."

38. *English Wycliffite Sermons*, vol. 1, Sermon 45, p. 424.

39. *English Wycliffite Sermons*, vol. 1, Sermon 45, p. 424.

40. *English Wycliffite Sermons*, vol. 1, Sermon 45, p. 426.

41. *English Wycliffite Sermons*, vol. 1, Sermon 45, p. 426. Interestingly enough, this same sermon contains an arresting reference to the playing of a Resurrection pageant. After having described Pilate's command for the sepulcher to be guarded until the third day to stop proclamations of resurrection, he adds, "An þis pagyn pleyen þei þat huyden þe trewpe of Godis lawe" (p. 425). For comments on this passage in reference to the common concern of Wycliffite social thought and the York Corpus Christi plays with the "mother tongue," see Ruth Nissé, "Staged Interpretations: Civic Rhetoric and Lollard Politics in the York Plays," p. 427.

42. Meg Twycross, "Playing the Resurrection," in *Medieval Studies for J. A. W. Bennett*, edited by P. L. Heyworth, p. 280. Twycross adds that the play goes some way to making this clear to us. Woolf, *The English Mystery Plays*, p. 275: "Amongst the English cycle plays York is alone in adopting the method of the early Latin plays."

43. The set design was Laurence Koppe's in a production put on by the Department of English in association with the Newman Center, University of Toronto, directed by Karen Sawyer. See her director's notes in the program to

The York Plays, University of Toronto, 20 June 1998. One could also envision a production in which two pageant wagons stood adjacent, one housing the action in Pilate's palace and one, the not-empty tomb, such that the proximity of the conspirators frames the laments of the women. See also Twycross, below, for other comments on staging the resurrection.

44. *York Plays,* pp. 397, 344.

45. *York Plays,* p. 348.

46. From the words of Appendix in *The Resurrection of Our Lord,* edited by J. Dover Wilson and Bertram Dobell (Oxford: Oxford University Press, 1912), p. 10.

47. *York Plays,* p. 354.

48. *York Plays,* p. 354.

49. *York Plays,* p. 345.

50. Twycross, "Playing the Resurrection," p. 281.

51. Williams, *Resurrection,* p.106.

52. For Mary Magdalene's inconsolability in the meditative play of *Christ's Burial,* in *Late Medieval Religious Plays of Bodleian MSS Digby 133 and E Museo 160,* edited by Donald C. Baker, John L. Murphy, and Louis B. Hall Jr. (Oxford: Oxford University Press, 1982), see Karma Lochrie, *Margery Kempe and the Translations of the Flesh,* pp. 187 ff. Patricia Badir also writes about medieval theatrical representations of resurrection in "Representations of the Resurrection at Beverley Minster Circa 1208: Chronicle, Play, Miracle," pp. 9–41.

53. *York Plays,* p. 357.

54. *York Plays,* p. 358.

55. Augustine, *Homilies on the Gospel of John,* vol. 7, *A Select Library of the Nicene and Post-Nicene Fathers* (New York, 1888), p. 437.

56. Augustine, *Homilies on the Gospel of John,* p. 427.

57. Augustine, *Homilies on the Gospel of John,* p. 438.

58. *English Wycliffite Sermons,* vol. 3, Sermon 65.

59. *York Plays,* p. 358: "Mi lorde Jesu, I knowe now þe."

60. See in this connection Pickstock's comments on the "necrophilia of modernity" in *After Writing,* p. 109: "It would seem that secularized death is the best example of an object there is." And see her chapter "The Resurrection of the Sign," p. 255: "For it is when the Eucharist is hypostatized as either a thing or a sign in separation from ecclesial and ecstatic action, that it becomes truly decadent."

61. *York Plays,* pp. 360 ff.

62. *York Plays,* p. 363.

63. I thank Chris Chism for her excellent comments on this point, which I have incorporated here.

64. Aers and Staley, *The Powers of the Holy,* p. 72.

65. Rosemary Woolf has made the suggestion that the York plays may show the influence of Langland. For her comments on the influence of *Piers*

Plowman B-text, Passus xviii, ll. 304–5, on the York Harrowing of Hell, see Woolf, *The English Mystery Plays,* p. 271.

66. Twycross, "Playing the Resurrection," p. 274.

67. Twycross, "Playing the Resurrection," p. 274.

68. T. G. Bishop, *Shakespeare and the Theatre of Wonder,* has put it the following way: "It is not enough that the historical fact of Resurrection and return be mimed by actors: somehow these plays must dramatize not merely ancient story, but the inner order to the story that shapes the audience's common present" (p. 58).

69. Roach, *Cities of the Dead,* p. 4.

70. Fischer-Lichte, *The Semiotics of Theater,* p. 7.

71. Martin Goldman, *The Actor's Freedom,* p. 114.

72. Herbert Blau, *The Audience,* p. 65.

73. Cavell, *Disowning Knowledge,* p. 85.

74. Paraphrasing Jonathan Bates, *The Genius of Shakespeare,* p. 325.

CHAPTER SIX

1. Perhaps the tendency of functionalism to stress integration in Corpus Christi has sidelined the complexity of the processes of that integration and the obstacles in the way of such integration.

2. The last words of this sentence are paraphrased from Gerard Loughlin's essay "The Basis and Authority of Doctrine," in *The Cambridge Companion to Christian Doctrine,* edited by Colin E. Gunton, p. 47. Loughlin defines the modern reduction of the multivalent figurations of allegorical exegesis to the "one literal meaning" of a text that is understood as its historical reference. Such a drastic reduction means that "what really happened," which is in any case accessible only now to science, redefines the interrelationship between scripture and doctrine. Henceforth, "Scripture is no longer understood as mutually constituted by the story it narrates and the community to whom it is narrated—a community already contained within the story, as the story within it" (p. 47). This changed understanding between scripture, history, and doctrine underlines much of the condescension toward the Corpus Christi plays and also renders difficult alternative means of understanding them. For they are understood as showing forth long distant events rather than articulating an interrelation between two cities that are not separate entities in time and space, one trying to model itself upon the other, but impossible to separate because their interaction concerns "each man's capacity to love what he loves," as Peter Brown puts it in his comments on Augustine's *City of God* in *Augustine of Hippo: A Biography,* p. 323. See *City of God* 15.8.10 and 16.3.70. In his book *Theology on the Way to Emmaus,* Nicholas Lash puts it in the following way: "The fundamental form of the Christian interpretation of scripture is the life, activity and organization of the believing community" (p. 43).

3. Rowan Williams, "Trinity and Revelation," p. 209. Indeed if theological

utterances are understood as knowledge "out there," they will be uncontaminated by our own agency in agreement and disagreement, their "truth" precisely secured by such outsiderdom. We do not have to be responsible for or known in them. And so as Rowan Williams explores in another essay, "The Suspicion of Suspicion," such forms of conceptualizing and trying to grasp knowledge may actually be considered a "flight from relation," a "quest for an impossible transparency or immediacy in relation" (pp. 50–51). These profoundly Wittgensteinian themes are explored in Cavell's extraordinary *The Claim of Reason*, especially pp. 351–52, and in *Must We Mean What We Say?*, especially the essay entitled "The Availability of Wittgenstein's Later Philosophy," p. 61. They are pursued in specifically theological directions by Fergus Kerr in his classic book *Theology After Wittgenstein* and more recently in *Immortal Longings*.

4. I think it is probably the emphasis on the "interior" and individual aspects of confession and contrition in the critical literature that has prevented critics from understanding the full force of the workings of Corpus Christi as penitential. The dualist distinction between an interior soul (the subject of confession) and a series of outward bodily gestures as they manifest themselves in theatrical and ritual forms is not a useful bifurcation. I deal with the creation and costs of this bifurcation, and how theater is itself a vehicle and instrument of them, more fully in chapter 7.

5. Patrice Pavis notes that in drama, "the fiction . . . is always at the mercy of . . . the enactment" (cited by Garner, *The Absent Voice*, p. 22).

6. H. J. Schroeder, trans. and ed., *Disciplinary Decrees of the General Councils*, pp. 259–60; cited in David Myers, *"Poor Sinning Folk": Confession and Conscience in Counter-Reformation Germany*, p. 28.

7. *Speculum Sacerdotale*, edited by E. H. Weatherly. Early English Text Society, o.s., 200 (London: Oxford University Press, 1936), p. 122. The *Speculum Sacerdotale* is a fifteenth-century English collection, British Museum Additional Manuscript 36791. It consists of narratives of the Virgin and the saints and biblical stories, expositions on ecclesiastical ritual, and a section on penance that forms a self-contained unit within the collection. This part of the collection uses both the Decretals of the Third Lateran Council of 1179 (under Pope Alexander III), the Pseudo-Augustinian *Liber de Vera et Falsa Poenitentia*, and some of the letters and sermons of Augustine that treat the subject of penance. The collection is obviously designed to help a priest "handle the sin" of penitents.

8. Greg Jones has recently examined the pervasive "internalization" and "privatization" of forgiveness in his book *Embodying Forgiveness: A Theological Analysis*, p. 50. "We find forgiveness," he writes, "not only by looking within ourselves but by being restored to communion with God and with one another in and through specific practices of forgiveness, thus embodying forgiveness as a way of life" (p. 50). It is with the sidelining of those "specific practices" and

their integrity both in late medieval penance and in the modern criticism about it that I have to do here.

9. *Speculum Sacerdotale,* p. 71.

10. *Speculum Sacerdotale,* p. 65.

11. Myers, *"Poor Sinning Folk,"* p. 28. See, for example, William Lyndwood in his canon on confession and penance derived from a fourteenth-century diocesan statute that specifies: "Also the priest should choose a common place to hear confessions, where he may be seen generally by all those in the church, and the priest shall not hear in secret places the confession of anyone, and especially not women, except in case of urgent necessity or because of the infirmity of a penitent" (*Provinciale, seu Constitutiones Angliae* [London, 1679]; quoted in Christopher Harper-Bill, *The Pre-Reformation Church in England 1400–1530,* p. 107).

12. The necessity for the priest to maintain the secrets of confession were spelled out in Canon 21 of Fourth Lateran: "But let him give strict heed not at all to betray the sinner by word or sign or in any other way, but if he need more prudent counsel let him seek it cautiously without any indication of the person: since we decree that he who shall presume to reveal a sin discovered to him in the penitential tribunals is not only to be deposed from the priestly office, but also to be thrust into a strict monastery to do perpetual penance" (cited by Karma Lochrie, *Covert Operations: The Medieval Uses of Secrecy,* p. 25). Much of the richest work on confession and penance has explored the uses of confession and penance for subjectivity. See, for example, the work of Lee Patterson, Linda Georgianna, Karma Lochrie, and Allen Frantzen cited in the bibliography. More recently David Myers and Mary C. Mansfield have explored the public, communal, and liturgical dimensions of this sacrament. A pioneer of this approach was Pierre-Marie Gy, "Histoire liturgique sacrament du pénitence," pp. 5–21.

13. Thomas of Chobham, *Summa Confessorum,* edited by F. Bloomfield (Louvain: Nauwelaerts, 1968), p. 13. The "private" penances were usually discretionary to the confessing priest. But solemn penance for serious crimes came under the jurisdiction of the bishop, a distinction articulated in canon law.

14. See, for example, Robert of Flamborough, canon-penitentiary of Saint-Victor at Paris, in his *Liber Poenitentialis,* edited by J. J. Francis Firth (Toronto: Pontifical Institute of Medieval Studies, 1971), p. 84: "Sed privata poenitentia nullum est sacramentum." And see Mary C. Mansfield, *The Humiliation of Sinners: Public Penance in Thirteenth-Century France,* p. 32.

15. The same courtesy is advised in Lyndwood: "Also the priest should enjoin upon a wife such penance that she be not suspected by her husband of any secret and great sin, and the same should be observed for a husband" (quoted in Harper-Bill, *Pre-Reformation Church,* p. 108).

16. *Speculum Sacerdotale,* p. 79. Perhaps this is to prevent vigilante acts of

vengeance that the whole operation of penance is designed to replace; in any case, the consequences and problems of the adjudication of private and public penance are easy to see.

17. *Speculum Sacerdotale*, p. 79.

18. Myers observes that the sacrament essentially was a "lower court for the discovery of acts that only authorities at the episcopal or papal court could forgive" (Myers, *"Poor Sinning Folk,"* p. 30). It was precisely the severing of pastoral from judicial concerns that renders a much more "privatized" sacrament after the Reformation.

19. Mary Erler has recently explored the eucharistic and theatrical interrelations of the Palm Sunday liturgy in her "Palm Sunday Prophets, Processions and Eucharistic Controversy," pp. 58–81; and see below. See also *Speculum Sacerdotale:* "And that day ye alle oweþ for to be at the procession and yche man that he be confessid to bere his palme" (p. 98).

20. Myers, *"Poor Sinning Folk,"* p. 52. Recitation of this psalm, the "neck-verse," was also considered a test of clerical status and could grant clerics the right to be tried in an ecclesiastical court in which they could escape the death penalty. Such contradictory aspects of the use of Psalm 51 are explored with delight and learning in the late medieval morality play *Mankind*, and this aspect of the play is treated in Janette Dillon, *Language and Stage in Medieval and Renaissance England*, p. 66.

21. *Speculum Sacerdotale*, p. 63.

22. This is actually the theology of Julian of Norwich. For excellent recent considerations of Julian's theodicy, see Denise Baker, *Julian of Norwich's "Shewings": From Vision to Book*, and Aers and Staley's important twin essays on Julian in *The Powers of the Holy*. And see John Milbank, *Theology and Social Theory*, p. 421.

23. Gratian, Peter Lombard, Abelard, Hugh of Saint Victor, and the earliest writers on the sacrament of penance held a markedly contritionist view. Thomas Aquinas articulates the sacrament of penance within the terms of scholastic sign and sacramental theory. If sacraments produced grace from the work of the person receiving them (*ex opere operantis*), then contrition could indeed be the efficient cause of forgiveness. But sacraments dispense grace *ex opere operato*, from the work performed. Although the disposition of the penitent is important, the efficacy of the sacrament, the automatic power of the sacramental sign, rendered the correct words of absolution by a properly ordained priest absolutely vital. Duns Scotus wanted to dispense with the trifold division of contrition, confession, and absolution altogether and sought to locate the essence of the sacrament in the sole absolution of the priest. Here the external sign and the correct form of words are all important: "Poenitentia est absolutio hominis poenitentis, facta certis verbis, cum debita intentione, prelatis a sacerdote, jursidictionem habente ex institutione divina, efficaciter significantibus absolutionem animae a peccato" (Duns Scotus, *Quaestiones*

in librum quartum sententiarum, vol. 18, *Opera Omnia* (Paris, 1894), p. 421, dis. 16 q. 1).

24. I have been arguing in this book that we have overlooked the intersubjective dimensions of sacramentality and that Corpus Christi theater animates those dimensions again, moving the sacraments away from the possession *of* the church and toward the relations performed between people. One might say that Corpus Christi is freed to look at sacraments *ex opere operantis.*

25. Myers, *"Poor Sinning Folk,"* p. 15.

26. De Heretico Comburendo of 1401 allows the church to pass over a heretic to the state for burning. The first martyr to be burned under this statute, William Sawtre, was a priest and a relapsed heretic. The statute of 1401 issued from joint ecclesiastical and parliamentary action. See Peter McNiven, *Heresy and Politics in the Reign of Henry IV: The Burning of John Badby;* and Paul Strohm, *England's Empty Throne: Usurpation and the Language of Legitimation 1399–1422,* especially chapter 2, for an account of these first heretic burnings; and see below. It should be noted, moreover, that heresy was an offense, the sole offense, for which a cleric could order the detention of a layman. A bishop could in fact arrest someone accused of heresy on mere suspicion. Heresy, therefore, was to be judged and could be judged by the church alone (Susan Brigden, *London and the Reformation,* p. 151; and F. Donald Logan, *Excommunication and the Secular Arm in Medieval England*).

27. For this understanding of secrets, see D. A. Miller, *The Novel and the Police;* and Eve Kosofsky Sedgewick, *Epistemology of the Closet;* and with specific respect to medieval subjects, Lochrie, *Covert Operations.*

28. "Of Confession," in *The English Works of Wyclif,* edited by F. D. Matthew. Early English Text Series, o.s., 74 (London: Kegan Paul, Trench, Trübner, 1880), p. 338.

29. "Of Confession," p. 335 (my italics).

30. "Of Confession," p. 341.

31. "Of Confession," p. 341.

32. *Fasciculi Zizaniorum: Magistri Johannis Wyclif,* edited by W. W. Shirley (London: Longman, 1858), p. 278. See also items 5 and 6 from Register of Thomas Polton, Worcester, St. Helen's Record Office, in Anne Hudson's essay "The Examination of Lollards," in *Lollards and Their Books,* p. 133. Wyclif's understanding that the priest's absolution could only be confirmatory, blasphemous if the penitent was not contrite, is outlined in his *Sermones,* vol. 2, 62/26 ff, 138/24 ff. For further references, see *Selections from English Wycliffite Writings,* edited by Anne Hudson (Cambridge: Cambridge University Press, 1978), p. 146.

33. A. G. Dickens quotes Johnson's abjuration from Wolsey's Register, fol. 131ᵛ, in *Lollards and Protestants in the Diocese of York 1509–1558,* p. 18.

34. Dickens, *Lollards and Protestants,* pp. 18–19. "Receiving discipline" means, of course, being scourged, usually whilst the Psalm 50 [51] was recited

over you. For a recent account of penances imposed on recalcitrant Lollards, see Norman Tanner, "Penances Imposed on Kentish Lollards by Archbishop Warham 1511–12," in *Lollardy and the Gentry in the Later Middle Ages*, edited by Margaret Aston and Colin Richmond, pp. 229–49.

35. Brigden, *London and the Reformation*, p. 148.

36. Stevens, *Four Middle English Mystery Cycles*, p. 82; citing Palliser, *Tudor York*, p. 234; and R. B. Dobson, "Admission to the Freedom of the City of York in the Later Middle Ages," p. 13.

37. Stevens also notes that during the Lammas Fair, held quite close in time to Corpus Christi in July, the archbishop of York had jurisdiction over the entire city (Stevens, *Four Middle English Mystery Cycles*, p. 82; Palliser, *Tudor York*, p. 182).

38. *Two Wycliffite Texts: The Sermon of William Taylor 1406 and Testimony of William Thorpe 1407*, edited by Anne Hudson, Early English Text Series, 301 (Oxford: Oxford University Press, 1993), p. 88.

39. Indeed this is the point of Arundel's repeated request for his submission to the church and Thorpe's repeated redefinition of the church to which he is willing to submit himself. Thorpe's response produces rage in Arundel ("And þan þe Archebischop, smytnyg wiþ his fist fersli vpon a copbord, spake to me wiþ grete spirit . . . ," p. 88), and this is not surprising because his formulations—for example, at p. 92—mean that he puts his own conscience above the authority of the church. See Anne Hudson's comments on this trial in "William Thorpe and the Question of Authority," in *Christian Authority: Essays in Honour of Henry Chadwick*, edited by G. R. Evans, pp. 127–28.

40. *Two Wycliffite Texts*, p. 89.

41. *The Testimony of William Thorpe* is examined as an argument over confession by Katherine C. Little, "Reading for Christ: Interpretation and Instruction in Late Medieval England," chap. 2. Little points out that although Thorpe's confession is not an annual auricular confession, but an examination for heretical belief, the link between these two practices had already been made in Fourth Lateran: part of the purpose of confession as established there was precisely the detection of heretical views.

42. Dickens, *Lollards and Protestants*, p. 18.

43. The kinds of recognition and misrecognition involved in this "casting" is also seen in Wyclif's claim that if Christ were to come back as an unknown priest, he would surely be excommunicated by the Roman curia, and if he did not recant, he would then be tried and burned as a heretic. See Wyclif, *Tractatus de Blasphemia*, edited by Michael Henry Dziewicki (London: Wyclif Society, 1893), p. 62: "In tantum, quod si Cristus prelatus incognitus visiteret peregrine prelatos istius ecclesie presencia corporali, instaretque inportune contra vocatos eius vicarios, sicut olim institit contra minorem avariciam sacerdotum, est evidens quod excommunicarent eum in curia romana et nisi veritatem revocare voluerit, condempnarent eum ad ignem tamquam hereticum, et blasfemam." See also p. 72. This is explored by David Aers in his essay

"Wycliffite Texts and *Piers Plowman*," in *The Powers of the Holy*, edited by Aers and Staley, p. 46; and see other works cited there.

44. David Aers has recently explored the acute contradictions in Wyclif's ecclesiology in a chapter entitled "John Wyclif's Understanding of Christian Discipleship," in *Faith, Ethics and Church in English Writing 1360–1410*. I thank him for permission to read the manuscript in advance of publication.

45. The sidelining of interiority—the consequence at once of a distrust of narrative forms of knowledge, as well as a fixation with defining their own community by means of the sins of the other, the clergy—is explored to great effect by Little in "Reading for Christ" and in her article "Catechesis and Castigation: Sin in the Wycliffite Sermon Cycle," pp. 213–44.

46. *The Towneley Plays*, edited by Stevens and Cawley, p. 401.

47. *A Tretise of Miraclis Pleyinge*, edited by Clifford Davidson (Kalamazoo, Mich.: Medieval Institute Publications, 1993), p. 95. In an utterly different reading of the logic of incarnation, the *Tretise* author writes: "the voice of Crist and the voice of the fleysh ben of two contrarious lordis" (p. 96).

48. Loughlin, "The Basis and Authority of Doctrine," p. 47.

49. Milbank, *Theology and Social Theory*, p. 397. See Milbank's important essay "The Name of Jesus," in *The Word Made Strange: Theology, Language, Culture*. I have found this rich essay a deep resource for my thinking about penance and theater. See also the work of Hans Frei, *Theology and Narrative: Selected Essays*, edited by George Hubsinger and William C. Placher.

50. Rowan Williams, "Postmodern Theology and the Judgement of the Word," in *Postmodern Theology and Christian Faith in a Pluralist World*, edited by F. B. Burham, p. 96.

51. Nissé, "Staged Interpretations," p. 436. See also Stevens's treatment of the Entry in his *Four Middle English Mystery Cycles*, pp. 50–51. The beast on which Christ rides is "comen" (207/57), belonging to the city as a whole, and it is by permission and to its honor that the city bears Christ in its midst.

52. Nissé, "Staged Interpretations," p. 444.

53. This is particularly true in the context of the fifteenth century. Aers explains the inextricability of questions of government and questions of devotion in the context of Arundel's England in the following manner: "As forms of dissent became classified as heresy (a contingent historical development, not some doctrinal and 'transcendent' necessity), as heresy became classified and dealt with as sedition (through parliamentary acts and the secular power), the ways in which the languages and practices of religion were inextricably bound up with the languages and practices of governance and politics became especially transparent" (Aers, "Faith, Ethics and Community," p. 350).

54. *York Plays*, pp. 217, 219.

55. Ernst Kantorowicz has explored the parallels between the Palm Sunday liturgy and royal entries in "The King's Advent and the Enigmatic Panels in the Doors of Santa Sabina," pp. 207–31, and in *Laudes Regiae: A Study in Liturgical Acclamations and Mediaeval Ruler Worship*. See also Gordon Kipling's ex-

ploration of royal entries, especially his analysis of King Henry VII's civic entry at York in 1486, in *Enter the King: Theatre, Liturgy and Ritual in the Medieval Civic Triumph*, p. 134, following the prospective account in *The York House Book*, pp. 137–42. This entry uses the Assumption pageant (*REED: York*, vol. 1, 145/33–34), so it is be expected that audiences would be alert to shared mechanics as well as metaphors. Lorraine Attreed has explored the occasionally tense politics of welcome in her article "The Politics of Welcome: Ceremonies and Constitutional Development in Later Medieval English Towns," in *City and Spectacle in Medieval Europe*, edited by Barbara Hanawalt and Kathryn Reyerson, pp. 208–31. In 1461 Palm Sunday saw the defeat of Henry VI's forces twelve miles from York. Edward had to grant the city a pardon for its previous disloyalty, and as Attreed comments, "the ceremonies served as a background for Edward's personal mission at York, namely the removal of his father's severed head from Micklegate Bar, on which it had been placed by the victorious Lancastrians after the Battle of Wakefield three months earlier" (p. 215). Micklegate is the gate through which the Corpus Christi pageants process as well as the gateway for royal entries following the same processional route to the Pavement.

56. Without mutual forgiveness, as Augustine said, "no one will be able to see God" (*City of God* 15.6, 19.24, 25, 26, 27); and see Milbank, where this insight informs the central final section of his book *Theology and Social Theory*. This understanding of presencing (that God in the body of Christ is visible or invisible in bonds of charity) is articulated in the rites of Easter. The images in the church are covered in Lent. When Dives asks Pauper why this might be the case in a late medieval dialogue, Pauper replies that the covering is a sign that we cannot see God's face when we are in deadly sin. When we make amends and do penance, it will become visible again, after the Lenten season. See, for example, *Dives and Pauper*, edited by Priscilla Heath Barnum. Early English Text Society 275, 280 (London: Oxford University Press, 1976): "In tokene þat qhyl men ben in dedly synne þey moun nought seen Goddys face ne þe seyntys in heuene, and þat God and al þe court of heuene hyden here face from man and womman qhyl þey been in dedly synne, tyl quanne þey welyn amendyn hem be srwe of herte and shryfte of mouthe and amendys-makynge" (p. 99).

57. Rowan Williams, *The Wound of Knowledge: Christian Spirituality from the New Testament to St. John of the Cross*, p. 3.

58. Stevens, *Four Middle English Mystery Cycles*, p. 59.

59. Pointed out by Stevens, *Four Middle English Mystery Cycles*, p. 76. See Pamela King for a recent examination of the York Trial plays in the context of contemporary medieval legislative practices, in "Contemporary Cultural Models for the Trial Plays in the York Cycle," in *Drama and Community: People and Plays in Medieval Europe*, edited by Alan Hindley, pp. 200–16.

60. Elza Tiner, "'Inventio,' 'Dispositio,' and 'Elocutio' in the York Trial Plays," p. 46, comments that the case is handled "as an affair of urgency effecting church and state."

61. *York Plays*, p. 254.

62. *York Plays*, p. 264.

63. *York Plays*, p. 301.

64. We are able to date the tilemakers' pageant of Christ before Pilate 2 reasonably accurately because the *Memorandum Book* records the tilemakers' assumption of responsibility for this pageant in a series of documents between 1422 and 1432. See Richard Beadle's comments on the York cycle in *The Cambridge Companion to Medieval English Theatre*, p. 104. Although we do not know the precise nature of the revisions undertaken, such a date suggests the proximity in time to the Lancastrian dispensations against heresy and the central symbol of the eucharist in such discussions; see Strohm, *England's Empty Throne*, and below.

65. Tiner, "'Inventio,'" p. 67.

66. If one thinks of Pope Gregory's letter to try and silence Wyclif, we should probably say from the 1370s. For an examination of the contexts of ecclesiastical law and censorship, see chapter 1 of Andrew Cole's unpublished Duke dissertation, "Revising Langland and Chaucer: Heresy and Literary Authority in Late Medieval England"; and A. K. McHardy, "De Heretico Comburendo," in *Lollardy and the Gentry in the Later Middle Ages*, edited by Margaret Aston and Colin Richmond, pp. 112–26.

67. McNiven, *Heresy and Politics*, p. 86; and see p. 41. Before 1382 the liaison between the church and the state was legally sanctioned by an act known as "De excommunicatio capiendo." If a person had already been excommunicated for heresy in an ecclesiastical court, the local bishop could obtain a writ ordering the sheriff to imprison the offender until he had reconciled himself with the church (McNiven, *Heresy and Politics*, p. 36). But as McNiven notes, although these measures were useful in disciplining certain kinds of essentially worldly offenses, they were not good at dealing with wandering preachers and heretics "whose very beliefs dictated their lack of concern for worldly ties" (p. 37). Even before the bishop could apply for a royal writ, the heretic had to be tried, convicted, and found "contumacious" but was given forty days, a good Lenten period, in order to plead against his arrest. These procedures understand excommunication as a really effective sanction and the intervention of the lay power as a truly last resort. But as McNiven points out, defiance of excommunication and of priestly and episcopal jurisdiction had actually become part of the Lollard heretical doctrine, and in this sense the teeth were taken out of what the church regarded as its most effective deterrent. For the standard work on excommunication, see Logan, *Excommunication and the Secular Arm in Medieval England.*

68. McNiven, *Heresy and Politics*, p. 37.

69. Tiner, "'Inventio,'" p. 56, says that Jesus is illegally arrested. And Jesus does say to Annas and Caiphas that they could have arrested him in the temple. But although Jesus is entrapped, his arrest is perfectly legal under the legislation of the 1380s, which functioned as summary *"sus"*laws.

70. Strohm, *England's Empty Throne*, p. 54.

71. McNiven, *Heresy and Politics*, p. 90.

72. See Strohm, *England's Empty Throne*, p. 34, who points out the analytic complicity of historians who perceive Lollardy as a preliminary threat for which machinery had subsequently to be created.

73. Aers's comments on the trial of William Thorpe become relevant here. Thorpe asks Arundel whether a "subject should obey a prelate who is 'unlaweful.'" To Arundel's response that this subject need have no anxiety because he or she is acting in faithful obedience, Thorpe merely responds, "Sere, I triste not herto." Aers comments that such a position is perfectly consonant with the Thomistic position whereby a human law becomes a perversion of the divine law when it deviates from right reason (Aers, "Faith, Ethics and Community," p. 358). It was perfectly common within the soteriology of the high Middle Ages to make arguments for the redemption in terms of the language of the lawsuit. Hugh of Saint Victor, for example, talked about the redemption as a "case" with three parties: God, man, and the devil (*De Sacramentis*, Book 1, part 8, chap. 4). Abelard, in his commentary on Saint Paul's Epistle to the Romans, argues against the grain of such readings that the redemption is not about law but about love; see Michael Clanchy, *Abelard: A Medieval Life*, p. 285.

74. *York Plays*, p. 252.

75. *York Plays*, pp. 252, 264. The notion that killing is an offense against his order is a transposition of John 18:31, as R. H. Nicholson points out in his article "The Trial of Christ the Sorcerer in the York Cycle," p. 133.

76. See the opening to Strohm's chapter "Heretic Burning: The Lollard as Menace and Victim," *England's Empty Throne*, p. 32.

77. John Foxe, *The Acts and Monuments of John Foxe: A New and Complete Edition*, edited by R. B. Seeley and W. Burnside (London, 1838), p. 127. I have checked Foxe's translations against the trial documents in *Registrum Johannes Trefnant*, edited by W. W. Capes (London: Canterbury and York Society, 1916).

78. Foxe, *Acts and Monuments*, p. 168. *Registrum Johannes Trefnant*, p. 329: ". . . mirandum est quomodo summus pontifex Romanorum audet anticipare iudicii diem ut iudicet aliquos esse sanctos, abhominibus honorandos, et alios iudicet peccatores cum demonibus eternaliter cruciandos."

79. McNiven, *Heresy and Politics*, p. 210.

80. Strohm, *England's Empty Throne*, p. 33.

81. John Wyclif, *De Eucharistia tractatus maior*, edited by Johann Loserth (London: Wyclif Society, 1892), pp. 327–43. McNiven, *Heresy and Politics*, p. 26.

82. Foxe, *Acts and Monuments*, p. 170. *Registrum Johannes Trefnant*, p. 333: "sed confiteri peccata sacerdoti tanquam iudici et ab eo recipere penas corporales ad satisfaciendum Deo pro peccatis commissis non video fundatum in veritate scripture."

83. Foxe, *Acts and Monuments*, p. 178. *Registrum Johannes Trefnant*, p. 344: "si Cristus unam pro peccatis offerens hostiam in sempiternum sedet in dex-

tera Dei et una oblacione consummavit in sempiternum sanctificatos, si Cristus semper assistit a dextera Dei ad interpellandum pro nobis, quid oportuit illum relinquere hic aliquod sacrificium pro peccatis nostris a sacerdotibus offerendum cotidie?" He also says even more trenchantly, "And every priest is ready daily ministering and often times offering like sacrifices, which can never take away sins. But this Jesus, offering one sacrifice for sin, sitteth evermore on the right hand of God, expecting the time till his enemies be made his footstool."

84. One thinks of the degradation of the priest William Sawtre; see Strohm, *England's Empty Throne*, p. 43.

85. *York Plays*, p. 303. See Pamela King's comments on the punctuation of the York plays by elevation lyrics in "Corpus Christi Plays and the 'Bolton Hours' 1: Tastes in Lay Piety and Patronage in Fifteenth Century York," p. 57.

86. *York Plays*, p. 295.

87. *York Plays*, p. 222.

88. *York Plays*, p. 302.

89. *York Plays*, p. 302.

90. *York Plays*, p. 251.

91. *Two Wycliffite Texts*, p. 92.

92. *York Plays*, p. 301.

93. *York Plays*, p. 302.

94. Aers, "John Wyclif's Understanding of Christian Discipleship," p. 143.

95. *York Plays*, p. 408.

96. They are judged as to whether they have performed the seven works of mercy, but they do not know when they have. See Woolf's comments on these scenes in *The English Mystery Plays*, pp. 295, 297.

97. *York Plays*, p. 409.

98. John Audelay describes this relationship: "þe pore schul be ade domysmen / Apon þe ryche at domeysday; / Let se houe þai cun onswere þen / For al here ryal, reuerant aray; / In hunger, in cold, in purs, weleawy? / Afftyr here almes ay waytyng / þay wold not vysete us nygt ne day / þus wyl þai playn ham to heuen Kyng / þat is aboue" (*The Poems of John Audelay*, edited by Ella Keats Whiting, Early English Text Society, o.s., 184 [London: Oxford University Press, 1931], pp. 9–10; cited in Marjorie McIntosh, "Finding a Language for Misconduct: Jurors in Fifteenth-Century Local Courts," in *Bodies and Disciplines: Intersections of Literature and History in Fifteenth-Century England*, edited by Barbara Hanawalt and David Wallace, p. 95).

99. The *saeculum* is a time not a place, and for Augustine knowledge is not a place seen but a time remembered (Milbank, *Theology and Social Theory*, p. 426).

100. I am paraphrasing from Adam Phillips's essay "Fears," in *Terrors and Experts*, p. 53: "Fear . . . is a state of mind in which the object of knowledge is the future, but it is, of course, a knowledge that can only be derived from the past."

101. *Select English Wycliffite Writings*, nos. 3/99, 16/110. See also *Dives and Pauper*, 1.lii.1–75, *Piers Plowman* B.xi.180. It should be noted that the plays do not hypostatize Christ in the image of the poor man either because the souls are not aware of the eschatological meaning of their actions.

102. *York Plays*, p. 410.

103. Theatrical deixis is always two-way.

104. William Cavanaugh, *Torture and Eucharist: Politics and the Body of Christ*, p. 206.

105. Stanley Hauerwas, *Sanctify Them in the Truth: Holiness Exemplified*, chap. 3, p. 79. He goes on to add: "It is as if the crucifixion covered our overdraft in God's universal bank making all humanity solvent again."

106. Cavanaugh, *Torture and Eucharist*, p. 221.

107. Cavanaugh, *Torture and Eucharist*, p. 269.

108. Milbank, "The Name of Jesus," p. 150: "The gospels can be read, not as the story of Jesus, but as the story of the (re)foundation of a new city, a new kind of human community."

109. Denys Turner, "Negative Theology and Eucharistic Presence," p. 154; also available in Sarah Beckwith, ed., *Catholicism and Catholicity: Eucharistic Communities in Historical and Contemporary Perspective*. Austin's distinctions are elaborated in *How to Do Things with Words*.

110. Turner, "Negative Theology," p. 154.

111. Turner, "Negative Theology," p. 155.

112. Pavis; cited in Garner, *The Absent Voice;* see above.

113. Cavanaugh, *Torture and Eucharist*, p. 212. Cavanaugh's argument has an important precursor in Henri de Lubac, *Corpus Mysticum: L'eucharistie et l'église au moyen âge*, especially pp. 290 ff.

114. See Hugh of Saint Victor, *De Sacramentis*, for the notion that the benefits of the passion are appropriated by the sacraments (1.8.7 and 2.1.5–7). It should be obvious that I think that the York plays do not systematically espouse an Anselmian or a devil's rights theory of salvation.

115. Brown, *Augustine of Hippo;* see note 2.

116. Milbank, "The Name of Jesus," p. 161.

117. Milbank, "The Name of Jesus," p. 153.

118. Cavanaugh, *Torture and Eucharist*, p. 234.

CHAPTER SEVEN

1. George Steiner, *Real Presences*, p. 147.

2. Alexandra Johnston, "The Word Made Flesh: Augustinian Elements in the York Cycle," in *The Centre and Its Compass: Studies in Medieval Literature in Honour of Professor John Leyerle*, edited by Robert A. Taylor et al., p. 225.

3. Ludwig Wittgenstein, *Philosophical Investigations*, no. 115, p. 48: "A *picture* held us captive. And we could not get outside it, for it lay in our language and language seemed to repeat it to us inexorably."

4. For the importance of "what we say when," see Cavell's explorations of

Austin's ordinary language philosophy and Wittgenstein in *Must We Mean What We Say?* (especially the title essay).

5. Glynne Wickham, *Early English Stages, 1300–1660*, 3 vols. vol. 2, part 1, p. 35. I have borrowed some sentences here and in the subsequent paragraph from my introduction to "The Cultural Work of Medieval Theater: Ritual Practice in England, 1350–1600," a special issue of *Journal of Medieval and Early Modern Studies* 29, no. 1 (winter 1999): 1–2.

6. Patrick Collinson, "The Elizabethan Church and the New Religion," in *The Reign of Elizabeth I*, edited by Christopher Haigh, p. 174.

7. See Peter Lake's excellent essay on our uses of the terms generated by sixteenth-century polemicists and our fear and unwitting repetition of those terms, "Religious Identities in Shakespeare's England," in *A Companion to Shakespeare*, edited by David Scott Kastan, pp. 58–59.

8. In Chester the plays had been moved to Whitsun in 1521. In David Mills's recent exploration of the Chester cycle, he speculates that the Chester cycle remained acceptable as York's cycle did not "because it conformed to what the sixteenth century imagined a medieval cycle should have been. Hence while in York it was the mayors of Catholic sympathies—William Allen in 1572 and Robert Cripling in 1579—who sought to revive the cycle, in Chester it was men of firm Protestant commitment—John Hankyn in 1572 and John Savage in 1575—in whose mayoralties the plays received their last performances" (Mills, "Chester's Mystery Cycle and the 'Mystery' of the Past," pp. 1–23). For final cessation of Corpus Christi performances, see Ian Lancashire, *Dramatic Texts and Records of Britain: A Chronological Topography to 1558*, p. xxx. A comparative analysis of the "end" of the cycles would be a useful diagnostic project. The plays had been performed at the end of the Corpus Christi procession until c. 1468, when the procession succeeded the feast day; see Alexandra Johnston, "The Procession and Play of Corpus Christi in York after 1426," pp. 55–62. For details of the regulation of the Corpus Christi procession and its relation to the guild of Corpus Christi, see Johnston, "The Guild of Corpus Christi and the Procession of Corpus Christi in York," pp. 372–84. After the dissolution (see below), the city had taken over the assets of the guild; during Mary's reign the procession is held again in 1555, 1556, and 1557 (p. 383).

9. *REED: York*, vol. 1, p. 293.

10. *REED: York*, vol. 1, pp. 331–32.

11. *REED: York*, vol. 1, p. 353, and below. See Alexandra Johnston, "The Plays of the Religious Guilds of York: The Creed Play and Paternoster Play," p. 65: "On February 15, 1567–68, the city council decided to stage the Creed Play instead of the Corpus Christi Play and made detailed preparations for its production." The Ecclesiastical Commissioners of the Council of the North heard of the production, and on 27 March Hutton sent his letter to the council (p. 65).

12. *REED: York*, vol. 1, p. 368.

13. *REED:York*, vol. 1, p. 365.

14. See Johnston, "The Plays of the Religious Guilds," p. 66: two aldermen requested "all suche þe bookes as pertayne this Cittie" from Grindal in 1575, but there is no record that he returned them. The earliest mention of the Paternoster play in York is in the Wycliffite *De Officio Pastorali*, cap. 15, in *The English Works of Wyclif*, pp. 429–30, where he uses it as an argument for vernacular translation of the Gospels: "herfore freris han tauȝt in Englond in þe pleye of Yorke and in many opere cuntreys siþen þe paternoster is part of matheus gospel, as clerkes knowen, why may not al be turnyd to English trewely as is þis part?" The Paternoster play was owned by the Paternoster guild, which was founded for the specific purpose of mounting the play. For the performance history, see Johnston, "The Plays of the Religious Guilds," pp. 72–76. The play, although originating as part of the educational activities of the friars, the property of a religious guild, was municipally controlled from the end of the fifteenth century until 1572.

15. Of course the consignment to script had been part of a centralization of control in the first place; see above.

16. *REED:York*, vol. 1, p. 390.

17. This seems true whether the plays in question are the Corpus Christi plays or the Paternoster play. With the religious guilds having been abolished, the guild plays were now civic property.

18. Both Grindal and Hutton were northerners, but their education in the universities, their acquaintance during their Marian exile with the Swiss and German reform centers as well as with Calvin, Bucer, and Peter Martyr, gave them evangelical pastoral aspirations quite antipathetic to the structures and habits of Yorkshire society, as well, arguably, to the very partial reformation of the English church and the royal settlement of 1559. Patrick Collinson in his biography of Grindal regards him as "an exemplary figure of the English Reformation in what was arguably its most creative phase" (*Archbishop Grindal 1519–1583*, p. 20). That is, he combined a passionate evangelical commitment with his office in a way that seemed quite impossible in the later bruising schisms of Protestantism, Anglicanism, and Puritanism. Hutton was a member of Grindal's circle at Cambridge, becoming his chaplain in 1561 and succeeding him as Master of Pembroke Hall. Like Grindal for Collinson, Hutton for Peter Lake represents a Protestant consensus somewhere between the more radically nonconformist views of Cartwright and conformists such as Perne or Curteys, a consensus increasingly impossible to maintain in the painfully polarized late sixteenth century, when it seemed that the choice could only be which side to espouse. Hutton was first dean of York, 1567–89, subsequently bishop of Durham, and in 1595 became archbishop of York. In his article on Hutton, Lake sees him as exemplary of the way "in which national institutions (here the church and the university), acting through the mechanism of upward social mobility and the propagation of a strongly protestant, indeed puritan

ideology, could integrate the local with the national and the national with the local" (Peter Lake, "Matthew Hutton—A Puritan Bishop?" p. 204).

19. *REED: York*, vol. 1, p. 353.

20. *REED: York*, vol. 1, p. 353.

21. Edward VI's Act of Uniformity was the first act of legal compulsion to church attendance, although here nonattendance was punished by the church not the state; see Alexandra Walsham, *Church Papists: Catholicism, Conformity and Confessional Polemic in Early Modern England*, p. 11; *Statutes of the Realm* 5, 6, Edward Vi c.1. nos. 1, iii. This injunction that is repeated frequently, for example, in 1571 when householders are charged to assure the presence of two members of their household to be present at sermons on Sundays and holidays.

22. W. R. Trimble, *The Catholic Laity in Elizabethan England: 1558–1603*, p. 23.

23. Trimble, *The Catholic Laity*, pp. 23–24.

24. In the end it might also be said to reveal the limits of that enforcement—see Grindal's famous letter of resignation to Queen Elizabeth in 1576, "concerning suppressing the prophecies, and restraining the number of preachers," which essentially reveals the limits of her reform policy (Edmund Grindal, *The Remains of Archbishop Grindal*, edited by Rev. William Nicholson. The Parker Society [Cambridge: The University Press, 1843], pp. 367–90).

25. J. C. H. Aveling, *Catholic Recusancy in the City of York: 1558–1791*; Patricia Badir, "Playing Space: History, the Body, and Records of Early English Drama," p. 146.

26. Badir, "Playing Space," p. 146.

27. J. A. Sharpe, *Early Modern England: A Social History 1550–1760*, p. 187.

28. Claire Cross, "Priests into Ministers: The Establishment of Protestant Practice in the City of York 1530–1630," in *Reformation Principle and Practice: Essays in Honour of Arthur Geoffrey Dickens*, edited by Peter Newman Brooks, p. 216.

29. For the discussions around "survivalism," church papism, and the Catholicism of the missions, see John Bossy, *The English Catholic Community 1570–1850*, and Christopher Haigh, "The Continuity of English Catholicism in the English Reformation," pp. 37–69. The Acts of 1581, 1587, and 1593 can only be interpreted as the most concerted attempt to eradicate upper-class nonconformity with their crippling twenty-pound fines and provision for land sequestration (Walsham, *Church Papists*, p. 11). For an examination of the bite of such statutes, see Michael C. Questier, *Conversion, Politics and Religion in England, 1580–1625*, especially chapter 6, "Heresy Is Dead and Policy Is the Life of Religion: State, Church, Conversion and Conformity," pp. 126–67.

30. Aveling, *Catholic Recusancy*, p. 53. This campaign intensifies in the 1580s. The 1581 Act puts the recusancy fine up to a crippling twenty pounds, and the injunctions of 1559, that "honest men" in each parish should supervise churchgoing, were actually enforced with a fine for dereliction of duty (p. 55).

31. Of course the language of "success" and "failure" is itself suspect and polarizing. For excellent analysis and commentary on this language, see Lake, "Religious Identities in Shakespeare's England," p. 72, where he points out that in overturning the partisan providentialism of the Whig traditions, revisionism has put in its place a picture that duplicates those traditions, expanding the term "Catholic" until it represents the most paranoid antipapist fears, and contracting the term "Protestant" until it looks like the most exclusive and self-selecting form of godliness. He comments, "On this basis, but only really on this basis, can the simple continuity of something called Catholicism through the English Reformation be vindicated and the failure—indeed, the status as nonevent—of the Reformation itself be asserted. But as we have seen, the period during which the master categories in terms of which the continuity argument is framed were being developed and contested, continually being shaped and reshaped by a whole host of ideological fractions and social groups, was precisely the same period during which their 'continuity,' their 'success' or 'failure' are being notionally tested or gauged by modern historians" (p. 72). For the inadequate notion that the "failure" of conformity is attributable to legislative incapacity, see Questier, *Conversion, Politics and Religion*, pp. 166-67. The point is that the kind of religiosity experienced as salvific for evangelicals is simply not susceptible, in the authentic movements of its uncompelled spirit, to administrative reach or convenience. See below for an exploration of the instability, the chronic gap between inner and outer, generated by a religion established by law.

32. Aveling, *Catholic Recusancy*, p. 50.

33. Aveling, *Catholic Recusancy*, p. 12.

34. Aveling, *Catholic Recusancy*, p. 52.

35. Aveling, *Catholic Recusancy*, p. 52. Aveling also mentions Askwith, a draper who is mayor in 1580 and again in 1593 and whose son becomes a recusant.

36. Gardiner, *Mysteries' End*, p. 75. Harbert and Beckwith refused to ride with the mayor on the occasion of the play.

37. Badir, "Playing Space," p. 153. And see *REED: York*, vol. 1, p. 366. See also *York Civic Records*, vol. 115, pp. 49-50. Harbert and Beckwith were confined to prison. They were discharged from prison and ordered to appear before the lord mayor to show their obedience. Since they "did obstynatly and disobediently refuse," they are disenfranchised from the city. It appears that on 23 June (sixteen days later), Harbert submitted himself to the council and was restored to his place on the city council. The record of his readmittance indicates that part of what made the corporation so infuriated was the allegiance and alliance of these men with the Council of the North: "Maister Harbert personally came before theis presents and did humbly submytt hymself to abide the ordre of the Lord Mayour and this worshipfull assemble for his disobediens to his Lordship and for sewyng hym before the Lord President and

Counsell in this North parties, beyng a foreryne courte, contrary to the ancient ordynuncs of this Citie . . ." (p. 50).

38. *REED: York,* vol. 1, p. 367.

39. Aveling, *Catholic Recusancy,* p. 53. And see also his mention in 1599 of Alderman Thomas Herbert's brother, who becomes a recusant. Margaret Clitherow, convert to mission Catholicism and the wife of a York butcher—according to her confessor and biographer Father Mush a saint—was pressed to death because she maintained total silence in the face of her accusers. A Yorkshireman trained in Douai and Rome in the newly founded college for missionary priests, Father Mush is Clitherow's chaplain and writes her life ("The Life of Margaret Clitherow," vol. 3, *The Troubles of Our Catholic Forefathers,* edited by John Morris [Farnborough: Gregg International Publishers, 1872]. Mush later signed a declaration of allegiance to Elizabeth in the last year of her reign; see Megan Matchinske, *Writing, Gender and State in Early Modern England: Identity Formation and the Female Subject,* p. 183 and chapter 2, "Framing Recusant Identity in Counter-Reformation England," pp. 53–85.

40. Perhaps the most influential account of the "suppression" of the Corpus Christi cycles assumes direct and overt suppression; see Gardiner, *Mysteries' End.* Bing Bills in "The Demise of the English Corpus Christi Play: A Re-examination of Attitudes and Perceptions in the Tudor Age of the Sixteenth Century," and in his article "The 'Suppression Theory' and the English Corpus Christi Play: A Re-examination," pp. 157–68, questions Gardiner's back projection of some late Protestant views onto the earlier part of the sixteenth century, finding no evidence for overt legislative suppression, and argues that the plays expire for largely economic reasons. However, as I have made clear in chapter 2, the kind of separation Bills envisages between the economic and the cultural is a separation created by the very version of the economic that he uses. Richard K. Emmerson and Paul Whitfield White have both developed more nuanced and precise ways of thinking about the Reformation and the Corpus Christi cycles in their essays in a special issue of *Journal of Medieval and Early Modern Studies* 29, no. 1 (winter 1999), "The Cultural Work of Medieval Theater: Ritual Practice in England, 1350–1600."

41. There is no Last Supper at Norwich or Coventry, a stage direction in Towneley ("Tunc comedunt") (*The Towneley Plays,* p. 215, l. 351), and a rendition of the historical institution of the Last Supper in Chester. It is hard to say how York represents the Last Supper in the bakers' pageant because there are fifty-three lines missing between lines 89 and 90. Beadle comments that it is not possible to say exactly when the missing link disappeared, but it is precisely at the point in the pageant where the institution of the eucharist is being discussed (Beadle, *The York Plays,* p. 230, and notes at pp. 443–44). Of the extant evidence, only N-town explicitly formulates a doctrine of transubstantiation as central to eucharistic action (*The N-town Play,* edited by Stephen Spector. Early English Text Society, s.s. 11–12 [Oxford: Oxford University Press, 1991],

p. 449). For these points, see Larry Clopper, "English Drama: From Ungodly Ludi to Sacred Play," in *The Cambridge History of Medieval English Literature,* edited by David Wallace, p. 761. For a detailed examination of Chester's institution scene, see David Mills, *Recycling the Cycle: The City of Chester and Its Whitsun Plays,* pp. 172–73.

42. See below. Hutton's attitude to the people of Yorkshire can be gauged from his letter to Burghley in 1568, declaring the need for a new archbishop—Grindal. The new archbishop should be "a teacher because the country is ignorant; a virtuous and godly man because the country is given to sift a man's life; a stout and courageous man in God's cause because the country otherwise will abuse him; and yet a sober and discreet man lest too much vigourousness harden the hearts of some that by fair means might be mollified" (quoted from P.R.O. S.P. Dom. 12/48/41, Hutton to Burghley, 31 November 1568; Lake, "Matthew Hutton," p. 184). Grindal's own comment about the state of Yorkshire on his arrival was that here was "another church, rather than a member of the rest" (Grindal to Cecil, 29 August 1570, *Remains of Archbishop Grindal,* pp. 325–36; quoted Collinson, *Archbishop Grindal,* p. 190).

43. In a letter of 8 July 1575 addressed by the city council to Grindal requesting the return of the playbooks of the Paternoster play, the council mention a "lawe of the realme (by means of which) they are to be reformed," but Bills, who mentions this formulation, can find no such law: "The Church could interfere with town plays when those plays contained material repugnant to the Queen's religion. However to forbid the towns their prerogatives to perform their plays would have been overstepping the powers of the Church" (Bills, "The Demise," p. 361). In 1572, after Henry, earl of Huntingdon, had been appointed to head the Council of the North, Grindal, having obtained an extension of the Ecclesiastical Commission from his province from the queen, manages to get the riding of Yule and Yule's wife abolished: "Forasmuch as the said disguysed rydyng and concourse aforsaid besyds other inconvenyences standeth also to the prophanyng of that day oppoynted to holy uses, and also withdraweth great multitudes of people from devyne service and sermons" (Bills, "The Demise," p. 366).

44. Quoted in appendix C in Wickham, *Early English Stages,* vol. 2, part 1, p. 330. *De Regno Christi* was written by Martin Bucer as a New Year's gift for Edward VI, in which he puts to work the model of a disciplined Christian community established over twenty-five years in Strasbourg. For Grindal's relation to Bucer, see Collinson, *Archbishop Grindal,* p. 53.

45. My understanding here of the structures and grammars of knowledge and acknowledgment is conceived and developed in the writings of Stanley Cavell, especially in *Must We Mean What We Say?* and part 4 of *The Claim of Reason.*

46. See Simon Shepherd and Peter Womack, *English Drama: A Cultural History,* p. 3.

47. Greg Walker, *The Politics of Performance in Early Renaissance Drama,*

pp. 230–31; appendix 1, pp. 225–31, details the censorship and regulation of printed drama.

48. William Worthen, *Shakespeare and the Authority of Performance*, p. 25, points out that prior to the institution of "literature," it is hard to even conceive of the stage as a vehicle for the reproduction of textual, literary authority at all.

49. Hence he removes the authority of the civic authorities, too, over the performance.

50. For details, see below and David Cressy, *Bonfires and Bells: National Memory and the Protestant Calendar in Elizabethan and Stuart England*. Authorized holy days appeared in red letters in the 1559 Book of Common Prayer. The Elizabethan legislation of holy days essentially preserved the Edwardian pruning of the ecclesiastical calendar; see Cressy, *Bonfires and Bells*, p. 7.

51. Cavanaugh, *Torture and Eucharist*.

52. See chapter 3.

53. D. M. Palliser, *The Reformation in York 1534–1553*, p. 12. Of the chantries, one-half are in the parish churches, two bridge chapels, and the rest are in the Minster (pp. 21–22).

54. Robert Whiting, *Local Responses to the English Reformation*, p. 99.

55. Whiting, *Local Responses*, pp. 66, 69. It should be noted that what is going on here is a device constantly exploited by the theater, that is to say, the resignification of one object for another. This has been Launce's point in *The Two Gentlemen of Verona* and my own in chapter 4.

56. P. J. FitzPatrick, *In Breaking of Bread: The Eucharist and Ritual*, p. 209.

57. Badir, "Playing Space," p. 87.

58. Badir, "Playing Space," p. 287.

59. Badir, "Playing Space," p. 276.

60. Walker, *The Politics of Performance*, p. 226.

61. See *REED: York*, vol. 1, pp. 1, 409, 419, 430, 436, 441, 442, 471, 476, 488, 491, 501, 521.

62. Peter Roberts, "Elizabethan Players and Minstrels and the Legislation of 1572 Against Retainers and Vagabonds," in *Religion, Culture and Society in Early Modern Britain: Essays in Honour of Patrick Collinson*, edited by Anthony Fletcher and Peter Roberts, p. 54.

63. John Wasson, "Professional Actors in the Middle Ages and Early Renaissance," pp. 1–11.

64. Robert Tittler, *Architecture and Power: The Town Hall and English Urban Community c. 1500–1640*, p. 140.

65. See Tittler, *Architecture and Power*, p. 141; and also see *Records of Early English Drama: Devon*, edited by John Wasson (Toronto: University of Toronto Press, 1986), p. xxv–xxvi. Wasson notes a distinction between the preferred playing places of local amateurs, who preferred the parish space, and professional players, who tended to prefer the guildhall.

66. Scott McMillan and Sally Beth McClean, *The Queen's Men and Their Plays*, p. 13.

67. Michael O'Connell, *The Idolatrous Eye: Iconoclasm and Theater in Early Modern England,* p. 16.

68. "A Fruitful dialogue declaring these words of Christ: This is My Body" (Grindal, *The Remains of Archbishop Grindal,* p. 43).

69. Judith Maltby, *Prayerbook and People in Elizabethan and Early Stuart England,* p. 3.

70. See *The Lay Folk's Mass Book,* edited by T. F. Simmons. Early English Text Society, o.s., 71 (London: N. Trübner, 1879). This collection makes it clear that the priest's words and the laity's words were separate, with actions and gestures coinciding at certain key moments such as the elevation of the host. Recently Virginia Reinburg and Eamon Duffy have reexamined the forms of participation possible in the mass; see Reinburg, "Liturgy and the Laity," pp. 526–48; and Duffy, "Lay Appropriation of the Sacraments," pp. 53–68.

71. For details on the books used for the use of the liturgy, see John Harper, *The Forms and Orders of Western Liturgy from the Tenth to the Eighteenth Century,* p. 58.

72. See Geoffrey Cuming, *The Godly Order: Texts and Studies Relating to the Book of Common Prayer,* p. 91, for details on how Cranmer modeled the mass. See Diarmaid MacCulloch, *Thomas Cranmer: A Life,* p. 464, for a discussion of Book 5 of the Defence, where Cranmer discusses the sacrifice. Cranmer uses Hebrews to contrast propitiatory sacrifices with sacrifices of Thanksgiving. See Thomas Cranmer, "Defence of the True and Catholic Doctrine of the Sacrament of the Body and Blood of our Saviour Christ," in *The Remains of Thomas Cranmer,* edited by Rev. Henry Jenkins, 4 vols., vol. 2 (Oxford: The University Press, 1833), pp. 291–92. It was Cranmer's view that Maundy Thursday is a holy communion and not a sacrifice, which happened alone on Good Friday.

73. See Cuming's comparison of the 1549 and 1552 rites (*The Godly Order,* pp. 110–22).

74. Cuming, *The Godly Order,* p. 94.

75. Quoted from an early attempt of Cranmer's revision of the Breviary in MS Royal 7B.IV, probably composed c. 1546–47; see Cuming, *The Godly Order,* p. 10.

76. Cuming, *The Godly Order,* p. 12.

77. Patrick Collinson, "Thomas Cranmer," in *The English Religious Tradition and the Genius of Anglicanism,* edited by Geoffrey Rowell, p. 84.

78. See Cressy, *Bonfire and Bells,* p. 4. In 1536 Henry VIII had forced Convocation to limit the holy days. Local parish dedication feasts scattered throughout the calendar henceforth were to take place on the first Sunday in October, and in this sense, too, the BCP commonly enforced a national and uniform liturgy. The holy days remaining were the Feasts of the Apostles, Blessed Virgin, Saint George, the Nativity, Easter Day, Saint John the Baptist, and Saint Michael the Archangel, as well as Ascension Day, All Hallows' Day, and Candlemas.

79. Hutton, *The Rise and Fall of Merry England,* p. 78.

80. Collinson, "Thomas Cranmer," p. 94.

81. See Edward Muir, *Ritual in Early Modern Europe,* p. 7.

82. Muir, *Ritual in Early Modern Europe,* p. 7; and see chapter 5, "The Reformation as a Revolution in Ritual Theory," pp. 155–84.

83. Roy A. Rappaport, *Ritual and Religion in the Making of Humanity,* p. 32.

84. "Against the Articles of the Devonshiremen," in Cranmer, *Remains,* p. 230. The eighth article of their complaint is "We will not receive the new service, because it is like a Christmas game: but we will have our old Service of Matins, Mass, Even-song, and Procession in Latin, as it was before" (p. 230).

85. Cranmer, *Remains,* p. 214.

86. Cranmer, *Remains,* p. 214.

87. Quoted in Lowell Gallagher, *Medusa's Gaze: Casuistry and Conscience in the Renaissance,* p. 22.

88. Walsham, *Church Papists,* p. 12. Churchgoing, rather than the eucharist, was the "legal standard for creedal consent" in Elizabeth's reign.

89. Collinson, "Thomas Cranmer," p. 91, commenting on the 1545 litany. Collinson talks about the way in which the 1549 liturgy is at odds with Cranmer's theology by saying that Cranmer didn't want to put into people's mouths "sentiments which were not wholly theirs" (p. 96).

90. Nicholas Ridley, "A Piteous Lamentation of the Miserable State of the Church of England in the Time of the Revolt from the Gospel," in *The Works of Nicholas Ridley,* edited by Rev. Henry Christmas. The Parker Society (Cambridge: The University Press, 1841), p. 50. Ridley's lamentation is written during the reign of Mary when the liturgy reverts to its Latin usage. And see *The Book of Common Prayer 1559: The Elizabethan Prayer Book,* edited by John Booty (Charlottesville: University Press of Virginia, 1976), p. 15: ". . . the service in this Church of England these many year hath been read in Latin to the people, which they understood not, so that they have heard with their ears only, and their hearts, spirit, and mind have not been edified thereby."

91. Walsham, *Church Papist,* p. 40.

92. Cressy, *Bonfires and Bells,* p. 12: "The Elizabethan Settlement settled nothing at all."

93. Lake, "Religious Identities," p. 64.

94. See Walsham, *Church Papist,* pp. 90–91, for forms of protestation against communion.

95. The name most characteristically associated with the uses of formal restriction in ritual is Maurice Bloch; see his *Ritual, History and Power: Selected Papers in Anthropology.* For a thorough examination of the characteristics associated with ritual activity, see Catherine Bell, *Ritual.*

96. See John H. Primus, *The Vestments Controversy: An Historical Study of the Earliest Tensions in the Church of England in the Reigns of Edward VI and Elizabeth,* p. 76.

97. Pierre Bourdieu, "Authorized Language: The Social Conditions for the Effectiveness of Ritual Discourse," in *Language and Symbolic Power*, edited by John B. Thompson, translated by Gino Raymond and Matthew Adamson, p. 115. This example, at once hilarious and deeply moving, is quoted from R. P. Lelong, *Le dossier noir de la communion solennelle*. In his analysis of it, Bourdieu contemplates the social conditions for the effectiveness of ritual discourse after J. L. Austin. He comments, "Ritual symbolism is not effective on its own, but only insofar as it *represents*—in the theatrical sense of the term—the delegation" (p. 115).

98. The case is described in detail in Claire Cross, "Lay Literacy and Clerical Misconduct in a York Parish During the Reign of Mary Tudor," pp. 10–15. The details are taken from testimony given in the church courts.

99. Cross, "Lay Literacy," p. 12. Cross is citing Borthwick Institute D and C CP 1556/1: deposition of Clerk. She notes (p. 15) that these two phrases misrepresent the burial service in the first instance and the first verse of Psalm 111, a vespers psalm, "Beatus vir, qui timet dominum: in mandatis eius volet nimis."

100. *Medieval Drama*, edited by Bevington, p. 27.

101. See Clopper, "English Drama," p. 742; see also E. K. Chambers, *The Mediaeval Stage*, 2 vols., vol. 2, p. 100. For Grosseteste, see Robert Grosseteste, *Roberti Grosseteste episcopi quondam lincolniensis Epistolae*, edited by Henry Richards Luard (London: Longman, Green, Longman and Roberts, 1861), pp. 72–74, 118–19, 161–62, 317–18. See also Clopper, "English Drama." And also see the contrasted responses of Honorius of Autun in *Medieval Drama*, edited by Bevington, p. 9; and Aelred of Rievaulx's *Speculum Caritatis* c. 1141–42, translated by Elizabeth Connor (Kalamazoo, Mich.: Cistercian Publications, 1990). See also the prohibitions against playing cited in Lancashire, *Dramatic Texts and Records of Britain*, pp. 51, 52, who adds Handlyng Synne (*Handlyng Synne* A.D. 1303 with those Parts of the Anglo-French Treatise on which it was Founded, William of Waddington's Manuel des Pechiez, edited by Frederick J. Furnivall. Early English Text Society, o.s. 119 [London: K. Paul, Trench, Trübner, 1901–3]), and two sermons at York synod; see Robert O'Brien, "Two Sermons at York Synod of William of Rymyngton 1372 and 1373," p. 49.

102. *Tretis of Miraclis Pleyinge*, p. 101. Heather Hill-Vasquez comments on the risking of sacramental power threatened by playing priests in her paper "The *Tretis of Miraclis Pleyinge* as Revisionist Text: Disputing the 'Pleyinge' of Christ's Body."

103. See Claire Sponsler and Robert Clark, "Othered Bodies: Racial Cross-Dressing in the Mistère de la Sainte Hostie and the Croxton Play of the Sacrament," pp. 61–88; Seth Lehrer, " 'Representyd now in yower syght': The Culture of Spectatorship in Late Fifteenth Century England," in *Bodies and Disciplines: Intersections of Literature and History in Fifteenth-Century England*, edited by Barbara Hanawalt and David Wallace, pp. 29–62; Stephen Spector, "Time, Space and Identity in the Play of the Sacrament," in *The Stage as Mir-*

ror: Civic Theatre in Late Medieval Europe, edited by Alan E. Knight, pp. 189–200.

104. *The Book of Common Prayer 1559,* p. 8.

105. Thomas More, "A Treatis upon the Passion," in *The Yale Edition of the Complete Works of Thomas More,* edited by Garry E. Haupt (New Haven: Yale University Press, 1976), vol. 13, p. 157. He goes on to give two examples of Christ appearing in forms other than his own that are resonant for the Corpus Christi cycles, for it is here that the inability to recognize the resurrected Christ is at the heart at once of eucharistic doctrine and of the uses of vision in theater. Christ, he says, appears "in fourme of a wayfaring man" and "in fourme of a gardener." More gives these examples to legitimate playing under other forms. Another way of talking about the example presented to us by More here is to say that its confidence lies in the way in which it assumes the performative magic whereby the name and title of prince is assured as a social essence. As Eric Santner has recently observed, "We cross the threshold of modernity when the attenuation of these performatively effectuated social bonds becomes chronic, when they are no longer capable of seizing the subject in his or her self-understanding" (Santner, *My Own Private Germany: Daniel Paul Schreber's Secret History of Modernity,* p. xii, and chapter 8).

106. Compare Nicholas Ridley in his "Treatise against the Error of Transubstantiation" made while Ridley was imprisoned in the Tower: "then do they godly and charitably . . . that do say that such do make the holy sacrament of the blessed body and blood of Christ nothing else, but a bare sign, or a figure, to represent Christ none otherwise than the ivy-bush doth represent the wine in a tavern: or as a vile person gorgeously apparelled may represent a king or a prince in a play . . ." (*The Works of Nicholas Ridley,* p. 10).

107. Michael Bristol, *Big-time Shakespeare,* p. 176. He goes on to say that it is for this very reason that theater has the capacity to theorize all redemptive media and to make visible the links between ritual, theater, and social contradiction.

108. Gash, "Carnival and the Poetics of Reversal," p. 93. My examples from *II Henry IV* and *Measure for Measure* are taken from Gash's excellent article. A rule of thumb for deploying the term "ritual" in analyses of medieval theater: that the categories of ritual and theater become at once more diagnostically nuanced and illuminating when the critic works from actual examples rather than finding ritual and theatrical forms that operate according to his preconceived model. By looking at how actors and their roles are modified and manipulated in ritual and theatrical settings, held in tension or conformity, by seeing the highly complex interrelations between the two forms, we will have a much more flexible and specific grasp of the full complexity of medieval speech acts.

109. Thomas Becon, "Displaying of the Popish Mass," in *Prayers and Other Pieces of Thomas Becon,* edited by Rev. John Ayre. The Parker Society (Cambridge: Cambridge University Press, 1844), p. 253.

110. Becon, *Prayers and Other Pieces,* p. 259.

111. Becon, *Prayers and Other Pieces,* pp. 264, 270. And, for example: "This done, ye set the chalice down again upon the altar, and ye cover with your corporass cloth for catching of cold. Then once again kneel ye down, and up again, like dive-doppels, and kiss the altar, and spread your arms abroad, as though ye would embrace some she-saint" (p. 276).

112. Becon, *Prayers and Other Pieces,* p. 282.

113. Becon, *Prayers and Other Pieces,* p. 282.

114. Walker, *Plays of Persuasion: Drama and Politics at the Court of Henry VIII,* pp. 169-70.

115. Walker, *Plays of Persuasion,* p. 169.

116. Paul Whitfield White, *Theatre and Reformation: Protestantism, Patronage and Playing in Tudor England,* p. 13.

117. Although the 1538 injunctions altered local parish worship and the fabric of medieval churches significantly, since they called for the extinguishing of lights (except for those on the altar, rood loft, and Easter Sepulchre) and the removal of images "abused with pilgrimages or offerings," and forbade the veneration of relics, in 1539 Henry still supported Palm Sunday palms, Ash Wednesdays ashes, and Candlemas candles as well as "creeping to the cross"; see Hutton, *The Rise and Fall of Merry England,* pp. 75-77.

118. Francis Beaumont, *The Knight of the Burning Pestle,* edited by Michael Hattaway (London: A & C Black, 1996).

119. Walker points out that nearly all the apparel in *King John* is clerical and that "a large supply . . . would have been available to Bale and his troupe by way of Cromwell's seizure of monastic property and valuables from February 1536." Walker also suggests that since the troupes performed at religious houses, some of these clothes could actually be borrowed (*Plays of Persuasion,* p. 191). See also John Bale, *The Complete Plays of John Bale,* edited by Peter Happe, 2 vols. (Cambridge: D. S. Brewer, 1985-86).

120. Coldeway has seen the Vestarian controversy as intimately connected with the demise of town drama. Popish rags, he argues, were desanctified and transformed into stage costumes to become part of the theatrical wardrobes maintained by the parish ("Some Economics Aspects," p. 77).

121. Peter Stallybrass, "Worn Worlds: Clothes and Identity on the Renaissance Stage," in *Subject and Object in Renaissance Culture,* edited by Margreta de Grazia, Maureen Quilligan, and Peter Stallybrass, pp. 289-320.

122. Stallybrass, "Worn Worlds," p. 305. He goes on to mention the "Monty Pythonesque absurdity of the transformations at King's College," when the liturgical garments that had been made into playing gear under Edward VI were turned back into priests' robes under Mary, only, presumably, to be turned back again into players' clothes a few years later (p. 306).

123. White in *Theatre and Reformation,* begins his book with a striking account of Bale's version of such iconoclasm by discussing the scene in John Bale's *Three Laws* (c. 1553) in which the vice Infidelity prompts the bishop Am-

bition to bend down, thereby transforming his prelatical miter into a wolf's gaping mouth (p. 1).

124. Edwin Shepard Miller, "The Roman Rite in Bale's *King John,*" pp. 802-22.

125. Bale, *King John,* vol. 1, p. 36.

126. Bale, *King John,* vol. 1, p. 51.

127. Bale, *King John,* vol. 1, p. 54.

128. John Alford, "'My Name Is Worship': Masquerading Vice in Medwall's *Nature,*" in *From Page to Performance: Essays in Early English Drama,* edited by John Alford, p. 154. Alford assumes this is because the genre lacks "artistic self-consciousness." I think though that such explanations with their assumptions of a genre's teleology (in this case the morality play) need to be rethought in relation to the widespread revolution in ritual theory, practice, and modes of worship from which playing, before the Tudor period, had never been separable.

129. *The N-town Play,* p. 248.

130. In *Wisdom Who Is Christ,* Lucifer wears a devil's dress over the costume of a gallant; see *Wisdom,* in *The Macro Plays,* edited by Mark Eccles. Early English Text Society, o.s., 262 (Oxford: Oxford University Press, 1969), ll. 373-80.

131. See Ann Wierum, "'Actors' and 'Play-Acting' in the Morality Tradition," pp. 189 ff., for these examples. For *Nature,* see Henry Medwall, *The Plays of Henry Medwall,* edited by Alan H. Nelson (Cambridge: D. S. Brewer, 1980).

132. *A New Interlude of Godly Queene Hester,* edited by W. W. Greg (Louvain: A. Uystpruyst, 1904).

133. Alford, "'My Name Is Worship,'" p. 160.

134. *Republica: An Interlude for Christmas 1553,* attributed to Nicholas Udall, edited by W. W. Greg. Early English Text Society (Oxford, Oxford University Press, 1952).

135. Shepherd and Womack, *English Drama,* p. 28.

136. One might say that it is not rebuilt again until Shakespeare.

137. Nicholas Davis, "The Playing of Miracles in England between c. 1350 and the Reformation," p. 162.

138. Bishop, *Shakespeare and the Theatre of Wonder,* p. 58; and also see the excellent exploration of this play by Nicholas Davis in "The Playing of Miracles," pp. 162 ff. See also Bishop where he argues that part of the point of medieval drama was precisely the extent to which sacrament and performance become integrated (p. 47).

139. Nicholas Davis, *"The Playing of Miracles,"* p. 162.

140. Lloyd Davis, *Guise and Disguise: Rhetoric and Characterization in the English Renaissance* (Toronto: University of Toronto Press, 1993), p. 5: "Disguise signifies a type of philosophical and semiotic paradox that operates in and underlies social actions."

141. FitzPatrick, *In Breaking of Bread,* p. 148.

142. FitzPatrick, *In Breaking of Bread,* pp. 148-49. Author's italics.

143. FitzPatrick gives the final example of an "x" on a sheet of paper: "Faced with an 'x' written on a torn-off scrap of paper, I may wonder whether it means a kiss, an illiterate's signature, the preamble to a bishop's signature, a mathematical or logical symbol, or the rejection of an answer submitted for evaluation. These several interpretations compete for assent, and we may or may not be able to make a decision in the matter. But there is no competition between the 'x' itself and the significance we attach to it, nor does the 'x' disguise any of its significances" (FitzPatrick, *In Breaking of Bread*, p. 149).

144. Fischer-Lichte, *The Semiotics of Theater*, p. 73.

145. Fischer-Lichte, *The Semiotics of Theater*, p. 76.

146. Cited in Wickham, *Early English Stages*, vol. 1, p. 116.

147. Cited in Meg Twycross and Sarah Carpenter, "Masks in Medieval English Theatre," p. 30.

148. FitzPatrick, *In Breaking of Bread*, p. 148.

149. Kerr, *Theology After Wittgenstein*, p. 147.

150. Wittgenstein, *Philosophical Investigations*, p. 178c (II.iv).

151. FitzPatrick, *In Breaking of Bread*, p. 158.

152. Kerr, *Theology after Wittgenstein*, p. 147.

153. Cavell, *The Claim of Reason*, p. 44.

154. Cavell, *The Claim of Reason*, especially, pp. 351 ff.

CHAPTER EIGHT

1. It might be noted here that Archdeacon George Austin is also firmly opposed to the ordination of women in the Anglican church.

2. Charles Spencer, "Enter God, Centre Stage," *Daily Telegraph*, 29 February 1996, p. 14. Other contenders included Joyce Nettles's choice of Judi Dench and Celestia Fox's of Sean Connery. I am sure we all have our own casting preferences. I will content myself with pointing out the ingenious casting of Reginald Hill's astonishing character Andy Dalziel as God in his book *Bones and Silence*. When this deliciously gross and bluff northerner gets to play God, it is an in-joke not just for lovers of the York plays, but for lovers of detective fiction, too. For here, generically speaking, justice is always just, and there are always signs, in the world of detective fiction called "clues," that point to the guilty one. Though Dalziel may not be quite ethereal enough to play God, at least he always nails the killer and upholds the law as just. I have argued at length in the previous chapters that in medieval Corpus Christi theater, the actors would not have been assumed to be imitating God, only signifying him.

3. Ritual, as I explained in chapter 7, seeks to create identities, and its conventionalism and invariance work to seal up the gap between actor and role, so that the priest becomes a priest and nothing else and he will also be a priest offstage, as it were.

4. In the 1951 productions, as I explored in chapter 1, the actor playing Christ was kept anonymous until the actual production.

5. The act of May 1606 was "for the preventing and avoiding of the great

abuse of the Holy Name of God in Stage playes, Interludes, Maygames, Shows and such like." Any person who jestingly or profanely speaks or uses the "Holy Name of God or Christ Jesus, or of the Holy Ghost or of the Trinity, which are not to be spoken but with fear and reverence," is to be fined ten pounds (*Statutes of the Realm*, vol. 4, part 2, p. 1097).

6. See Richard Findlater, *Banned! A Review of Theatrical Censorship in Britain.* The first man to appear as a modern Christ as opposed to a medieval Christ was Vittorio Gassmann, who appeared in Gian Paolo Calligan's play *The Man Who Murdered Pilate* in 1948. Initially, the lord chamberlain specified that only his voice should be heard, forbidding an actual stage appearance. He later allowed the stage appearance with the proviso that it should be made clear that no impersonation was involved. When the actor plays Christ, it is therefore staged as a metadrama since it is made clear that the actor is only rehearsing a passion play.

7. The Toronto productions of the summer of 1998 featured predominantly university-based theater groups but also some church-based groups. The other major tradition of Corpus Christi playing in York—the productions regularly performed as part of the York Arts Festival—has been written about by Elliott, *Playing God.*

8. For commentary on these academic productions, see Sponsler, "The Culture of the Spectator."

9. Barry Unsworth, *Morality Play* (London: Penguin, 1996), first published by Hamish Hamilton in 1995. Subsequent quotations from *Morality Play* will be from the Penguin edition and will appear in parentheses in the text.

10. "So it was decided among us to make a place with curtains against the wall of the yard in the corner close to where they were playing" (Unsworth, *Morality Play*, p. 86; and see p. 127). In this sense *Morality Play* is an allegory of theater history and the "growth of the stage." Unsworth mentions the Corpus Christi plays as big-town productions that compete with small-scale troupes for audiences.

11. See Nicholas of Martin, p. 103: "It comes to me sometimes again, his triumph as he held up the purse with both hands, in the very gesture of the celebrant priest."

12. And Stephen has been the actor who is always not only most wedded to the authority of the script, but also most truly deferential to the very authority he now so movingly indicts. Stephen has always played the parts "requiring dignity and state," and he has always had the "best memory for lines" (p. 21).

13. Notice also the Weaver's antitheatricality. Unsworth has done his homework.

14. As in the weaver's association of him with the anti-Christ.

15. "The man was dying unshriven, there might have been time to hold out the Cross to him, but I was afraid to approach. *Mea maxima culpa*" (p. 3). And it is significant here that he recognizes that he *cannot* give absolution.

16. The associations of sodomy, confession, and penance are long and

complex; see Allen Frantzen, *Before the Closet: Same-sex Love from Beowulf to Angels in America*, and Mark Jordan, *The Invention of Sodomy in Christian Theology.*

17. Denys Arcand, *Jésus de Montréal,* p. 7.

18. François Ramasse, "Denys Arcand: Être tendre malgré lui," pp. 12–17.

19. Ramasse, "Denys Arcand," p. 16.

20. Ramasse, "Denys Arcand," where Arcand describes what it is like being flavor of the month after the success of *The Decline of the American Empire.*

21. Excerpts from *Towards a Poor Theatre* in Richard Schnechner and Lisa Wolford, eds., *The Grotowski Sourcebook,* p. 27.

22. Schnechner and Wolford, *The Grotowski Sourcebook,* pp. 34–35.

23. Schnechner and Wolford, *The Grotowski Sourcebook,* p. 33.

24. Richard Cardinal has earlier been identified as a satanic figure in that he has "tempted" Daniel with the riches he could have if he "cashed in" the success of the passion performances.

25. Cavell, *Must We Mean What We Say?,* p. 327.

26. Lloyd Baugh, *Imaging the Divine: Jesus and Christ-Figures in Film,* p. 129.

27. Stanley Cavell, *The World Viewed: Reflections on the Ontology of Film,* pp. 25, 188.

28. Shepherd and Womack, *English Drama,* p. 350.

29. Elliott, *Playing God,* p. 11.

30. Cited in Shepherd and Womack, *English Drama,* p. 41.

31. Shepherd and Womack, *English Drama,* p. 310.

32. Loren Kruger, *The National Stage: Theatre and Cultural Legitimation in England, France and America,* p. 6.

33. Shepherd and Womack, *English Drama,* p. 41.

34. Shepherd and Womack, *English Drama,* p. 34.

35. Shepherd and Womack, *English Drama,* p. 313.

36. Shepherd and Womack, *English Drama,* p. 317.

37. See, for example, the following plays: John Arden's *The Business of Good Government* (1969), Edward Bond's *Passion* (1969), Dennis Potter's *Son of Man* (1969), David Edgar's *O Fair Jerusalem* (1985), Howard Barker's *The Castle* (1985) and *The Last Supper* (1999), and Peter Barnes's *Red Noses* (1985) and *Sunset and Glories* (1990). Elizabeth Angel-Perez has suggested that "modern playwrights are not content with seeking their material in the Middle Ages; they expose the very mechanisms inherent in medieval drama that they find of use to their political purpose" (Angel-Perez, "The Revival of Medieval Forms in Recent Political Drama," in *Drama on Drama: Dimensions of Theatricality on the Contemporary British Stage,* edited by Nicole Boireau, p. 16).

38. Tony Harrison, *The Mysteries.*

39. Harrison, *The Mysteries,* p. 162. This moment, of course, echoes and recalls the earlier moment in the first part of *The Mysteries* (the Passion) where it is a miner who takes up the words of the centurion from the York plays as

the light from his helmet shines "first on the face of [the crucified] Jesus, then, questioningly, on the faces of the audience": "What may these marvels signify / That here was showed so openly / Unto our sight?" (Harrison, *The Mysteries*, p. 155).

40. Harrison, *The Mysteries*, p. 162.

41. See Irving Wardle in *The Times*, 21 January 1985; and Bernard Levin, *The Times*, 19 April 1985, for example.

42. Levin, *The Times*, 19 April 1985.

43. See, for example, Clifford Davidson, "Positional Symbolism and English Medieval Drama"; and Daryll Grantley, "The National Theatre's Production of the *Mysteries:* Some Observations," who calls it a parody of medieval drama in his review (p. 73).

44. Meg Twycross, "The Theatricality of Medieval English Plays," in *The Cambridge Companion to Medieval English Theatre*, edited by Richard Beadle, p. 38. I do not think we can decide in advance what is recoverable or irrecoverable. The fascinating thing about performance is how things do live on.

45. Interview with Katie Mitchell in *Moral Mysteries: Essays to Accompany a Season of Medieval Drama at the Other Place*, edited by David Jays, p. 40.

46. *Moral Mysteries*, p. 40.

47. *Moral Mysteries*, p. 40.

48. *Moral Mysteries*, p. 41.

49. Katie Normington, "'Little Acts of Faith': Katie Mitchell's The Mysteries," p. 101.

50. Katie Mitchell and Edward Kemp, *The Mysteries, Part 1: The Creation*, p. x.

51. Mitchell and Kemp, *Mysteries, Part 1*, p. x.

52. Katie Mitchell and Edward Kemp, *The Mysteries, Part 2: The Passion*, p. xvi. Jack Miles's "biography" of God, which thinks about God as a "character," may have been an influence on them here, too; see Jack Miles, *God: A Biography*.

53. Fundamentalism, as James Barr, among others, has pointed out, is very much the child of the Enlightenment and not sixteenth- and seventeenth-century Protestantism.

54. Mitchell and Kemp, *Mysteries, Part 2*, p. x.

55. Mitchell and Kemp, *Mysteries, Part 2*, p. x.

56. Mitchell and Kemp, *Mysteries, Part 2*, p. xi.

57. My own observations are based on the production I saw at the Other Place in 1997 at Stratford, but Kemp and Mitchell appeared to change the production still further when they took it to the Barbican. Charles Spencer talks in a particularly negative review about the liberal doses of Rilke, Dostoyevsky, and Bulgakov now added to the text and the new setting of Bosnia.

58. For further examples of this stripping away, see Mitchell and Kemp, *Mysteries, Part 1*, p. xiii: "We became more and more rigorous about removing material that did not have biblical support"; and *Mysteries: Part 2*, p. v: "remov-

ing layers of medieval Catholicism in search of what lay beneath"; and pp. v–vi: "stripping away to the skeleton of the biblical source and building up from there." What you get from this is actually a rampantly gung-ho (all the more for being so unwitting) return to the fundamentalism of nineteenth-century Protestantism and a far cry from the pre-Reformation values that they had originally searched for. No one has yet tried a medieval production that might fully animate and understand the relation to a plastic and material culture. This remains a utopian project.

59. *Moral Mysteries*, p. 51.

60. *Moral Mysteries*, p. 82. So they decide not to do it in medieval costume because they think that it would locate the play too securely and enclosedly in the medieval world.

61. *Moral Mysteries*, p. 83.

62. *Moral Mysteries*, p. 84.

63. Mitchell and Kemp, *Mysteries, Part 2*, p. xiv.

64. And it's hard to see in fact that it is anything other than "a hang-over from our original starting point" (Mitchell and Kemp, *Mysteries: Part 2*, p. xiv).

65. "The finding of an object is a re-finding of it" (Sigmund Freud, "Three Essays on the Theory of Sexuality," in Vol. 7, *Standard Edition*, translated and edited by James Strachey, Anna Freud, Alix Strachey, and Alan Tyson, 7:222).

Works Cited

PRIMARY SOURCES

Aelred, of Rievaulx. *Speculum caritatis.* Translated by Elizabeth Connor. Kalamazoo, Mich.: Cistercian Publications, 1990.

Anselm. *Monologium.* Translated by Sidney Norton Deane. La Salle, Ill.: Open Court, 1951.

Aquinas, Thomas. *Commentary on Aristotle's Politics.* Translated by Susan Ziller, Cary Nederman, and Kate Langdon Forhan. In *Medieval Political Theory—A Reader: The Quest for the Body Politic 1100–1400,* edited by Cary Nederman and Kate Langdon Forhan, 136–48. London: Routledge, 1993.

———. *Summa Theologiae.* London: Blackfriars, 1964–80.

Audelay, John. *The Poems of John Audelay.* Edited by Ella Keats Whiting. Early English Text Society, o.s., 184. London: Oxford University Press, 1931.

Augustine. *City of God.* Translated by Henry Bettenson. Harmondsworth: Penguin, 1984.

———. "Commentary on John." *Patrologia Latina cursus completus: series latina,* edited by J.-P. Migne. Vol. 35, col. 1463. Paris, 1844–65.

———. *Confessions.* Translated by Henry Chadwick. Oxford: Oxford University Press, 1991.

———. *Homilies on the Gospel of John.* Vol. 7, *A Select Library of the Nicene and Post-Nicene Fathers.* New York, 1888.

Bale, John. *The Complete Plays of John Bale.* Edited by Peter Happe. 2 vols. Cambridge: D. S. Brewer, 1985–86.

Beard, Thomas. *The Theatre of God's Judgements.* London, 1631.

Beaumont Francis. *The Knight of the Burning Pestle.* Edited by Michael Hattaway. 1969. Reprint, London: A & C. Black, 1996.

Becon, Thomas. *Prayers and Other Pieces of Thomas Becon.* Edited by Rev. John Ayre. The Parker Society. Cambridge: Cambridge University Press, 1844.

The Book of Common Prayer 1559: The Elizabethan Prayer Book. Edited by John Booty. Charlottesville: University Press of Virginia, 1976.

Christ's Burial, in *Late Medieval Religious Plays of Bodleian MSS Digby 133 and E Museo 160.* Edited by Donald C. Baker, John L. Murphy, and Louis B. Hall Jr. Oxford: Oxford University Press, 1982.

Cranmer, Thomas. *The Remains of Thomas Cranmer,* edited by Rev. Henry Jenkins. 4 vols. Oxford: Oxford University Press, 1833.

Dives and Pauper. Edited by Priscilla Heath Barnum. Early English Text Society 275, 280. London: Oxford University Press, 1976.

Drake, Francis. *Eboracum: or, The History and Antiquities of the City of York, From its Original to the Present Times. Together with the History of the Cathedral Church, and the Lives of the Archbishops of that See.* 2 vols. London: Printed by William Bowyer for the author, 1736.

Duns Scotus, John. *Quaestiones in librum quartum sententiarum.* Vol. 18, *Opera Omnia.* Paris, 1894.

The English Works of Wycliff. Edited by F. D. Matthew. Early English Text Series, o.s., 74. London: Kegan Paul, Trench, Trübner, 1880.

English Wycliffite Sermons. Edited by Anne Hudson and Pamela Gradon. 5 vols. Oxford: Clarendon Press, 1983–96.

Fasciculi Zizaniorum: Magistri Johannis Wyclif. Edited by W. W. Shirley. London: Longman, 1858.

Foxe, John. *The Acts and Monuments of John Foxe: A New and Complete Edition.* Edited by R. B. Seeley and W. Burnside. London, 1838.

Grindal, Edmund. *The Remains of Archbishop Grindal.* Edited by Rev. William Nicholson. The Parker Society. Cambridge: The University Press, 1843.

Grosseteste, Robert. *Roberti Grosseteste episcopi quondam lincolniensis Epistolae.* Edited by Henry Richards Luard. London: Longman, Green, Longman and Roberts, 1861.

Handlyng Synne A.D. *1303 with those Parts of the Anglo-French Treatise on which it was Founded, William of Waddington's Manuel des Péchiez.* Edited by Frederick J. Furnivall. Early English Text Society, o.s., 119. London: K. Paul, Trench, Trübner, 1901–3.

Hugh of Saint Victor. *Didascalicon.* Translated by J. Taylor. New York: Columbia University Press, 1961.

———. *On the Sacraments of the Christian Faith.* Translated by Roy J. Deferrari. Cambridge, Mass.: Medieval Academy of America, 1951.

Humbert of Romans. *Beati Umberti sermones.* Venice, 1603.

Julian of Norwich, *The Shewings of Julian of Norwich.* Edited by Georgia Ronan Crampton. Kalamazoo, Mich.: Medieval Institute Publications, 1993.

Lanfranc. "Liber de corpore et sanguine domini." Vol. 150, *Patrologia Latina cursus completus: series latina.* Edited by J.-P. Migne, cols. 407–42. Paris: 1844–65.

Langland, William. *The Vision of Piers Plowman.* Edited by A. V. C. Schmidt. London: J. M. Dent, 1978.

The Lay Folk's Mass Book. Edited by T. F. Simmons. Early English Text Society, o.s., 71. London: N. Trübner, 1879.

Medieval Drama. Edited by David Bevington. Boston: Houghton Mifflin, 1975.

Medwall, Henry. *The Plays of Henry Medwall.* Edited by Alan H. Nelson. Cambridge: D. S. Brewer, 1980.

Middle English Sermons. Edited by Woodburn O. Ross. Early English Text Society, o.s., 209. London: Humphrey Milford, 1940.

Mirk, John. *Mirk's Festial: A Collection of Homilies by Johannes Mirkus.* Edited by Theodor Erbe. Early English Text Society, e.s., 96. London: Kegan Paul, Trench, Trübner, 1905.

More, Thomas. *The Yale Edition of the Complete Works of Thomas More.* Edited by Garry E. Haupt. New Haven: Yale University Press, 1976.

Mush, Father. "The Life of Margaret Clitherow." Vol. 3, *The Troubles of Our Catholic Forefathers.* Edited by John Morris. Farnborough: Gregg International Publishers, 1872. Reprint, 1970.

A New Interlude of Godly Queene Hester. Edited by W. W. Greg. Louvain: A. Uystpruyst, 1904.

The N-town Play. Edited by Stephen Spector. Early English Text Society, s.s., 11–12. Oxford: Oxford University Press, 1991.

Provinciale, seu Constitutiones Angliae, edited by William Lyndwood. London, 1679.

Records of Early English Drama: Devon. Edited by John Wasson. Toronto: University of Toronto Press, 1986.

Records of Early English Drama: York. Edited by Alexandra F. Johnston and Margaret Rogerson. 2 vols. Toronto: Toronto University Press, 1979.

Das Register Gregors VII. Edited by E. Casper. 2 vols. Berlin: MGH Epistolae selectae II fasc. 1–2, 1920–23.

Registrum Johannes Trefnant. Edited by W. W. Capes. London: Canterbury and York Society, 1916.

Regularis Concordia. Translated by Thomas Symons. London: Nelson, 1953.

Respublica. Edited by W. W. Greg. The Early English Text Society. Oxford: Oxford University Press, 1952.

The Resurrection of Our Lord. Edited by J. Dover Wilson and Bertram Dobell. Oxford: Oxford University Press, 1912.

Ridley, Nicholas. "A Piteous Lamentation of the Miserable State of the Church of England in the Time of the Revolt from the Gospel." In *The Works of Nicholas Ridley,* edited by Rev. Henry Christmas. The Parker Society. Cambridge: The University Press, 1841.

Robert of Flamborough. *Liber Poenitentialis.* Edited by J. J. Francis Firth. Toronto: Pontifical Institute of Medieval Studies, 1971.

Selections from English Wycliffite Writing. Edited by Anne Hudson. Cambridge: Cambridge University Press, 1978.

Shakespeare, William. *The Two Gentlemen of Verona.* Edited by Clifford Leech. London: Methuen, 1969. Reprint, London: Thomas Nelson and Sons, 1997.

Smith, J. Toulmin. *English Gilds.* Early English Text Society, o.s., 40. London: Humphrey Milford, 1870.

Speculum Sacerdotale. Edited by E. H. Weatherly. Early English Text Society, o.s., 200. London: Oxford University Press, 1936.

Statutes of the Realm. 9 vols. London, 1810–28.

Thomas of Chobham. *Summa Confessorum.* Edited by F. Bloomfield. Louvain: Nauwelaerts, 1968.

The Towneley Plays. 2 vols. Edited by Martin Stevens and A. C. Cawley. Early English Text Society, s.s., 13–14. Oxford: Oxford University Press, 1994.

A Tretise of Miraclis Pleyinge. Edited by Clifford Davidson. Kalamazoo, Mich.: Medieval Institute Publications, 1993.

Two Wycliffite Texts: The Sermon of William Taylor 1406 and Testimony of William Thorpe 1407. Edited by Anne Hudson. Early English Text Series, o.s., 301. Oxford: Oxford University Press, 1993.

Wisdom. In *The Macro Plays.* Edited by Mark Eccles. 203–15. Early English Text Society, o.s., 262. Oxford: Oxford University Press, 1969.

Wyclif, John. *De Eucharistia tractatus maior.* Edited by Johann Loserth. London: Wyclif Society, 1892.

———. *Sermones.* Edited by Johann Loserth. 4 vols. London: Wyclif Society, 1887–90.

———. *Tractatus de Blasphemia.* Edited by Michael Henry Dziewicki. London: Wyclif Society, 1893.

York Civic Records. Vols. 1–8. Edited by Angelo Raine. Wakefield: York Archeological Society Record Series, 1938–52.

York Memorandum Book: Vol. 1 (1376–1419). Edited by Maud Sellers. Durham, Eng.: Surtees Society, 1912.

York Memorandum Book: Vol. 2 (1388–1493). Edited by Maud Sellers. Durham, Eng.: Surtees Society, 1915.

York Mystery Plays: A Selection in Modern Spelling. Edited by Richard Beadle, and Pamela King. Oxford: Clarendon Press, 1984.

The York Play: A Facsimile of British Library MS Additional 35290, Together with a Facsimile of the "Ordo Paginarum" Section of the A/Y Memorandum Book, and a Note on the Music by Richard Rastall. Edited by Richard Beadle, and Peter Meredith. Leeds: University of Leeds, 1983.

The York Plays. Edited by Richard Beadle. London: Edward Arnold, 1982.

The York Plays. Edited by Lucy Toulmin Smith. Oxford: Clarendon Press, 1885.

SECONDARY SOURCES

Aers, David. "Faith, Ethics and Community: Reflections on Reading Late Medieval English Writing." *Journal of Medieval and Early Modern Studies* 28, no. 2 (spring 1998): 341–70.

———. "John Wyclif's Understanding of Christian Discipleship." In *Faith, Ethics and Church in English Writing 1360–1410.* Woodbridge: Boydell and Brewer, 2000.

Aers, David, and Lynn Staley. *The Powers of the Holy: Religion, Politics, and Gender in Late Medieval English Culture.* University Park: Pennsylvania State University Press, 1996.

Agnew, Jean-Christophe. *Worlds Apart: The Market and the Theater in Anglo-American Thought, 1550–1750.* Cambridge: Cambridge University Press, 1986.

Alford, John. "'My Name Is Worship': Masquerading Vice in Medwall's *Na-*

ture." In *From Page to Performance: Essays in Early English Drama*. East Lansing: Michigan State University Press, 1995.

Alter, Jean. *A Sociosemiotic Theory of Theatre*. Philadelphia: University of Pennsylvania Press, 1990.

Angel-Perez, Elizabeth. "The Revival of Medieval Forms in Recent Political Drama." In *Drama on Drama: Dimensions of Theatricality on the Contemporary British Stage*, edited by Nicole Boireau. 15–29. (Basingstoke: Macmillan, 1997).

Arcand, Denys. *Jesus de Montréal*. Montreal: Boreal, 1989.

Ascherson, Neal. "Why Heritage Is Right-Wing." *Observer*, 8 November 1987.

Ashley, Kathleen. Introduction to special issue of *Journal of Ritual Studies* 6, no.1 (winter 1992).

———. "Sponsorship, Reflexivity and Resistance: Cultural Readings of the York Cycle Plays." In *The Performance of Middle English Culture: Essays on Chaucer and the Drama in Honor of Martin Stevens*, edited by James J. Paxson, Lawrence M. Clopper, and Sylvia Tomasch, 9–24. Cambridge: D. S. Brewer, 1998.

Ashley, Kathleen, and Pamela Sheingorn. "An Unsentimental View of Ritual in the Middle Ages or, Sainte Foy Was No Snow White." *Journal of Ritual Studies* 6, no. 1 (winter 1992): 63–85.

Attreed, Lorraine. "The Politics of Welcome: Ceremonies and Constitutional Development in Later Medieval English Towns." In *City and Spectacle in Medieval Europe*, edited by Barbara Hanawalt and Kathryn Reyerson, 208–31. Minneapolis: University of Minnesota Press, 1994.

Austin, J. L. *How to Do Things with Words*. Oxford: Oxford University Press, 1962.

Aveling, J. C. H. *Catholic Recusancy in the City of York: 1558–1791*. St. Albans, Hertfordshire: Catholic Record Society, 1970.

Badir, Patricia. "Playing Space: History, the Body, and Records of Early English Drama." *Exemplaria* 9, no. 2 (fall 1997): 255–79.

———. "Representations of the Resurrection at Beverley Minster Circa 1208: Chronicle, Play, Miracle." *Theatre Survey* 38, no. 1 (May 1997): 9–41.

Bainbridge, Virginia. *Gilds in the Medieval Countryside: Social and Religious Change in Cambridgeshire c.1350–1558*. Rochester, N.Y.: Boydell Press, 1996.

Baker, Denise. *Julian of Norwich's "Shewings": From Vision to Book*. Princeton: Princeton University Press, 1994.

Bartlett, Martin. "The York 'Crucifixio Cristi.'" Master's thesis, University of York, 1987.

Bates, Jonathan. *The Genius of Shakespeare*. London: Picador, 1997.

Baucom, Ian. *Out of Place: Englishness, Empire and the Locations of Identity*. Princeton: Princeton University Press, 1999.

Baugh, Lloyd. *Imagining the Divine: Jesus and Christ-Figures in Film*. Kansas City: Sheed and Ward, 1997.

Bauman, Zygmunt. *Postmodern Ethics*. Oxford: Blackwell, 1993.

Beadle, Richard. "The Shipwright's Craft." In *Aspects of Early English Drama,* edited by Paula Neuss, 50–61. Cambridge: D. S. Brewer, 1983.

———. "The York Cycle: Texts, Performances, and the Bases for Critical Enquiry." In *Medieval Literature: Texts and Interpretation,* edited by Tim William Machan, 105–19. Binghamton: Center for Medieval and Early Renaissance Studies, 1991.

———, ed. *The Cambridge Companion to Medieval English Theatre.* Cambridge: Cambridge University Press, 1994.

Beckwith, Sarah. *Christ's Body: Identity, Culture and Society in Late Medieval Writings.* London: Routledge, 1993.

———. Introduction to "The Cultural Work of Medieval Theater: Ritual Practice in England 1350–1600." Special issue of *Journal of Medieval and Early Modern Studies* 29, no. 1 (winter 1999): 1–5.

———. "Ritual, Church and Theatre: Medieval Dramas of the Sacramental Body." In *Culture and History: Essays on English Communities, Identities and Writing,* edited by David Aers. 65–90. Hemel Hempstead: Harvester Wheatsheaf, 1992.

———, ed. *Catholicism and Catholicity: Eucharistic Communities in Historical and Contemporary Perspectives.* Oxford: Blackwell, 1999.

Bell, Catherine. "Discourse and Dichotomies: The Structure of Ritual Theory." *Religion* 17 (April 1987): 95–118.

———. *Ritual.* Oxford: Oxford University Press, 1997.

———. *Ritual Theory, Ritual Practice.* Oxford: Oxford University Press, 1992.

Bills, Bing. "The Demise of the English Corpus Christi Play: A Re-examination of Attitudes and Perceptions in the Tudor Age of the Sixteenth Century." Ph.D. diss., University of Iowa, 1974.

———. "The 'Suppression Theory' and the English Corpus Christi Play: A Re-examination." *Theatre Journal* 32 (1980): 157–68.

Bishop, T. G. *Shakespeare and the Theatre of Wonder.* Cambridge: Cambridge University Press, 1996.

Black, Anthony. *Guilds and Civil Society in European Political Thought from the Twelfth Century to the Present.* Ithaca, N.Y.: Cornell University Press, 1984.

———. *Political Thought in Europe: 1250–1450.* Cambridge: Cambridge University Press, 1992.

Blau, Herbert. *The Audience.* Baltimore: Johns Hopkins University Press, 1990.

———. *Take Up the Bodies.* Chicago: University of Illinois Press, 1982.

Bloch, Maurice. *Ritual, History and Power: Selected Papers in Anthropology.* London: Athlone, 1989.

Boireau, Nicole. *Drama on Drama: Dimensions of Theatricality on the Contemporary British Stage.* Basingstoke: Macmillan, 1997.

Bommas, Michael, and Patrick Wright. "Charms of Residence: The Public and the Past." In *Making Histories: Studies in History, Writing and Politics,* edited by Richard Johnson et al., 253–301. Birmingham: Centre for Contemporary Cultural Studies, 1982.

Bossy, John. *The English Catholic Community 1570–1850*. London: Darnton, Longman and Todd, 1975.

Bourdieu, Pierre. "Authorized Language: The Social Conditions for the Effectiveness of Ritual Discourse." In *Language and Symbolic Power*, edited by John B. Thompson, translated by Gino Raymond and Matthew Adamson. 107–16. Cambridge: Harvard University Press, 1991.

———. *The Logic of Practice*. Translated by Richard Nice. Stanford: Stanford University Press, 1990.

———. *Outline of a Theory of Practice*. Translated by Richard Nice. Cambridge: Cambridge University Press, 1977.

Brecht, Bertolt. "The Curtains." In *Poems on the Theatre*, translated by John Berger and Anna Bostock. Lowestoft, Suffolk: Scorpion, 1961.

Brenkman, John. "Theses on Cultural Marxism." *Social Text* 7 (spring/summer 1983): 19–33.

Brenner, Robert. *The Brenner Debates: Agrarian Class Structure and Economic Development in Pre-Industrial Europe*. Edited by T. H. Aston and C. H. E. Philpin. Cambridge: Cambridge University Press, 1985.

Brigden, Susan. *London and the Reformation*. Oxford: Clarendon Press, 1989.

Bristol, Michael. *Big-time Shakespeare*. London: Routledge, 1996.

Brown, Peter. *Augustine of Hippo: A Biography*. Berkeley: University of California Press, 1967.

Brown, Raymond. *The Death of the Messiah: From Gethsemane to the Grave*. 2 vols. New York: Doubleday, 1994.

Browne, Martin. "Producing the Mystery Plays for Modern Audiences." *Drama Survey* 3 (1963): 5–15.

Burke, Kenneth. *The Rhetoric of Religion*. Boston: Beacon Press, 1961.

Camille, Michael. *The Gothic Idol: Ideology and Image-Making in Medieval Art*. Cambridge: Cambridge University Press, 1989.

Carnley, Peter. *The Structure of Resurrection Belief*. Oxford: Clarendon, 1987.

Carruth, Cathy, ed. *Trauma: Explorations in Memory*. Baltimore: Johns Hopkins University Press, 1995.

Carruthers, Mary. *The Book of Memory: A Study of Memory in Medieval Culture*. Cambridge: Cambridge University Press, 1990.

Castoriadis, Cornelius. *The Imaginary Institution of Society*. Translated by Kathleen Blamey. Cambridge, Mass: MIT Press, 1987.

Cavanaugh, William. *Torture and Eucharist: Politics and the Body of Christ*. Oxford: Blackwell, 1998.

Cavell, Stanley. *The Claim of Reason: Wittgenstein, Skepticism, Morality and Tragedy*. Oxford: Oxford University Press, 1979.

———. *Must We Mean What We Say?* Cambridge: Cambridge University Press, 1976.

———. *Disowning Knowledge in Six Plays of Shakespeare*. Cambridge: Cambridge University Press, 1987.

———. *The World Viewed: Reflections on the Ontology of Film*. Cambridge: Harvard University Press, 1979.

Chambers, E. K. *The Mediaeval Stage.* 2 vols. Oxford: Clarendon, 1903.

Champion. "The Gilds of Medieval Beverley." In *The Medieval Town in Britain,* edited by P. Riden. Cardiff: Cardiff Papers in Local History, 1980.

Clanchy, Michael. *Abelard: A Medieval Life.* Oxford: Blackwell, 1997.

Clarke, Simon. "Socialist Humanism and the Critique of Economism." *History Workshop* 8 (1979): 137–56.

Clopper, Lawrence. "English Drama: From Ungodly Ludi to Sacred Play." *Cambridge History of Medieval Literature,* edited by David Wallace, 739–66. Cambridge: Cambridge University Press, 1999.

———. "Lay and Clerical Impact on Civic Religious Drama and Ceremony." In *Contexts for Early English Drama,* edited by Marianne G. Briscoe and John C. Coldeway, 102–36. Bloomington: Indiana University Press, 1989.

Coldeway, John. "Some Economic Aspects of the Late Medieval Drama." In *Contexts for Early English Drama,* edited by Marianne G. Briscoe and John C. Coldeway, 77–101. Bloomington: Indiana University Press, 1989.

Cole, Andrew. "Rewriting Langland and Chaucer: Heresy and Literary Authority in Late Medieval England." Ph.D. diss., Duke University, 2000.

Coletti, Theresa. "Reading REED: History and Records of Early English Drama." In *Literary Practice and Social Change in Britain: 1380–1530,* edited by Lee Patterson, 248–84. Berkeley: University of California Press, 1990.

Collinson, Patrick. *Archbishop Grindal 1519–1583.* Berkeley: University of California Press, 1979.

———. "The Elizabethan Church and the New Religion." In *The Reign of Elizabeth I,* edited by Christopher Haigh, 169–94. Houndmills, Basingstoke: Macmillan, 1984.

———. "Thomas Cranmer." In *The English Religious Tradition and the Genius of Anglicanism,* edited by Geoffrey Rowell, 79–103. Wanbridge: IKON, 1992.

Comaroff, Jean, and John Comaroff. "Bodily Reform as Historical Practice." In *Ethnography and the Historical Imagination.* Boulder: Westview Press, 1992.

Connerton, Paul. *How Societies Remember.* Cambridge: Cambridge University Press, 1989.

Copjec, Joan. *Read My Desire: Lacan Against the Historicists.* Cambridge, Mass.: MIT Press, 1994.

Cowling, Douglas. "The Liturgical Celebration of Corpus Christi in Medieval York." *REED Newsletter* 2 (1976): 5–9.

Cramer, Peter. *Baptism and Change in the Early Middle Ages c. 200–c. 1150.* Cambridge: Cambridge University Press, 1993.

Cressy, David. *Bonfires and Bells: National Memory and the Protestant Calendar in Elizabethan and Stuart England.* Berkeley: University of California Press, 1989.

Crockatt, William. *Eucharist: Symbol of Transformation.* New York: Pueblo Publishing, 1989.

Cross, Claire. "Lay Literacy and Clerical Misconduct in a York Parish During the Reign of Mary Tudor." *York Historian* 3 (1980): 10–15.

———. "Priests into Ministers: The Establishment of Protestant Practice in the City of York 1530–1630." In *Reformation Principle and Practice: Essays in Honour of Arthur Geoffrey Dickens,* edited by Peter Newman Brooks, 205–25. London: Scolar Press, 1980.

Crouch, David. "Paying to See the Play: The Stationholders on the Route of the York Corpus Christi Play in the Fifteenth Century." *Medieval English Theatre* 13 (1991): 64–111.

Cuming, Geoffrey. *The Godly Order: Texts and Studies Relating to the Book of Common Prayer.* London: Alcuin Club, SPCK, 1983.

DaMatta, Roberto. *Carnivals, Rogues and Heroes: An Interpretation of the Brazilian Dilemma.* Translated by John Drury. Notre Dame: University of Notre Dame Press, 1991.

Davidson, Clifford. "Positional Symbolism and English Medieval Drama." *Comparative Drama* 25, no. 1 (spring 1991): 66–76.

Davis, Lloyd. *Guise and Disguise: Rhetoric and Characterization in the English Renaissance.* Toronto: University of Toronto Press, 1993.

Davis, Nicholas. "The Playing of Miracles in England between c. 1350 and the Reformation." Ph. D. diss., Cambridge University, 1978.

Dawson, Anthony B. "Performance and Participation: Desdemona, Foucault and the Actor's Body." In *Shakespeare, Theory and Performance,* edited by James Bulman, 29–45. London: Routledge, 1996.

Derrida, Jacques. *Limited Inc.* Evanston, Ill.: Northwestern University Press, 1988.

Devlin, D. S. "Corpus Christi: A Study in Medieval Eucharistic Theory, Development, and Practice." Ph.D. diss., University of Chicago, 1975.

Dickens, A. G. *Lollards and Protestants in the Diocese of York 1509–1558.* Oxford: Oxford University Press, 1959. Reprint, London: Hambledon Press, 1982.

Dillon, Janette. *Language and Stage in Medieval and Renaissance England.* Cambridge: Cambridge University Press, 1998.

Dobb, Maurice. *Studies in the Development of Capitalism.* 1946. Rev. ed. London: Routledge and Kegan Paul, 1963.

Dobson, R. B. "Admission to the Freedom of the City of York in the Later Middle Ages." *Economic History Review* 26, 2d ser., no. 1 (1973): 1–22.

———. "Craft Guilds and City: The Historical Origins of the York Mystery Plays Reassessed." In *The Stage as Mirror: Civic Theatre in Late Medieval Europe,* edited by Alan E. Knight, 91–106. Cambridge: D. S. Brewer, 1997.

———. *The Jews of Medieval York and the Massacre of March 1190.* York: St. Anthony's Press, 1974.

———. "The Risings in York, Beverley and Scarborough, 1380–1." In *The English Rising of 1381,* edited by R. H. Hilton and T. H. Aston. Cambridge: Cambridge University Press, 1984.

———, ed. *The Peasant's Revolt of 1381.* London: Macmillan, 1970.

Douglas, Mary. *Natural Symbols: Explorations in Cosmology.* Harmondsworth: Penguin, 1973.

Duffy, Eamon. "Lay Appropriation of the Sacrament in the Later Middle Ages." *New Blackfriars* 77, no. 900 (January 1996): 53–68.

———. *The Stripping of the Altars: Traditional Religion in England c. 1400–c. 1580.* New Haven: Yale University Press, 1992.

Dumoutet, Edouard. *Le désir de voir l'hostie et les origines de la dévotion au saint-sacrement.* Paris: Beauchesnes, 1926.

Durkheim, Emile. *The Elementary Forms of Religious Life.* London: Allen and Unwin, 1915.

———. *The Elementary Forms of Religious Life.* Translated by Joseph Ward Swain. New York: The Free Press, 1965.

Eco, Umberto. "Semiotics of Theatrical Performance." *The Drama Review* 21 (March 1977): 107–17.

Elam, Keir. *The Semiotics of Theatre and Drama.* London: Methuen, 1980.

Elliott, John. *Playing God: Medieval Mysteries on the Modern Stage.* Toronto: University of Toronto Press, 1989.

Emmerson, Richard K. "Contextualizing Performance: The Reception of the Chester *Anti-Christ.*" *Journal of Medieval and Early Modern Studies* 29, no. 1 (winter 1999): 89–119.

Enders, Jody. "Medieval Snuff Drama." *Exemplaria* 10, no. 1 (1998): 171–206.

———. *The Medieval Theater of Cruelty: Rhetoric, Memory and Violence.* Ithaca: Cornell University Press, 1999.

Erler, Mary. "Palm Sunday Prophets, Processions and Eucharistic Controversy." *Renaissance Quarterly* 48, no. 1 (spring 1995): 58–81.

Festival Program of 1988. *York Festival Collection.* York City Library, 1988.

Findlater, Richard. *Banned! A Review of Theatrical Censorship in Britain.* London: MacGibbon and Kee, 1967.

Fischer-Lichte, Erika. *The Semiotics of Theater.* Bloomington: Indiana University Press, 1992.

FitzPatrick, P. J. *In Breaking of Bread: The Eucharist and Ritual.* Cambridge: Cambridge University Press, 1993.

Flanigan, Clifford. "The Liturgical Drama and Its Tradition: A Review of Scholarship 1965–1975." *Research Opportunities in Renaissance Drama* 18 (1975): 81–102 and 19 (1976): 109–36.

Foot, Michael. *Aneurin Bevan: Volume Two 1945–60.* New York: Atheneum, 1974.

Fradenburg, Louise. "Voice Memorial: Loss and Reparation in Chaucer's Poetry." *Exemplaria* 2, no. 1 (March 1990): 169–202.

Frantzen, Allen. *Before the Closet: Same-sex Love from Beowulf to Angels in America.* Chicago: University of Chicago Press, 1998.

Frei, Hans. *Theology and Narrative: Selected Essays.* Edited by George Hubsinger and William C. Placher. Oxford: Oxford University Press, 1993.

Freud, Sigmund. "Mourning and Melancholia." In Vol. 14, *The Standard Edi-*

tion of the Complete Psychological Works of Freud, translated and edited by James Strachey, Anna Freud, Alix Strachey, and Alan Tyson. London: Hogarth Press, 1953–74.

———. "Three Essays on the Theory of Sexuality." In Vol. 7, *Standard Edition,* translated and edited by James Strachey, Anna Freud, Alix Strachey, and Alan Tyson. 24 vols. London: Hogarth, 1953–74.

Frisby, David. *Simmel and Since: Essays on Georg Simmel's Social Theory.* London: Routledge, 1992.

Gallagher, Lowell. *Medusa's Gaze: Casuistry and Conscience in the Renaissance.* Stanford: Stanford University Press, 1991.

Gardiner, Harold C. *Mysteries' End: An Investigation of the Last Days of the Medieval Religious Stage.* New Haven: Yale University Press, 1946.

Garner, Stanton. *The Absent Voice: Narrative Comprehension in the Theater.* Urbana: University of Illinois Press, 1989.

———. *Bodied Spaces: Phenomenology and Performance in Contemporary Drama.* Ithaca: Cornell University Press, 1994.

Gash, Anthony. "Carnival and the Poetics of Reversal." In *New Directions in Theatre,* edited by Julian Hilton, 87–119. New York: St. Martin's Press, 1993.

Georgianna, Linda. *The Solitary Self: Individuality in the* Ancrene Wisse. Cambridge: Harvard University Press, 1981.

Geary, Patrick. *Phantoms of Remembrance: Memory and Oblivion at the End of the First Millennium.* Princeton: Princeton University Press, 1994.

Girard, René. *Things Hidden since the Foundation of the World.* Stanford: Stanford University Press, 1987.

Goldberg, P. J. "Craft Guilds, the Corpus Christi Play and Civic Government." In *The Government of Medieval York: Essays in Commemoration of the 1396 Royal Charter,* edited by Sarah Rees Jones, 141–63. York: Borthwick Institute of Historical Research, 1997.

———. "Performing the Word of God: Corpus Christi Drama in the Northern Province." In *Life and Thought in the Northern Church c. 1100–1700,* edited by Diana Wood, 145–70. Woodbridge, Eng.: Boydell Press, 1999.

———. "Urban Identity and the Poll Taxes of 1377, 1379 and 1381." *Economic History Review* 43, 2d ser., no. 2 (1990): 194–216.

———. *Women, Work and Life-Cycle in a Medieval Economy: Women in York and Yorkshire, 1300–1520.* Oxford: Clarendon Press, 1992.

Goldman, Martin. *The Actor's Freedom.* New York: Viking Press, 1975.

Goose, Nigel. "English Pre-Industrial Urban Economies." *Urban History Yearbook* (1982): 27–30.

Grantley, Darryll. "The National Theatre's Production of the Mysteries: Some Observations." *Theatre Notebook* 40 (1986): 70–73.

Green, Mrs. J. R. [Alice Stopford]. *Town Life in the Fifteenth Century.* 2 vols. London: Macmillan, 1894.

Greenblatt, Stephen. "Remnants of the Sacred in Modern England." In *Subject and Object in Renaissance Culture,* edited by Margreta de Grazia, Maureen Quilligan, and Peter Stallybrass, 337–45. Cambridge: Cambridge University Press, 1996.

Gross, Charles. *The Gild Merchant: A Contribution to British Municipal History.* 2 vols. Oxford: Clarendon Press, 1890.

Grossberg, Lawrence. "Teaching the Popular." In *Theory in the Classroom,* edited by Cary Nelson, 177–200. Urbana: University of Illinois Press, 1986.

Grotowski, Jerzy. *Towards a Poor Theatre.* New York: Simon and Schuster, 1969.

Gy, Pierre-Marie. "Histoire liturgique sacrament du pénitence." *La Maison-Dieu* 56 (1958): 5–21.

Haigh, Christopher. "The Continuity of English Catholicism in the English Reformation." *Past and Present* 93 (1981): 37–69.

Halbwachs, Maurice. *On Collective Memory.* Translated by Francis J. Ditter and Vida Yazdi Ditter. New York: Harper and Row, 1980.

———. "Marxism and Culture." *Radical History Review* 18 (fall 1978): 5–14.

Handelman, Don. *Models and Mirrors: Towards an Anthropology of Public Events.* Cambridge: Cambridge University Press, 1990.

Handke, Peter. *Kaspar and Other Plays.* Translated by Michael Roloff. New York: Farrar, Straus and Giroux, 1969.

Hanning, Robert. " 'You Have Begun a Parlous Pley': The Nature and Limits of Dramatic Mimesis as a Theme in Four Middle English 'Fall of Lucifer' Cycle Plays." *Comparative Drama* 7 (1973): 22–50.

Harbison, Robert. *The Built, the Unbuilt and the Unbuildable: In Pursuit of Architectural Meaning.* London: Thames and Hudson, 1991.

Hardison, O. B. *Christian Rite and Christian Drama in the Middle Ages: Essays in the Origin and Early History of Modern Drama.* Baltimore: Johns Hopkins Press, 1965.

Harper, John. *The Forms and Orders of Western Liturgy from the Tenth to the Eighteenth Century.* Oxford: Clarendon, 1991.

Harper-Bill, Christopher. *The Pre-Reformation Church in England 1400–1530.* Harlow: Longman, 1989.

Harrison, Tony. *The Mysteries.* London: Faber and Faber, 1985.

Harrop, John. *Acting.* London: Routledge, 1992.

Harvey, David. *The Condition of Postmodernity.* Oxford: Blackwell, 1989.

Hauerwas, Stanley. *Sanctify Them in the Truth: Holiness Exemplified.* Nashville: Abingdon Press, 1998.

Hennessy, Peter. *Never Again, Britain 1945–51.* London: Vintage, 1993.

Hill, Reginald. *Bones and Silence.* New York: Delacorte Press, 1990.

Hill-Vasquez, Heather. "The *Tretise of Miraclis Pleyinge* as Revisionist Text: Disputing the 'Pleyinge' of Christ's Body." Paper presented at Modern Language Association, Toronto, 1997.

Hilton, Rodney. *English and French Towns in Feudal Society: A Comparative Study.* Cambridge: Cambridge University Press, 1992.

Hobsbawm, Eric, and Terence Ranger, eds. *The Invention of Tradition.* Cambridge: Cambridge University Press, 1983.

Holl, K. *Der Kirchen begriff des Paulus in seinem Verhaltnis zu dem der Urgemeinde.* In *Gesammelte Aufsätze zur Kirchengeschichte.* Tübingen: J. C. B. Mohr, 1921.

Holston, James. *The Modernist City: An Anthropological Critique of Brasilia.* Chicago: University of Chicago Press, 1989.

Holt, Richard, and Gervase Rosser. Introduction to *The English Medieval Town: A Reader in English Urban History 1200–1530.* London: Longman, 1990.

Homan, Richard. "Ritual Aspects of the York Cycle." *Theatre Journal* 33, no. 3 (October 1981): 303–15.

Howell, Martha. *Women, Production and Patriarchy in Late Medieval Cities.* Chicago: University of Chicago Press, 1986.

Hoyau, Philippe. "Heritage and Consumer Society: The French Case." In *The Museum Time-Machine,* edited by Robert Lumley, 27–35. London: Routledge, 1988.

Hudson, Anne. *Lollards and Their Books.* London: Hambledon Press, 1985.

———. "William Thorpe and the Question of Authority." In *Christian Authority: Essays in Honour of Henry Chadwick,* edited by G. R. Evans, 127–37. Oxford: Clarendon Press, 1988.

Hughes, Andrew. "Liturgical Drama: Falling between the Disciplines." In *The Theatre of Medieval Europe,* edited by Eckehard Simon, 42–62. Cambridge: Cambridge University Press, 1991.

Hunt, Lynn. "The Sacred and the French Revolution." In *Durkheimian Sociology: Cultural Studies,* edited by Jeffrey C. Alexander. Cambridge: Cambridge University Press, 1988.

Hutton, Patrick. *History as an Art of Memory.* Hanover: University of Vermont, 1993.

Hutton, Ronald. *The Rise and Fall of Merry England: The Ritual Year 1400–1700.* Oxford: Oxford University Press, 1994.

Hutton, Will. "Stopping the Rot in a State of Decay." *Guardian Weekly,* 1 October 1995.

Jacques, Sister Bernarda. "Ancient Magic Distilled: The Twentieth Century Productions of the York Mystery Plays." Ph.D. diss., Tufts University, 1971.

James, Mervyn. "Ritual, Drama and Social Body in the Late Medieval English Town." *Past and Present* 98 (1983): 3–29.

Janovitz, Anne. *England's Ruins: Poetic Purpose and the National Landscape.* Oxford: Basil Blackwell, 1990.

Jays, David, ed. *Moral Mysteries: Essays to Accompany a Season of Medieval Drama at the Other Place.* Stratford: RSC Publications, 1997.

Johnson, Richard. "Thompson, Genovese and Socialist-Humanist History." *History Workshop* 6 (1978): 79–110.

Johnston, Alexandra F. "The Continental Connection: A Reconsideration." Paper presented at "The Stage as Mirror: Civic Theatre in Late Medieval Europe." Penn State, March 1993. Reprinted in Alan E. Knight, ed., *The Stage as Mirror: Civic Theatre in Late Medieval Europe.* Cambridge: D. S. Brewer, 1997.

———. "The Guild of Corpus Christi and the Procession of Corpus Christi in York." *Mediaeval Studies* 38 (1976): 372–84.

———. "The Plays of the Religious Guilds of York: The Creed Play and Paternoster Play." *Speculum* 50 (1975): 55–90.

———. "The Procession and Play of Corpus Christi in York after 1426." *Leeds Studies in English* 7 (1973–74): 55–62.

———. "The Word Made Flesh: Augustinian Elements in the York Cycle." In *The Centre and Its Compass: Studies in Medieval Literature in Honour of Professor John Leyerle,* edited by Robert A. Taylor et al. Kalamazoo, Mich.: Medieval Institute Publications, 1993.

———. "The York Corpus Christi Play: A Dramatic Structure Based on Performance Practice." In *The Theatre in the Middle Ages,* edited by Herman Braet, Johan Nové, and Gilbert Tournoy, 362–73. Leuven: Leuven University Press, 1985.

Jones, Greg. *Embodying Forgiveness: A Theological Analysis.* Grand Rapids, Mich.: William B. Eerdmans, 1995.

Jones, Paul. *Christ's Eucharistic Presence: A History of the Doctrine.* New York: P. Lang, 1994.

Jordan, Mark. *The Invention of Sodomy in Christian Theology.* Chicago: University of Chicago Press, 1997.

Justice, Alan. "Trade Symbolism in the York Cycle." *Theatre Journal* 31 (1979): 47–58.

Justice, Steven. *Writing and Rebellion: England in 1381.* Berkeley: University of California Press, 1994.

Kantorowicz, Ernst. "The King's Advent and the Enigmatic Panels in the Doors of Santa Sabina." *Art Bulletin* 26 (1944): 207–31.

———. *Laudes Regiae: A Study in Liturgical Acclamations and Mediaeval Ruler Worship.* Berkeley: University of California Press, 1946.

Kaye, Harvey. *The British Marxist Historians: An Introductory Analysis.* Cambridge: Polity Press, 1984.

Kelly, John, and Martha Kaplan. "History, Structure, and Ritual." *Annual Review of Anthropology* 19 (1990): 119–50.

Kennedy, V. L. "The Moment of Consecration and the Elevation of the Host." *Mediaeval Studies* 6 (1944): 121–50.

Kermode, Jennifer. "Merchants, Overseas Trade and Urban Decline: York, Beverley and Hull c. 1380–1500." *Northern History* 23 (1988): 51–73.

———. "Urban Decline?: The Flight from Office in Late Medieval York." *Economic History Review* 35 (1982): 179–98.

Kerr, Fergus. *Immortal Longings.* Notre Dame: University of Notre Dame Press, 1997.

———. *Theology after Wittgenstein.* Oxford: Basil Blackwell, 1986.

King, Pamela. "Calendar and Text: Christ's Ministry in the York Plays and the Liturgy." *Medium Aevum* 67 (1998): 30–59.

———. "Contemporary Cultural Models for the Trial Plays in the York Cycle." In *Drama and Community: People and Plays in Medieval Europe*, edited by Alan Hindley, 200–16. Brepols: University of Hull, 1999.

———. "Corpus Christi Plays and the 'Bolton Hours' 1: Tastes in Lay Piety and Patronage in Fifteenth Century York." *Medieval English Theatre* 18 (1996): 46–62.

———. "Spatial Semantics and the Medieval Theatre." In *The Theatrical Space.* Vol. 9, *Themes in Drama*, edited by James Redmond, 45–58. Cambridge: Cambridge University Press, 1987.

Kipling, Gordon. *Enter the King: Theatre, Liturgy and Ritual in the Medieval Civic Triumph.* Oxford: Clarendon Press, 1998.

Kirwan, Christopher. *Augustine.* London: Routledge, 1989.

Knight, Alan E., ed. *The Stage as Mirror: Civic Theatre in Late Medieval Europe.* Cambridge: D. S. Brewer, 1997.

Kobialka, Michal. *This Is My Body: Representational Practices in the Early Middle Ages.* Ann Arbor: University of Michigan Press, 1999.

Kolvé, V. A. *The Play Called Corpus Christi.* Stanford: Stanford University Press, 1966.

Kowzan, Tadeusz. *Littérature et spectacle.* The Hague: Mouton, 1975.

Kramer, Stella. *The English Craft Gilds: Studies in Their Progress and Decline.* New York: Columbia University Press, 1927.

Kruger, Loren. *The National Stage: Theatre and Cultural Legitimation in England, France and America.* Chicago: University of Chicago Press, 1992.

Kubiak, Anthony. *Stages of Terror: Ideology and Coercion as Theatre History.* Bloomington: Indiana University Press, 1991.

Kuhn, Sherman M., ed. *Middle English Dictionary, O–P.* Ann Arbor: University of Michigan Press, 1975.

Lake, Peter. "Matthew Hutton—A Puritan Bishop?" *History* 64 (1979): 182–204.

———. "Religious Identities in Shakespeare's England." In *A Companion to Shakespeare*, edited by David Scott Kastan, 57–84. Oxford: Blackwell, 1999.

Lancashire, Ian. *Dramatic Texts and Records of Britain: A Chronological Topography to 1558.* Toronto: University of Toronto Press, 1984.

Laroque, François. *Shakespeare's Festive World: Elizabethan Seasonal Entertainment and the Professional Stage.* Translated by Janet Lloyd. Cambridge: Cambridge University Press, 1991.

Larson, Gary. *The Far Side Gallery.* London: Futura, 1989.

Lash, Nicholas. *Easter in Ordinary: Reflections on Human Experience and the Knowledge of God.* Charlottesville: University of Virginia Press, 1990.

————. *Theology on the Way to Emmaus.* London: SCM Press, 1986.

Lawton, David. *Faith, Text and History: The Bible in English.* Charlottesville: University Press of Virginia, 1990.

Lefebvre, Henri. *The Production of Space.* Translated by Donald Nicholson-Smith. Oxford: Blackwell, 1991.

Lehrer, Seth. " 'Representyd now in yower syght': The Culture of Spectatorship in Late Fifteenth Century England." In *Bodies and Disciplines: Intersections of Literature and History in Fifteenth-Century England,* edited by Barbara Hanawalt and David Wallace, 29–62. Minneapolis: University of Minnesota Press, 1996.

Lelong, R. P. *Le dossier noir de la communion solennelle.* Paris: Mame, 1972.

Lipphardt, Walther, ed. *Lateinische Osterfeiern und Osterspiele.* 7 vols. Berlin: De Gruyter, 1975–.

Little, Katherine C. "Catechesis and Castigation: Sin in the Wycliffite Sermon Cycle," *Traditio* 54 (1999): 213–44.

————. "Reading for Christ: Interpretation and Instruction in Late Medieval England." Ph.D. diss., Duke University, 1998.

Lochrie, Karma. *Covert Operations: The Medieval Uses of Secrecy.* Philadelphia: University of Pennsylvania Press, 1999.

————. *Margery Kempe and the Translations of the Flesh.* Philadelphia: University of Pennsylvania Press, 1991.

Logan, F. Donald. *Excommunication and the Secular Arm in Medieval England.* Toronto: Pontifical Institute of Medieval Studies, 1968.

Loughlin, Gerard. "The Basis and Authority of Doctrine." In *The Cambridge Companion to Christian Doctrine,* edited by Colin E. Gunton, 41–64. Cambridge: Cambridge University Press, 1997.

Lozar, Paula, ed. and trans. "The 'Prologue' to the Ordinances of the York Corpus Christi Guild." *Allegorica* 1 (1976): 94–113.

Lubac, Henri de. *Corpus Mysticum: L'eucharistie et l'église au moyen âge.* Paris: Aubier, 1949.

Lumley, Robert, ed. *The Museum Time-Machine.* London: Routledge, 1988.

MacCulloch, Diarmaid. *Thomas Cranmer: A Life.* New Haven: Yale University Press, 1996.

Macpherson, C. B. "Capitalism and the Changing Concept of Property." In *Feudalism, Capitalism and Beyond,* edited by Eugene Kamenka and R. S. Neale, 104–25. London: Edward Arnold, 1975.

————. *The Political Theory of Possessive Individualism: Hobbes to Locke.* Oxford: Clarendon Press, 1962.

Macy, Gary. "The Dogma of Transubstantiation in the Middle Ages." *Journal of Ecclesiastical History* 45 (January 1994): 11–41.

Maltby, Judith. *Prayerbook and People in Elizabethan and Early Stuart England.* Cambridge: Cambridge University Press, 1998.

Manning, Roger. *Village Revolts: Social Protest and Popular Disturbances in England 1509–1640.* Oxford: Clarendon Press, 1988.

Mansfield, Mary C. *The Humiliation of Sinners: Public Penance in Thirteenth-Century France.* Ithaca: Cornell University Press, 1995.

Marx, Karl. *Capital. Collected Works.* Vols. 35–37. New York: International Publishers, 1975–95.

———. *The German Ideology. Collected Works.* Vol. 5. London: Lawrence and Wishart, 1976.

Massey, Doreen. "A Global Sense of Place." In *Studying Culture: An Introductory Reader,* edited by Ann Gray and Jim McGuigan. London: Edward Arnold, 1993.

Matchinske, Megan. *Writing, Gender and State in Early Modern England: Identity Formation and the Female Subject.* Cambridge: Cambridge University Press, 1998.

McHardy, A. K. "De Heretico Comburendo." In *Lollardy and the Gentry in the Later Middle Ages,* edited by Margaret Aston and Colin Richmond, 112–26. New York: St. Martin's Press, 1997.

McIntosh, Marjorie. "Finding a Language for Misconduct: Jurors in Fifteenth-Century Local Courts." In *Bodies and Disciplines: Intersections of Literature and History in Fifteenth-Century England,* edited by Barbara Hanawalt and David Wallace, 87–122. Minneapolis: University of Minnesota Press, 1996.

McLaren, Peter. "On Ideology and Education: Critical Pedagogy and the Politics of Empowerment." *Social Text,* nos. 19/20 (fall 1988): 153–85.

McMillan, Scott, and Sally Beth McClean. *The Queen's Men and Their Plays.* Cambridge: Cambridge University Press, 1998.

McNiven, Peter. *Heresy and Politics in the Reign of Henry IV: The Burning of John Badby.* Woodbridge, Eng.: Boydell Press, 1987.

McRee, Benjamin. "Religious Guilds and Civic Order: The Case of Norwich in the Late Middle Ages." *Speculum* 67 (January 1992): 69–97.

Meredith, Peter. "John Clerke's Hand in the York Register." *Leeds Studies in English* 12 (1981): 245–71.

———. "The York Cycle and the Beginning of Vernacular Religious Drama in England." In *Le Laudi Drammatiche umbredelle Origini.* Viterbo: Union Printing, 1981.

Merleau-Ponty, Maurice. *The Visible and the Invisible,* edited by Claude Lefort. Evanston, Ill.: Northwestern University Press, 1968.

Merrington, John. "Town and Country in the Transition to Capitalism." In *The Transition from Feudalism to Capitalism,* introduction by Rodney Hilton, 170–95. London: Verso, 1978.

Milbank, John. "The Name of Jesus." In *The Word Made Strange: Theology, Language, Culture.* Oxford: Blackwell, 1997.

———. *Theology and Social Theory.* Oxford: Blackwell, 1990.

Miles, Jack. *God: A Biography.* New York: Alfred A. Knopf, 1995.

Mill, Anna J. "The Stations of the York Corpus Christi Play." *Yorkshire Archeological Journal* 37 (1948–51): 492–502.

Miller, D. A. *The Novel and the Police.* Berkeley: University of California Press, 1990.

Miller, E. "Medieval York." In *Victoria History of the Counties of England: A History of Yorkshire, the City of York,* edited by R. B. Pugh. Oxford: Oxford University Press, 1961. 25–113.

Miller, Edwin Shepard. "The Roman Rite in Bale's *King John.*" *PMLA* 64 (1949): 802–22.

Mills, David. "Chester's Mystery Cycle and the 'Mystery' of the Past." *Transactions of the Lancashire and Cheshire Historical Society* 137 (1988): 1–23.

———. *Recycling the Cycle: The City of Chester and Its Whitsun Plays.* Toronto: University of Toronto Press, 1998.

Mitchell, Katie, and Edward Kemp. *The Mysteries.* London: Nick Hern Books, 1997.

Moi, Toril. "I Am a Woman." In *What Is a Woman?: And Other Essays.* Oxford: Oxford University Press, 1999.

Moore, Henrietta. *Space, Text and Gender: An Anthropological Study of the Marakwet of Kenya.* Cambridge: Cambridge University Press, 1986.

Muir, Edward. *Ritual in Early Modern Europe.* Cambridge: Cambridge University Press, 1999.

Mulhall, Stephen. *Philosophy's Recounting of the Ordinary.* Oxford: Clarendon Press, 1994.

Myers, David. *"Poor Sinning Folk": Confession and Conscience in Counter-Reformation Germany.* Ithaca: Cornell University Press, 1996.

Nairn, Tom. *The Enchanted Glass: Britain and Its Monarchy.* London: Hutchinson Radius, 1988.

National Heritage Memorial Fund Annual Report of 1981. London: HMSO, 1981.

Neuss, Paula. "God and Embarrassment." In *Themes in Drama.* Vol. 5, *Drama and Religion,* edited by James Redmond, 241–53. Cambridge: Cambridge University Press, 1983.

Nicholson, R. H. "The Trial of Christ the Sorcerer in the York Cycle." *Journal of Medieval and Renaissance Studies* 16, no. 21 (fall 1986): 125–69.

Nissé, Ruth. "Staged Interpretations: Civic Rhetoric and Lollard Politics in the York Plays." *Journal of Medieval and Early Modern Studies* 28, no.2 (spring 1998): 427–52.

Nora, Pierre. "Between Memory and History: Les Lieux de Mémoire." Translated by Marc Roudebush. *Representations* 26 (spring 1989): 7–25.

———. *Les lieux de mémoire.* 7 vols. Paris: Gallimard, 1984–92.

———. *Realms of Memory.* Translated by Arthur Goldhammer under the direction of Pierre Nora. 3 vols. New York: Columbia University Press, 1996–98.

Normington, Katie. "'Little Acts of Faith': Katie Mitchell's The Mysteries." *New Theatre Quarterly* (1998): 99–110.

O'Brien, Robert. "Two Sermons at York Synod of William of Rymyngton 1372 and 1373." Cîteaux Commentarii Cisterciensis, 1968.

O'Connell, Michael. *The Idolatrous Eye: Iconoclasm and Theater in Early Modern England.* Oxford: Oxford University Press, 2000.

Official Handbook of the Festival of Britain. London: HMSO, 1951.

Outram, Dorinda. *The Body and the French Revolution.* New Haven: Yale University Press, 1989.

Ozouf, Mono. *Festivals and the French Revolution.* Translated by Alan Sheridan. Cambridge: Harvard University Press, 1988.

Paden, William. "Before the 'Sacred' Became Theological: Rereading the Durkheimian Legacy." *Method and Theory in the Study of Religion* 3, no. 1 (1991): 10–23.

Pagels, Elaine. *The Gnostic Gospels.* New York: Random House, 1981.

———. "Visions, Appearances, and Apostolic Authority: Gnostic and Orthodox Traditions." *Gnosis, Festschrift für Hans Jonas,* edited by B. Aland, 415–30. Gottingen: Vandenhoeck und Ruprecht, 1978.

Palliser, D. M. "The Trades Guilds of Tudor York." In *Crisis and Order in English Towns 1500–1700,* edited by Peter Clark and Paul Slack, 86–116. London: Routledge and Kegan Paul, 1972.

———. *The Reformation in York 1534–1553.* Borthwick Papers No. 40. York: St. Anthony's Press, 1971.

———. *Tudor York.* Oxford: Oxford University Press, 1979.

Patterson, Lee. "The *Miller's Tale* and the Politics of Laughter." In *Chaucer and the Subject of History.* Madison: University of Wisconsin Press, 1991.

Phillips, Adam. "Fears." In *Terrors and Experts,* 46–63. Cambridge: Harvard University Press, 1996.

Phythian-Adams, Charles. "Ceremony and the Citizen: The Communal Year at Coventry, 1450–1550." In *Crisis and Order in English Towns, 1500–1700,* edited by Peter Clark and Paul Slack, 57–85. London: Routledge and Kegan Paul, 1972. Reprinted in *The Early Modern Town,* edited by Peter Clark. Longman: Open University Press, 1976.

———. *The Fabric of the Traditional Community.* Milton Keynes, Eng.: Open University Press, 1977.

———. *Rethinking English Local History.* Leicester: Leicester University Press, 1987.

Pickstock, Catharine. *After Writing: On the Liturgical Consummation of Philosophy.* Oxford: Blackwell, 1998.

Pierce, Charles. *Collected Papers.* Cambridge: Harvard University Press, 1931–58.

Postan, M. M. *The Medieval Economy and Society.* Harmondsworth: Penguin, 1975.

Primus, John H. *The Vestments Controversy: An Historical Study of the Earliest Tensions in the Church of England in the Reigns of Edward VI and Elizabeth.* Kampen: J. H. Kok, 1960.

Program for the 1969 Corpus Christi Productions, *York Festival Collection,* York City Library.

Questier, Michael C. *Conversion, Politics and Religion in England, 1580–1625.* Cambridge: Cambridge University Press, 1996.

Ramasse, Françoise. "Denys Arcand: Être tendre malgré lui." *Positif* 340 (June 1989): 12–17.

Rappaport, Roy A. *Ritual and Religion in the Making of Humanity.* Cambridge: Cambridge University Press, 1999.

Reinburg, Virginia. "Liturgy and the Laity in Late Medieval and Reformation France." *Sixteenth Century Journal* 23, no. 3 (1992): 526–48.

"Report of the Board of the York Festival Society." 14 October 1952. *York Festival Collection,* York City Library.

Reynolds, Susan. "Medieval Urban History and the History of Political Thought." *Urban History Yearbook* (1982): 14–26.

Rigby, Stephen. *Marxism and History.* Manchester: Manchester University Press, 1987.

Righter, Anne. *Shakespeare and the Idea of the Play.* New York: Barnes and Noble, 1963.

Roach, Joseph. *Cities of the Dead: Circum-Atlantic Performance.* New York: Columbia University Press, 1996.

Roberts, Peter. "Elizabethan Players and Minstrels and the Legislation of 1572 Against Retainers and Vagabonds." In *Religion, Culture and Society in Early Modern Britain: Essays in Honour of Patrick Collinson,* edited by Anthony Fletcher and Peter Roberts, 29–55. Cambridge: Cambridge University Press, 1994.

Rogerson, M. "The York Corpus Christi Play: Some Practical Details." *Leeds Studies in English,* n.s., 10 (1978): 97–101.

Rubin, Miri. *Corpus Christi: The Eucharist in Medieval Culture.* Cambridge: Cambridge University Press, 1991.

———. "Religious Culture in Town and Country: Reflections on a Great Divide." In *Church and City 1000–1500: Essays in Honour of Christopher Brooke,* edited by D. Abulafia, M. Franklin, and Miri Rubin, 3–22. Cambridge: Cambridge University Press, 1992.

———. "Small Groups: Identity and Solidarity in the Late Middle Ages." In *Enterprise and Individuals in Fifteenth-Century England,* edited by Jennifer Kermode, 132–50. Stroud: Alan Sutton, 1991.

Sacks, David Harris. "The Corporate Town and the English State: Bristol's 'Little Businesses' 1625–1641." *Past and Present* 110 (1988): 69–105.

Samuel, Raphael. *Theatres of Memory.* Vol. 1, *Past and Present in Contemporary Culture.* London: Verso, 1994.

Santner, Eric. *My Own Private Germany: Daniel Paul Schreber's Secret History of Modernity.* Princeton: Princeton University Press, 1996.

———. *Stranded Objects: Mourning, Memory and Film in Postwar Germany.* Ithaca: Cornell University Press, 1990.

Sawyer, Karen. Director's notes in program to *The York Plays,* University of Toronto, Toronto, Ontario, 20 June 1998.

Schillebeeckx, Edward. *Christ: The Sacrament of the Encounter with God.* London: Sheed and Ward, 1963.

Schnecher, Richard, and Lisa Wolford. *The Grotowski Sourcebook.* London: Routledge, 1997.

Schroeder, H. J., trans and ed. *Disciplinary Decrees of the General Councils.* St. Louis: B. Herder Book Co., 1937.

Sedgewick, Eve Kosofsky. *Epistemology of the Closet.* Berkeley: University of California Press, 1990.

Segundo, Juan. *The Community Called Church.* Maryknoll, N.Y.: Orbis Books, 1973.

Sharpe, J. A. *Early Modern England: A Social History 1550–1760.* Bungay, Suffolk: Edward Arnold, 1987.

Sheingorn, Pamela. *The Easter Sepulchre in England.* Kalamazoo, Mich.: Medieval Institute Publications, 1987.

Shepherd, Simon, and Peter Womack. *English Drama: A Cultural History.* Oxford: Blackwell, 1996.

Sider, Gerald. *Culture and Class in Anthropology and History: A Newfoundland Illustration.* Cambridge: Cambridge University Press, 1986.

Silver, Jeremy. "Astonished and Somewhat Terrified: The Preservation and Development of Aural Culture." In *The Museum Time-Machine,* edited by Robert Lumley. London: Routledge, 1988.

Simmel, Georg. "Soziologie des Raumes." *Jahrbuch für Gesetzgebung, Verwaltung und Volkswirtschaft* 27 (1903): 27–71.

Sissons, Michael, and Phillip French, eds. *The Age of Austerity: 1945–51.* Harmondsworth: Penguin, 1964.

Skura, Meredith Anne. *Shakespeare the Actor and the Purposes of Playing.* Chicago: University of Chicago Press, 1993.

Smith, Jonathan Z. *To Take Place: Toward Theory in Ritual.* Chicago: University of Chicago Press, 1987.

Smith, R. M. " 'Modernization' and the Corporate Village Community in England: Some Skeptical Reflections." In *Explorations in Historical Geography,* edited by A. R. H. Baker and D. Gregory, 140–79, 234–45. Cambridge: Cambridge University Press, 1984.

Sokolowski, Robert. *Eucharistic Presence: A Study in the Theology of Disclosure.* Washington, D.C.: Catholic University of America Press, 1994.

Spector, Stephen. "Time, Space and Identity in the Play of the Sacrament." In *The Stage as Mirror: Civic Theatre in Late Medieval Europe,* edited by Alan E. Knight, 189–200. Cambridge: D. S. Brewer, 1997.

Sponsler, Claire. "The Culture of the Spectator: Conformity and Resistance to Medieval Performances." *Theatre Journal* 44 (1992): 15–29.

———. *Drama and Resistance: Bodies, Goods, and Theatricality in Late Medieval England.* Minneapolis: University of Minnesota Press, 1997.

Sponsler, Claire, and Robert Clark. "Othered Bodies: Racial Cross-Dressing in the Mistère de la Sainte Hostie and the Croxton Play of the Sacrament." *Journal of Medieval and Early Modern Studies* 29, no. 1 (winter 1999): 61–88.

Stallybrass, Peter. "Worn Worlds: Clothes and Identity on the Renaissance Stage." In *Subject and Object in Renaissance Culture,* edited by Margreta de Grazia, Maureen Quilligan, and Peter Stallybrass, 286–320. Cambridge: Cambridge University Press, 1996.

Stallybrass, Peter, and Allon White. *The Politics and Poetics of Transgression.* London: Methuen, 1986.

States, Bert. *Great Reckonings in Little Rooms: On the Phenomenology of Theater.* Berkeley: University of California Press, 1964.

———. *The Pleasures of the Play.* Ithaca: Cornell University Press, 1994.

Steiner, George. *Real Presences.* Chicago: University of Chicago Press, 1989.

Stevens, Martin. *Four Middle English Mystery Cycles: Textual, Contextual and Critical Interpretations.* Princeton: Princeton University Press, 1987.

Stewart, Susan. *On Longing: Narratives of the Miniature, the Gigantic, the Souvenir, the Collection.* Baltimore: Johns Hopkins University Press, 1984.

Strohm, Paul. *England's Empty Throne: Usurpation and the Language of Legitimization 1399–1422.* New Haven: Yale University Press, 1998.

Strong, Roy. *A Tonic to the Nation: The Festival of Britain 1951.* London: Thames and Hudson, 1976.

Swanson, Heather. "The Illusion of Economic Structure: Craft Guilds in Late Medieval English Towns." *Past and Present* 121 (1988): 29–48.

———. *Medieval Artisans: An Urban Class in Late Medieval England.* Oxford: Basil Blackwell, 1989.

Tanner, Norman. "Penances Imposed on Kentish Lollards by Archbishop Warham 1511–12." In *Lollardy and the Gentry in the Later Middle Ages,* edited by Margaret Aston and Colin Richmond, 229–49. New York: St. Martin's Press, 1997.

Terdiman, Richard. "Deconstructing Memory: On Representing the Past and Theorizing Culture in France since the Revolution." *Diacritics* 15 (winter 1985): 13–36.

———. *Present Past: Modernity and the Memory Crisis.* Ithaca: Cornell University Press, 1993.

Thomas, Keith. *Religion and the Decline of Magic.* London: Weidenfield and Nicholson, 1970. Reprint, London: Peregrine, 1980.

Thompson, E. P. *Customs in Common: Studies in Traditional Popular Culture.* New York: The New Press, 1993.

Tiner, Elza. "'Inventio,' 'Dispositio,' and 'Elocutio' in the York Trial Plays." Ph.D. diss., University of Toronto, 1987.

Tittler, Robert. *Architecture and Power: The Town Hall and English Urban Community c. 1500–1640.* Oxford: Clarendon Press, 1991.

Tönnies, Ferdinand. *Community and Society.* Translated by Charles P. Loomis. New York: Harper and Row, 1963.

Toro, Fernando de. *Theatre Semiotics: Text and Staging in Modern Theatre.* Translated by John Lewis. Toronto: University of Toronto Press, 1995.

The Transition from Feudalism to Capitalism. Introduction by Rodney Hilton. London: Verso, 1978.

Travis, Peter. "The Social Body of the Dramatic Christ in Medieval England." *Early English Drama, Acta* 13 (1985): 17–36.

Trimble, W. R. *The Catholic Laity in Elizabethan England: 1558–1603.* Cambridge: Belknap Press, 1964.

Turner, Denys. "The Darkness of God and the Light of Christ: Negative Theology and Eucharistic Presence." In *Catholicism and Catholicity: Eucharistic Communities in Historical and Contemporary Perspectives,* edited by Sarah Beckwith, 31–46. Oxford: Blackwell, 1999.

———. "Negative Theology and Eucharistic Presence." *Modern Theology* 15, no. 2 (April 1999): 143–58.

Twycross, Meg. "'Places to Hear the Play': Pageant Stations at York, 1398–1572." *REED Newsletter* 2 (1978): 10–33.

———. "Playing the Resurrection." In *Medieval Studies for J. A. W. Bennett,* edited by P. L. Heyworth, 273–96. Oxford: Clarendon Press, 1981.

———. "The Theatricality of Medieval English Plays." In *The Cambridge Companion to Medieval English Theatre,* edited by Richard Beadle, 37–84. Cambridge: Cambridge University Press.

Twycross, Meg, and Sarah Carpenter. "Masks in Medieval English Theatre." *Medieval English Theatre* 3 (1981): 7–41, 69–113.

Ubersfeld, Anne. *L'école du spectateur.* Paris: Belin, 1981.

Ulin, Robert. *Understanding Cultures: Perspectives in Anthropology and Social Theory.* Austin: University of Texas Press, 1984.

Underdown, David. *Revel, Riot and Rebellion: Popular Politics and Culture in England 1603–1660.* Oxford: Oxford University Press, 1987.

Unsworth, Barry. *Morality Play.* London: Hamish Hamilton, 1995. Reprint, London: Penguin, 1996.

Uzzell, David. "The Hot Interpretation of War and Conflict." In *Heritage Interpretation,* edited by David Uzzell. 2 vols. London: Belhaven Press, 1989.

Veltrusky, Jiri. "Man and Object in the Theater." In *A Prague School Reader on Esthetics, Literary Structure, and Style,* edited by Paul Garvin. Washington, D.C.: Georgetown University Press, 1964.

Walker, Greg. *The Politics of Performance in Early Renaissance Drama.* Cambridge: Cambridge University Press, 1998.

———. *Plays of Persuasion: Drama and Politics at the Court of Henry VIII.* Cambridge: Cambridge University Press, 1991.

Wallace, David, ed. *The Cambridge History of Medieval English Literature.* Cambridge: Cambridge University Press, 1999.

Walsham, Alexandra. *Church Papists: Catholicism, Conformity and Confessional Polemic in Early Modern England.* Bury St. Edmunds, Suffolk: Boydell Press, 1993.

Wasson, John. "Professional Actors in the Middle Ages and Early Renaissance." *Medieval and Renaissance Drama in England* 1 (1984): 1–11.

Weimann, Robert. *Shakespeare and the Popular Tradition in the Theatre.* Baltimore: Johns Hopkins University Press, 1978.

Wenzel, Siegfried. "Somer Game and Sermon References to a Corpus Christi Play." *Modern Philology* 86 (1989): 274–83.

West, William, "The Idea of a Theater: Humanist Ideology and the Imaginary Stage in Early Modern Europe." In *Renaissance Drama*, n.s., 28. Evanston: Northwestern University Press, 1999.

Wheeler, Wendy. "After Grief? What Kinds of Inhuman Selves?" *New Formations* 25 (summer 1995): 77–95.

White, Allon. *Carnival, Hysteria, and Writing: Collected Essays and Autobiography.* Edited by Stuart Hall and Jacqueline Rose. Oxford: Clarendon Press, 1993.

White, Eileen. "People and Places: The Social and Topographical Context of Drama in York 1554–1609." Ph.D. diss., University of Leeds, 1984.

———. "Places for Hearing the Corpus Christi Play in York." *Medieval English Theatre* 8, no. 2 (1986): 23–63.

———. *The York Mystery Play.* York: Yorkshire Architectural and York Archeological Society, 1984.

White, Paul Whitfield. "Reforming Mysteries' End: A New Look at Protestant Intervention in English Provincial Drama. *Journal of Medieval and Early Modern Studies* 29, vol. 1 (winter 1999): 121–87.

———. *Theatre and Reformation: Protestantism, Patronage and Playing in Tudor England.* Cambridge: Cambridge University Press, 1993.

Whiting, Robert. *Local Responses to the English Reformation.* Houndmills, Basingstoke: Macmillan, 1998.

Wickham, Glynne. *Early English Stages, 1300–1660.* 3 vols. London: Routledge and Kegan Paul, 1959–81.

Wierum, Ann. " 'Actors' and 'Play-Acting' in the Morality Tradition." *Renaissance Drama*, no. III (1970): 189–214.

Williams, Raymond. "Base and Superstructure in Marxist Cultural Theory." In *Problems in Materialism and Culture: Selected Essays.* London: Verso, 1980.

Williams, Rowan. *On Christian Theology.* Oxford: Blackwell, 2000.

———. "Postmodern Theology and the Judgement of the Word." In *Postmodern Theology and Christian Faith in a Pluralist World,* edited by F. B. Burham, 92–112. San Francisco: Harper and Row, 1989.

———. *Resurrection.* London: Darton, Longman, and Todd, 1982.

———. "The Suspicion of Suspicion." *The Grammar of the Heart: New Essays in Moral Philosophy and Theology.* Edited by Richard Bell, 36–53. San Francisco: Harper and Row, 1988.

———. "Trinity and Revelation." *Modern Theology* 2 (1986): 197–212.

———. *The Wound of Knowledge: Christian Spirituality from the New Testament to St. John of the Cross.* London: Darton, Longman, and Todd, 1990.

Willis, Paul. "The Weight of Sin in the York Crucifixio." *Leeds Studies in English* 15 (1984): 109–16.

Wilshire, Bruce. *Role Playing and Identity: The Limits of Theatre as Metaphor.* Bloomington: Indiana University Press, 1982.

Wittgenstein, Ludwig. *Philosophical Investigations.* Oxford: Blackwell, 1953.

Wood, Ellen Meiksins. "Capitalism and Human Emancipation." *New Left Review* 167 (1988): 3–20.

———. "Falling through the Cracks: E. P. Thompson and the Debate on Base and Superstructure." In *E. P. Thompson: Critical Perspectives,* edited by Harvey Kaye and Keith McClelland, 125–52. Philadelphia: Temple University Press, 1990.

———. *The Pristine Culture of Capitalism: A Historical Essay on Old Regimes and Modern States.* London: Verso, 1991.

———. "The Separation of the Economic and the Political in Capitalism." *New Left Review* 127 (May–June 1981): 65–95.

Woolf, Rosemary. *The English Mystery Plays.* Berkeley: University of California Press, 1972.

Worthen, William. *Shakespeare and the Authority of Performance.* Cambridge: Cambridge University Press, 1997.

Wright, Patrick. "Heritage and Danger: The English Past in the Era of the Welfare State." In *Memory: History, Culture and Mind,* edited by Thomas Butler. Oxford: Blackwell, 1989.

———. *On Living in an Old Country: The National Past in Contemporary Britain.* London: Verso, 1985.

Yates, Frances. *The Art of Memory.* Chicago: University of Chicago Press, 1966.

York City Scrapbook of the Festival, Box Y394.

Young, Karl. *Drama of the Medieval Church.* 2 vols. Oxford: Clarendon Press, 1933.

Index

Abelard, 240 n. 73

actors: amateur, 135; and audience, 89, 133; bodies of, 3, 59, 64, 66–67, 100, 115; clergy as, 147; in *Jesus of Montreal,* 174–76, 179; in *Morality Play* (Unsworth), 163–66, 173; professional, 8, 17, 132–35. *See also* performance; theater

Acts of Suppression and Uniformity, 125–26, 245 n. 21

Adam, 45

Aers, David, 87, 111, 240 n. 73

Agnew, Jean-Christophe, 209 n. 88

Alford, John, 151

Allen, William, 127

Alter, Jean, 223 n. 23

Annas, in York plays, 81–83, 108–9

Anselm, 44

anticlericalism, 79–80

Aquinas, Thomas, 24, 61, 71, 234 n. 23

Arcand, Denys, 163, 174. *See also Jesus of Montreal*

architecture: and Festival of Britain, 6

Arundel (archbishop), 99, 105

Ascheron, Neal, 14, 199 n. 66

atonement. *See* penance

Attlee, Clement, 7

Audelay, John, 241 n. 98

audience: of film, 180; of theater, 87–89, 112, 148

Augustine, Saint, 4, 44, 79, 84–85, 193 n. 6, 212 n. 4

Austin, George, 161

Austin, J. L., 115, 139

Badby, John, 105, 107

Badir, Patricia, 131

Bale, John: *King John,* 148–53; iconoclasm in, 149; as parody, 149–50

Banerjee, Victor, 199 n. 72

Banham, Rayner, 194 n. 18

Barley Hall (museum), 14

Bartlett, Martin, 68

Baucom, Ian, 196 n. 40

Beadle, Richard, 54

Beard, Thomas: *The Theatre of God's Judgements,* 64

Beaumont, Francis: *The Knight of the Burning Pestle,* 149

Becon, Thomas: "Displaying of the Popish Mass," 145–48

belief, and community, 88

Bell (bishop), 8

Bell, Catherine, 28–29

Berengar, 60

Bevan, Aneurin, 194 n. 17

Bible: and clericalism, 82. Books of: I Corinthians, 29, 78; Hebrews, 69; Isaiah, 69; John, 29, 75, 83–85; Luke, 75; Mark, 75, 78, 178; Matthew, 46, 75, 79–80, 112; I Peter, 69; Psalms, 96–97, 234 n. 20. *See also names of biblical figures*

Bills, Bing, 247 n. 40

Bishop, T. G., 153

Blasphemy Laws (1606), 3, 161, 192 n. 1

Blau, Herbert, 62, 64, 88

body: of actor, 3, 31, 59, 64; as bearer of meaning, 31–32; of Christ (*see* Christ, body of); and creation, 46; distrust of, 140; eucharistic, 78; and fall of man, 45–46; resurrected, 179; as symbol, 39–40

Book of Common Prayer, 135–40; language of, 136; and national church, 139–40; on theater, 143–44

Bourdieu, Pierre, 27–28

Brecht, Bertold: *Galileo,* 176

287